THE

GUILT OF SLAVERY

AND THE

CRIME OF SLAVEHOLDING,

DEMONSTRATED FROM THE

HEBREW AND GREEK SCRIPTURES.

BY

REV. GEORGE B. CHEEVER, D.D.,
PASTOR OF THE CHURCH OF THE PURITANS.

NEGRO UNIVERSITIES PRESS
NEW YORK

Originally published in 1860
by John P. Jewett & Co., Boston

Reprinted 1969 by
Negro Universities Press
A DIVISION OF GREENWOOD PUBLISHING CORP.
NEW YORK

Library of Congress Catalogue Card Number 69-16586

SBN 8371-1380-6

DEDICATION AND PREFACE.

I DEDICATE this volume to REV. WM. G. SCHAUFFLER, D. D., of Constantinople, who expressed to me, in his last visit to this country, his conviction of the truth and accuracy of the views on the subject of slavery, presented by me in the BIBLIOTHECA SACRA, and now embodied in the present work. I know the feelings of abhorrence and of anguish in the hearts of some of our missionaries abroad, in regard to the prevalence of this gigantic sin. They dare not let the heathen know that such an iniquity is tolerated by Christians; much less, that the very Missionary Boards that send the gospel abroad maintain and sanction, in any of the churches at home, such a violation of all its precepts.

May the Lord God bring speedily the time when the churches and the ministry, at home and abroad, shall unite in the condemnation and removal of this monstrous abomination!

The slaveholding tyranny established in this country over the blacks has rapidly ripened into a despotism full blown, with all the arts and terrors of proscription against even the free whites, who prefer liberty to slavery, and dare express an independent opinion, or maintain an independent spirit. The masters and managers of this despotism, defying all the fundamental principles of jurisprudence, as well as of revealed religion, have set up slavery even on the throne of Justice, confounding and concentrating, out of the maxims and prejudices of past wickedness and darkness, the present rule of slaveholding piety and policy, *that black men have no rights that white men are bound to respect.* They are, as MR. COLERIDGE did not hesitate to designate them, A LEG BANDITTI OF MEN-STEALERS, and they are ready to hang at the nearest lamp-post all who resist or even disavow the laws of their brotherhood. But, as EDMUND BURKE said of the leaders of the French Reign of Terror, " Their *tyranny* is complete in their *justice*, and their *lanterne* is not half so dreadful as their *court.*"

Their religion is still worse than either, being a perversion of the gospel of love into a law of malignity and cruelty, so that every virtuous and honest man must, by the necessity of truth and conscience, be an unbeliever, and only a depraved heart could receive such pretended revelation. It is the conviction of the impossibility of any such revelation sanctioning so diabolical a cruelty and crime as that of human slavery, that has led to the preparation of this volume, in every part of which I•have adhered to the logic of God's word, and while dealing with the original have made the argument plain and simple to the English reader.

The ground studies of the work, so far as the Old Testament is concerned, were published in several successive numbers of the BIBLIOTHECA SACRA, in the years 1855 and 1856. Out of the intolerable pressure of the accusation that the Old Testament sanctioned slavery, the investigation was begun, and has been continued; the result is the demonstration in this volume, which, being drawn from God's word, we fear not to challenge the overthrow of it by the defenders of slavery as an impossibility. A similar survey of the teachings of the Bible on this subject had been admirably presented, in part, in a tract on the Mosaic system of servitude, by the late venerated and lamented Judge Jay, whose services to his country as a Christian jurist, statesman, philanthropist and patriot, the bitter enemies of his abolitionism have vainly attempted to depreciate or conceal.

I have demonstrated the power and duty of the church and ministry with the Word of God against this sin. Indifference and neutrality in this conflict are treason. "He who supports the system of slavery," said the ABBÉ RAYNAL, "is the enemy of the whole human race, and whoever justifies it deserves the utmost contempt from the philosopher, and from the negro a stab with his dagger." RAYNAL here states a principle of desert, not a rule of action. But again he says, "If there existed a religion which tolerated or authorized, though only by its silence, such horrors; if, occupied with idle questions, it did not thunder without ceasing against the authors and instruments of this tyranny; if it made it a crime for the slave to break his chains; if it endured in its bosom the unjust judge who would condemn the fugitive; if such a religion existed, would it not be necessary to bury its ministers under the ruin of their own altars?"*

The Abbé Raynal was a Roman Catholic, but he wrote like a prophet, and he describes the religion of Protestants, if they sanction this iniquity. The right of slavery, he justly declares, is the right to commit every species of crime; so that a church defending this right is no more a church of Christ, but a synagogue of Satan.

Let those who have affirmed that American slavery could not exist out of the church, were it not protected in it, THEMSELVES PREACH AGAINST IT; let the churches and the ministry not merely denounce it in Confessions and General Assemblies, but proclaim the word of God against it from the pulpit, and apply the law of Christ in its excommunication, and our whole country would speedily be redeemed from the infinite curse and crime. We have been too justly called a people of Good Resolutions; and the publication of strong *whereases* and *resolves* gains, generally, sufficient reputation for anti-slavery principles, without any necessity or intention of practising upon them. May God give us grace to do, as well as say.

As Republicans and Christians let us adopt the generous sentiment of SIR SAMUEL ROMILLY. "A genuine love of liberty is not a selfish feeling confined to ourselves, and to the contracted circle of our privi-

* ABBÉ RAYNAL, Histoire Philosophique des deux Indes, Vol. VI., pp. 94-111, and Vol. I., 28.

CONTENTS.

INTRODUCTION.

The argument which we propose to develope, demonstrating the iniquity of slavery, is fourfold; philological, statutory or legal, historical, and moral. The argument from consequences is both historical and moral.

In pursuing the philological argument we begin with the Hebrew, from which, through the Septuagint translation, it passes into the New Testament, where it is merged in the moral and retributive, and closes with the great decisive judgment, He that is unjust, let him be unjust still.

I. The philological argument is baptized throughout with the idea of the virtue, manliness, honorableness and Christian integrity of voluntary paid or rewarded labor, as the characteristic of a truly free and benevolent social state. An admirable German writer has thrown a great light, even in a few suggestions, upon the darkness in which this subject has been involved in the Biblical literature of his own country. He notes and corrects some of the errors of Michaelis. He notes the fact that the Hebrew language has no word that stigmatizes a part of the laboring community by a degrading *brand mark*, or separates them from the others as slaves, but only an honorable generic expression for all who stand in the serving relation. He affirms that among a people so occupied with agriculture, whose Lawgiver, Moses, and whose Kings, Saul and David, passed immediately to their high vocation from the care of their flocks and the labors of the plow, there could no degrading significance ever be attached to any appellation of labor; for the name of the Servant of God is the honorable title of Moses and the pious.*

THERE IS NO WORD IN THE HEBREW LANGUAGE FOR SLAVE, and this grand fact speaks volumes. The glorious necessity and penury of that divine language in this respect, (a penury the consequence of wealth), •dragged in triumph the Greek words which human depravity had applied to slavery, and made a show of them openly, having bound them to the service of a universal and Christian freedom. In the work of translation, for want of another pure language that had not been created out of despotism and servility, the Greek words for service, though stamped with the superscription of slavery, had to be taken as the exponents of the nobler Hebrew. But the grand old Hebrew significance held on and triumphed, being indeed additionally elevated and transfigured by the Gospel.

The Greek was not laid aside, nor unclothed, but clothed upon with the divineness of the Hebrew; and the words that are thus transfigured must be viewed as reflecting the glory of that Redeemer, whose incarnation, death, and work of redemption gathered all mankind into one free family.† To look at them otherwise, in their usage in the New Testament, would be as if one of the disciples could have stripped Moses and Elias of their glory, and compelled them to appear in their earthly and mortal habiliments. There is no exaggeration in this. If any man will examine carefully the works of those scholars who have written on the principles of interpretation as applied to the Greek of the New Testament, he will find that though this particular view might not have been in

* SAALSCHUTZ. Das Mosaiche Recht. Mosaic System of Laws. Vol. 2, ch. ci, p. 697.

† SEILER. Biblical Hermenuetics. Part 2, Sec. ccxlii. "The language of the New Testament had its origin from the Greek Jews, and the religion of the New Testament is based on the writings of Moses and the prophets. The first and principal helps for investigating the usage of words in the writings of the Evangelists and Apostles are the text and the Greek translation of the Old Testament."

the mind of those writers, yet the demonstration is inevitable from their principles.*

(1.) The leading word ennobled by this process is δοῦλος, with its cognates, as used for the varieties of service. And here what is needed is simply to rescue the text from the insane thraldom which the defenders of slavery put upon these words, of being compelled into the service of that social and civil abomination and crime, as if no other meaning than that of slavery could possibly be connected with them. The question is triumphantly asked, Does not δοῦλος mean slave? The pro-slavery interpreters have melted down the king's coin, and brought it to their mint, for this base image and superscription. They have taken the basest and most degraded meaning of the Greek, and have set that as the standard of usage in Divine Inspiration. All that is necessary in regard to δοῦλος is to prove that the New Testament writers used it as the synonyme of the free old Hebrew word עֶבֶד, the proof of which is incontrovertible through the Septuagint translation.† "As this version became the Bible of all the Jews, who were dispersed throughout the countries where Greek was spoken, it became the standard of their Greek language."‡ It became their grand classic library, and in it the word that among the Greeks designated *slaves* was redeemed from that degradation, and applied to freemen, to the free servants of freemen, and to the children of God. But, in addition to this, it can be proved that even in classic usage, so called, this word and its cognates were not exclusively applied to slaves; so that in no case can their occurrence prove that slaves or the system of slavery were recognized or meant. These words necessarily all received a baptism of freedom from

---

* WINER, Grammar of Idioms of the Greek Language of the N. T., pp. 34, 31. "The religious dialect of the Jews, even in the Greek, naturally approached the Hebrew, and had its type in the Septuagint." "Their Greek style took the general complexion of their mother tongue. Hence originated a Jewish Greek, which native Greeks generally did not understand and therefore despised."

† Lightfoot's Works, Vol. 4, p. 31. PLANCK, Greek Diction of N. T. ROBINSON, Philology N. T.—TITTMAN on Forced Interpretations. THOLUCK, Lexicography N. T.

‡ Marsh's Lectures, p. 3, sec. xiv.

the Hebrew, by being employed in its translation in so many cases where no meaning of slavery could attach to them; and then afterwards by being applied ordinarily to signify the domestics in Judean families, the servants who were Jews themselves, and could not possibly be slaves.

In the great and glorious fugitive law, in Deut. xxiii., 16, the words used are אֶבֶד for the Hebrew, a *servant*, and δοῦλος for the Greek, a servant. Now if, in this case, it could even be proved that both these words, both the Hebrew and the translation, meant *slave* and slave only, then the argument would be destructive of the whole claim of slavery as having any sanction in God's Word. For the person here described as a slave is evidently one who in God's sight has a perfect right to his freedom, and the same right as to men also, no matter what may be their claims or their laws in regard to him. Those claims and laws are so unrighteous, when they treat him as a slave, that he has a perfect right to break away from them, and God himself forbids any man from interfering with that right, but commands every man to defend it, and to protect the fugitive in its enjoyment, without any regard to wicked human enactments.

But the stranger and the native were placed upon the same footing, for certainly God would not have inserted in his laws for his own people a privilege in behalf of the heathen which could have been denied in behalf of the Hebrew citizen. So that, if the word describing the fugitive means slave, it is as clear as the day that slavery is unjust and wrong in God's sight, that the claim of property in man is sinful and good for nothing, not to be respected, but rejected, and reprobated, and defied.

And if it does not mean slave, then it means a freeman unjustly treated as a slave; so that we have here a case, in the very instance and principle, in the very text and law, on which the Epistle of Paul to Philemon is grounded, of the utter repudiation of slavery, the denial of the possibility of its being sanctioned by divine permission, the assertion of the duty of protecting the oppressed servant, of the claim of the fugitive slave to freedom, and

of the duty, on the part of Christians, to give freedom to the oppressed fugitive, whether slave or servant, to give freedom to the
δοῦλος, and on no account return him into the power of the
oppressor.

The Septuagint usage of the word δοῦλος, for free service, may
be known by comparing the following instances : Ex. xxi., 2 ; Josh.,
i., 1, xiv., 7, xxii., 4 ; Judges vi., 27, xix., 19 ; 1 Sam. xvii., 9, xviii.
5, xxv., 10 ; 2 Sam. ix., 10, xii., 18, xix., 17 ; 1 Kings xii., 7 ; 2
Kings iv., 1 ; 1 Chron. vi., 49 ; Neh. ix., 14 ; Dan. ix., 11 ; Eccl.
v., 11, where it is for עֹבֵד, the sleep of a laboring man is sweet.
These cases, in comparison with others, prove incontrovertibly a
very general use of δοῦλος, where the meaning of slave can not
be admitted or intimated ; and no Jew, in any of the instances in
which it was applied to any of his own nation, would endure the
signification of slavery. It thus passed into the New Testament
as a synonyme of the old, free, honorable Hebrew word עֶבֶד, and
was employed by the writers of the New Testament, as of the Old,
indifferently, to signify servants in families, servants of God, servants of Christ, servants among the Pagans, servants among Christians ; and if at any time it refers to slaves, it is with no intimation of any sanction of slavery, but rather (as in 1 Tim. vi., 1, 2)
in the supposition that only out of the church of Christ, only
among Pagans and unbelievers, can there be found persons who
will hold slaves ;* and that when Christians are so unfortunate as
to be held under such a yoke, they must endure it to the honor of
God, in the hope of the conversion of their heathen masters, al-

---

* SAALSCHUTZ. DAS MOSAISCHE
RECHT. Laws of Moses, vol. 2., 715.
He remarks on the impossibility of
the system of slavery having prevailed among the Hebrews, in the
sense of that word in modern times,
and among the nations out of Judea;
and states the impropriety of the
term slavery being applied to the
Hebrew system of domestic service,
from which every element of slavery
was excluded. He points out what
he designates as a most pernicious
mistake brought in by Machaelis,
that of giving the title of bondage or
slavery to the system of Jewish service, when it was not slavery at all,
and did not allow of slavery. The
work of Saalschutz was published in
Berlin, in 1846.

though, if they can be made free, they must not be slaves, but should gain and keep their freedom.*

(2). The same is true in regard to the word δουλεια, *service*, often rendered *bondage* in English, but which in the original is so often used of the work or ministry of a free person that there can be no argument of slavery drawn from its usage any where, unless the context plainly proves that slavery is the subject of discourse.† The usage in the Septuagint may be seen from the following instances: Gen. xxx., 26, of Jacob's service to Laban; 1 Kings v., 6, of Hiram's and Solomon's servants; 1 Kings xii., 4, Solomon's service upon the people of his kingdom; 1 Chron. vi., 48, service of the Levites for the Tabernacle; xxv., 6, service of the singers in the house of God; Psalm civ., 4, herb for the *service* of man; Ez. xxix., 18, Nebuchadnezzar's service and hire unto God.

* CAMPBELL on the Gospels, vol. 2. Note on Matt. xx., 27, declares that by the word δουλος is meant a *servant* in general, whatever kind of work he be employed in, as well as a slave. "It is solely from the scope and connection that we must judge when it should be rendered in the one way, and when in the other." The mention of the subject, or the occurrence of the word, does not justify the relation or the sin. Neither does the silence of the sacred writer imply a sanction; no more than the silence of Christ, when John was beheaded by Herod, implied the sanction of that murder. See also DR. F. A. COX, (England) Scriptural Duty to Slaveholders, etc. He describes δουλος as "a generic term, applied to all the relations of servitude and acts of service, even when no inferiority of rank or condition is predicable."

† JOSEPHUS. Antiq. B. xvi., ch. 1. He is speaking of the impossibility, under the law of Moses, of there being such a thing as the slavery of the Jews to foreigners. He says that in case of crime, a thief, if he have not enough property to make restitution for his theft, may be sold for the amount of his theft, that is, his services may be sold to such an amount and he may be compelled to work till his labor shall have amounted to such a sum. But he can not be sold to foreigners at any rate, neither to one of his own nation in such manner as to be under perpetual slavery, for he must have been released after six years. This is a very positive and striking proof of the meaning of the Jewish system of service as limited and voluntary; and inasmuch as δουλειαν is the word used by Josephus (translated, however, in English, *slavery*), it is clear that such phraseology does not of necessity mean slavery, but is used for the service of hired laborers and freemen.

(3). The usage of δουλευω is under the same conditions. It is employed in the Septuagint for the Hebrew verb עָבַד, *to labor*, and receives and retains a signification of freedom in being used as the exponent of that word.* It is employed where slavery could not be meant,† as for example, in Gen. xiv., 4, of tributary confederates *serving* Chedorlaomer, and Gen. xxv., 23, the elder shall serve the younger; xxix., 15, of Jacob serving Laban; xxxi., 6, of the same; Ex. xxi., 2, 6, of the service of the Hebrew servant; Deut. xv., 18, worth a double hired servant in *serving* six years; Hosea xii., 12, Israel *served* for a wife.

(4). The word οικετης is another term employed in the New Testament for servants, which might mean slave, if the context rendered it necessary, if the subject matter was that of slaves or slavery; but also it is used for freemen and free servants, and might be applied, and was applied, in that sense.

Now οικετης is rendered by Calvin in the Latin word *famulus*, and he notes that inasmuch as it is not δοῦλοι, but οἰκέται, that is used in 1 Pet. ii., 18, the passage may be understood to refer to free servants as well as slaves.‡ And Bretschneider says that οικετης is used not merely of slaves, but also of freemen, of the wife and the children.§ Josephus employs this word for servants of the Hebrews, who could not possibly be slaves.‖ It is em-

---

* JOSEPHUS, Antiq., B. 3, ch. xii., sec. 3. He describes the fiftieth year as "a jubilee, in which debtors were freed from their debts, and the servants were set at liberty, which servants (translated *slaves* in the English) became such, though of the same stock, by transgressing." The Greek is not *slaves*, but being employed of Hebrews certainly signifies a free service on a voluntary contract; οἱ δουλεύοντες ελευθεροι ἀφίενται, *those engaged at service were set free*. This phraseology is that used also by JUSTIN MARTYR in his Dialogue with

Trypho, where he employs the word εδουλευσεν to signify the labor of Jacob in the service of Laban. This was not slavery, but a free, voluntary contract. See Gen. xxix., 15, 20.

† STEPHANUS, Thesaurus. He gives an instance from Diogenes Laertius of δουλευω applied to working for wages.

‡ CALVIN, Com. in 1 Peter ch. ii.

§ BRETSCHNEIDER, Lex. "Non solum de servis, sed etiam de liberis."

‖ JOSEPHUS against Apion, B. 2, Sec. 19, and elsewhere.

ployed in the SEPTUAGINT for those who were not and could not
be slaves.* In the same way it is employed in the New Testament. Stephanus, Liddell and Scott, Schleusner, refer to a similar
usage in classical writers, so that it is sometimes opposed to δοῦλον
(Herodotus, example, also Xenophon), and in the N. T. there could
be no indication or intimation from it of the existence of slavery.

Now Facciolatus renders *famulus* by the Greek word υπηρετης,
and the Latin words *minister, servus.†* At the same time he says
that *famulus* is employed concerning a free man serving another,
and ministering. Hence Ulpian is quoted showing that all, even
free men, are comprehended under the name of *familiæ*, who are
in service; *famulus* is also used concerning ministers of the gods.

Again, *servus* is rendered by Facciolatus as *famulus*, and δοῦλος
and θεραπων are presented as synonyms in the Greek. But he
quotes Cicero pro Cluentio as saying, *Legum id circo omnes servi
sumus, ut liberi esse possimus*, we are all for this very purpose
servants to the law, that we might be free. A wise and beautiful
apothegm, not a little like the language of Paul in regard to our
being servants of Christ, that we might have perfect freedom.
And even concerning the word *verna,‡* a home-born slave, Facciolatus says that it was used sometimes in application to a freeman
born at Rome. But as to θεραπων, which Facciolatus has set
with δοῦλος, as the translation of *servus*, the lexicographers affirm
that in Homer and the old authors it always differs from δοῦλος,
as implying free and honorable service. But in Chios θεραποντες
was the name for their slaves.

Now θεραπων is the word used by the Septuagint, instead of
δοῦλος, in several instances, concerning Moses, as a translation of
the Hebrew עֶבֶד, the word for servant, though, as is well known,
the word δοῦλος is most commonly employed for all forms and
qualities of service. But θεραπων is also the word employed by

---

* SEPT. Trans. Gen. xxvii., 37;
Lex. xxv. 42, 55; Num. xxxii., 5;
Prov. xxii, 7; Deut. xxxii., 5, (of
Moses).

† FACCIOLATUS, Lex. Lat. FAMULUS.
‡ BECKER, Gallus, 213. " *Vernæ*,
children resulting from the contubernium among the slaves."

Paul in the epistle to the Hebrews (ch. iii., 5), in regard to Moses, and it is the only instance in all the New Testament in which this word is used, while δοῦλος is used in cases without number, of free men in free, voluntary and honorable service. All this shows (1) how closely the usage in the New Testament follows that of the Septuagint, and (2) how impossible it is to draw any conclusion from the use of any word, which, in the classical Greek writers, may have ordinarily meant *slave*, that such is the meaning of the word in the New Testament. The Septuagint translators of the Hebrew Scriptures were the classics of the New Testament writers, although Paul was familiar, perhaps, with all the Greek literature of his time.

The proof from the use of the word θεραπων is conclusive as to the freedom of the domestic service and of servants among the Hebrews. It is used not only of Moses, in Numbers and Joshua, but of Job, in the book of Job, (i., 8; ii., 3; xlii., 7;) and by Job himself concerning his own servants, (xix., 16,) I called my servant, and he gave me no answer, and (xxxi., 13,) If I did despise the cause of my man-servant or of my maid-servant, etc., and of servants generally, (iii., 19,) the servant is free from his master, and (vii., 2,) as a servant earnestly desireth the shadow, etc. It is used also in Numbers xxxii., 31, of the children of Gad and Reuben. The use of this word by Paul, in the Epistle to the Hebrews, in speaking of Moses, was adopted, there cannot be a doubt, because the Septuagint translation used it in places which referred to Moses as God's faithful servant over God's house.

Moses is also called in the Septuagint οικετης (as in Deut. xxxiv., 5). In the New Testament οικετης no more indicates a slave than οικετης or θεραπων in the Septuagint translation of the Old Testament. Trommius renders the word, domesticus, famulus, servus.* And *domesticus* is the word employed by Lardner for οικειοι, in rendering the text Eph. ii., 19, " no more strangers, but fellow citizens with the saints, and of the household of God." You

---

* Trommii Concord. Græc. Vet. Test. οικετης.

have equal rights of citizenship with the people and natives of the country, and are God's domestics.* Whether domesticus, or famulus, or servus, in the translation into Latin be employed, or οικετης, or διακονος, or δοῦλος, or θεραπων, in the Greek, there is no more indication of slavery than when the Hebrew word for servant עֶבֶד is employed in the Old Testament,† and rendered by the Greek translators οικετης,‡ or δοῦλος, or θεραπων, or by the Latin vulgate servus, or famulus, or domesticus, or verna.

(5.) An examination of the Septuagint usage of the words δοῦλη, *maid-servant*, and παιδισκη, *maiden, damsel, servant*, as employed for the Hebrew words אָמָה and שִׁפְחָה, reveals the same conditions. These Greek words received the same free significance from the Hebrew, and carried it into the dialect of the New Testament. In Ruth iii., 9, δοῦλη, *handmaid*, is applied to Ruth herself; so in ii., 13. So, 1 Sam. i., 11, 16, 18, of Hannah; and chapter xxv., several times of Abigail; 2 Sam. xx., 17. Saalschutz and others have noted the free signification of these Hebrew words; improperly, at any time, translated by words that convey the meaning of slavery. *Bondwoman* is not the proper translation of the word designating Hagar in Hebrew as Sarah's maid.

(6.) The usage of παιδισκη is subject to the same law. Gen. xxi., 10, 12, 13; xxx., 3; xxxi., 33; Ex. xx., 10, 17; xxi., 20, 32; xxiii., 12; Deut. xii., 12, 18; xv., 17; xvi., 11, 14; Ruth ii., 13; iv., 12; 1 Sam. xxv., 41; Jer. xxxiv., 9, 11, 16. The examination demonstrates its usage of free persons. To translate it by the word *bondwoman* or *slave* would be to convey a falsehood under the claim of revelation.

All these words are used in the New Testament of free persons.

---

* LARDNER on Peter. Works, Vol. 6, p. 218.

† SAALSCHUTZ. Laws of Moses, Vol. 2, 714. With what justice (this writer well demands) can any one apply the term of servile thraldom or slavery to a free system like that among the Hebrews? Persons that were free by law every seventh year could not be called slaves. They were in no sense such. He exposes the falsehood of any such appellative to the system.

‡ BRETSCHNEIDER. Lex. N. T. οικετης, applied to free persons, *non solum de servis sed etiam de liberis, uxore, filiis*.

And though some of them generally, and others often, were applied in classic Greek, out of Judea, to the state and custom of slavery, they were prepared for Christianity and for the state of freedom, first as Hebrew proselytes in the Septuagint, second, as adopted into the family of Christ, where there is neither bond nor free.* Such is the course of the argument in all its branches, from Genesis to Revelation, under the guidance and presence of the free system and words of the Hebrew dispensation.

II. The second great form of the argument, the legal or statutory, runs on in the same manner, under the same influences. The whole system is a system for freemen, and there is no legislation for slaves. Something of the power of the argument from the system of laws comes out in the way of contrast. Ye shall not commit the crimes which ye have seen committed by the Egyptians, but ye shall set yourselves against them. Ye were oppressed in Egypt, ye shall not oppress one another; ye were strangers in Egypt, ye shall love the stranger as yourselves.†

This general principle prevailed, and excluded the possibility of caste, or prejudice against color or labor, from ever getting a foothold. It was a law of Egypt that the murder, whether of a

---

* CAMPBELL. Preliminary Diss. to the Interp. N. T. Dis. 2. part ii. The words Greek, but the spirit Hebrew. Campbell's acute and interesting instances of the naturalization laws in regard to words, and the causes and methods of their operation, might be carried, with great weight, into the illustration of the subject of slavery. With the antique pagans slavery was a virtue of society, with the Christians it was a vice. With modern pagans it is a vice, with modern Christians (but only in the United States) it is a virtue, established by law. Not without just ground did the celebrated Humboldt record his sarcasm against professedly Christian slaveholders and churches in America, that it is not now the saints but the infidels that call in question the justice of slavery. HUMBOLDT, Kingdom of New Spain, Vol. 1, chap. vii.

† MARSHAM. Lex Mosaic. Ex *malis* Egyptiorum *moribus, bonæ* Israelitarum *leges*, remarks Marsham, with as much truth as antithesis. Out of the wicked manners and morals of the Egyptians sprang the admirable laws of the Israelites. God never permitted his people to be personal slaves till the crucifixion of the Saviour and destruction of Jerusalem. But out of the hard bondage laid upon them by Pharaoh grew the legal provisions against personal slavery through all generations. Lev. xix., 34; Deut. x., 19.

freeman or a slave, was to be punished with death;* and Heeren regarded this equality of the penalty, together with the law forbidding imprisonment for debt, as among some proofs of an advancement in moral culture among the Egyptians, such as few of the nations of antiquity have made.† It was a law, Diodorus has noted, that if any man slew another, or seeing him suffer violence, did not rescue him, though he were able, he should be put to death. Compare with this, Prov. xxiv., 11, 12, "If thou forbear to deliver them that are ready to be slain," etc. There was no difference, among the Hebrews, as to the claims of benevolence, between the native and the stranger. Michaelis notices particularly the fact of "the inequality between citizens and strangers being counteracted by a law which ordained crimes, at least of various kinds, to be punished precisely in the same manner on both." There shall be one and the same law for the native and the stranger.‡

These principles, laid down in the law book of the nation, are such, that not only among themselves, but in regard to strangers, all manner of oppression was forbidden and excluded. No form of slavery could exist with such constitutional safeguards against it, any more than a monarchical form of government could exist under the Constitution of the United States. Not till the spirit of the people had departed could the forms of constitutional law be violated; and when they were violated, then the wrath of God descended. The law of freedom was not only national, but particular, extending even to the treatment of the fugitive by each individual, the duty of each and every person being to maintain and defend freedom for each and every other person. The law was of liberty every man to his brother, and every man to his neighbor. The attempted violation of this law in the time of

---

* DIODORUS SICULUS. But Plato thought there ought to be different laws for freemen and slaves; a word for a freeman, a blow for a slave, and so in proportion. See BECKER'S Charicles. Excursus, *Slaves.*

† HEEREN. Ideen uber die Politik, etc., der alten welt, 347.

‡ MICHAELIS. Laws of Moses. Vol. 2, art. cxxxviii.

Jeremiah sent the whole nation into captivity; so that here both the reality and significance of the law are demonstrated, and the abhorrence of God against slavery, in such manner as cannot be mistaken. The law laid upon every man a responsibility of freedom for his neighbor.

Entering upon the New Testament, it is not to be imagined that the glorious elevation and scope of this commandment would be ignored and contradicted. Accordingly, in the Epistle to Philemon, we find the rule of giving liberty every man to his brother and every man to his neighbor reëstablished, and slavery abolished. The law of freedom, by the love of Christ, accomplishes in the New Testament what the law of God had appointed in the Old.

III. The historical argument is intimately connected with the legal, running along with it, illustrating it, and illustrated by it. In exactly the same manner it is baptized with the spirit of freedom, being not the history of slavery, but of God's providence, word and grace, against slavery, and of the destruction and misery of the nation through the very attempt to establish slavery. The attempt comes out, as the climax of Jewish wickedness, in the thirty-fourth chapter of Jeremiah's prophecy, the punishment of which cured the madness and the crime. The later history discloses a nation and a social system, the legitimate growth of laws excluding slavery, and rendering individual labor, and especially the labors of agriculture, free, honorable and ennobling. Every man received a just recompense of wages for his work, whether the contracted time were longer or shorter.* No idea is clearer

---

* CAVE on the Mosaical Dispensation (Lives of the Apostles), 82. He quotes Antigonus Sochæus, two hundred and eighty-four years before Christ, exhorting his disciples not to be like mercenary servants, who serve merely for the wages they can get from their masters, but to serve God for himself, without expectation of reward. This plainly shows the custom of society to have been that of voluntary labor upon hire, upon contract between the parties, and not that of slavery, where the master owned the man, and paid him nothing for his work, and was not supposed to be under any obligation to pay him any thing. There was no such slavery in Judea.

or more common, throughout the New Testament, than that of the voluntary choice of masters and of service, with agreement of the price, the conditions, and the payment of stipulated wages. The supposition of such voluntary, paid service runs through the whole gospels and epistles.

And whereas the history in the Old Testament discloses a law for the protection of fugitives, exactly such as might be expected to follow in the train of a system of legislation that condemned the making merchandise of man to the punishment of death, the current of the New Testament brings us to the fulfillment of that law, under the gospel; brings us to just such a state of society as we might suppose would grow out of such a system of laws, in conjunction with the spirit and precepts of the gospel, with the injunction upon the Christian master, in the name of Christ and his love, to receive that fugitive as a free brother, no longer a servant, but a brother beloved, both in the flesh and in the Lord. The historical argument is here perfect and complete, having traveled all along with the legal, and now uniting with it in a harmony of proof as impressive and instructive as it is delightful. This history of the conduct of Paul and Philemon, in regard to this matter, was presented, doubtless, for this very purpose, to show that the Hebrew laws against slavery and in behalf of fugitives and freedom were not a temporary speculation, but enjoined a practical, essential form of virtue, justice and piety, to last as long as the world stands.

A striking part of this history is the record of the first sermon of the Lord Jesus, in Nazareth, on the text in Is. lxi., 1, 2. He hath anointed me to preach deliverance to the captives, the acceptable year, the jubilee year of the Lord. The last jubilee, the closing jubilee of the history of the Jewish nation, "fell with the year of the death of the Redeemer."* Lightfoot notes it as a

---

* LIGHTFOOT. Harmony. Part 3. Works, vol. v., 135. "Not only a year of jubilee, in a spiritual sense," says Lightfoot, "but also a year of jubilee in the literal and proper sense indeed." Lightfoot's chronological reckoning makes the last jubilee of the Jewish nation, (freedom to all the inhabitants of the land), correspond with the year of the crucifixion.

year of jubilee in the literal and proper sense indeed. But what a lamentable confusion and destruction of the prototype and prophetic history would there have been, if, when the time for this closing jubilee had come, being a festival instituted as a jubilee of personal liberty to all the inhabitants of the land, the old divine statutes of personal freedom had been abrogated, and in their stead the gospel had sanctioned and established personal slavery! Instead of this, the gospel abolished all slavery, and brought in a new and perfect freedom in Christ Jesus. The gospel law abolished every thing evil, and fulfilled and carried to the uttermost perfection every thing good. This law of advancement from that which was transitory and imperfect to that which was to be permanent and perfect, wanting nothing, is so plain, so unquestionable, that it is amazing that any human being could so far forget and confound it as to admit the possibility of a form of oppression which had been branded in the Old Testament as a crime worthy of death, being exalted in the New into a sacred, civil and domestic system, the supporters, defenders and practisers of which were to be received as owners of slaves, making merchandise of men, into the communion of the Christian church!

An astonishing example of such confusion is found even in the pages of such a writer as Olshausen, who admits that "the institution of slavery could not be approved by Christianity, for it was the product of sin;"* but afterwards intimates that inasmuch as it was an institution established in the world, and the apostles found it established, "therefore they did not forbid it!" "The apostles," he says, "would have blamed severely the *introduction* of slavery, if it had not existed when the gospel came into the world!" Just as if the fact of a sin being established gave it a solid moral claim, and exempted it from moral reprobation! And again he says, "The defenders of *negro* slavery can not appeal to Paul, for *negro* slavery is recent, and not from the earliest times, but was introduced by Christians themselves, to their everlasting disgrace, and is kept up only by fraud and kidnapping."

---

* OLSHAUSEN on Ephesians vi., 5, etc.

In this singular reasoning we have a decisive reprobation of slavery, as contrary to the law and essence of Christianity, and yet its possession of the world, when Christianity comes, is presented as a higher law than Christianity, or as constituting nine tenths of the law, and imposing silence on the gospel in regard to it.* By the same method of reasoning the apostles were bound to have said nothing against idolatry, that also being an established institution of society, when and where the gospel came, an institution involving civil rights and relations, with which the gospel must not interfere. But this is neither the law, nor the spirit, nor the history, neither of Judaism nor Christianity, which are both as united against slavery as they are against idolatry.

IV. The moral argument is a combination of the philological, legal and historical, which all converge in the great lesson of universal charity taught by the gospel, Whatsoever ye would that men should do to you, do ye even so to them, and, Thou shalt love thy neighbor as thyself. These laws lay hold also of the great announcement in the New Testament that God hath made of one blood all the races of men that dwell upon the face of the earth; with the other great fact that every wall of caste, color, national peculiarity and prejudice, is broken down in Christ, and that in him, in the church, there is neither Jew nor Greek, circumcision nor uncircumcision, Barbarian nor Scythian, bond nor free. Whatsoever contravenes or violates these laws of love must be abolished by the gospel; no reasoning can stand that disregards

* OLSHAUSEN on Coloss. iv., 1. Give unto your servants that which is just and equal. To avoid the inevitable conclusion of the abolition of slavery from this passage, Olshausen affirms that this direction "can not mean equality with masters, for that would be to abolish slavery, which was contrary to Paul's intention! It means rather the equal treatment of all the slaves, not preferring one at the expense of another." And this is supposed by a Christian commentator to be the interference of divine inspiration in behalf of slaves with their masters, not to give more to one than to another! If a peck of meal a week were the rule, the master must not give a peck and a half to any favored slave, for that would not be just and equal to the rest! So deep down into the common sense as well as piety of the church and of modern theology has the poison of slavery infused itself!

them; no piety is true that does not seek their perfect and complete fulfillment.

The moral argument, like the legal, *is against the relation itself*, as intrinsically unjust, cruel and wicked. And the historical and statistical developments, the argument from consequences, prove incontrovertibly the disastrous effect of admitting the relation as compatible with Christianity. If in the outset the piety of the church had faithfully applied the law of God, had taken that law, with its legitimate, intended conclusions and consequences, and driven it against the relation of slavery, as incompatible with Christianity, then would slavery have been expelled from the world wherever the church was established. If the church had applied the law of God against slavery as against murder, judging the relation of the slaveholder to the slave as it judges the relation of the murderer to his victim, then it would have been as impossible for slavery to have obtained a foothold in the church, or a sanction in the world, as for murder.

But the instant it was admitted that the relation, being civil and political, must not be interfered with, and might be innocently continued, while it was left to the spirit of Christianity, so called, to abolish the reality, that instant the whole authority of the church against it was paralyzed; for it was manifest that the reality of slavery consisted in the relation, and if that were permitted and sanctioned in the word of God as just, and not to be disturbed, then the reality was just and permanent likewise. Accordingly, under such treatment, the iniquity held on, till it not only destroyed the Roman empire, but ran through the Middle Ages, prevailing greatly, even in the church, notwithstanding that here and there, as in the cases of Augustine and Isidore,* eminent remonstrances were uttered in opposition to it, and now and then churches and monasteries, and, in general, the monastic spirit and rules, were set against it.† Nevertheless, when it passed from

---

* NEANDER, Church Hist. Bohn's, edit. vol. 3.

† EUSEBIUS, Life of Constantine and NEANDER, Memorials of Christian Life. One of the earliest laws in regard to it is mentioned by Eusebius, in the life of Constantine, who enacted "that no Christian should remain in

the form of Roman and Greek slavery into the form of the *serfage* of the Dark and Middle Ages, the reality was still that of slavery,* and it was submitted to and maintained, even by the church and its corrupt Christianity,† because the church had never applied, the law of God and the gospel of Christ against *the relation itself,*

servitude to a Jewish master, on the ground that it was wrong for the ransomed of the Saviour to be subjected to the yoke of slavery by a people who had slain the prophets and the Lord. The slave was to be set at liberty, and the master punished by a fine." It is obvious that such legislation did not strike at the relation or reality of slavery as in itself unjust, and forbidden in God's word, nor had the corrupt Christianity of that or a later age either the purity or power to enforce the word of God against it, or to produce a legislation accordant with humanity.

* THIERRY, History of the Norman Conquest, 89, 288, 293. In the famine in 1070, "the Saxon, wasted and depressed by hunger, would come and sell himself and all his family to perpetual slavery." The effect of slavery in the depreciation of property, and running of the land to waste, was remarkable. "The land on which the Englishmen o. exalted rank had lived in plenty, maintained, after the conquest, only two laborers, poor and enslaved, who scarcely returned to their Norman lord a tenth part of the revenue of the ancient free cultivators."

"About the year 1381, all those who were called bond in England, that is, all the cultivators, were serfs in body and goods ; the lord could sell them, together with their houses, oxen, children and posterity, which, in the English deeds, was expressed

in the following manner, Know that I have sold A. B., my knave, and all his offspring, born, or to be born." The word *bondage*, in the Norman tongue, expressed at that time all that was most wretched in the condition of humanity. Yet this word, from the Anglo-Danish word *bond*, meant, originally, a free cultivator, and joined to the Saxon word *hus*, denoted the master of the house, the *husbond*, or, in modern English, *husband*.

† GUIZOT, Hist. Civilization, vol. 2, in his Table of the Councils of the Gallic Church from the fourth to the tenth century, refers to several canons of different councils, as in the years 538 and 541, making the above-named distinction between Jews and Christians, doubtless following out that very law of Constantine referred to by Eusebius, and concluding that while it was sinful for a Jew to hold a Christian as a slave, and an opprobium and distress not to be endured by a Christian, it might be very just and proper for the Christians to enslave the Jews. The Christian bishops are forbidden from restoring runaway Christian slaves to their Jewish masters. And in the year 567 a law is quoted which declares that inasmuch as many persons, to the ruin of their souls, have made captives of others by violence and treason, such persons, if they neglect to restore such slaves to their freedom, shall be excommunicated.

of property in man, the relation of slaveholding, as by the divine judgment under all circumstances the guilt of man-stealing.

There always followed, with the relation,* and grew out of it, all the excesses, all the cruelties, all the degradations and oppressions, all the annihilations of right, and disregard of justice and humanity,† all the treatment, in fine, of human beings as brutes, always inevitable on the tolerance and practice of slavery as a system, under whatever name.‡ In all ages, whatever wickedness has been passed into law, whatever has been sanctioned and defended by any form of government, there have always been a sufficient number of Christians, so called, to defend the divine right of such wickedness, and give it a respectable place and standing in the church of God. On the other hand, God has always kept his witnesses against such inhuman and anti-Christian Christianity, and sometimes has so exalted them as martyrs, (in the modern age from Latimer and Sidney down to John Brown) that the light of their burning sheds the radiance of God's own law and gospel over whole ages, even in the midst of the excesses of atheism and depravity. " It hath been ever hereupon observed," said one of those noble martyrs, " that they who most precisely adhere to the laws of God, are least solicitous concerning the commands of men, unless they are well grounded ; and those who

* GAILLARDIN. Histoire du Moyen Age. Tom. 1, 117. He refers to a law of Rotharis, of the Lombards, which sets the slave in the rank of things, chattels, and treats the women in slavery as brutes. " Met l'esclave au rang des choses, et traite la femme esclave comme une vache ou une jument ; servum aut ancillam, *seu alias res mobiles.*"

† GEIJER. History of the Swedes, ch. vii, 86. To " beat one like a slave," to have " as little right as a scourged house girl," or female slave, are expressions found in the laws. But as early as 1335, serfdom, or thraldom, was abolished in Sweden. The old diabolic feature always remained with it, while slavery lasted, of the impossibility of slaves contracting marriage. A volume might be written on the infernal reason and philosophy of this one fixture of the great vice.

‡ THIERRY. Hist. Norman Conquest, 288. WALLON. Hist. d'Esclavage. Vol. 2, ch. v., 177. BECKER. Gallus, Slave-family ; and Charicles, Exc. Slaves, compared with BLAIR, Inquiry ; FUSS. Roman Antiq. POTTER. Greek Antiq. GROTE. Hist. Greece, Vol. 3, 95.

most delight in the glorious liberty of the sons of God, do not only subject themselves to Him, but are most regular observers of the just ordinances of man, made by the consent of such as are concerned, according to the will of God."*

Now by the Word of God we are bound to meet and conquer every thing that opposes itself to the will of God; for the weapons of our warfare are not carnal, but mighty through God to the pulling down of strongholds; and it is the business of the church and ministry to wrestle with the Word of God against the rulers of the darkness of this world. The relation of slaveholding must be sentenced by the church as in itself an immoral relation, and the claim of property in man must be presented as it stands in God's Word, as a moral guilt equivalent with the crime of murder.

It is the great responsibility of the modern church, the great work before it, the great honor and privilege offered to it from God, to turn the lightning of his Word against this gigantic iniquity of the modern age, that, as in the grand imagery of the prophet Daniel, "the beast may be slain, and his body destroyed, and given to the burning flame." The conquest of this sin through the Word and Spirit of the living God, ministered by a fearless church and ministry, would be so celestial a triumph, would be such a proof of Divine Inspiration, such a demonstration of divine power and grace, that it would stir the whole world as with the trumpet of an archangel. Let the church of God in our country assume this position of authority, and exercise this power, and straightway the Gentiles would come to her light, and kings to the brightness of her rising.

And it is a terrible position which those have taken, who stand in the way of such a demonstration, and refuse to admit the light of God's Word upon this great wickedness. They stand between the world and its salvation. They trample the world into infidelity and darkness, for the sake of supporting a despotic, death-dealing, popular sin.

* ALGERNON SIDNEY. Discourses on Government, Vol. 1, 315.

CHAPTER I.

IMPORTANCE OF THE INVESTIGATION.—THE MOOD OF MIND REQUISITE FOR IT.—THE EFFECT OF PREJUDICE.—IMPIETY OF DESIRING AND SEEKING IN THE SCRIPTURES A SANCTION OF MEN'S SINS.—MANUFACTURE OF INFIDELITY BY THE SANCTION OF SLAVERY.

A MORE solemn and important question than that of the verdict in the word of God in regard to slavery, can not occupy our attention. If God's judgment is really revealed against slavery as sin, then we, as a people, are condemned and guilty beyond any other nation under heaven. The investigation of the matter can not but be intensely interesting to us as men, as citizens, as Christians, to whom the welfare and salvation of our country are dear. If we dare oppose this giant iniquity, or hope for success in the conflict, we must fight the battle against it by the word of God. If it be not condemned there, it is in vain that we struggle for its overthrow. If it be not condemned of God, men will maintain it, and we have no power against it, nor any right to denounce it as sin. One side or the other, it must divide society into extreme parties, for there is no middle ground, and every man ought to know where he stands in regard to it, and by what authority. Every man ought to take one side or the other, by the word of God. Every man will be compelled to do this, sooner or later, and the part of wisdom is to take the right position now, on God's side, and for God's truth and righteousness, while a battle can be fought and gained on these grounds.

To constitute an impartial juror as to the judgment of the word of God in such a case, it is not necessary that a man's humane instincts, or preferences of liberty, should be denied, or abrogated, or put in abeyance. It is rather requisite that the heart should guide the understanding, and take, at the very outset, the side of the oppressed against the oppressor. There should be, in the first place, a preference of freedom above slavery, and second, a sympathy in behalf of the oppressed, and not in favor of the oppressor.

We have sometimes found men whom we have supposed sincere in their professed abhorrence of slavery, evidently bent, nevertheless, on discovering something in the Bible to shield it from unlimited reprobation. It has filled us with astonishment and sadness, on engaging in the argument, to discover a manifest desire that you may be defeated in your endeavor to produce from the sacred Scriptures an indisputable indictment of slavery as sin. And even when the demonstration has been presented, they have resorted to sophistry and special pleading to evade its power. Such men come to the word of God not desiring to find the verdict against slavery, but with preferences leaning in its favor, and on the lookout for something to justify the oppressor, rather than to vindicate and righten the oppressed.

This is not a mood of mind in which men can possibly investigate fairly. If called to sit upon a jury, they would be peremptorily and justly challenged as being interested witnesses and judges. The understanding is darkened, the judgment is bribed, the power of discernment is perverted. Such a prejudice is as a strong magnet, or a box of steel tools, close by the compass, that will turn a ship out of her way, on the plainest, smoothest, easiest sea ever navigated.

Moreover, such a disposition of mind is contrary to every rule of investigation and of judgment, *even where an acknowledged criminal is to be tried*, and where the doubt, if doubt there be, is to go in favor of humanity, and of the prisoner at the bar. How much more where the question is as to the right of millions of our fellow-men to be treated as freemen like ourselves, or their destination to be held in bondage as felons. The doubt in such a case must certainly, by all Christian obligation, by all moral sentiment and conscience, weigh in favor of those held in bondage, and not in favor of those claiming the right to enslave them. If we are to remember them that are in bonds as bound also with them, and there is any doubt in regard to the justice of their being kept bound, we ought unquestionably to side *with them*, and not with those who bind them. A verdict for the binding can not righteously be rendered, without the clearest, most indisputable, most unquestionable title.

And so with the argument from the Scriptures, in which so much is involved besides the fate of those held or proposed to be held in bondage. The slaveholder must show a clear title to hold, and in such a case the doubt is fatal to his title. The principle laid down by Paul comes into play, and he that doubteth is damned if he eat this morsel with a hesitating conscience, because it is not a question of a mere act of harmless self-indulgence, more or less, as whether he shall have turkey or corned beef for his dinner, whether he shall go clad in broadcloth or sackcloth, whether he shall eat two oranges or half a dozen for his dessert, the determination of which questions does not at all concern the interests or rights of others, much less violate them; but it is, whether he shall eat his own dinner or steal and consume that which belongs to another man; whether he shall take of his own flock and his own herd for his own purposes, or lay hands on the little ewe lamb that is his poor neighbor's; nay, more than that, whether, in fact, he shall eat a sheep that belongs to him, or a man that does not. He has got to settle, beyond dispute, that slavery, at the present day and in our own country, is sanctioned of God, and that, by God's ordinance, the slave he claims *belongs to him*, before he can take him.

Nor is it enough, if he could prove, which he can not, that the practice of slavery was once permitted to a particular people or a designated individual; in order to adopt it *as his own right*, he must show a similar designation *in his own case*, an appointment from God *for himself to act as a slaveholder*. For the thing for which he is seeking supernatural sanction, being the taking and holding of a man as his property, is not only an infringement of God's ownership as the Creator, a robbery of God, but also a robbery of man, and the highest violation of all natural right; and if not, if it were naturally right, what need to seek such a supernatural sanction? We do not go to the word of God to ask whether we may eat bread, or drink tea and coffee, and wear raiment, or build houses and live in them, or pay our just debts, or burn wood or anthracite coal in our fire-places.

And the going to God's word for a sanction of what all mankind feel to be villainy, is a dreadful sacrilege and impiety, especially for a professed Christian. It is worse iniquity than that of forging the name of your friend as an indorsement on your note, which, without that name, would have been worthless. He, it is true, is sure to reject the note as spurious, and the forgery will be discovered as soon as the paper is presented for payment, but, meanwhile, what mischief, confusion and misery may be the consequence. And suppose a company, aware of the existence of such forged notes, that should combine to keep up their credit in order to profit by them, passing them from one to another, and making the world believe them trustworthy, what language could severely enough characterize such fraud? By and by God will protest the forgery of his name and authority on the back of these notes of hand claiming property in human beings, and he will search out the wickedness for a terrible retribution, but, meanwhile, what mischief and misery are enacted by the forgery! And if a company take it up, and make a business of it, how wide and dreadful the destruction!

It is like a corporation of wreckers destroying the lights on a coast for the sake of profit in their piracy. It is as if you could put chemical poison into the fountain of our sunlight

for the sake of a more complete and rapid bleaching process
in an article of your private, profitable monopoly and manufacture. It is as if the physicians in a place, in order to keep
up their business, should poison the wells and fountains, or set
malaria in the atmosphere for the purpose of producing or
maintaining a chronic epidemic. It is as if you should adul-
terate all the flour of the year's harvest with plaster of Paris,
or even with arsenic, to make it weigh heavier. These frauds
depreciate the genuine article, even if there were no other
suffering or mischief from them.

Just so the Bible becomes a suspicious book under these
immoral operations conducted by virtue of its authority. Its
credit is diminished just as that of a bank is diminished, when
a company of forgers and counterfeiters have succeeded in
forcing into the market a quantity of false notes and counter-
feits. And suppose that, these villains having been very successful in their work, so as to become a great moneyed power,
with much command of the market, the directors of the bank,
for fear of a combination against their own business, should
conclude, instead of protesting the false bills, and prosecuting
their authors, to guarantee them, and strike a bargain for mutual benefit and insurance, assuming the false in order to gain
acceptance for the true; through how many generations, or
in how many nations, could such a bank maintain its credit?

Now a man coming to the Scriptures, in search of some excuse of slavery there, comes despairingly in regard to every
other refuge, comes driven thither for a shield and defense
against the condemnation of humanity, comes acknowledging
that the moral sense of mankind is against it, and desiring to
disgrace that moral sense as a dangerous radicalism and fanaticism. But what a diabolical hypocrisy and sacrilege for a
man to come to the word of God, in the hope of proving an
acknowledged injustice and inhumanity to be no sin ; in the
hope of finding some sanction and excuse for the deliberate
voluntary protection and continuance of that which is confessed

to be a vast evil! What shall we say as to the moral enormity of a Christian man's sympathies being in favor of the sin, and against the condemnation of it, against the finding of a verdict of such condemnation in the Scriptures.

The moral sense of mankind being against slavery, and there being something in the heart and conscience of every investigator of the subject, which tells him that it certainly is not one of the Christian graces, and it being indisputable that the world regard it as selfishness and oppression, every Christian man might be supposed to hope that the book which he considers and teaches to be the only written revelation from Jehovah, the only infallible guide as to morality and religion, will be found so clearly on the side of justice and humanity, as to leave no doubt what is justice and humanity; and that, when God has laid down the great rule, Whatsoever ye would that men should do to you, do ye even so to them, he will not be found sanctioning that which is the completest violation of that rule. One would think that the sympathies of every true Christian would lead him to desire a verdict in the Scriptures in behalf of freedom and against slavery, and that he would come to the Bible, not to find some ground for defending slavery from the spontaneous and all but universal reprobation of mankind, or some apology for holding human beings in bondage, or some protection of a system admitted to be the source and concatenation of boundless crime and misery, but some irresistible weapons for its overthrow. How can it be, that any man should not come with a mind open to conviction, and a heart ready to hail the condemnation of such a system, instead of being drawn by the argument like a bullock to the slaughter? We have sometimes been amazed to meet with an evident disappointment in the minds of professed Christians, on having it demonstrated to them that there was nothing in favor of slavery in the word of God; the admission has been extorted, unwilling, and the acknowledgment resisted and evaded every step of the way.

Any thing miraculous in God's word, we can believe, because its morality is so heavenly, because the revelation is for man's good, and tends to make a heaven upon earth; but it is impossible to believe an institution that grows out of theft, cruelty, and murder, and perpetuates all those iniquities; an institution which is the climax and support of all villainy, to have come down from God.

The book being a transcript of God's holiness, we must believe it to have come from him, for without it, and before it, men did not know God; but the moment we should find it to be a transcript, apology and sanction of men's vices, we must inevitably reject and despise it. It is to be supposed that every true Christian would desire to remove every shade of doubt or darkness cast upon the holy Scriptures, every cloud that dims the brightness of their evidence as the word of God, every barrier of ignorance and prejudice against the clear shining of that evidence: "Thy word is very pure, therefore thy servant loveth it." You do not desire to find adultery sanctioned in the word of God, nor forgery, nor murder.

If the moral delinquencies of the Koran and the book of the Mormons are admitted to be insuperable objections against any supposition of those books being from God, so as to take away all obligation upon any person even to examine their claims, would not the sanction of human slavery, as known by its fruits, and for the sake of its fruits, much rather release a man from any such obligation? Let a man know what slavery is—its origin, its results, and the means by which it is sustained and propagated—and then tell him that *such as it is*, it is supported and commanded in this book, and would he not have reason to say, "This being the case, I am not bound to examine any farther. I know that this book can not be from God?"

There are things in the Bible which men *wrest*, not for the sake of good, but for evil, and for their own destruction; and such are the texts which they have endeavored to torture into the likeness of some permission of this sin. They might as well plead, while keeping a class of men, for their own profit, ground down and debased in an employment which would inevitably make them cruel, profane, insensible, and reckless, that they were sanctioned in so doing by the passage which says that God hardened Pharaoh's heart. The men, ministers, and churches, who plead Scripture as the shield and sanction of slavery, are wholesale manufacturers of infidelity.*

* These errors and immoralities of opinion and of practice have been extended and perpetuated even through the medium of books prepared for children, and books of piety. Take the following for one example, by the American Sunday School Union.

"Slavery seems to have existed before the flood. Noah speaks of it as a thing well known. Among the ancient patriarchs it was very common. The servants, of whom we hear in the history of their times, were properly slaves, who might be bought and sold without any regard to their own will. Some of the richer shepherds, like Abraham and Job, appear to have had thousands of them belonging to their households."

This passage occurs in a work by Rev. John W. Nevin, D. D., entitled, "Summary of Biblical Antiquities, for the use of Schools, Bible Classes and Families." Every sentence in the paragraph is the statement of an absolutely false assertion, even from the first, for not a word nor a hint is to be found in the Bible concerning slavery before the flood. Yet these falsehoods are for the instruction of children!

In a valuable work on the Legal Rights of Women, by E. D. Mansfield, the writer declares that Hebrew wives were bought with money or produce, and that this was the consequence of the right of the father to *sell his children as slaves!* He refers to Michaelis for proof. Yet the thought hardly seems to have suggested itself how dreadful a reproach this throws upon the Bible, and how impossible it is to maintain as a divine revelation a book which could be proved to have permitted and enjoined the traffic in human beings, and the selling of children by their parents as slaves! CALMET, and the Encyclopedias generally, have circulated the same error. REES is an honorable exception.

The same monstrous assertion we find transferred to the pages of the Commercial Gazetteer, published by the Harpers, and there also we are referred to Michaelis, as the authority, being informed that in Judea, and in Rome alike, parents had the power of selling their children for slaves! See the corrections of Michaelis, by SAALSCHUTZ, *Das Mos. Recht,* Laws of Moses, Vol. II.

CHAPTER II.

THE argument against slavery, both from the Old and New Testament, is various and ample, amounting to a demonstration of God's abhorrence of this sin, as palpable and cogent as the demonstration against idolatry itself. We have, first, the historic record of a state of society appointed of God, in which there is no trace of slavery to be found; the first and only indisputable case of it, or of men's availing themselves of its existence, being marked as a case of man-stealing, aggravated and monstrous.

Second, we have the record of God's reprobation of such an approximation to slavery as was witnessed in the oppression of the Hebrews by the Egyptians, and of God's vengeance against their oppressors for such a crime.

This is accompanied and followed, thirdly, by a perpetual injunction against ever imposing on any other race any similar bondage; and we have a series of the divine precepts for the humane and generous treatment of the stranger, the outcast, the unprotected and oppressed, and repeated warnings from God never to treat any human beings, but especially the weak and friendless, with unkindness; *à fortiori*, the culmination of cruelty and oppression in the system of chattel slavery much more intensely reprobated and forbidden of God.

Fourth, we have a series of explicit divine statutes, appointing the system of domestic service, marking its bounds, guarding against the possibility of its passing into oppression or slavery, protecting the rights of the servants as carefully as those of the masters, forbidding servants to be sold as slaves, and rendering the establishment of slavery impossible.

Fifth, we have separate, fundamental, unlimited statutes, condemning with the penalty of death that crime which is the origin and essence of slavery, *man-stealing*, *holding*, and *selling*, and forbidding any restoration to his master of any servant a fugitive from his master. The conclusion from these statutes is unavoidable, that the claim of property in man is not only without foundation in justice, but is a crime equivalent in guilt to that of murder.

Sixth, we have historical and legal decisions and precedents, growing out of these statutes, and settling their interpretation.

Seventh, we have great and solemn recorded cases of the divine wrath in consequence of the violation of those statutes, and the divine judgment against the transgressors.

Eighth, we have the curse of God attached to unjust law, and men forbidden to obey it.

Ninth, we have the commentaries of the prophets upon the laws, in a body of denunciations against oppression and slavery, and injunctions of freedom, and demands of justice and benevolence towards the oppressed, the like of which are not to be found the world over, nor ever existed in the jurisprudence or literature of any nation; and which, if slavery had been sanctioned in the law of God, would stand forth in glaring contradiction and condemnation of that law.

Tenth, we have in other forms the principles of the morality of love, of which that law is the exponent, and on which it is grounded, and descriptions of the actual life of social freedom, benevolence and prosperity which it produces, in such histories as those of the books of Ruth and Job.

Eleventh, we have terrible and oft repeated curses pronounced against both the act and the system of taking men's labor without giving them wages; curses without any restriction, and belonging logically, morally and expressly to any system of which this wickedness is a fundamental element, as of slavery it is.

Twelfth, we have God's requisitions upon men to protect, defend and restore such as were defrauded of their freedom and their rights, and his demand, as in Isaiah, that every yoke be broken, and the oppressed set free; and to this may be added the forms of prayer for deliverance from the oppression of man, that so we may keep God's statutes, and the forms of promise, that in the coming of God's kingdom, he will save the children of the needy and break in pieces the oppressor; a thing which he could not do, if at the same time the severest possible oppression had been sanctioned by his law.

In all these ways, the consummation of proof, as well as its variety, is perfect. Nor is the interpretation of particular statutes left to opinion or to reasoning merely, but God takes the broken statute, for example, and shows its meaning, if there could be any doubt in regard to it, by pronouncing sentence, and executing the penalty. How dare any man assert that God ever sanctioned slavery in his statutes, when the historical record stands undisputed and indisputable, of his public indictment and punishment of the whole nation for the introduction and attempted establishment of slavery, *contrary* to his statutes? God himself, a thousand years after the framing of the statutes, calls the people into court, states again the substance and meaning of the statutes, reads the indictment for their transgression of them, and promulgates and inflicts the sentence; and the one crime is that of slavery. The comparison of the thirty-fourth chapter of Jeremiah with the twenty-second of Ezekiel, and the examination of concurrent and immediately succeeding circumstances and events prove this, and fasten the application with an awful emphasis and solemnity.

"I made a covenant of freedom with your fathers, freedom not for yourselves merely, but for your servants, to all time, that ye should proclaim liberty for them and not slavery; but ye have rebelled against my statutes, and brought your servants into subjection, at your pleasure, and not theirs. Ye have not proclaimed liberty, every man to his neighbor and his brother, therefore I proclaim liberty for you, saith the Lord, to the sword, to the pestilence and the famine, and ye shall be removed into all nations of the earth." That was the sentence, and immediately it was executed, almost as swiftly as the bolt follows the lightning. This is one example of God's own interpretation of his own laws. And so we are confronted from generation to generation in God's word, with furrows of light, mountain ranges of light, precedents like volcanoes, where the flame and the red-hot lava forbid all possibility of mistake.

Thus the history grows out of the laws, and is a commentary upon them; and every lawyer, and every historic scholar knows the value of such testimony. If any old English statutes of Edward the Fourth's reign, for example, were in doubt, and a case can be found two or three hundred years afterwards, clearly attested, in which the statute in doubt was applied, and judgment issued, and sentence executed for its violation, that would settle the matter; that is the very perfection of interpretation. And thus, in regard to God's own law, God's *judgments* are said by him to be as the light that goeth forth. And such is the interpretation of the Mosaic statutes by the sacred history.

And negatively there is the same light as positively. For xample, in the statutes we have *man-selling* forbidden as well as man-stealing; consequently, in the history there are no instances ever of any sale of human beings, any traffic in slaves. In the statutes again we have a law forbidding the restoring of fugitive servants to their masters; consequently, in the history we have servants running away, but never any cases of their restoration, nor any signs of marshals or judges of probate appointed for slave commissioners, nor any indications of the institution of bloodhounds to hunt for fugitives, nor court houses with chains for their trial, nor jails to imprison them, nor arrangements for having them sold to pay their jail fees. All the conditions and junctures of society that would inevitably have grown out of the existence and influence of slavery, had it been sanctioned by law, are wanting; the inevitable consequences of slave legislation, proving its reality and its character, are not to be found. On the contrary, all the fixtures of society are found, and all the events happen, that would naturally grow out of a state of freedom, the result of a system of laws intended for the perpetual establishment of freedom, and the prevention, suppression and extinction of slavery.

Thirteenth. Coming down to the New Testament, we find, first of all, the illustration of this correspondence between institutions, and the laws that have produced them, in the absence of slavery from the land and nation governed by the legislation of the Old Testament. We find that in Judea there was no such thing as slavery in the social life and customs of the Hebrews. This iniquity does not appear, as inevitably it must have done, had it been a fixture in the divine laws for the Jewish people. Had it been a domestic institution ordained of God, the whole land would have been, in the progress of so many ages, overrun with slaves; the whole nation would have been crowded with them. They would have constituted the great article of wealth and luxury. There would have been slave markets in every city; and in Jerusalem, in the very temple, not only those that sold doves, but those that sold slaves would have had their places for such merchandise—their stalls for traffic in human flesh.

For either it is the worst of all theft, or the most sacred of all property. But there is not the remotest indication of slavery, or involuntary servitude, or the selling and buying of men as property. On the contrary, every presentation of manners, every picture of society, and the very parables of the Lord Jesus, show the customs of free voluntary service;

as, for example, the parable of the householder and his hired
laborers, in the twentieth of Matthew. Five several times
the householder goes forth to look up and hire his laborers,
on a free mutual contract for wages, and there is no intimation
that there is such an accursed thing as slavery, instead of free
labor, in existence. So in the parable of the prodigal son,
"How many hired servants of my father's," etc. "Make me
as one of thy hired servants." And so in the very next chapter, Luke xvi. 13, "No servant can serve two masters, for
either he will hate the one, and love the other, or else he will
hold to the one, and despise the other."

Fourteenth. But, more particularly and expressly, we have
the law of love repromulgated by our Saviour, "Thou shalt
love thy neighbor as thyself," and "Whatsoever ye would
that men should do to you, do ye even so to them," with such
commentaries thereon, as to fasten its application particularly
to the oppressed African race as claiming our compassion. We
have the truth of the universal brotherhood of man proclaimed
anew, and the oneness of all races in Christ so insisted on,
that in their treatment there shall neither be Jew nor Gentile,
bond nor free.

Fifteenth, we have the distinct averment that if a man
be converted to Christ in a state of bondage to an earthly
master, and may be made free, he is by all means to choose
his freedom; the logical consequence of which, on the other
side, is the duty of his master, as a Christian, to set him free.

Sixteenth, we have, in the epistle to the Hebrews, the express injunction to remember them that are in bonds, as bound
also with them; intimating an habitual consideration of such
bondage as the greatest of calamities and wrongs upon those
who endured it, who were to be made unceasingly the subjects of prayer and of sympathy; but if so, the conclusion is
absolute of its being a sin against God for any person under
the light of his word to hold any fellow-creature in such bondage.

Seventeenth, we have, in the epistle to Timothy, a direct reference to the fundamental Hebrew law against men-stealers, as a law of God, in full force under the gospel, with an injunction to apply it with and by the gospel; and assuredly, in such application, whatever law of justice and mercy was given under the old dispensation, had an enlarged significance and scope, and a more direct and intense authority under the new. Nothing in this respect was taken from the new, but much was added.

Eighteenth. Then in the epistle to Philemon, we find the Apostle Paul, with that old fundamental fugitive slave law before him for his guide, acting on its principles; first, giving to Onesimus, a runaway slave, a shelter with him till he became converted, and then, with his own consent—and not till then—sending him back to Philemon, with the distinct averment that he was now no longer a servant, but a brother beloved; and to guard against the interpretation of his being merely a Christian brother, but still a slave, it was carefully added that he was a brother, not only in the Lord, but in the flesh, no longer a servant in either way; and the confident belief was added that Philemon, as a Christian, recognizing the same law of duty that Paul recognized, would go even farther than Paul chose to suggest, in the fulfillment of his whole duty towards this liberated brother.

Nineteenth. In several epistles we have the command, "Masters, give unto your servants that which is just and equal;" an injunction proving that no such class of servants was admissible, was to be supposed existing in the household of any Christian master, as were considered property—no class that were not parties to a compact of service for wages received; proving that all servants under the Christian law were servants on wages, consequently not possible to have been slaves, but their masters subject to the rules for the treatment of servants laid down in the holy Scriptures, which forbade any other than free paid service.

Twentieth, we have the institution of Christian churches, with their equality of membership and citizenship in Christ, without respect to persons, or to class, caste, or color; and in the church we have the whole family relationship renewed, and so sanctified in Christ, together with the reciprocal duties of husbands and wives, parents and children, so distinctly affirmed for all mankind, irrespective of classes, as to render the system of slavery impossible, without defying the authority of God, and violating every one of those sanctities: so that, for the possibility of the preservation of God's ordinances, slavery must be abolished, the condition of slaves, and the system of slave laws and usages, being incompatible with the keeping of the divine commandments, and the prevalence of the system impossible, without the defilement, degradation, and at length abolition of the most precious gifts of Heaven to man.

Twenty-first. Take, for example, the sacrament of marriage, with its wondrous transfiguration in such holy loveliness and glory, in the epistle to the Ephesians, where the sacredness and closeness of the union between the husband and the wife is likened to the union between Christ and the church. The passage begins, " Wives, submit yourselves unto your own husbands, as unto the Lord," and it concludes, " Let every one of you in particular so love his wife, even as himself, and the wife see that she reverence her husband."*   Now let us apply this to slavery, and we see instantly that for the miserable creatures under the crushing despotism of this damning sin, it is impossible; this blessedness was never made for slaves; from the paradise of marriage they are eternally excluded ; and slavery does not need a stronger demonstration of its guilt, than is presented by this terrific impossibility of the realization of that holiness and happiness appointed of God for the whole race redeemed in Christ Jesus.   Husbands, love your wives ; wives, be obedient to your husbands; as the church is subject

* Eph. v., 22, 23.

to Christ, so let the wives be to their own husbands in every thing. Conceive of this as addressed to the millions of American chattels reduced to a state of concubinage for slave-breeding, and instantly one of the divinest chapters in the word of God becomes a hideous and horrible satire.

Twenty-second. The same may be said of the instructions to parents and children, and of the reciprocal privileges and duties of Christian nurture and obedience; including the ordinance of the baptism of children, and the responsibility of their consecration to God. The whole household relationship is swept away, and the very existence of the family, as God has appointed it, is rendered impossible by a system that forbids marriage; forbids children to obey their parents; makes both classes the mere property of the master, and forbids parents from training up their children under any other nurture and admonition than that of the slave-market and the auction block, in the most absolute chattelism the world ever saw. We need, therefore, no other argument to show the infernal nature of this American system of Christian slaveholding than such a trial of it on the word of God. It is like the torture of the boots, the thumb-screws, and the wedges on the human system. You might as well say that your lungs were intended to breathe fire or the fumes of sulphuric acid, or that you can live upon the oil of vitriol, or that the crystals of prussic acid were appointed for the strengthening of your stomach, as that this dreadful scheme of iniquity grows out of Christianity, or can possibly be consistent with it. On the contrary, it destroys for its victims every ordinance of Christianity, and every possibility of participation in its blessings; and it must corrupt every element of true religion in the hearts of those who practice and defend the system. It creates one class of selfish despots, for whom the word of God, so frightfully perverted, is made just only a minister to their avarice and cruelty; at whose will, and for the convenience of their lusts and interests, all the rights and claims of

others, even to the elementary privileges of Christianity, are
denied and refused, or parceled out at man's bidding, not
God's. It degrades and distorts another class into a set of
creatures for whom the instructions in the word of God are
inadmissible, or if any of its privileges are offered, it is only
at the will of the masters, under whose legislation and administration, Christianity itself becomes a perversion of the
attributes of God, a sneering, tantalizing mockery and torture, a fable of charity, but a reality of prejudice, injustice
and cruelty.

Now we may not pass from this sketch of the course of
argument in the word of God against the sin of slavery, without remarking how eminently and closely scriptural it is as
a subject of investigation, how appropriate as a subject for
preaching and teaching, through what highways of light, of
divine instruction, of the glorious revelation of God's attributes and ways, and what disclosures of duty and happiness,
it leads the mind; so that, notwithstanding the wicked, inhuman prejudice against having the claims of the oppressed
presented from the word of God, and the iniquity of such oppression demonstrated, no subject could be more interesting
and enlivening, and none more suitable for the Sabbath and
the pulpit.*

* See GRANVILLE SHARPE, Declaration of Natural Right, 179. And
ABBÉ RAYNAL, Histoire Des Indes,
compared with GROTIUS and others,
showing that the Law of Nations and
of Natural Right runs parallel with
this whole line of argument from the
Scriptures. "The Law of Nature is
founded on the primary and eternal
laws of God, and whatsoever is contrary to any of these is *malum in se*,
which no authority on earth can make
lawful." "*Non sunt statuta, sed cor-
ruptelæ*, the laws against Natural
Right ARE NOT LAWS, BUT CORRUP-
TIONS," which the will of God requires every man to disobey. COKE,
BRACTON, and others, cited by SHARPE.

scattering abroad of the nations, admit one hundred and fifty years; this would leave from the confusion of tongues to the lifetime of Abraham a couple of centuries. This is the only interval in which the inequality and oppression of slavery can be supposed to have had any commencement. But there is no indication of it whatever, and in the very nature and necessity of the freedom of society at that time, its existence would have been impossible; not till a later period, and a greater multiplication of human beings, could caste and service have ripened into slavery, even in Egypt.

At the age of seventy-five, A. M. 2083, B. C. 1921, after the death of Noah, Abraham departs out of Haran, and begins his patriarchal wanderings, journeying towards the south. Three hundred years after the division of tongues we find him, by stress of famine, with his household, sojourning in Egypt, on terms of friendship with Pharaoh, with much riches of sheep and oxen, and he-asses, and men-servants and maid-servants, and she-asses and camels. On his departure out of Egypt, he is described as very rich in cattle, in silver and gold, and Lot also is described as possessing flocks and herds and tents; and the only description of servants specified are herds-men. They are not catalogued as property, but they have the charge of Abraham's and Lot's property, and they quarrel, as opposing clans, among themselves. There is not a trace among the servants of the household of any thing but voluntary, free service. There was no mode of compulsion by which either Abraham or Lot could have procured or maintained any other service. The supposition of any other is wholly groundless and gratuitous. It is one of the most insolent assumptions that can be conceived, without the remotest ground of argument or probability, without the slightest fact or hint of sacred or profane history to build upon, when the apologist or defender takes up the idea of the code and principles of modern American slavery, and carries it back to the household of Abraham, and from that assumption argues as if it were a reality. There is not only nothing to justify, but every thing to contradict and forbid this conclusion.

Let us consider it closely. The households of Abraham are brought before us and described, in the way of a brief classification, in several passages, as in Gen. xiv. 14; xvii. 12, 13, 23, 27. The first classification is of those fit for war, and drawn out for that purpose; the second is with reference to circumcision, and the classes to be submitted to that rite; both classifications are of males only, but they include *all* the males of every description. In the first classification, only those born in his own house are included, to the number of three hundred and eighteen. The Hebrew phrase (Gen. xiv. 14) is יְלִידֵי בֵיתוֹ *yelidhi betho, the born of the house,* the born of his house, or his household; a phrase distinguishing the natives of Abraham's community, those born within the families under his jurisdiction, of his tribe, in his service, and under his protection, as their head; a phrase distinguishing them from those who were born abroad, and had entered into his service, from the families of "strangers," from tribes or races other than his. These are not called servants, but instructed ones, or persons trained and experienced, persons of proved fidelity and skill, who could be relied upon. He armed, or led forth in battle array, these trained, tried, disciplined ones, the *experts*, of tried character, born and educated in his own patriarchal settlement or household. They were certainly not born in his own tent, nor beneath his own roof, but were simply the children of families dwelling in tents or tabernacles, owning a patriarchal allegiance to him, not owned by him, not his property, but connected with him in the voluntary, definite obligations which bound the community of families together. Among these families were found three hundred and eighteen males capable of bearing arms, and so trained as to be able to act efficiently as soldiers. He set them in battle array as such, and not either as servants or slaves. They are not only not called servants here, but in the twenty-fourth verse, instead of being mentioned as servants, they are called "the young men," חַנִּעָרִים, *hanaarim*, certainly, beyond all question, freemen. The Hebrew phrase describing them as drawn out, is נַיָּרֶק חֲנִיכָיו, *vayarek henikav, eduxit milites ad bellum* (Gesenius), חָנִיךְ, *initiatus, hinc peritus, probatœ fidei, initiated, skilled, of proved faithfulness. He drew out his trained ones to war.*

So much for the first classification, founded on the circumstance of having been born in the families of Abraham's patriarchal household, and the quality of being able and instructed to bear arms, to serve as soldiers. If we add to the males an equal number of females, we have six hundred and thirty-six, say from the age of twenty to thirty or upwards. Add an equal number from infancy up to twenty, and we should have twelve hundred and seventy-two, born of the house. Now as to the second classification in reference to circumcision, the division of males is as follows. In the 12th verse of the 17th chapter, the whole household of Abraham is divided into "those born in the house, or bought with money of any stranger, which is not of thy seed, every man-child in your generations." In the 13th verse, "He that is born in thy house, and he that is bought with thy money." In the 23d verse, "All that were born in his house, and all that were bought with his money, every male among the men of Abraham's house." In the 27th verse, "All the men of his house, born in the house, and bought with money of the stranger." All but Abraham and Ishmael are comprehended in these two classes.

In these passages, the division of the whole household community is into those born in the house, members by birth of Abraham's tribe-families, and those bought with his money of the stranger, and not of his seed. There were three hundred and eighteen of the first class, old enough and instructed enough to serve as soldiers in a military expedition; on the lowest average computation there would be at least as many more, too young and inexperienced for such service, making together six hundred and thirty-six. It is assumed by those who assert that Abraham was a slaveholder, that these were all slaves, for it is assumed that the phrase *born in the house* means slaves, and if this were the case, then Abraham had, at this time, six hundred and thirty-six slave born, and if you add as many more females, of all ages twelve hundred and seventy-two.

Now if those born in the house were slaves, what were those bought with money ? They constituted all the remaining portion of Abraham's household, and if they also were slaves, then it follows that every male in Abraham's whole patriarchal jurisdiction and community was a slave, and he and Ishmael his son were the only free persons among them. Supposing those bought with his money to be one half as many as the others, here would be a community of some nine hundred males in the state of slavery and only two free persons among them, the owner and his son ! If you add as many more females, then a community of eighteen hundred slaves in the same case. And this would constitute the whole of an independent tribe, a nomadic, roving community, eighteen hundred slaves and the owner and his son; no laws to bind them to him in subjection, no military or civil power or process by which such subjection could be maintained, or the slavery enforced; and the owner dependent on one half or one third of these chattels acting as a band of soldiers to keep the other half from being carried away captive by surrounding royal marauders !

If only those born in the house were Abraham's slaves, and if those obtained from strangers, those bought with his money, and not of his seed, were not slaves, then the absoluteness and sacredness of the chattelism were just in proportion to the nearness of relationship on the part of the chattels to their owner. Those that were born in Abraham's house, and were of his own race in nearer or more distant degrees of affinity, just in proportion to their home relationship, were in a worse condition than the strangers, more absolutely and entirely enslaved!

But in opposition to such extreme absurdities, we find by examination of the phrases *born in the house* and *bought with money*, that neither of them intimates a state of slavery, nor can, without violence, be so interpreted. This will be demonstrated in pursuing the philological argument; at present the comparison of a few passages will be sufficient, as of Exodus, xii. 43–49; Leviticus, xxii. 10, 11; Leviticus, xviii. 9; Exodus, xxi. 2; Jeremiah, ii. 14; Ecclesiastes, ii. 7. In these passages the usage of the phrases "born in the house," "home-born," "sons of the house," is demonstrated as a common usage in reference to free persons; indeed, not a solitary instance can be found of their application to slaves. In Genesis xv. 3, Abraham says, "One born in my house, בֶּן־בֵּיתִי *ben bethi*, is mine heir;" certainly not a slave. Bishop Blayney translates Jeremiah ii. 14: יְלִיד בַּיִת, *yelidh beth, child of the household*, and affirms that it answers to the Latin words *filius familias*, and stands *opposed* to a slave.* But this is precisely the same word as in Genesis xiv. 14, "*born in his own house*." So in Leviticus xxii. 11, of a person born in the priest's house, the same phrase. In Exodus xii. 48, 49, the *home-born* is referred to as אֶזְרַח הָאָרֶץ, *etzrah haarets, the born of the land*, free-born.

In Leviticus xviii. 9, we have an example of corresponding usage in connection with בַּיִת *beth*, as of free persons, "The daughter of thy father or daughter of thy mother, *born at home*, מוֹלֶדֶת בַּיִת, *moledheth beth, the born of the house ;* and there is no more proof that the phrase in Genesis xiv. 14, means a slave, or means any other than a freeman, than there is that the daughter is a slave, because called *the born of the house.*

It is impossible to interpret Genesis xv. 3, *one born in my*

* Blayney's Jeremiah—note on verse 14, chapter ii.

house, is mine heir, of a slave. But the three hundred and eighteen in Genesis xiv. 14, *born in his own house,* were all of the same class, and the phrases are synonymous. The children of the Hebrew servants were as free-born as the children of their masters; there was no such thing as chattelism in existence among them, nor any such infamous law or custom as that which brands the child as the property of the master, because the parent was claimed as such, or had been employed in his service at the time of the babe's birth. Yet nothing less than this infamy of infamies is attributed to Abraham and his household, by those who assert that the phrase *born in his own house* is to be interpreted of slaves.

But, second, the phrase *bought with money,* מִקְנַת־כֶּסֶף, *miqnath keseph,* Genesis xvii. 12, is equally demonstrated as a usage applying to freemen, and not to slaves. This is proved by Leviticus xxv. 51, spoken in regard to a Hebrew, who could by no possibility be a slave, מִקְנָתוֹ מִכֶּסֶף *miqnatho mikkeseph, the money that he was bought for,* the money of his purchase, the phrase always used of obtaining a Hebrew servant. So in Exodus xxi. 2 : " *If thou buy a Hebrew servant,"* the same verb of *obtaining,* as used likewise in Ruth iv. 10 ; " Moreover, Ruth, the Moabitess, the wife of Mahlon, *have I purchased* to be my wife," קָנִיתִי *kanithi, bought,* that is *obtained* with a dowry, for Ruth was not a slave. So likewise Genesis iv. 1 ; used in regard to the first-born of Eve, who was not a slave ; Eve said, I have *bought* a man from the Lord, קָנִיתִי *kanithi, gotten, obtained.* So likewise Hosea iii. 2 ; the prophet's purchase of his wife, *I bought her to me,* the word from כָּרָה being the word employed, which is placed by Gesenius as synonymous with קָנָה *kanah, to obtain.*

Now clearly if from the phrase, *bought with his money,* it would be proper to assume that those servants, whose service was thus obtained, were Abraham's slave property, and consequently to assume that it is right for us to buy human beings and hold them as slaves, because *by this assumption* Abraham did the same, then from the same phrase we can demonstrate, first, that the Hebrew servant was a slave, to be bought and sold as property, and consequently, secondly, that all our servants are slaves; thirdly, that Ruth, the wife of Boaz, was the slave property of Boaz, his chattel; and fourthly, that the wife of the prophet Hosea was his slave, his property; and consequently, fifthly, to conclude that it would be right for pious men now to hold their wives as slaves, and dispose of them as property. On the contrary, it is incontrovertible that the use of this idiom furnishes no more indication of slavery in Abraham's household, than it did in Adam and Eve's; no more than the use of the phrase in our language at the present day, I have got me, at a very fair price, a good coachman, or, I have got me, for a reasonable sum, ten good clerks for our new warehouse, or, I have procured, at a good bargain, twenty hands for the farm during the summer, or fifteen carpenters for the buildings, would prove that the coachman and the clerks, the farmers and the carpenters, were all chattels, slaves, property, bought, sold, transferred, as you might transfer a horse and carriage, a wheelbarrow, plow, carpenter's bench, or clerk's writing desk.

So likewise the phrase, *born in his house*, has no connection with slavery, and can not be shown to have the least meaning or intimation that way. But in order to gain the first beginning of a sanction for American slavery from Abraham's household, its defenders have got to prove that God ordained for him a law that every child born of any of his servants was, therefore, by law of such birth, a chattel, a slave, a piece of Abraham's property, and that that quality of property, supreme above every other, inhered in that race, generation after generation. Men assume this in order to sustain this iniquity among themselves; they can not appeal to Abraham without such an assumption. And let every thinking man consider the hideous and horrible perversion of thus carrying back the most atrocious feature of the slavery of our time, and setting that up,

that enormity of the theft of children from their parents, as
the meaning of the phrase, born in his own house, a meaning
which that phrase never bears anywhere, nor ever did bear;
as if Abraham laid his grasp on every new-born child under
the jurisdiction of his patriarchal authority, and said, This is
my property, my slave, by virtue of the father and the mother,
or the mother alone, having been in my service, under my patriarchal supervision, when the babe came into the world! This
is monstrous, and would scandalize the pages of a divine inspiration, if foisted among them. And slavery is altogether a
thing so positive and dreadful, that mere suppositions or hints
are not to be endured in the place of proof in regard to it;
but you rightfully demand the most positive and palpable
demonstration of its existence, especially if men are going to
claim for themselves, by virtue of its alleged practice in Abraham's family, the right, four thousand years afterwards, of
property in human beings, the right of enslaving another race
for ever. If men dare attempt to bring Scripture to sanction
such iniquity, they must be held to the most irresistible and
undeniable demonstration.*

---

* BUTLER'S ANALOGY, Christianity
as a republication of natural religion.
The carelessness of men, though themselves opposed to slavery, and regard-
ing it as criminal and pernicious in
the extreme, yet admitting, or taking
for granted, its existence by authority
of Divine Revelation, is inexplicable.
Yet even WALLON, a recent French
historian of slavery, suggests, without a
single proof, that Abraham's *slaves* (!!)
composed, with his flocks, the heritage
which he transmitted to his son Isaac,
and that Moses did not merely refer to
such slavery, but maintained and established it by law! "What authority
is thus given to usage," exclaims this
writer, "by a Word, which Christians
revere as the voice of God! Slavery,
otherwise only a human establishment,
becomes thus a divine institution!"
And yet, the whole drift of this writer's
work, which is voluminous, and very
learned, is against slavery, and a
demonstration of the duty of every
people to abolish it. How dreadful
the supposition, could it be made to
prevail, that the voice of God is thus
in antagonism with the dictates of
natural justice and humanity! Compare JAY'S WORKS, Letter to Bishop
Ives, and Reproof of Am. Church.
Compare, also, GISBORNE on the
Morals of Slavery, 144, 155, and
GRANVILLE SHARPE'S Declaration of
Natural Right, 29.

CHAPTER IV.

Now it is to be marked, in this argument, that when God
revealed himself to Abraham, and began in his person the
foundation of a new religious dispensation and race, he plucked
him away from the manners and the morals of the world as it
was, and consecrated him as the person in whom all the families of the earth should be blessed, a progenitor of nations,
and the framer of such a discipline and policy for his children
and his household after him, that they should keep the way
of the Lord, to do justice and judgment. A system of justice
was to be established in opposition to the prevalence of injustice and selfish power, and a system of righteous judgment
instead of despotic violence and wrong, and of this Abraham
was chosen to be an example and head.

Justice and judgment! These are the attributes of God,
infallible, immutable, in principle and in action. A God of
truth and without iniquity, just and right is he. As he is just
in himself, just in all his attributes, just in all his ways, so he
will not, can not sanction injustice or unjust judgment in
others; he can not and will not set at the foundation of society any example of injustice, any fountain or precedent of
unrighteousness for after generations and ages.

It is monstrous impiety to attempt to foist such deformities
into a divine revelation. When we remember with what fiery
indignation and wrath God has proclaimed vengeance against
all manner of oppression and injustice: "Wo unto him that

buildeth his house by unrighteousness, and his chambers by wrong; wo unto him that taketh his neighbor's work without wages, and giveth him not for his hire;" when we remember how every page of this holy book shines with the glory of God's righteousness, and that of old it passed into a proverb, that justice and judgment are better than all sacrifices, it is impossible to admit that in the first household life and constitution, through which God declared he would make all nations blessed, he should have set a fountain of sin and misery, the streams of which make every nation that drinks thereof accursed.

It is equally a monstrous supposition, inadmissible at the outset, that a man should be chosen of Jehovah to receive and promulgate, or to plant and exemplify, the great commanding principles of right and wrong in human society, the manner of feeling and of conduct, of personal and social intercourse, pleasing to the Deity, and then that this chosen ambassador or missionary of religious ethics should have been left to take his pattern of life and manners from the heathen world—from tribes and nations destitute of a divine revelation, having corrupted, and at length extinguished that which the race originally received. It is impossible to suppose, that in such an essential part, both of natural and revealed morality, as the rights of men to personal liberty, and the respect due to those rights, Abraham should have been instructed or permitted of God to take just what he found in the brutal and idolatrous, or half-civilized and barbarous tribes around him, and to set *that* as the example in his own household, and transmit it as the will of God to posterity. If the system of human slavery had been established and transmitted, it would inevitably have left no room for doubt as to its reality; the results of its establishment would have proved it beyond a question. The passage of the lava from a volcano would not be more surely traced by its effects, the position of an extinct volcano could not be more surely known in after ages by the discovery of its crater, than the existence of slavery by its fruits in the laws, policy, and history of the people.

If in any thing we are in doubt as to the details of the social system appointed of God, in Abraham's exemplification or foundation of it, we rightly look for information to the manner in which we find it developed in his posterity. From that development we can argue back to what must have been commenced as the source of it in Abraham's own life. In default of any specific, unquestionable knowledge as to Abraham's domestic laws and habits, we have to look at the after result of the system which he set a going; the earliest point where the arrangements plainly crop out, as it were, shows us what his own practice must have been. If a fountain is so deep down in the rifts under a mountain that we can not get at its depths, to analyze it there, we must be satisfied with the nearest accessible point, where the stream comes rippling through the green meadow, or brawling over the cliff. God chose Abraham for the purposes of his righteousness, and grafted upon him the graft of a new society. He did not choose Abraham to sanction and perpetuate in him the manners and morals of a violent and unregenerate age, but to set in him the example and the spring of a Christian society, a benevolent community, a society under the divine law. Now whatever that law and those principles are found to be, when they come to be clearly and unmistakably revealed and developed in an after age, they must have been in Abraham's planting and commencement of them. As the stream is known by its fountain, so the fountain is known by its stream.

If you wished to ascertain the original fruit of the parent tree in an orchard a hundred years old, which you knew by the records of the farm that your grandfather planted and grafted with his own hands, the kind of fruit, we mean, which the tree yielded the first time after grafting, would you not appeal to the whole orchard, and to the kind of apples it has borne in your time? But suppose that some one should set before you the bitter, unwholesome fruit of a wild crab-apple tree, the product of the wilderness, affirming *that* to have been the fruit which your grandfather chose for his orchard, and intended to perpetuate, arguing that it must have been so, because that bitter-crab tree had grown wild in the forest for hundreds of years, and the fact of its being in the neighborhood of the grounds of your grandfather when he grafted his orchard, proves that the orchard must have been grafted with slips of that wild crab tree. Thou fool, you would say, the orchard does not bear crab-apples, and never did, on the contrary, it has always been a law of the farm that if any were found they should be cut down, and we know that the fruit the trees bear now is the very same that our grandfather grafted, and used in his own family. Does not the fruit of a grafted tree always prove the nature of the graft? If I have half a dozen pear trees in my garden, that bear the most delicious St. Michael's, and I know that those pear trees were grafted by my father, do I not know that he grafted the very fruit which every autumn I use at my table, and not the choke pear, which even my hogs scarcely put up with? Will you tell me that the choke pear was the one which my father was fond of, and which he carefully cultivated, and intended for my table? How then does it happen that the trees which he grafted bear the St. Michael's?

When God converts a man, does he convert him to perpetuate by him the works of the devil, or to destroy the works of the devil, and introduce the fruits of grace? When a man is cut out of the wild olive, and grafted into the true olive, is it for the purpose of fruit or is it to perpetuate poison? When God brings a drunkard to repentance, does he do it in order to set up a new rum shop on the man's premises, under his care, and so to sanctify the sale of rum by his example? When God converts a Pagan, does he do it in order to bring in Pagan rites into his church, and to sanctify the worship of Pagan images? When God chose Abraham, did he do it in order to set the seal of his approbation upon one of the greatest enormities of the idolatrous world, slavery and the slave-trade, in order to bring in that iniquity, and establish it in the household policy of his own people? This is the argument of those who assume that Abraham held slaves and then appeal to his example as being God's sanction of the crime of American slavery. That which, if Abraham had let it alone, would have been branded as a crime, would have stood in the annals of Sodomic and Egyptian history as a crime, by being taken up into Abraham's life, as a domestic example, is baptized for a virtue. This is a horrible perversion, and blasphemy against the justice and holiness of God.

But we say, let the records of that household policy answer. They are before us, they are plain, from the time of Abraham downwards. If Abraham had had slaves, had bought and sold men as property, had grown rich in that way, his slave property would have been more valuable than all his other riches, and Isaac and Jacob would have inherited his possessions and his claims, and by the very law of propagation and of entail in slave property would have vastly accumulated it. Isaac would have had the whole three hundred and eighteen home-born, or six hundred and thirty-six of both sexes, and twelve hundred and seventy-two of all ages, or more than eighteen hundred of all classes, on his father's plantation, besides all the increase of hands for more than fifty years, for Abraham, when he died, gave all that he had unto Isaac, and fifty years would have increased the number, at the lowest computation, to some ten or twelve thousand. And the same inheritance descending inevitably from Isaac, and accumulating through the lifetime of Jacob for more than a hundred years, even if divided between Esau and Jacob, must have constituted a great multitude. It is impossible that all this slave property, as a sanctified domestic institution, could have vanished into thin air; or if a missionary institution, Jacob would not have been allowed to put it up at auction, or dispose of it at a price, on account of the famine in Canaan. When Jacob went down into Egypt, we should certainly have found slaves in his household, for he took his journey with all that he had, and there is great particularity in the enumeration both of souls and substance, but not the faintest shadow of the presence of slavery do we find there, not the most distant intimation of slaves or slave property being a patriarchal fixture. What has become of the three hundred and eighteen, or the six hundred and thirty-six, or the twelve hundred and seventy-two, or the eighteen hundred, and their increase of many thousands, left to his children by their great slaveholding grandfather? Slavery never dies out, but by the law of human cupidity holds on and makes itself more and more manifest. Abraham never *sold* slaves; nobody accuses him of that; and even those who assume that he was a slaveholder, can find no trace of any such transaction. What, then, became of his three hundred and eighteen, or six hundred and thirty-six, or twelve hundred and seventy-two, or eighteen hundred? They did not descend to Isaac, they were not inherited by him as a property, for then also we should have found them in the family of Jacob, since Isaac never sold slaves. But all traces of them disappear, and neither in Jacob's family nor Esau's can we discover the least indication of slavery or slave property.

On the contrary, the only instance of the selling and buying of a human being in a record of more than four hundred years is that of Joseph, distinctly branded by him, in describing the transaction, as man-stealing. And until that transaction, there is no positive proof of slavery existing anywhere; so that, to resume our illustration of the orchard and the grafted fruit, this wild tree, which the advocates of slavery assume to have been adopted by Abraham, as a universal growth of society, is not certainly discovered in all that region till at least three hundred years after the calling of Abraham, and then comes up as a crime. If, instead of being crime, slavery had been a domestic institution, appointed of God and sanctioned as a patriarchal right, we should certainly have found some trace of human beings held as property when the Israelites went up out of Egypt.

Instead of that, we find such property forbidden, and the origin of it, and the traffic in it, denounced as an iniquity to be punished with death. We find a net-work of admirable legislation, woven with direct reference to the exclusion of this iniquity, so as to render slavery for ever impossible in the land. And these laws are beyond question an embodiment of the great principles of common law and custom that had prevailed since Abraham set them. They are the grand precedents of judgment and of justice which God declared that Abraham was appointed to transmit to his posterity, reduced to specific written forms; the principles that had been transmitted from the patriarchal life of Abraham, for otherwise the Israelites could not possibly have been prepared for such legislation, nor brought submissively under it.

The legislation appointed of God was not that of a break-up in their habits, not a revolutionary legislation, but a legislation in concord with the system of morals and manners set in power by Abraham, and consolidated for five hundred years. The great idea of the sacredness of personal freedom was not a new unknown idea; if it had been, no code of laws could have communicated it, so as to make it instantly pervade the nation as a life. And, on the other hand, the despotic and dreadful idea of the righteousness and sacredness of slave property, the justice and benevolence of buying and selling men as chattels, if *that* had been a custom and an heirloom from Abraham downwards, could not have been opposed without disturbance, could not have quietly yielded and vanished and given place to the unexampled system of freedom and kindness revealed through Moses. If the people had been slaveholders, with the example of Abraham to sanction them, and Moses had undertaken to put a stop to that system, and to strike the fetters from their slaves, he would have found a

shall I do when God riseth up? and when he visiteth, what shall I answer him? Did not he that made me in the womb make him? and did not one fashion us in the womb?" Compare these sentiments of justice and humanity, this acknowledgment of natural equality and mutual right, this recognition of mutual obligation and duty, with the tone of opinion, feeling, and language prevailing at the South towards a race of slaves.

Now, as a patriarch chosen of God, and appointed as the beginning and head of a mighty religious dispensation, it is not to be supposed that Abraham was *less* advanced in morals and religion, after this divine call, than Job. Wherever Abraham sojourned under the divine guidance, he certainly must have carried and maintained, as the friend and prophet of God, those principles to which God himself referred, when he said, "I know Abraham, that he will command his children and his household after him, and they shall keep the way of the Lord, to do justice and judgment." It is not to be supposed that Abraham copied the institutions of the tribes around him, or adopted the manners and morals of the people among whom he journeyed, but, on the contrary, he must have had a standard of his own, and preserved his own principles. If slaves were presented to him by kings, they passed out from the ungodly and oppressive rule under which they had been held as chattels, into a household under divine teachings, where they were regarded as human beings with rights, and not as articles of property. When Abraham received them, it is not to be imagined that he received into his household, along with them, the slave-code and slave-usages, or supposed them to be creatures without rights, whose service he could take without wages. Their slavery ceased the moment they became his servants; and the rite of circumcision, by which they were all equally consecrated to God, and adopted in the divine covenant as the objects of his care and favor, was in itself a most impressive seal of personal freedom and responsibility, and a recognition of the sacredness of individual rights.

CHAPTER V.

Cockatrices' Eggs Laid by Lexicographers, and Hatched by Commentators.—Assumptions and Misrepresentations, and Consequent Prejudices and Errors.—Difficulty of the Dislodgment of Old Tenant Lies.—Necessity of their Exorcism from Theological Literature.

It is under the guidance of such views that we have to come to the consideration of the legislation in the Old Testament on the subject of the nature and times of domestic servitude. When that legislation was ordained of God, there was no such thing as slavery in the nation, either to be regulated or extirpated. Its asserted existence is the merest imagination and assumption, without one particle of proof; a figment more groundless than that of the Blue Laws of Connecticut. They who assume its existence, are bound to show their authority in the clearest terms, for it is one of those things that can not be admitted without positive demonstration. But in the absence of all evidence, the assumption of such an enormous system of wickedness is monstrous.

The very assumption rests on the fastening of the word *bondman* into the divine revelation in the English version, when there is no such word in the original; and on the use of the word *slave* in the lexicons and commentaries, instead of the word *servant*, which is the Hebrew word of the Scriptures, there being no word for *slave* in the Hebrew language. In the history of languages, there is hardly an instance of greater perversion and violence; probably no instance of so vast a conclusion, with such dreadful consequences, being founded upon the wrong translation of a word. The iniquity of American slavery, with all its atrocities, builds and perpet-

uates itself upon the sanction thus pirated for it in the word of
God. The lexicographers, translators and commentators have
acted as borers for the slaveholding interest, and have laid
the eggs of this sin in the bark of the word, where its monstrous developments are defended as the legitimate product
of God's righteous sovereignty. As was said of old, "None
calleth for justice, nor pleadeth for truth; they trust in vanity
and speak lies; they conceive mischief and bring forth iniquity.
They hatch cockatrices' eggs, and weave the spider's web; he
that eateth of their eggs dieth, and that which is crushed
breaketh out into a viper."

Without the slightest examination of the original, without
a question as to the justice or injustice of slavery, its inconsistency with the benevolence commanded in the Scriptures,
apparently with not a thought as to the bearing of its sanction upon the character and claims of a divine revelation, or
its manner of representing the attributes of God, the great
tide of commentators and of readers has swept on. Some of
the best writers have, in one sentence, adopted the common
representation of the existence of slaves and slavery in Judea,
and in the next given such details of that slavery, so called, as
proved that there was nothing of slavery in it, and that this
term could not, without a sweeping falsehood, be applied to it.

As an instance of such singular carelessness, we may take
the admirable work of Dean Graves on the Pentateuch (especially the third Lecture, Part II., on the Moral Principles of
the Jewish Law), in which the iniquity and abominations of
modern slavery and of the slave trade are denounced as "an
aggravated guilt publicly known and nationally tolerated, so
as to fill the minds of the pious and reflecting with the most
alarming expectation that the signal judgments of God will
awfully chastise such depravity." The writer says, speaking
of the justice of the death penalty, "On this subject it is
necessary to observe, that *as liberty is equally valuable with
life*, the Jewish law, with the STRICTEST EQUITY, ordained that

if any man were convicted of attempting to reduce any fellow-citizen to slavery, he should be punished with death." Part ii., Lect. iii., p. 154. Yet in the very same lecture he applies the word SLAVE to the Jewish *servant*, and remarks that "the penal code of the Jews guarded the person of the servant and the slave, as well as of the freeman; the injunction, 'Whosoever smiteth a man that he die, shall surely be put to death,' equally protected all." "The chastity of *female slaves* was guarded by strict regulations, and no Jew could be a slave for longer than seven years." Again, "Compare the Mosaic regulations respecting *female slaves* with the universal and abominable licentiousness which polluted every ancient nation in their intercourse with slaves."

Here the Hebrew servant, making a contract of service for six years, is called a *slave*, and *female slaves* are spoken of as if such a class really existed, at the same time that the very fact of the limitation of service to six years, and the law of freedom when such service has expired, demonstrate that such a servant was in no sense a slave, and such service in no sense slavery! And with the admitted and applauded fact that God denounced the bringing of any person into slavery, as a crime to be punished with death, yet is slavery spoken of as one of the institutions of the Mosaic law, and, of course, an institution appointed and established of Jehovah! That very condition, into which, if one man were found reducing another, he should be put to death, is nevertheless represented as being a condition of domestic society, not merely permitted, but made, by the divine will, an integral and essential fixture of the social life!

A still more remarkable instance occurs in Jahn's Biblical Archæology, where the writer gravely affirms, in the 169th section of his work, which he has entitled *Respecting Slaves*, that "it is probable that some of the patriarchs, as was sometimes the case at a later period, with individuals in Greece and Italy, possessed many thousands of them!" Again, he makes the following astounding declaration : " The *Canaanites* could not be held in slavery. For them, under the then existing circumstances, *slavery was regarded as too great a privilege !*" He then proceeds to enumerate some of the ways in which men might find themselves endowed with this same privilege !

And so the march of misrepresentation and mistake has continued.* And such has been the indifference and fatuity of the world, such the carelessness of commentators, ready to echo one another's opinions without examination, and such the power of long-continued prejudice, that the very apparatus of study, except only the original sacred text itself, has been tortured and discolored, so as to throw false lights upon the subject, and set things in a false position. It is just like having your tables of logarithms falsified, or the glasses of your telescope misplaced, confounded, or the screws of your compound microscope reversed, or your chemical tests wrongly labeled. Under the deception produced by such undiscovered and unquestioned tricks, some of the ablest commentators on the laws of Moses have gravely considered slavery as an unquestioned and indisputable fact, not less certain than the existence of leviathan. The lexicons have translated the word *servant* by the word *slave.* The phrase *buying a serv-*

* See, for other examples, "Illustrated Commentary on the Holy Bible," London : 1840, vol. i., page 32. Also, the comment on Gen., chapter xv. The writer makes the monstrous declaration that "the word translated *servant* generally denotes what we should call *a slave.*" He then goes on to say that the mass of the servants mentioned in the Scripture history were absolute and perpetual slaves. They and their progeny were regarded as completely the property of their masters, who could exchange or sell them at pleasure, could inflict what punishments they pleased, and even in some cases put them to death. ABRAHAM'S SERVANTS WERE MANIFESTLY OF THIS DESCRIPTION."

There can be no excuse for such extravagant ignorance or falsehood. In an interpreter of the word of God the carelessness of such assertions becomes worse than careless, when the subject is of so solemn a weight and importance as that of the judgment in the word of God in regard to slavery. Under such teaching, no form or prevalence of error could be surprising. It is a demoniac possession that must be exorcised, or wherever it remains it excludes the truth, and foams and rages against it.

ant has been set in our language, without any indication of
its Hebrew usage, just as if it meant the traffic in human
beings as property. Learned and able archæologists, and
writers of introductions, have prepared and printed whole
sections on the treatment of *Hebrew slaves*, and have adduced
passages as proof-texts, which, rightly examined and interpreted, prove that no such thing as slavery was permitted.*

These errors and prejudices were begun at a time when, in
England, and all over the world, not only slavery, but even
the African slave trade, was sustained and practiced without
scruple, even by Christians ; so that there was nothing in the
assertion of slavery being sanctioned, or even enjoined of

---

* Horne's Introduction, vol. iii., page
419: The most singular concatenation
of examples of such heedless mistakes,
is to be found in the fifth chapter of
the fourth part of the third volume
of this work. Assertions are made,
and texts referred to, as if in proof of
them, which, on examination, refute
the assertions. See, for instance, the
note on Deut. xv. 18. The word
slave is heedlessly applied to persons
at voluntary service, and perfectly
free. By such inaccurate use of
terms, reverberated from writer to
writer, there has come to be an accumulation of apparent authorities for
the opinion that slavery was established under God's sanction. The
Hebrew *servants* are called *slaves*, and
by the same process, historians and
commentators on the domestic life
and customs of the free States, could
prove incontrovertibly that chattel
slavery was a domestic institution,
universally established among them.

Bonar on Leviticus, pages 444 and
463, speaks with the same unfortunate carelessness of "every Hebrew
slave," and at the same moment of
the freedom to "leave his servitude;"

the latter qualification rendering the
former condition an impossibility,
though the inconsistency does not
seem to have once occurred to the
mind of the writer.

The manner in which opinion has
been manufactured and sustained is
exemplified in assertions such as the
following: "The Lord wished to
punish the Canaanites and other heathen nations, because of their heathenism; and of course the Lord has
a right so to do. His decree, therefore is this: that *heathens* shall be exposed to bondage, and Israel shall
take them as their slaves."

If this had been true, the punishment, in such a case, would have
been a reward, for the slavery was
freedom into which they passed; and
the curse inflicted was their elevation
to all the religious and civil privileges
of God's own chosen people! Singular enough to see a writer declaring that God cursed and punished
the heathen for their heathenism, by
adopting them into his own church,
and bestowing franchises upon them,
of which, in their heathen condition,
they knew nothing!

God, so startling or incredible, as to induce an examination of the Scriptures in regard to it. The great Hebrew lexicographer, Gesenius, probably never gave it a thought, and hardly had occasion to mark any distinction between a servant and a slave, as to the question of any morality or immorality in the relation.

In consequence of all this, we come to the Bible argument under great disadvantages. Long defended titles to opinion, supposed incontestable, have to be contested, and decisions based upon misinterpretations have to be set aside, and precedents established by men of great authority have to be resisted. We have not only to prove property, but to disprove false claims. We have to bring expensive actions for ejectment before we can take possession of our own. By a species of squatter sovereignty, the advocates of slavery have settled down in the Scriptures, as the Scribes and Pharisees did in Moses' seat, with their traditions, under the authority of father Abraham; and possession being nine tenths of the law, it takes nine times as much argument and conscience to dislodge, as it did confidence and ignorance to squat.

Even if there had been such a thing as slavery among the Hebrews, God's allowance of it among them would have been no justification of American slavery, no more than Noah's planting a vineyard would justify our getting drunk on cider-brandy. Even supposing God to have admitted, for a season, a degree of slavery, under laws for its regulation and abolition, supposing the Hebrews to have held slaves by permission, this could be no justification for an American slaveholder retaining the African race in bondage, or holding any human being as property. To plead Hebrew slavery in excuse or authority for American, is just to act like a rumseller in one of the cities of Scotland, convicted of selling bad liquors; but he alleged in defense of the practice the fact stated in the second chapter of John, verse tenth, Every man at the beginning doth set forth good wine, and when men have well drunk, then that which is worse; but thou hast kept the good wine until now. He said, they must have used up a great deal of bad wine in this process, and our Lord Jesus said not one word in condemnation of it to the bridegroom; and it was altogether as proper for him to provide bad spirits for his customers as it was for that family to provide it for their guests. That is just the amount of the whole alleged Bible argument in regard to slavery, namely, that if the Hebrews, at God's command, or under his revealed permission, could enslave the heathen, then the Americans, without God's permission or command, have the same right to enslave Africans; an attempted justification so weak, so worthless, so unprincipled and hypocritical, that it is hardly fit for a sober notice.

It is a reproach to the word of God to admit for a moment that a thing so unjust and full of evil has any existence or sanction whatever in it. And it has not. And on this ground we stand. We affirm that at the very outset of the Hebrew legislation there was no such thing as slavery among the Hebrews to be regulated. Not one text can be brought to prove its existence, nor any intimation that it was any way in practice when God revealed the Hebrew code of laws to Moses. The whole spirit of the Bible, from beginning to end, is against it. The first legislation in regard to domestic servitude was for freedom, not slavery; it was to guard against slavery, and prevent the possibility of its coming in from abroad.

God himself referred to that great fact in the announcement of his last vengeance on the kingdom and people for their attempt to set up slavery instead of liberty; for that was just the essence of their crime. I made a covenant of liberty *in the day that I brought your fathers out of Egypt*, out of the house of bondage, liberty every man to his neighbor. The covenant so made, so established, and so referred to, was of freedom *against* slavery, not in toleration or regulation of it. The nation was about to enter on a series of conquests, and to be brought in contact with other nations, where slavery might be found prevailing, and where temptations would arise to practice and establish the iniquity themselves, and under those circumstances, in preparation for future junctures, such admirable laws were passed, as rendered slavery and the slave traffic, either domestic or foreign, either of Hebrews or heathen, impossible. If those laws were obeyed, then, under God's old covenant, as well as new, such a crime as that of holding men as property, or maintaining the claim of property in man, was impossible.

There are volumes of commentaries, from which it may be plainly seen what blindness and insensibility have rested even on the church of God in regard to this subject, and what extravagances, yea, what madnesses of opinion, and complications of falsehood, have grown out of such stupidity and ignorance, what monstrosities even good men have gravely and calmly swallowed, what doctrines, as bad as the vilest immoralities of the Hindoo or heathen mythology, have been accepted as parts of divine revelation. As a remarkable instance, we may refer to the Rev. Dr. Pyle's paraphrastic commentary on the Scriptures, published at London in several volumes in 1717. In the first volume, in the commentary on the twenty-first chapter of Exodus, taking it for granted that the system of slavery was an established institution of the state, and, as a domestic institution, committed of God to the fostering care of the government and the magistrates, for its perpetuity by natural increase, the author thus explains the fourth verse in regard to the Hebrew servant's family relations. "If a wife," says he, "were procured him by his master, or appointed him by the magistrates that sold him, *only to breed slaves by*, then, if he leaves his service, he shall leave the wife and children, *as the master's proper goods and possessions !*" Could there be a manifestation of more profound insensibility, darkness, and consequent perversion of the moral sense, than this?

It is difficult to conceive how a Christian man, a minister of the gospel, certainly not ignorant of the first and lowest laws and principles of justice and of moral purity, could put such a monstrosity as this in writing, as part of a divine revelation for the teaching of virtue, benevolence, and piety. How any man could deliberately affirm that such a diabolical state of society as this enactment would constitute was sanctioned of Heaven, was protected, authorized, commanded by a holy God, passes our comprehension; how he could suppose that other men, with an enlightened moral sense, could receive such enactments of impurity and cruelty as the dictates and records of divine inspiration, worthy of a solemn commentary, is equally amazing. But, with a theological literature baptized in such opinions, the tenacity and despotism are not strange, with which the supposition of there being some sanction of slavery in the Scriptures has knotted itself upon the general mind, has become rooted and grounded as a common principle, an axiom, a root of bitterness and error, a possession, indeed, by the father of lies, and the murderer from the beginning.

Is it any wonder that under such teachings, and from a baptism with such habits of thinking, and such doctrines of devils, as the supposed water of life, a man like John Newton should have been enabled even to continue in the slave trade for some time after his conversion, without any compunction, any misgiving, any discovery or sense of its injustice, its sinfulness against God? We have the same insensibility to contend against now, and the same difficulty to persuade men to go back of the fact of present lawful possession, and inquire if the original guilt of man-stealing does not, by the divine law, as well as by common justice, inhere in the very claims of a present property in man, as that same crime. We have to cut down a whole forest of lies before we can open a pathway to the truth. It is therefore essential that we take slavery and the slaveholder, and carry both the sin and its abettors back to its reprobated origin, and set them under the judgment of the word of God.

CHAPTER VI.

"Now these are the judgments which thou shalt set before them. If thou buy a Hebrew servant, six years he shall serve, and in the seventh he shall go out free for nothing. If he came in by himself, he shall go out by himself; if he were married, then his wife shall go out with him. If his master have given him a wife, and she have borne him sons or daughters, the wife and her children shall be her master's, and he shall go out by himself. And if the servant shall plainly say, I love my master, my wife, and my children; I will not go out free; then his master shall bring him unto the judges; he shall also bring him to the door, or unto the door post; and his master shall bore his ear through with an awl; and he shall serve him for ever." Exodus, xxi. 1–6.

If we should take the first clause in this body of enactments, and connect it with the last, thus, If thou buy a Hebrew servant, his master shall bore his ear through with an awl, and he shall serve him for ever; it would be no unfair example of the torture by which it is attempted to pervert Scripture, and sanctify slavery from the word of God. In the first place, there is the phrase, *If thou buy ;* in the second place, there is the phrase, *He shall serve him for ever.* What phrases in the English language could describe slavery, it might be asked, if these do not?

But a candid and careful reader, even of the English alone,

on reading only the first verse in this series of enactments in regard to domestic service, would see at once the falsehood of any conclusion of *property* as the meaning of the word *buy ;* for this buying is only a contract of service for six years; six years shall he serve, and *in the seventh he shall go out free for nothing.*

In the second place, he would see the impossibility of property, from the fact of its being a *voluntary* contract between two persons, equal parties in the contract, and not with reference to a third person. The bargain for a *slave* is the purchase from a third person, while the person *bought* stands by as a *chattel,* a thing, to be disposed of with no more consultation of himself than if he were a wheelbarrow. There is no such traffic as this admitted in the Scriptures. Such buying and selling is forbidden as *man-stealing,* to be punished with death; and such buying and selling is the great sin of our country, against God and man. There is never a case of the purchase of a servant from a third person, as a piece of property is purchased; but only the *service* of the servant, *for a limited, specified time,* was purchased, and always from himself, the sole owner.

In the third place, the contract, in the words, *he shall serve him for ever,* is equally demonstrated to be a purely voluntary contract, and for a limited, specified time, and no longer. But how do you prove this, when the language is unlimited, *for ever ?* Simply by the institution of the jubilee. At the recurrence of each fiftieth year liberty was proclaimed throughout all the land, *unto all the inhabitants thereof.* Consequently, by that known institution it is incontrovertible that the words, *he shall serve him for ever,* mean only he shall serve him to the longest period remaining for any service between that time of the contract and the next coming year of jubilee.

Just so with that passage in Leviticus, xxv. 45, 46, which the defenders of slavery are accustomed so triumphantly to fling in the face of those who demonstrate its inherent, eternal and immutable wickedness. "Moreover, of the children of the stranger that do sojourn among you, of them shall ye buy, and of their families that are with you, which they begat in your land; and they shall be your possession. And ye shall take them as an inheritance for your children after you, to inherit a possession; they shall be your bondmen for ever." This the defender of slavery avers to be proof positive of perpetual bondage; and if he can but succeed in making his hearer ignore, or exclude from court, the corresponding and explanatory passages, if he can prevent him from going behind the English phrases, and showing what is meant, if he can persuade him into a judgment, without investigation of the merits of the case, he can prove the existence of slavery to the satisfaction of any man who is willing to darken his conscience and handle the word of God deceitfully, that he may indulge his sins in peace.

But the same investigation pursued as with the other passage, dissipates the darkness, removes every vestige of involuntary bondage, and leaves no manner of doubt as to the buying being simply a voluntary contract between two parties of service for a limited and perfectly definite time, guarded by the jubilee itself from all possibility of perpetuity. The investigation proves that the buying of servants among the children and families of the heathen sojourning in the land no more meant slavery for them, than it did for the Hebrews. The Hebrews were no more permitted to make slaves of them, than they of the Hebrews. The word for servant is the same. The process of obtaining servants is the same. The heathen were perfectly free to serve or not serve, to go or stay; and if they were able, they had the same right to buy Hebrews, if the Hebrews were willing to enter their service, that the Hebrews had to buy them. Again and again one manner of law was commanded both for the heathen and the Hebrews. "Love ye therefore the stranger, for ye were strangers in the land of Egypt. Thou shalt not pervert the judgment of the stranger, nor of the fatherless, but thou shalt remember that thou wast a bondman in Egypt, and the Lord thy God redeemed thee thence; therefore I command thee to do this thing. Thou shalt not oppress the stranger. And if a stranger sojourn with thee in your land, ye shall not vex him. But the stranger that dwelleth with you shall be unto you as one born among you, and thou shalt love him as thyself, for ye were strangers in the land of Egypt."

Thou shalt love him as thyself. By the interpretation of those who seek to falsify the word of God for a sanction of the wickedness of slavery, this means, Thou shalt thrust him into a worse bondage than ever thou thyself didst endure in Egypt. Thou shalt take all his rights from him, thou shalt buy and sell him as a camel, or a camel's furniture; thou shalt make a mere chattel of him. Thou shalt range up and down the land, as a tyrant over him, with him for thy lawful property and possession. Thou shalt lay thy grasp upon his children whenever and wherever it pleases thee, and buy and sell them, for the slaves of thy children to the latest generation. Thou art delivered and appointed to exercise this cruelty upon the heathen, and to set an example of God's benevolence and righteousness in these abominations in the sight of all the nations.

If such blasphemy were credited, how could it do otherwise than make infidels out of all honest men, for who could accept such immoral horrors as the stuff of a divine revelation? It could be only a satanic, selfish exultation, that could take delight in the discovery of such sanction of sin, and a dishonesty equally satanic that could make a man boast of such sanction, as a proof, satisfactory to his mind, that the book containing it came from a holy, just, and righteous God. Yet there is such wickedness among men. It is described in the fiftieth Psalm: "Thou thoughtest that I was altogether such an one as thyself. When thou sawest a thief, then thou consentedst with him, and hast been partaker with adulterers. What hast thou to do to declare my name?"

Just so, again, with the passage in Exodus, xx. 20, 21 : "If a man smite his servant, or his maid, with a rod, and he die under his hand, he shall surely be punished. Notwithstanding, if he continue a day or two, he shall not be punished, for he is his money." What can be greater proof of property in man than this? exclaims the slaveholder; *for he is his money.* But now if you look back to the second verse, and trace the context, you find it is *purchased voluntary service* that is spoken of, and nothing else. It is the *service of the Hebrew,* who could not possibly be a slave, or be bought or sold as property; but that limited *service* being bought and paid for beforehand, for six years, the man from whom it is owing is described as the master's *money,* because he had invested money for his services in hiring him for six years; and it is argued that he being worth so much to his master, for a service contracted and paid for, that master could not be supposed to have intended to kill him; and therefore, though it would be proper to punish his cruelty, yet not to punish him for murder, a crime which he did not intend to commit. The presumption that he did not, is founded on the supposition that he could not have intended to throw away his own money, which he would have done, in killing him, as truly as if he had thrown it into the Jordan or the Dead Sea. If he had intended to kill him, he would have done it at once; if such were his object and his malice, he would have murdered him on the spot, and would have been put to death for it. But the continuance of the smitten servant for a season, affords a second presumption that the killing was unintentional. Such presumptions not unfrequently shield a criminal, justly, from the highest penalty of the law, because they present to the jury a doubt, which must go in favor of the prisoner. When it is said, he shall not be punished, it can hardly be supposed to mean that no punishment shall be inflicted at all, but simply that he shall not be avenged with the blood-vengeance by the avenger, but with some lesser penalty. The case in the verses next preceding is similar, and throws still more light upon the matter. "If men strive together, and one smite another with a stone, or with his fist, and he die not, but keepeth his bed ; if he rise again, and walk abroad upon his staff, then shall he that smote him be quit ; only he shall pay for the loss of his time, and shall cause him to be thoroughly healed."

Not only does the enactment under consideration prove that the transaction of buying, so called in our English translation, excluded the possibility of property in man, but it incidentally brings out what will be more definitely noted, the sacredness of marriage among servants as among masters. There could be no separation of husband and wife. Husbands, love your wives ; wives, obey your husbands ; were privileges, duties, obligations, as inviolable for servants as for masters. The marriage tie alone, with the domestic constitution growing out of it, was a shield and sanctity of independence and freedom for servants, that rendered the degradation of them into slaves, and the claim of property in man over them, impossible. This, of itself, demonstrates the crime and guilt of American slaveholding. The slaveholder is hunted in the word of God by principles and texts surer than his own bloodhounds ; nothing in Divine revelation but holds him, in the guilt of his claim of property in his fellow-man, to an inexorable retribution.

The passages sometimes adduced in support or sanction of men's wickedness prove the very opposite, and cut the presumptuous, audacious sinner to the heart. The word of God, in the hands of these daring, but awkward ignoramuses, is like a South American *boomerang*. They think they have seized a great passage for their purpose, and are shying it away at their adversaries ; and at first it goes this way, then that, then seems as if it were making straight for the target,

when, in the most astounding manner, by an involution of
eccentric hidden law and power of right motion, it comes
back upon themselves. The man who thought he was going
to prostrate his opponent with it is knocked down by it.
When a great piratical sinner, or captain of one of Satan's
men-of-war, undertakes to grapple upon his intended victim a
coil of perverted Scriptures, it sometimes runs out almost
as quick as lightning, and carries himself overboard before he
is aware of the entanglement, or can get his legs out of the
knot. It is a pithy proverb, Give rope to a villain, and he'll
hang himself. He doubles and twists the noose for others,
and holds the rope ready for the body of his victim; but suddenly and unexpectedly the noose is knotted about his own
neck, and at the nearest gallows tree of God's providence the
fool is swinging in the air, till his bones rattle and bleach for
a universal warning.

So men are holden by the cords of their own sins, and their
own snares entrap them. There is the same fatality in a
wicked state policy, only this takes a broader sweep, and the
principles of an immoral expediency close upon their authors
as the lid of a great sepulcher. The wicked precedents and
laws run on for a while in great seeming prosperity, but at
length they come round face to face in conflict, as great glaring hyenas, with the victim of their rage right between them,
the nation and the church that set them on fire, and sanctified
them, to be devoured by them. "Wo to thee that spoilest,
and thou wast not spoiled; when thou hast done spoiling,
then they shall spoil thee." Like Daniel's lions, when the authors of such wickedness are given up to its operation, their
own agents will break all their bones in pieces before even
they have reached the bottom of their own den of villainy.

CHAPTER VII.

WE proceed with the analysis of the ground-passage in the
system of enactments in Exodus, xxi. 2–6, both for development of the argument, and removal of objections.

The very first command limited the ordinary term of service to six years, but, at the same time, made an enlarged term
optional as a matter of choice and agreement, solemnly entered
into before judges. We proceed to draw out the argument
from this first stand-point, and it carries us nearly over the
whole ground. *If thou buy a Hebrew servant.* The first
question arising is this : From whom is the purchase made?
If from a third party, considered as an owner, this would go
far to prove the existence of some kind of slavery. This,
then, is a matter of the very first importance. But a second
question arises, as to the nature of the purchase, the determination of which goes far to settle the first question, and is
likewise of the highest importance. Is the *buying* which is
here brought to light a transfer of ownership, such as we are
accustomed to indicate by the terms buying and selling, or is
there a peculiarity in the usage of the Hebrew term, which
can not be conveyed by our word *buy*, but on the contrary a
wrong meaning is conveyed ? The closest examination of the
Hebrew usage, along with the known tenure of the service in
question, proves that the word does not mean to purchase as
an article of property, the idea of property in a person not

being comprehended in the transaction, nor admissible. The word in the original is the same which is used when it is said that the prophet Hosea *bought* his wife, not, certainly, of any third party who owned her—for in this astonishing instance she was under no man's authority or power—but of herself, by agreement with herself. Just so, Boaz *bought* Ruth, certainly not of any third party, nor as an article of property. So in Ecclesiastes, ii. 7, "*I got* me servants and handmaids," the same word translated in the case before us, buy, but meaning simply *I obtained*, with precisely the same signification as when we say, I have got me a good cook or a good chambermaid, or, I have obtained an excellent servant. If a gentleman in this country should hire a coachman, agreeing to keep him for six years, and he, on his part, to stay for six years, he might just as properly be said to have purchased his coachman as any Hebrew gentleman to have bought his servant. This word, then, does *not* mean traffic, as of an article of property, but indicates a bargain, free and voluntary on both sides; a bargain between two, and not the transfer of a chattel from the ownership of one person to the ownership of another person as his property.

This, then, of itself, goes far to determine the first question in regard to buying a Hebrew servant, namely, of whom? The answer is, not of any third party, but of himself, developing this grand peculiarity in the phraseology used as to obtaining servants, that the person hiring himself as a servant is described in Hebrew idiom, in relation to the person engaging his services, as selling himself, and himself receiving the purchase money. He simply sells his services for so long a time, but the Hebrew idiom takes the *Niphal* form of the verb to sell, and describes him as selling himself, though he is as truly a freeman, and as far from being a slave, or an article of property, as ever. And the person obtaining his services, and paying for them, is said to purchase him of himself, not of any owner or master to whom he belongs, for he belongs to himself, and is perfectly free to hire himself or not to whomsoever he pleases.

This idiom and meaning are proved, 1st, from the similar usage of the terms in other transactions, as we have seen; 2d, from comparison with Leviticus, xxv. 39, 47, where the case is supposed of a free Hebrew getting poor, and, as our translation has it, *being sold*, that is, in the original, selling himself unto thee. Of course, being a freeman, no third party could sell, or has any power over him, and yet this case is one in which an ordinary reader, from the very necessity growing out of the form of the translation (*be sold unto thee*), would suppose a sale from a third party. The second case is of a Hebrew in like manner falling poor, and going into service, in consequence, in the family of a heathen, a stranger, and the same expression precisely in the original is used to describe the contract, but in this case it is translated *sell himself* unto the stranger—no third party intimated.

3d. A third proof demonstrative of the idiom and meaning, as excluding any third party, is the prescribed time of the contract, six years, no more, no less. These six years in the man's life nobody owned, nobody was the master of, but himself. He only could sell them. The bargain for his services was made with himself, not with any third party. Yet he is described as being sold, and the man who engages his services is described as buying him.

4th. The same demonstration is renewed in the fact that his master, at the end of six years, if he enters into a new and longer contract for his services, has to buy them over again of himself, not of any other person; no third party comes in, nor does the master gain any right of possession by the fact of six years' previous service. The servant is as free to enter into a new contract as the master.

This matter being settled, the question comes up, whether the same idiom prevailed as to the obtaining of heathen servants, and it is proved that it did. *If thou buy a heathen serv-*

ant, would mean precisely the same, as to the parties and the purchase, as in the case of the Hebrew servant. But inasmuch as nothing is here specified in regard to any other than Hebrew servants, it might have been argued that there was no allowance of heathen servants at all among the Hebrews, because every part of this domestic arrangement was so carefully ordered by law. Accordingly, the legal provision was inserted, and the terms on which the heathen might be obtained for servants were explicitly settled. And the phraseology employed in regard to them, as to buying them, and as to their selling themselves, has precisely the same meaning, and no signification of slavery in it. In their case, there could no more be the buying of servants of a third party than in the case of the Hebrews. There were express provisions against such an enormity, of which provisions the great fugitive slave law in behalf of servants, not of masters, constituted one; which law, if we apply it exclusively to the heathen, as some contend, made the slavery of the heathen absolutely impossible, bringing it to an end the moment they touched the Hebrew soil. For, by that fugitive law, any heathen slave was at liberty to renounce the service of his master at any moment, and betake himself to the Hebrews for protection, and every Hebrew was bound to protect his freedom. So far, therefore, were the Hebrews from the wholesale privilege of making slaves of the heathen, or buying them as slaves, that they were by law compelled to receive and shelter as free, and to preserve and defend from oppression, every heathen slave who preferred freedom. No heathen could be obtained by any Hebrew as a servant without his own consent, without a free contract entered into, and the time specified and the wages paid.

Now, then, a third point is this very point of the length of time. "If thou buy a Hebrew servant, *six years shall he serve;*" but there may be a longer period of service, if he chooses to engage for it, and if the master agrees to it also on

shut up to these words alone, as to a legal writ, back of which we could not inquire, the enactment and procedure would look very arbitrary, would seem cruel and oppressive, if we had to give an opinion without examination of the other side? If a slaveholder could take this passage and some others, and fling them in our faces, restricting us from inquiring what they mean, what witnesses they can bring as to their meaning, just as he can prevent his slaves from testifying against any cruelties, however horrible, of white men, then he might say, as he can of his own wicked statutes, these are my justification for holding immortal beings as property, and you are not permitted to go behind these extracted verses to learn from the context what they really mean, or to gain that explanation which the word of God itself affords in regard to them.

In those days of early simplicity and nobleness, a man seeking a wife was not hunting for a fortune; he sought his wife, if he followed Jacob and Boaz's example, out of love; he considered his wife herself as his fortune, and was willing to give a large dowry for her, instead of demanding a dowry with her. The matches in the Bible are love matches, and Jacob's courtship was a courtship of seven years' service to the father of the damsel. And the father is sometimes described as selling his daughter, as in the very chapter before us, when he gave her in betrothal to her future husband, but certainly without the most distant shadow of that ignominious meaning which we justly attach to the infamous transaction, not uncommon in American slavery, of a man selling his own daughter for gain. But more generally the father is described as giving his daughter, even while the husband is described as buying her. Just so, in the case before us in Exodus, the statute having perhaps been framed with reference to the very example of Laban with Jacob and Rachel. And the moment we find that the dowry a man was expected to pay for a wife amounted, in the case of a laborer like Jacob, to seven years' steady and faithful apprenticeship and service, then we see that the master making such a grant, such a contract of marriage with his servant, has a claim for the payment from him. If it was right for Laban, it was right for any master; if it was a just rule for Jacob, it was just for any servant.

And as he could not take his wife and children away without having paid the just dowry, so neither would the law allow him to take the children from their mother, but they must remain with her. Under these circumstances the servant might at once engage with his master for the long term of service, and the covenant had to be ratified before judges in the most solemn manner, for the protection of the rights of either party, and for security on all sides against oppression and fraud. The service money in these contracts would seem, from some very plain indications, to have been paid beforehand, or a great part of it; and hence the necessity of a contract before judges, and also the precaution of boring the servant's ear, to constitute a proof positive of his obligations, if at·any time he should undertake to deny them, and to cheat his master out of the service he still owed to him. But every thing was voluntary on either side.

Now the contract for this longest period of service ever allowed is expressly described as a contract for ever; *he shall serve him for ever.* Yet it is demonstrated to have been only till the jubilee; for at that time, in the great recurring fiftieth year, by the central, fundamental, governing law, to which all contracts of business, of possessions, and of service were subordinate and amenable, every inhabitant of the land was free, and all arrangements of hiring and paying were calculated with reference to that time and that event, when every previous engagement came to an end. The conclusive proof of this is in Leviticus, xxv. 47–54 and 39–41: "He shall serve thee unto the year of jubilee, and then shall he depart from thee, both he and his children with him." The term for ever, applied to domestic service, is necessarily restricted in its meaning; at any rate, it can not refer to eternity. The limits of the restriction have therefore to be sought and explained from known circumstances. Under the law of jubilee it was perfectly plain, and could not be extended. It could not mean perpetual servitude, nor through the lifetime, because the time at which the contract was made might have been only ten years, or less or more, before the recurrence of the jubilee, and then, by the great controlling law, menservants, maid-servants, and children all went out free.

This term *for ever*, thus applied to the contract with Hebrew servants, being thus indisputably demonstrated and confessed to mean only to the jubilee, is in the same way demonstrated to mean the same thing, to be under the same restriction, when applied to the contract with heathen servants. They also might in like manner be bound by the *for ever* contract, but, in like manner, also, and by the same limitations, it came to its close for them at the jubilee. They too might be engaged for the shorter or for the longer period, but it was just as voluntary with them as with the Hebrews, and optional to make whichever contract the law allowed ; all contracts whatsoever coming to an end at the jubilee, when liberty was proclaimed to all the inhabitants of the land, whether Hebrew or heathen, natives or strangers.*

---

* JOSEPHUS. Antiq., B. III., ch. xii. Josephus intimates no restriction, but says, in the most general terms, οἱ δουλεύοντες ελευθεροι ἀφίενται, *the servants are set free.* Immediately previous he has said, speaking of the freedom of the fruits of the earth to all in common in the seventh and fiftieth years, that there was no distinction in that respect between their own countrymen and foreigners. If in minor things, much more in this great law of justice and benevolence, would the grand principle be fulfilled, Ye shall have the same manner of law for the stranger and the native. It was thus that the Jubilee, as the year of Redemption and of Liberty, universal, was so lively a type of the coming of Christ, and the ransom by him of sinners of every race. See, also, LIGHTFOOT. Works, Vol. V., 136. Lightfoot quotes Zohar in Lev. xxv., "As at the jubilee ALL SERVANTS WENT FREE, so at the last redemption," etc. Also, Vol. III., 110, 111. Compare SAALSCHUTZ, Laws of Moses, Vol. II., 714. Also, KITTO'S CYCLOP., Art. Slave. See, also, remarks in STILLINGFLEET'S Origines Sacræ, Vol. I., ch. vii.

CHAPTER VIII.

FREEDOM AND RIGHTS OF THE CHILDREN OF SERVANTS.—ESSENCE OF AMERICAN SLAV-
ERY.—PERVERSION OF THE MARRIAGE RELATION INTO A SLAVE-BREEDING FACTORY.
—IMPOSSIBILITY OF SUCH A MONSTROSITY AND ATROCITY BEING SANCTIONED OF GOD.

AND now we have a fourth point, of immense importance in
this investigation, growing directly out of this clause before
us in the twenty-first chapter of Exodus, the point, namely,
as to the position and rights of the children of servants born
in the households of their masters. Did they belong to the
master, or to their own parents? The bare statement of the
question is enough to settle it, but we patiently pursue the
investigation. From the length of the contracts with servants,
both ordinary and extraordinary, both the six years' contract
and that up to the jubilee, it follows, necessarily, that there
might be, must be, children of servants born in the house. If
these had belonged to the master, and not to the parents,
then the ordinance of marriage would have been, as to servants among the Hebrews, neither more nor less than a slave-
breeding institution, a perpetual manufacture of property in
human flesh, for the sole profit of the owner, the manufactory
being established and protected by the same divine law which
said, "Thou shalt love thy neighbor and the stranger as thyself." It would have broken up and destroyed the parental
relation, and changed the children of the servants into household cattle of the master, owned by him, and owing obedience
to him only. It would have cut off one whole commandment
in the decalogue from its application to parents and children,
"Honor thy father and mother," and transferred the authority and claim of obedience to the master and owner, the rela-

tion between father and mother being only that of factors, that of agents for the owner, to prepare, stamp, and make over into his possession, for his riches, new articles of property belonging to him.

If any one can believe that a marriage institution, of a nature so barbarous and diabolical as this, was set up by the divine law among the Hebrews, such a man can believe in any iniquity as divine. And to this extent a man must go in order to find any sanction of the system of American slavery in the word of God. For the essence of American slavery, the central, fundamental element of cruelty and crime, by which it is sustained and made perpetual, is just this, namely, the incessant and perpetual stealing of children from their parents, by the factorship of the marriage relation, perverted, corrupted, diabolized, into an engine of anguish and debasement to the parents, and of gain to the masters, that hath on it, more than any thing else in this world, the stamp of hell. But of this indescribable and infinitely atrocious wickedness there can not be a trace discovered in the Hebrew laws or domestic usages. The children of servants could no more be taken for property, or converted into property, or claimed by the master as belonging to him, than the servants themselves.

It would be infinitely monstrous to suppose that whereas the parents were free to hire themselves out as they chose, and could not be challenged as owing service to any one longer than six years, or, if for a longer period, only by a definite, voluntary contract, and never were, nor could be slaves, never could become the property of their masters; that their children, by the accident of being born to them while they were engaged in his service, became, not their children, but his property! Where are the articles of such villainy, or any indications of them? Where did ever the parents exist on earth that would consent to it? The supposition of such a thing among Hebrew parents, such an admission of child-stealing as an article of domestic service, would be an impious buffoonery. Such a thing could not exist, such an operation could not take place, but by divine command, and upon a voluntary contract. Was there ever such a command, or, even among the imported forms of idolatry, was there ever such an incarnation of Pandemonium, bad enough to suggest, or fierce enough to enforce it? Was there ever a set of servants so servile and dehumanized as to obey it or admit it? Did they ever make such a contract? Did they ever agree that, though the master had no power over *them*, no claim upon them as property, he should nevertheless have the right to grasp and hold as his property the objects of their affection, the children given to them of God, and dearer to them than themselves, just by reason of the fact that they were born in his household?   Could a more incredible, impossible monstrosity of oppression and of cruelty be laid to the charge of a divine revelation?   Nothing but a system which is "the sum of all villainies" could ever give birth to the imagination of such an atrocity.

Even if the tenure of service on the part of the parents had been such as to admit some idea of property in themselves, bought and paid for by the master as their owner, which it does not, still there could be no claim, except by a separate agreement and purchase, to the children; and such agreement there never was, nor ever the possibility of such purchase provided for. Even if the law could be shown to have given you property in the father, it gives you none in the child. Not one step can you go in this wickedness beyond the bond. If the law could allow your pound of flesh, it gives no drop of blood; above all, it does not allow you to take the heart's blood of the parent, in consigning the children, from the very womb, to the degradation and hopeless misery of a breathing and sensitive article of property and traffic. For the sanction of such an abomination, you have got to show a law in Hebrew legislation for claiming the children of servants, without right, without equivalent, without consent, a law demonstrating that for all that portion of the human family who work for wages, children are not a heritage from the Lord, but an heir-loom for the owner's avarice and cruelty. Such a law you *can* show in American slavery, and it brands the page where it is recorded, and the whole legislation that admits and sustains it, to everlasting execration, as the climax of iniquity and cruelty. But you can not, dare not, claim *that* as an essential element of Christianity; yet you must, in order to find the least sanction of American slavery in God's word, produce in that word the exact model of that devilish law.

There is, certainly, no natural right to enslave. It must be the creation of law, and of law framed on purpose for oppression, on purpose to establish, as legal, that which is naturally unjust. It were blasphemy to suppose this done by Jehovah. But assume, if you please, the existence in Judea of servants bound for life, bought for life. Is there any natural claim upon the children in consequence of such purchase of the parents? Did they, when they sold their own services, stand as the federal head of a race consigned by that purchase as the property of their masters for ever? Is there the slightest indication of such a monstrosity? Is *that* the meaning of God's embrace of the children in his covenant of mercy and love to the fathers? Was that the meaning of the Lord Jesus, when he said, Suffer the little children to come unto me, and forbid them not, for of such is the kingdom of heaven? All these enormities are essential to the existence of slavery, of that American slavery which claims to be sanctioned of Jehovah in his word. It constitutes and perpetuates, under pretense of divine law, nay, and of divine benevolence, such an accursed race, a race given over as the property of another race, without equivalent, without purchase, without payment.

The examination of the point before us is as an observation by the quadrant at sea, whereby we bring down the sun to demonstrate our exact position in relation to this sin; we learn the position of this sin in morals, and the depth and advancement of our depravity if we maintain it. We guage the guilt both toward God and man by this test, and show the impossibility of there ever having been the least sanction of it on the pages of a divine revelation. The institution of marriage was for all mankind, and not for certain aristocratic or governing classes merely. The unity of the family circle, with its privileges of sanctity, freedom and independence that could not be invaded, was not for the wealthy merely, while the laborer, the servant, was to be excluded from it, and put under the law of the *contubernium* for the master's profit ;* under the operation, in a slave-breeding manufactory, of a promiscuous concubinage so diabolical, that that worse than heathen monstrosity, set apart of God with a special seal of wrath branded upon it, should become no uncommon reality, " That a man and his father should go in unto the same maid."†

The institution of marriage, so adulterated, in combination

---

* Fuss, Roman Antiq., of Slaves, sec. 51, 52, 54, 56. The frightful similarity is to be noted between Roman and American slavery—Roman under the system of Paganism, American under Christianity — and especially the oneness and monstrosity of both in the same Sodomic licentiousness and adultery, on principle and for profit. It has been gravely decided that the marriage contract not being possible in law between slaves, the crime of adultery is done away among them, and they having no marital rights, no man can be punished for any violation of them.

† Amos, ii. 7. The startling apparition of the grossest and most horrid iniquities engendered from the mingling of the worship of Moloch and of God, in full blossom and power under the light of the gospel, is the most remarkable proof of the efficacy of the system of American slavery, as a hot-house of exotic abominations that could have been reared nowhere else under heaven, under no climate, in no tropic of pure, unadulterated native religion, but only where the capacities of natural depravity were assisted by the artificial combinations of a gangrened and perverted Christianity, made the efficient instrument of deadliest sin. While they promise the perfection of liberty, the supporters of this system are themselves the servants of corruption, speaking great swelling words of vanity, out of a heart exercised with cursed practices, and presenting to the world an amalgamation of the gospel in a form of most vaunted orthodoxy with the most wanton antinomianism under heaven.

with the law of domestic service, must have constituted, if that service was the system of slavery, the excommunication, to the latest generation, of all the posterity of servants from all the privileges of freedom, and the creation and consecration of children and children's children, for and under the curse of chattelism, to be cast out and trodden down of society with a ban worse than any ever contrived or fastened on mankind by the Man of Sin and Son of Perdition. Where is the covenant of such an abomination? In what part of the charter of divine mercy for mankind does it lie enshrined or buried? Under what literal or typical swathing, with what winding sheets of grave-clothes, laid away for the millennium of its resurrection? It has been reserved for the false Messiahs of a modern slaveholding Christianity to stand at this sepulcher, and bid this festering carcass come forth, commanding the church and the ministry to loose him and let him go. And this is the missionary Lazarus, whom the modern interpreters of divine providence are to charter and send out as the great power of God, the wonder-working, missionary, providential agency, whereby Ethiopia shall soon stretch forth her hands unto heaven!

The entailment of slavery among the Hebrews, the law of its hereditary succession, the abrogation of marriage by it, and the substitution of a system of concubinage and adultery instead of that divine ordinance, would have changed the whole condition and history of the nation. If the children of servants had been of necessity and by birth slaves, if such had been the law, and consequently the practice, the result would have been inevitable, a slave population in Judea increasing more rapidly than the free Hebrews themselves. But for a thousand years there is not the least trace of such a population, or law, or traffic; and the last crime that filled up the measure of the nation's iniquities, and brought down upon them the wrath of God without remedy, was the attempt to set aside their free constitution, which made such a slave race impossible, and to establish slavery in its stead.

We see, very plainly, some of the reasons of God's extreme severity in punishment of that last mighty crime. The moment that free constitution, which had been appointed of God, was set aside, and the people took their servants and said, You shall be ours at our pleasure, our property for ever, it made them all, at one blow, men-stealers—a nation of men-stealers. And if they proceeded to take the children also, as they would have done, it would make⋅them double men-stealers, that is, stealers of the children first from their parents, second from themselves, without any price or equivalent paid to any one. But in the very same chapter of laws in which God had restricted the period of Hebrew domestic service to six years, there was written out also the great divine law against man-stealing and selling: "He that stealeth a man, and selleth him, or if he be found in his hand, shall surely be put to death." Now the stealing of mere property was never punished by death; and if men had been considered as property, there would have been no such penalty as that against the stealing of men. But they were not; and because the converting of them into property was a perpetual moral assassination of them and their posterity, destroying the children through their parents, therefore, not only the act of stealing, but the claim of property in a human being, the holding of him as property, and the making merchandise of him, was, in the sight of God, as great a crime as killing him; it was an iniquity set in the same category for its punishment as murder.

And such a system as that of slavery could not possibly have been established without this crime and guilt of man-stealing; for even supposing any persons ever to have been sold as slaves *for crime* (of which there never was an instance, and could not be), the law strictly defended *the children* from being affected by that punishment. The children could never have been held in bondage because the parents were; there was no attainder, or entailment of vengeance, permitted. "The fathers shall not be put to death for the children, neither shall the children be put to death for the fathers, but every man for his own sin." Deuteronomy, xxiv. 16. And the practical enforcement of this law we may find in 2 Chronicles, xxv. 4, where Amaziah punished the murderers of the king, his father, " but slew not their children, but did as it is written in the law of the book of Moses, where the Lord commanded, saying, "The fathers shall not die for the children, nor the children for the fathers, but every man for his own sin." God also says in Ezekiel, in reference to the same thing, " Behold, all souls are mine ; as the soul of the father, so also the soul of the son is mine." Ezekiel, xviii., 4.

There was, therefore, no possible way in which children could be enslaved without man-stealing ; and when the nation, in the last stage of corruption and decay, undertook so to change their constitution and laws, as that servants and their children should be the property of their masters, they became a nation of man-stealers ; and for that crime God swept them from the face of the country. This same iniquity it is, which constitutes the great guilt of our own nation, and makes American slaveholders a people of men-stealers. They may aver that they bought the parents and paid for them, but the children they have stolen, stolen them from themselves, from their parents, from society, from God, without one farthing ever paid for them, with no claim upon them, save only the unrighteous and cruel enslavement of their parents before them.

Man-stealing and man-selling are the sole origin especially of American slavery. The progenitors of the human beings now bought and sold as chattels in this country were stolen from their native land, and they who first bought them knew that they were stolen. And their paying the price for them to the slave trader could not and did not take away from the poor stolen creatures their own right of ownership in themselves, but they remained stolen men and women, just as truly after being bought and paid for as before; and they who bought them and paid for them and claimed them as property, knowing them to have been stolen, were accessory to the crime, just as, by common law, the receiver of stolen property is party with the thief. If buying and paying, without just title, constituted lawful property, then what infinite villainies would be hourly committed with perfect safety! You, A B, declaring yourself to be the owner of any piece of property in the city or the country, could sell it to C D for five hundred or a thousand dollars, could sell any man's house over his own head, and the payment of that thousand dollars would make that buyer the owner, though you had no more right to sell, no more authority on the premises, than the nakedest beggar in Australia!

The absurdity is palpable, when the article thus bought and sold is an ordinary item of estate or merchandise; but the moment the subject of such buying and selling is a human being with a dark skin, it is enough for the buyer to aver that he has paid for him. In the case of ordinary articles of traffic, in the transfer of property, justice watches both sides, and the seller must establish his title to sell, or the buyer's having paid forty thousand dollars for the property could not make it his. In the case of a negro, it is enough for any white man to swear that he purchased him, and that makes the purchased black man a slave without remedy. How dreadful is this guilt! How sinful in the sight of Heaven such perfect disregard and annihilation of the right of each human being to the ownership of himself! The transmission of such property by inheritance is merely the transmission of a crime; no title can be transmitted where none existed. A man's slave property being inherited gives *him* no title as heir, since it was stolen at the outset, and all the increase by natural propagation is just merely the increase of the theft, the race on his hands being a stolen race. It is impossible, by transmission, to convert the crime into an innocent transaction. No man can innocently buy a fellow-man as property, or acquire any right of property in him, though he should give for him the cost of the whole solar system, if that could be weighed in God's balances, and put into his hands. The essential element of man-stealing is in the very title by which you claim any creature of those human beings whom you hold as property.

It is this perpetuating of injustice, this predestination and legacy of it as an inheritance, which the heirs of the estate plead that they are compelled to accept, as its guardians, that makes the system infinitely horrible and monstrous. The elements of evil in this iniquity, as well as the living subjects of oppression, run on increasing from generation to generation. You had perhaps two slaves bequeathed to you; yourself create five others and bequeath them. If you merely transmitted the two that you received, the system would be comparatively harmless; but it is a wickedness redoubled by every successive race of owners, who in their turn not only receive the stolen goods of those that preceded them, but themselves steal a new community, themselves claim a new and separate circle of human beings as their property, and maintain that all this is by the sanction of God Almighty.

Now, if such iniquity as this, and such propagation of it, had been rendered impossible in no other way, it would have been by the great law of jubilee, which was a universal, unconditional emancipation of all the inhabitants of the land every fifty years, making it absolutely impossible for any man's race or posterity ever to be enslaved. And that was one great object of this law, while at the same time it provided a preparatory discipline of heathen servants, to fit them also for the perfect freedom of the Hebrews.

It took them from the influences and examples of heathenism, and kept them, on an average, twenty or twenty-five years under the power and teachings of the divine law, and then they were free. The service of the heathen was by voluntary contract, and not an involuntary servitude; it was for wages paid, according to agreement, and made no approximation to slavery; and the law extending the term of contract to the jubilee operated as a naturalization law of benevolent probationary freedom for those who had perhaps been idolaters and slaves. They were put under such a system as made them familiar with all the religious privileges and observances which God had ordered and bestowed; a system that admitted them to instruction and kindness, and prepared them to pass into integral elements of the nation. But all engagements were voluntary. No Hebrew could compel any heathen to serve him; no Hebrew could buy any heathen servant of a third party as an article of property. No such buying or selling was ever permitted, but every contract was to be made with the servant himself. The forty-fourth verse of the twenty-fifth chapter of Leviticus proves this. "Both thy men-servants and thy maid-servants, which shall be to you of the heathen that are round about you, of them shall ye buy the man-servant and the maid-servant." And the forty-fifth verse continues, "Moreover, of the children of the strangers that do sojourn among you, of them shall ye buy, and of their families that are with you, which they begat in your land; and they shall be to you for a possession." Of the children of the strangers shall ye buy; that is, ye shall take the children themselves, as many as are willing to enter your service on this contract, not from a third party, but from themselves, by their own free choice, and from their families begotten among you; and those so taken, so engaged, shall, as to their time and service for the period for which they engage themselves, belong to you, be to you for a possession, a fixture of service, up to the period of jubilee. "Ye shall take them as an inheritance for your children after you to inherit a possession; ye shall serve yourselves with them for ever."

This language is the same with that used before concerning the Hebrew servant, under the same long contract till the jubilee, and what it means in the one case, precisely the same it means in the other; that is, they shall be your servants for the longest period admitted by your laws for any service or any contract, even till the jubilee. And as engaged by such contract, and paid on such terms, ye do take them, and may take them, as an inheritance for your children after you, for any part of the term of such service which may remain unexpired, when you, the head of the family, are taken away. Then those servants, by you engaged and paid for an apprenticeship till the jubilee, shall be for your children to inherit as a possession, the possession of their time and service, which, by your contract with them, as rightfully belongs to your children as to you, until the stipulated period come to an end.

Hebrew servants thus engaged themselves, or sold themselves to families of strangers, and it was called selling themselves *to the stock of the stranger's family ;* that is, selling themselves for a possession to the children of the family, until the jubilee ; thus constituting a fixture, a possession, as to time and service that had been engaged and paid for, in the family stock. This was done *by Hebrews themselves,* who, nevertheless, were perfectly free, and in no sense slaves ; it was done in exactly the same way by the heathen, on a contract exactly as free, and they were nevertheless in no sense slaves. But this jubilee contract, once entered into, was a contract *belonging to the family ;* it was a contract by which the servant's time and labor having been purchased, if ten, or forty years, was due to the family for that period. It had been purchased by the master for himself and his household, his children ; and the servant so apprenticed would belong, that is, his time and service would belong, to the family, to the children, if the master died before the time of the contract expired. If, for example, the master entered into such a contract the seventh year after the jubilee, it would be a contract for forty-three years to come. Now, suppose the master to die ten years from that time, then manifestly the time and service of the

Hebrew servant would belong to the family as their inheritance; it would belong to the children as their possession, after their father; and, again, if they all died within the next ten or twenty years, and the servant lived, then ten or twenty years of the unexpired service would still belong to the grand-children, as *their* possession; and so on till the jubilee. It would be an inheritance for the master, and his children after him, to inherit a possession; inasmuch as his death, ten years after a contract made and paid with a servant for forty years, did not and could not release that servant from his obligation to complete the service for which he had been paid before-hand.

Meantime, the servant could, on his own score, trade with the money which he had thus received, could turn it to the most remunerative account possible; for he was not owned by his master; and if any inhuman, oppressive claim were set up over him as property, he could flee away from such tyranny, and every man was bound to shelter and protect him; no man was permitted to return him to his master. He was protected by other definite provisions, likewise, from the cruelty of a bad master; of which provisions the enactment in Exodus, xxi. 27, is an example: "If he smite out his man-servant's tooth, or his maid-servant's tooth, he shall let him go free for his tooth's sake." We shall proceed to develop the peculiarities of freedom and benevolence in these remarkable laws, and demonstrate their operation.*

---

* See SAALSCHUTZ, Laws of Moses, on the provisions by which the servant could trade on his own account, and on the nature of the service rendered by Jacob to Laban.   Also, KITTO'S CYCLOP., article Slave.   See, also, BARNES on the privileges of Hebrew servants.   Inquiry into Scrip. Views of Slavery, ch. v.   Compare GRANVILLE SHARPE, Law of Retribution against Tyrants, Slaveholders, and Oppressors.   Compare, also, Judge JAY on Hebrew Servitude, one of the best productions of that eminent philanthropist.   Compare, also, STILLINGFLEET, Origines Sacræ, Vol. I., ch. vii. remarks on the duration of the Jubilee Contract.

CHAPTER IX.

God's Fugitive Law for Protection of the Runaway.—Comparison of it with Laws for the Restoration of Property.—Demonstration from it of the Impossibility of Property in Man.—The Guilt of such a Claim.—Slaveholding Punished with Death.-

"Thou shalt not deliver unto his master the servant which is escaped from his master unto thee. He shall dwell with thee, even among you, in that place which he shall choose, in one of thy gates, where it liketh him best. Thou shalt not oppress him." Deuteronomy, xxiii. 15, 16. This is part of God's personal liberty bill for a free people, who, if they would preserve their own freedom, must respect that of others, must protect the liberties of all, without respect of person. The benevolence and generosity of the Mosaic legislation against slavery, with the running fiery commentary of the prophets, denouncing this and every form of oppression, will for ever remain among the most convincing proofs of a divine revelation. A rainbow over the gates of Paradise, a cataract of liquid ruby or diamond bursting into spray, with the sun shining on it, a dome of the celestial city, with a phalanx of angels floating around it, would not be more beautiful, more wonderful, than these verses, in contrast with the slave legislation of the world. This divine fugitive law is a suitable companion for the law against man-stealing, completing the demonstration against the possibility of property in man.

It proves that in the divine estimation, no man could own another man in such a sense, as to have any claim upon him against his own will, without his own consent, in a contract of voluntary service; no man could own another man as property; and if he set up such a claim, the poor oppressed creature so claimed had the right to run away, the right to take possession of himself as his own, no matter how much his alleged owner might have paid for him. He had the right to run away, and every righteous man was bound to help him run away, and to give him shelter and protection. His master could not righteously demand him, for he could not and did not own him, could not righteously have bought and held him as property. The bargain of purchase and sale, by which he pretended to have acquired possession of him, was not only null and void, but was a theft, a robbery, an act of man-stealing. And so, instead of returning the fugitive, it would be incumbent on the law to seize the master making such a demand as his professed owner, and to indict and punish him for that crime. But the fugitive could never be treated as a slave; the whole nation, and every individual in it, were bound and compelled to regard and protect him as a freeman. He could never have been justly bought or sold as property, and the claim in him as such was forbidden on pain of death.

If he could have been justly, at any time, bought as property, then he would have been justly owned, he would have been the buyer's property; and if he had fled away, would have been himself the thief, and by the law of God, every Hebrew would have been bound to aid in capturing and restoring him to his owner. For it was expressly provided that all manner of lost or stolen *property* should be restored to the owner; and the Hebrew code had a specific closeness of detail and pertinacity of justice in this respect, that never marked the jurisprudence of any other people. If any man's ox, or ass, or sheep strayed from him, and any man found it, he was bound not only to advertise the owner, but even if he were his enemy, to bring it back to him again. If the owner was not known, or lived at a distance, then the law ran, " Thou shalt bring it to thine own house, and it shall be with thee until thy brother seek after it, and thou shalt restore it to him again. In like manner shalt thou do with his ass, and so shalt thou do with his raiment, and with all lost things of thy brother's, which he hath lost and thou hast found, shalt thou do likewise ; thou mayst not hide thyself."*

All lost things thou shalt deliver unto the owner. Now it is clear that if a slave were a thing, or if there had been such a thing as a slave recognized or lawful, such a possibility as that of property in man, there would have been no withdrawing that kind of thing, that kind of property, from under the operation of these laws. The obligation of restoring all lost things, all escaped, or runaway, or stolen property, must have included the most valuable of all property ; and the law would inevitably have read, Thou shalt especially restore unto his owner his lost slave. But it reads the reverse, Thou shalt *not* deliver unto his master the servant which is escaped from his master unto thee. The conclusion is inevitable, the proof from God impregnable, that man can not own property in man. If the servant could have been property, then he would have been the most valuable of all property, and the man detaining him from his owner would have been the greatest of all thieves. If he could have been property, as an ox or a sheep is property, then the obligation to restore him to his owner would have been by as much greater as a man is more valuable than a sheep. By the market price, on the comparison of lost things, according to the southern tariff, there would be at least fifty or a hundred times a greater obligation to deliver up a man than a sheep. The thing, therefore, is unqualified demonstration, and by this line of argument alone, from this one statute only, it is plain that there can be no such thing as property in man. This is God's judgment.

But God has made the case still stronger. By the statute in Exodus, xxii. 1–4, if a man steal an ox or a sheep, and kill it or sell it, he shall restore five oxen for an ox, and four sheep for a sheep. But if the theft be certainly found in his hand alive, whether ox, ass, or sheep, he shall restore double. The thief

* Deuteronomy, xxii. 1–3.

of mere property was not otherwise punished than by such fine, but never with death ; but he must make restitution, in some cases seven-fold. Now, according to this measure, if a man could have been property, like an ox, if there had been, or could be, or could have been, under God's law or permission, such property as a slave, then the thief stealing *a man* and selling *him* as a slave, or helping him to run away, would have been bound to restore at least five slaves for the one he stole and sold, or helped to escape ; but if the stolen man were found in his hand, then he would have to restore two slaves for one.   And if any man, considered as a slave, considered as property, ran away from his owner, and were caught, then, having been himself his own thief, he would be bound to become two men returning ; he must restore two slaves instead of one to his master. If any other man stole him and sold him, or helped him to run away, he must have restored five slaves to his owner, instead of the one he had helped to escape. Such must have been the law, if a man could have been property, if property in man had been admitted or possible.

Now read the law in regard to stealing a man. HE THAT STEALETH A MAN, AND SELLETH HIM, OR IF HE BE FOUND IN HIS HAND, HE SHALL SURELY BE PUT TO DEATH. As a man can not possibly be property, and as the making of him such was an injury that could never be recompensed, any more than the injury of murder, the scale of retribution instantly ascends to the highest penalty possible for crime on earth, and he that stole, sold, or held a human being as a slave was inevitably to be put to death. The claim of property in man was such a crime, that any connivance with it was worthy of death ; and any legal toleration or establishment of its possibility would be a wrong against man so immeasurable and a sin against God so infinite, that to admit it even by implication in a just code was impossible. God forbade the very supposition of property in man.

Slavery is the holding and treating of a human being as property. It is buying, selling, making merchandise of him. The *making merchandise* of him is set by itself as the same crime with the *stealing* of him, and is condemned of God to the punishment of death. The holding of him as a chattel, a thing of merchandise, is in like manner forbidden on pain of death. The first law against this crime ran as follows: "He that stealeth a man, and selleth him, or if he be found in his hand, he shall surely be put to death." A man, any human being; the statute comprehended both Jew and Gentile. The note of Grotius on this text shows the interpretation given to it by one of the most impartial and learned jurists in the world, and one of the most careful and accurate students of the Scriptures. It is a testimony of great value, as being the opinion of a competent judge, without bias, without prejudice, on a matter not then in controversy, the meaning of a statute perfectly explicit in its terms, and the extent and particularity of its application.

This emphatic note was adopted by the General Assembly of the Presbyterian Church in the United States, in the publication of the Larger Catechism appended to the Confession of Faith, and it stood there for a number of years, a faithful testimony from the word of God against the iniquity of slaveholding. The note of the Assembly was on the first paragraph of the answer to the question, "What are the sins forbidden in the eighth commandment?" Answer, "The sins forbidden in the eighth commandment, besides the neglect of the duties required, are theft, robbery, man-stealing, and receiving any thing that is stolen." Note, "1 Timothy, i. 10. The law is made for whoremongers, for them that defile themselves with mankind, for MEN-STEALERS. This crime among the Jews exposed the perpetrators of it to capital punishment (Exodus, xxi 16), and the Apostle here classes them with sinners of the first rank. The word he uses, in its original import, comprehends all who are concerned in bringing any of the human race into slavery, or in detaining them in it. *Hominum fures, qui servos vel liberos abducunt, retinent, vendunt, vel emunt. Stealers of men are all those who bring off slaves or freemen, and keep, sell, or buy them.*" "To steal a freeman," says Grotius, "is the highest kind of theft. In other instances, we only steal human property, but when we steal or retain men in slavery, we seize those who, in common with ourselves, are constituted, by the original grant, lords of the earth." Gen., i. 28. *Vide* Pol. Synopsin, *in loc.*

This direct and faithful testimony against the sin of slave-holding stood for years in the book of the Presbyterian Confession of Faith. Editions of it were published and freely circulated at the South,* where the testimony could not be contradicted, and as being the testimony of the church, in her received standards, was of the highest authority and importance, to be carefully maintained and constantly and without hindrance proclaimed. It was worth more than all that has since been put in its place, by any or all Assemblies since the year when it was expunged from the volume. For expunged it was, and that too at a time when its voice was becoming more and more powerful and necessary, and a long and compromising note in the year 1818 was set in its place.

The first law against man-stealing, holding, and selling, recorded in Exodus, was promulgated of God in the year B. C. 1491. Forty years afterwards, this statute appears in another form, or rather, an additional statute is enacted, not taking the place of the other, nor in any way abrogating it, or restricting its application, but particularizing the native Hebrew, the Israel-

---

* The edition before me is that of the year 1801, at Wilmington and Baltimore. The title page is as follows: "The Constitution of the Presbyterian Church in the United States of America, containing the Confession of Faith, the Catechisms, the Government and Discipline, and the Directory for the Worship of God. Ratified and adopted by the Synod of New York and Philadelphia, held at Philadelphia May the 16th, 1788, and continued by adjournments until the 28th of the same month. Wilmington: Printed and sold by Bonsall & Niles; also sold at their bookstore, No. 173 Market street, Baltimore. 1801."

ite, as the object of a special protection. This statute (in Deut., xxiv. 7) runs as follows: "If a man be found stealing any of his brethren of the children of Israel, and maketh merchandise of him, or selleth him, then that thief shall die; and thou shalt put away evil from among you."

If we inquire the reason for the repetition of the old statute against man-stealing, in this new form, we shall probably find it in the fact of the tendency of the appointed system of domestic service among the Hebrews, as an apprenticeship, ordinarily of six years, to pass, in the hands of a cruel householder, into oppression; the temptation for him to take advantage of the power given him by this contract, to hold the servant for a longer period, and in fact attempt to enslave him. A man might possibly endeavor to do this in regard to a Hebrew servant, who would not dare attempt it, in the face of the old law, in regard to any heathen freeman, or any man, the stealing of whom required the commission of the whole crime, without any foundation of previous legal service to build upon. The making merchandise of any of his brethren would be the changing of him from a voluntary servant into a slave; it would be the act of man-stealing, if he held him as a servant against his will, without contract, with the claim of property in him, and the claim and usurpation of the right of disposing of his services, or of his person, to others as property. Such a transfer of him would be a crime worthy of death; and any man who entered into the conspiracy against him, receiving him as property, and in his turn maintaining the claim of property in him, and treating him as merchandise, committed the same crime, and came under the same condemnation.

Now it is plain that this crime, if the fact of its being committed at second-hand deprived it of any of its primeval wickedness, might have passed in Judea into a domestic institution, a possession, an organized sin, with connivance and protection of the law; just as it has done in our own land, where the very same iniquity, forbidden by law as piracy, in the primal act, in the first taking of a human being as property and making merchandise of him, is, by simple transfer through other hands, transfigured from crime into righteousness, from theft into lawful possession, from man-stealing into a just domestic right and honorable mercantile transaction; is established and protected by law as an institution, is defended by divines, and received into the bosom of the Church as a Christian and missionary sacrament!

God would not suffer such horrible perversion of justice, and enshrinement of iniquity as righteousness, among his ancient people, and therefore statute after statute was enacted to render it impossible. The stealing, the selling, the making merchandise in any way, not only of a man, a heathen, a stranger, but of a Hebrew, though he were a servant, or of any of the children of Israel, under whatever pretense of service due, was forbidden on pain of death. Whosoever was found detaining or claiming any human being for such purpose, or conspiring with others to maintain such a claim, was found guilty of stealing a man, and was to be punished with death for it. There is doubtless, in the particularity of these statutes, a reference to the crime by which Joseph was sold to the Ishmaelites by his brethren, which act was, in both the sellers and the buyers, the act of man-stealing, and was so described by the record in Genesis. Joseph was stolen by his brethren in being sold by them; and if they had been the buyers instead of the sellers, if they had bought him as merchandise, instead of selling him, the crime would have been the same; the making merchandise of a human person being under all forms and circumstances, no matter through how many transfers, by how many parties soever, the crime of man-stealing.

Men-stealers, in the words of the original note in the Presbyterian Catechism, comprehended all who were concerned in bringing any of the human race into slavery, OR IN DETAINING THEM IN IT. Now the slaveholder, the holder of human beings as property in slavery, is, in all cases, the man who is concerned and employed in detaining the victims of this oppression in it. The slaveholder may say that he only received the stolen property, and that he paid for it in receiving it. But one of the sins forbidden in the eighth commandment is the receiving any thing that is stolen; and one of the forms and methods of this sin, to be punished with death by the law of God, was the *holding* of any human being in slavery as property; not the mere stealing of him, which was the more palpable form of the crime, but also THE HOLDING OF HIM IN SUCH BONDAGE, AS PROPERTY, (which might more easily have escaped notice,) WAS THE WHOLE CRIME, and was as certainly to be punished with death as the original stealing. This disposes of every slaveholder before God, and sets the crime of slaveholding just where it ought to be set—under the gallows.*

* Compare GRANVILLE SHARPE'S powerful scriptural presentation of this guilt, in his Law of Retribution against Tyrants, Slaveholders, and Oppressors; and Aristotle's definition of a slave, κτημα και οργανον του δεσποτου εμφυχον, *an animated tool and piece of property for the master's use;* with the slave laws by which this definition is carried into detail; and the fearful severity with which in all ages these laws have been executed; and the manner in which the slaveholder makes merchandise of unborn generations, and brands the babes of his slaves, as soon as they are born, with the Pagan's brand for an immortal being. All things taken into consideration, no man can wonder at God's awful severity and wrath against the crime of making merchandise of man, which is the crime of slaveholding. Compare GROTIUS and CLARKE on Ex. xxi., 16, and 1 Tim. i., 10, with DYMOND'S Essays on Morality, ch. xviii.; STEPHEN'S Merciless Laws of Slavery, and WALLON, Histoire d'Esclavage, Vol. II., ch. v.; also FUSS, Rom. Antiq.; and BECKER, Manual, Account of Rom. Slavery in Bib. Sac., 1845. Compare BECKER'S Charicles, Excurs. *slaves,* and Gallus, Excurs. *slave family;* also JUDGE JAY'S Works, Reproof of the Church, and Letter to Ives; also STROUD, Slave Laws; and GOODELL, Am. Slave Laws, Part I.

PART II.

DEMONSTRATION

FROM

THE HEBREW ORIGINAL

INVESTIGATION

OF WORDS AND STATUTES.

CHAPTER X.

THE handling of the word of God deceitfully, and all the miseries and mischiefs consequent thereupon, may begin in a very small, unnoticed way. It is insects, with their microscopic eggs, that work the greatest ruin with the most precious plants and flowers. By the capture of single words, by setting his mark upon them, perhaps clipping and *milling* them, and then setting them in circulation as the true coin, Satan has gained vast possessions. Perverted phrases, occupied with false interpretations, become the strongest citadels of the adversary of men's souls. We have adverted to some remarkable instances of inveterate and obstinate perversion and mistake; a volume might be occupied in tracing their origin and progress.

The fruits and forms of religious truth, poisoned by such malignant error at the fountain, have become like gnarled apricots and apples, stung by the *curculio ;* and men have become so habituated to the poisoned fruit, and the fair, sound, wholesome plum has become such a stranger, that at length they claim the knotted, bitter work of the *curculio* as the perfect work of God, and the attempt to excommunicate it from the market, and introduce the true fruit in its stead, is denounced as the work of infidelity and fanaticism.

Such errors acquire a singular tenacity by time. They conglomerate and adhere, till all the neighboring theology is like an old Roman wall, or like the *birs Nimroud*, with the bricks so fast in the rocky asphaltum, that no power can separate them; the whole is as one solid rock, through the tenacity of the mortar. One built up a wall, and another daubed it with untempered mortar; but the mortar in this case is tempered with vehement passion and power, and the most diabolical wickedness is protected by it.

It is a work of great difficulty to break down these prejudices. Precedents of mistake and wickedness, instead of the divine law, are made to constitute the highway of theology, the great military road. It follows some tortuous sheep-track, the highway of God's truth having been deserted, the precedent having been set by some bell-wether of the flock passing through a gap in the wall, and imitated by others, till the great route of theological traffic has become established over the breach of God's own commandments. The error has run on, age after age giving it sanction, till the support of it has become a mark of theological conservatism; and he who endeavors to stand in the way of the multitude, and direct the stream of opinion and of trade into the good old paths of God, is in danger of being himself run over and trampled to death, or cut down as a heretic and fanatic, or treated with a commission of lunacy. If he be not, of a truth, an angel, armed with the sword of the Spirit, and trusting wholly in God, Balaam on his ass will ride over him for an interview and compromise with Balak.

A few vicious precedents, especially if of high authority, are sufficient, even in the church of God, to overlay or shove aside the law, till they are at length *adopted as* the law; precisely according to the example of usurpation set by the Scribes and Pharisees in Moses' seat, thrusting the traditions of the elders in the place of the divine statutes, or alongside with them, as their supreme interpreters. Error is thus taught by rote, while the rule of God's word is disregarded or perverted. When things have run on in this manner, unchecked, unquestioned for a while, the vital elements of religion suffer, and a poison unsuspected is intruded into our daily food. The whole province of theology is in danger of becoming an infected region, as a fair inviting country, beneath whose soil the seeds of disease lurk for activity.

There is a great work of under-draining needed, for we are as a people who have built upon ground infested with concealed fountains of marsh malaria, and filled in for the purposes of building, with soil thrown over those feverish and pestilential springs; which, being thus partially restrained and suffocated, diffuse their noxious effluvia and seminal principles through every square foot of soil, into every cellar, beneath every basement. There is no possibility of outliving, or ignoring, or defying this invisible mischief. There can be no remedy, no security, but in a thorough under-draining of our ecclesiastical and theological marshes by the word of God. The fever and ague of a false piety is in every shovel-full of soil thrown up out of such stagnant centuries of error; every furrow turned over by the plow of such theology emits a vapor that smites the very husbandman with disease. All the quinine of the Tract volumes, all the tonics of the most stringent Calvinism, can not keep out the sickness from the system, while its elementary principles are diffused as health. The whole piety that builds over such foundations will be the condemned victim of *the shakes*, a fitful, unreliable, antinomian religion, now burning, now freezing; furious and proud in the extremes of a boasted orthodoxy, and confident at the same time in the indulgence and defense of the worst licentiousness. God must overturn and overturn and overturn, working according to Hebrews, xii. 27, and removing the things that are or can be shaken, till the principle of fever and ague is banished, and that alone which can not be shaken remains. In this work of sacred radicalism, there is the divine assurance of receiving a kingdom which can not be moved.

Our survey thus far has been general and introductory. We now proceed to a careful investigation of the words, or periphrastic expressions, employed in the original Hebrew for *servants* and *bond-servants*, *servitude* and *bondage*. Not a little is depending on their history and usage, and we have already noted the remarkable fact, that there is, in reality, no word for *slave*, or *bondman*, in the Hebrew tongue; there is no Hebrew word, into which these English terms, with our ideas attached to them, could properly be translated, or by which they could be conveyed. The Roman, Greek, or modern definition of the word slavery can not, with the least propriety or truth, be assumed as the meaning of the word used for servant or bond-servant in the Hebrew Scriptures. This is a most important fundamental consideration.

ORIGINAL WORD FOR SERVANT.

The ordinary word for *servant* is עֶבֶד, *evedh*. The verb עָבַד, *avadh*, *to labor*, constitutes the root. The primary signification of the verb has nothing to do with that afterwards attached to the noun, but is independent, separate, generic. It is an honorable meaning; for labor is the vocation of freemen, or was so before the fall, when the father of mankind was put into the garden of Eden to dress it and to keep it, and to till the ground; to *work* upon the ground, to cultivate it. The first instance of the use of the verb is in Genesis, ii. 5: *There was not a man to till the ground,* לַעֲבֹד, *laavodh, to labor upon it, to cultivate it.*

So in Genesis, iii. 23: The Lord God sent him forth from the garden of Eden, *to till the ground*, from whence he was taken; לַעֲבֹד, *laavodh, to work upon it.*

So in Genesis, iv. 2: Cain was a tiller of the ground, עֹבֵד, *ovedh*, a man *working* the ground; that was his occupation.

Also, Genesis, iv. 12: in the sentence of Cain, the same word is made use of, the verb in the second person; *when thou tillest the ground*, תַעֲבֹד *taavodh.*

The generic signification of the word, and the only signification possible in primeval society, is that of *labor, work,* personal

occupation. The same universal meaning is in the commandment, Six days shalt thou *labor*, תַּעֲבֹד, *taavodh*. Exodus, xx. 9.

In process of time comes the secondary meaning, with the
idea included of laboring for another; that additional idea
constitutes, indeed, the *secondary* meaning. At first it is only
the idea of working for another willingly, or for a consideration, for wages; as might be done by brothers and sisters, or
other blood relatives in the same family. See Malachi, iii. 17:
As a man spareth his own son that *serveth* him, הָעֹבֵד, *haovedh*.
There is yet no signification of subjection or of servitude. In
Genesis, xxix. 15, it is used concerning the service of Jacob
to Laban: *Shouldst thou serve me* for nought? Tell me what
shall thy wages be? וַעֲבַדְתַּנִי, a voluntary service. And Jacob
served, etc., וַיַּעֲבֹד, *vayavodh*, xxix. 20. *For the service which
thou shalt serve*, xxix. 27, בָּעֲבֹדָה אֲשֶׁר תַּעֲבֹד.

Next comes the added significance of *subjection*, first, politically, the subjection of tributary communities under one lord,
as in Genesis, xiv. 4: Twelve years they served Chedorlaomer,
עָבְדוּ אֶת כְּדָרְלָעֹמֶר, *avdhu*. So in Deuteronomy, xx. 11: All the
people shall be tributaries unto thee, and *they shall serve thee*,
וַעֲבָדוּךָ, *vaavadhu*. So in Genesis, xxv. 23, of the subjection
of Esau to Jacob: The elder *shall serve* the younger, יַעֲבֹד,
avodh. Also, Genesis, xxvii. 40, in Isaac's prediction: *Thou
shalt serve* thy brother, תַּעֲבֹד, *avodh*. Also in Jeremiah,
xxv. 11: These nations *shall serve* the king of Babylon,
וְעָבְדוּ אֶת־מֶלֶךְ. So Genesis, xxvii. 29: Let people *serve* thee,
וַיַעַבְדוּךָ

Second, both politically and personally. Genesis, xv. 13,
spoken of the bondage in Egypt: *Thy seed shall serve them*,
עֲבָדוּם, *avadhum*. Genesis, xv. 14: That nation *whom they
shall serve*, will I judge, אֶת־הַגּוֹי אֲשֶׁר יַעֲבֹדוּ. Also, Exodus,
i. 13: The Egyptians made the children of Israel *to serve* with
rigor, וַיַּעֲבִדוּ, *avidhu*. Also, Exodus, xiv. 12: Let us alone, *that
we may serve* the Egyptians, וְנַעַבְדָה אֶת־מִצְרָיִם. Also, Jeremiah,
v. 19: *Ye shall serve* strangers in a land not yours, תַּעַבְדוּ

taavdhu. Also, Jeremiah, xvii. 4: I will *cause thee to serve* thine enemies, אֹיְבֶיךָ וְהַעֲבַדְתִּיךָ

Third, spoken of personal servitude. Exodus, xxi. 2, concerning a Hebrew servant: *Six years shall he serve thee,* יַעֲבֹד שֵׁשׁ שָׁנִים, *avodh.* Exodus, xxi. 6: *Shall serve him for ever,* וַעֲבָדוֹ לְעֹלָם, *avadhu.* Leviticus, xxv. 39: *Thou shalt not compel him to serve as a bond-servant,* לֹא־תַעֲבֹד בּוֹ עֲבֹדַת עָבֶד. Leviticus, xxv. 40: *Shall serve thee,* unto the year of jubilee, עַד־שְׁנַת, *yaavodh,* הַיֹּבֵל יַעֲבֹד. The personal servitude embraces the idea of laboring for another, in subjection and inferiority, either on contract for wages, or as an oppression without wages. And thus the meaning and reality of the verb עָבַד passes gradually from voluntary labor for oneself into service performed for another, either for wages, or under oppression.

There are several other modes of usage in which the verb is employed, as, first and most commonly, *of the service of God.* Deuteronomy, vi. 13: Thou shalt fear the Lord thy God, and *serve him,* תַעֲבֹד, *taavodh.* Joshua, xxii. 5: To love the Lord your God, *and to serve him,* וּלְעָבְדוֹ. 1 Samuel, vii. 3: Prepare your hearts unto the Lord, *and serve him* only, וְעִבְדֻהוּ. Also, 1 Samuel, vii. 4: The children of Israel *served the Lord* only, וַיַּעַבְדוּ אֶת־יְהֹוָה. Psalm lxxii. 11: All nations *shall serve him,* יַעַבְדוּהוּ.

Second, of the service of idols. Psalm xcvii. 7: Confounded be all they that *serve graven images,* כָּל־עֹבְדֵי פֶסֶל. Ezekiel, xx. 39: *Serve ye* every one his idols, עֲבֹדוּ, *avodhu.* Deuteronomy, xii. 2: The nations *served their gods,* עָבְדוּ־שָׁם. Deuteronomy, xvii. 3, and Judges, x. 13: *Served other gods,* וַיַּעֲבֹד אֱלֹהִים אֲחֵרִים. 2 Kings, xxi. 3, worshiped all the host of heaven, *and served them,* וַיַּעֲבֹד אֹתָם. Jeremiah, xxii. 9: Worshiped other gods, *and served them,* וַיַּעַבְדוּם, *avdhum.*

Third, it is used once as synonymous with עָשָׂה, to perform, in the sense of presenting sacrifice to God; doing sacrifice, as our translation has it, Isaiah, xix. 21: The Egyptians *shall do sacrifice and oblation,* וְעָבְדוּ זֶבַח וּמִנְחָה.

Fourth, imposing labor on others. Exodus, i. 15: All their service wherein *they made them serve,* כָּל־עֲבֹדָתָם אֲשֶׁר־עָבְדוּ בָהֶם, *service served upon them.* Similar is Leviticus, xxv. 46, rendered unjustly in our translation, *They shall be your bondmen for ever,* בָּהֶם תַּעֲבֹדוּ, *taavodhu, on them ye shall impose service.* So Jeremiah, xxii. 13: With his neighbor's *service* without wages, בְּרֵעֵהוּ יַעֲבֹד חִנָּם, upon his neighbor *imposeth work* for nothing. Jeremiah, xxv. 14: Greek kings shall *serve themselves of them,* עָבְדוּ־בָם, *avdhu.* Jeremiah, xxx. 8: Strangers shall no more *serve themselves of him,* that is, of Israel, עוֹד זָרִים וְלֹא־יַעַבְדוּ־בִי, *yaavdhu;* shall no more *impose servile labor* on him, shall no more play the bond-master with him. This is as far as the verb ever goes toward the signification *to enslave,* an expression for which there is no equivalent in Hebrew, though the verb מָכַר, *to sell,* is used for the transaction, as in the enslaving of Joseph, when his brethren sold him to the Ishmaelites.

Now upon the verbal עֶבֶד, *evedh,* which is the word all but universally employed in Hebrew for servant, it is the secondary meaning, and not the primary, that has descended from the verb עָבַד, *avadh.* The noun עֶבֶד, *evedh,* never means a laborer, a worker, in the generic sense, as Adam and Noah were laborers, but always a worker with reference to the will of another, a worker in subjection, either on contract by hire, or by compulsion. In Ecclesiastes, v. 12, it is said, Sweet is the sleep *of a laboring man;* but there the verb is used, and not the noun; הָעֹבֵד, *haovedh,* him that worketh, or him working, the working man. The noun עֶבֶד means, indeed, a working man, but always under direction of another, or in subjection as a servant, a *serving* man. This is the generic meaning of the noun; not labor, but labor as service.

In Deuteronomy, xxvi. 6, 7, we have examples of several words used for labor in the same connection, that is, the condition of Israel in bondage: The Egyptians laid upon us *hard bondage,* עֲבֹדָה קָשָׁה, hard *labor.* And the Lord looked on *our labor and our oppression,* עֲמָלֵנוּ וְאֶת־לַחֲצֵנוּ. עָמָל is the verb frequently used for *laboring* to weariness, and עָמָל, the verbal from it, for wearisome *toil,* employed frequently in Ecclesiastes, as in Ecclesiastes, ii. 10, 11, 19–22, both the verb and the noun, both concerning labor of the mind and the body. So Psalm cxxvii. 1 : They labor in vain, עָמְלוּ.

In Psalm cxxviii. 2, yet another word for labor, which is frequently used, יְגִיעַ, thou shalt eat *the labor of thy hands,* יְגִיעַ, the verbal, used also in Genesis, xxxi. 42, Haggai, i. 11, Job, x. 3 : *The labor of the hands.* But none of these words besides עֲבֹרָה are used of servile labor exclusively, or with any definition that restricts their meaning, and decides it as applied to service for another, as is the case with עֶבֶד and עֲבֹדָה, for example, in Leviticus, xxv. 39, עֲבֹדַת עָבֶד, rendered in our translation, *the labor of a bond-servant.*

Then, secondarily, עֶבֶד, *evedh,* is applied by persons of noble station and life in speaking of themselves to other noble personages, instead of using the personal pronoun *me.* It is an oriental peculiarity. Genesis, xxxiii. 5, in Jacob's address to his brother Esau : The children which God hath graciously given *thy servant,* עַבְדֶּךָ. So Genesis, xlii. 13 : *Thy servants* are twelve brethren, עֲבָדֶיךָ. In the same manner, speaking of their father Jacob, Genesis, xliv. 27 : *Thy servant* my father said unto us, עַבְדְּךָ. So in Isaiah, xxxvi. 11, the style of Eliakim, Shebna and Joab with Rabshakeh, Speak, I pray thee, unto *thy servants,* עֲבָרֶיךָ.

This is the style of deference, politeness, humility. It may be the formal style of equals toward one another in high life, or the style of the inferior towards the superior. The effect is an elaborate and elegant courtesy toward equals, and a deferential, respectful homage towards superiors. The abruptness of an immediate address is prevented, and the form of language seems to have the effect of employing an ambassador or mediator between potentates. That which, in the courtesy of a formal politeness, is connected by us with the signature at the bottom of letters, as, *your obedient and humble servant*, or, *faithfully and truly your friend and servant*, the men of the East applied in daily conversation. See, for example, David's interview with Saul, 1 Samuel, xvii. 34 : Thy servant kept his father's sheep, etc. Also, David's conversation with Jonathan, 1 Samuel, xx. 7, 8 : Thou shalt deal kindly with thy servant. Also, Abigail's address to David, 1 Samuel, xxv. 24–31 : When the Lord shall have dealt well with my lord, then remember thine handmaid. And likewise David's address to Achish, 1 Samuel, xxviii. 2 : Surely thou shalt know what thy servant can do. See also Daniel, i. 12 : Prove thy servants. Also ii. 7, the address of the Chaldean astrologers to the king: Let the king tell his servants the dream.

Now to trace the delicate distinctions of intercourse in the use or neglect of such a form, and the manner in which the necessity of an independent spirit may compel its abandonment, let the reader mark the fact that Shadrach, Meshach, and Abednego, in their interview with Nebuchadnezzar, when they encountered the rage and authority of the king in full conflict with the authority of God, threw aside utterly the formal and deferential mode of address, and exclaimed, in the first person: "O Nebuchadnezzar, we are not careful to answer thee in this matter. Be it known unto thee, O king, that we will not serve thy gods, nor worship the golden image which thou hast set up." This defiance of the tyrant was far more bold, direct, and energetic, than if they had said : "The king's servants will not worship the image of the king." But their indignation annulled this form of homage, and even the intimation of being the king's servants, so grateful to the sense of power, they rejected from their language, and, rising to the dignity of equals and of freemen, they said: We, O king, will not obey thee, be it known unto thee. We will not serve thy gods. It was much as when, with us, to make defiance stronger, it is added, I tell thee to thy face, I will not heed thee.

But this deferential form is more especially and commonly the usage of the word עֶבֶד, *evedh*, in all addresses to God, and in prayer. Genesis, xviii. 3 : My Lord, if now I have found favor in thy sight, pass not away, I pray thee, from thy servant. And so 1 Kings, viii. 28–32 and 1 Chronicles, xvii. 17–19 : What can David speak more to thee for the honor of thy servant, for thou knowest thy servant ? So Psalm xxvii. 9 : Put not thy servant away in anger. Psalm xxxi. 16 : Make thy face to shine upon thy servant. Daniel, ix. 17 : O our God, hear the prayer of thy servant, אֶל־תְּפִלַּת עַבְדְּךָ.

In the same manner in which the verb עָבַד, *avadh*, is used to signify the *service* of God, the verbal עֶבֶד, *evedh*, is also used to signify the *servant* of God ; whether the application be to men of piety generally, those who trust in God, or to persons called and appointed of God to particular offices and undertakings. Psalm xxxiv. 22 : *The Lord redeemeth the soul of his servants,* פּוֹדֶה יְהוָה נֶפֶשׁ עֲבָדָיו. Nehemiah, i. 10 : Now these are *thy servants,* עֲבָדֶיךָ. Psalm cv. 42 : He remembered Abraham *his servant,* עַבְדּוֹ. Psalm cv. 26 : He sent Moses, *his servant,* עַבְדּוֹ. So likewise the verbal עֲבֹדָה, *avodha,* is used of the service of God, and of his temple, and of the righteous, as in Numbers, iv. 47 and Isaiah, xxxii. 17, the verbal מַעֲשֶׂה, *mauseh,* from עָשָׂה, *to do,* being here also used as synonymous with עֲבֹדַת, *avodhath.* 1 Chronicles, ix. 13 : Able men *for the work of the service* of the house of God, עֲבוֹדַת בֵּית־הָאֱלֹהִים מְלָאכֶת. The expression in Numbers, iv. 47, is illustrative לַעֲבֹד עֲבֹדַת עֲבֹדָה וַעֲבֹדַת מַשָּׂא, to do *the service of the ministry,* and the *service of the burden* in the tabernacle of the congregation.

Now then, we have seen how the meaning of the verb עָבַד, *avadh,* passes from the general idea of *labor,* to that of service for *another,* at first for wages, afterwards in bondage. But the derivative, the verbal עֶבֶד, *evedh,* is never used in any sense corresponding to the first and generic sense of the verb to labor, a laborer. It never means an independent laborer, as when it is said that Cain was a tiller of the ground. The verb, or participle, has to be used with reference to Cain, and not the noun, for as yet, the thing answering to the noun, the *servant*, was not; there is no mention of service at the will or wages of another, no intimation of labor for hire, and no mention of servants.

> "When Adam delved, and Eve span,
> Where was then the serving man?"

Cain was a tiller of the ground, Genesis, iv. 2, הָיָה עֹבֵד אֲדָמָה. He was a man tilling the ground, a man cultivating it, but he was not a servant. There was labor, but as yet no servitude; it is the participle employed, but not the noun. It is somewhat remarkable that the noun is never once employed, nor does the word *servant* come into view in the sacred record, till after the history of the antediluvian posterity of Adam is finished. Doubtless there was the reality of servitude; there must have been oppression in some of its worst forms, for the earth was filled with violence; but there is no intimation of slavery, and the example of some modern nations is sufficient to show that there may be violence, despotism, and oppression of the most terrible nature, even where the system of personal slavery does not exist.*

---

* If there had been slavery before the deluge this would certainly be no argument in its favor, no more than than the mention of bond and free in connection with the Judgment Day. Natural justice and right are as much against slavery as against murder; both crimes are forms of assassination. See the ABBÉ RAYNAL'S energetic and powerful reasoning (Histoire Philosophique des deux Indes, Vol. VI., 90–112), compared with GRANVILLE SHARPE'S Declaration of Natural Right. RAYNAL observes that if Pope Alexander III. had been inspired with the love of justice and humanity, instead of saying merely that Christians ought not to be slaves, he would have declared that MAN was never born for slavery, that none can lawfully hold a human being as a slave, that if the slave can not break his chains by force, he may flee, and his pretended master is an assassin if he punishes with death an action authorized by nature.

CHAPTER XI.

FIRST INSTANCE OF THE WORD FOR SERVANT.—THE CURSE UPON CANAAN NOT SLAV-
ERY, BUT NATIONAL DOMINION. — EGYPT AFTER FIVE HUNDRED YEARS FROM THE
DELUGE.—WORDS USED FOR MAID-SERVANTS.

THE curse pronounced upon Canaan contains the first instance of the use of the word עֶבֶד, *evedh*, Genesis, ix. 25, *a
servant of servants*, עֶבֶד עֲבָדִים. No mention had been made
of servants or slaves in the whole antediluvian history. There
were neither servants nor slaves in the ark. There was no
slave upon the earth when God entered into covenant with
Noah. The whole earth was peopled with freemen, for God
would have the new experiment begin with such, and the
curse of servitude, predicted and denounced *as* a curse, grew
directly out of sin. " Cursed be Canaan; *a servant of servants*
shall he be unto his brethren."

MEANING OF THE CURSE ON CANAAN.

The use of the word עֶבֶד, *evedh*, by Noah, as a word of degradation, a word of inferiority and subjection, the meaning
of which was well understood, shows that the thing indicated
by it was not then a new and strange thing. At the same
time the after history of the word, and its indiscriminate application to servants in general, and service of all kinds, proves
conclusively that it was not a *specific* word for that *kind* of
servitude which we call slavery. But if there had been the
thing there would have been the name, and if Noah had intended *the particular thing*, he would have used *the specific
name*. If slavery had existed among the antediluvians, it can

not be questioned that there would have been a term exclusively denoting it ; and if Noah had designed to threaten *that* curse, or to predict it, concerning a part of his posterity, he would inevitably have used that term, and not a term applied to all kinds of service. There is no word for slavery in the Hebrew language, answering to *our* word slavery, nor to the Greek word δουλεία, although that word is sometimes employed in the Septuagint to translate the Hebrew עֲבֹדָה, *avodha*, as in Exodus, vi. 6, for מֵעֲבֹדָתָם, *from their bondage*, viz., *Egyptian bondage.* It is certainly a fact of no unimportant significance, that there is no word in Hebrew which specifically signifies *slave* or *slavery ;* and there is the best of all reasons for it : the reality did not exist, and from the outset, when the language was formed, the root-word *labor* was of necessity taken for *service,* and from that the various constructions have been formed, and no word for slavery has been created.

In this curse upon Canaan there is, therefore, no proof that what we call slavery was intended ; no proof that the state of slavery was either in the mind of the speaker, Noah, or in the will of God, considered as inspiring the prediction. There is, indeed, no declaration that either the curse or the prediction was God's, no intimation that Noah was inspired of God in uttering it, no more than in planting his vineyard ; and were it not for the gift of the land of Canaan to Abraham, and the subjection of the Canaanites to the Hebrews, there would be no reason for supposing a divine inspiration in the case, since there is no reference anywhere to the prediction as inspired. But whether it were or not, it is not probable that the word *servant,* used by Noah, had the signification sometimes attached to it a thousand years afterwards. They assume too much who suppose that slavery existed among the antediluvians, there being not the least trace of it, and no more proof of it than that the immediate posterity of Adam were idolaters. It is most likely that man-stealing and man-

selling came into practice along with idolatry, fit accompani-
ments or consequences of such wickedness, after the deluge.

The use of the words עֶבֶד, *evedh*, *servant*, and עֶבֶד עֲבָדִים,
evedh avadhim, *servants*, by Noah, can not, therefore, be assumed to mean any thing more than servants and under-
servants, even were the passage applied in a personal sense,
which, however, is not the sense of the prediction.

It is applied, as in many other cases, to the subjection of
nations. The same word precisely is used by Isaac in regard
to the dominion of Jacob over Esau, Jacob's posterity being
the subject of Isaac's prediction as the dominant power.
Genesis, xxvii. 37 : All his brethren have I given to him *for*
servants, לַעֲבָדִים. I have made him (Jacob) *thy lord*, גְּבִיר.
This did not mean that Jacob and his posterity were to be
slaveholders, and Esau and his posterity slaves, but that one
nation should be under the government of the·other. *Let*
people serve thee, יַעַבְדוּךָ עַמִּים, Genesis, xxvii. 29. Just so in
the original prediction, Genesis, xxv. 23 : *The elder shall*
serve the younger, יַעֲבֹד, *yaavodh ; nation in subjection to na-*
tion ; the phrase employed by Gesenius is *populus populo ;*
people shall be tributary to people. The prediction in the
blessing given to Esau, as well as that to Jacob, and the completion of both, leave no doubt as to the meaning of the word,
and the nature of the service designed. See Genesis, xxvii.
40 : *Thou shalt serve thy brother*, אָחִיךָ תַּעֲבֹד, but shalt break
his yoke from off thy neck. So accordingly in 2 Samuel,
viii. 14, the posterity of Esau are recorded as in subjection
to the posterity of Jacob, but not as slaves. David put gar-
risons in Edom, and all they of Edom became David's *serv-*
ants, עֲבָדִים, *avadhim*. But in 2 Kings, viii. 22, it is recorded
that under the reign of Jehoram, 892 B. C., Edom revolted from
under the hand of Judah, and made a king over themselves.
This kind of service and rebellion is recorded in similar language in Genesis, xiv. 4 : Twelve years they *served* Chedorlaomer, עָבְדוּ, *avdhu ;* in the thirteenth, rebelled, מָרָדוּ, *maradhu.*

applied to Hagar, and designating her situation in Abraham's
family. These are the Hebrew words שִׁפְחָה, *shiphhah*, and אָמָה,
amah. Hagar is first introduced to us under the name שִׁפְחה,
shiphhah, Genesis, xvi. 1, 2, 4, 5, 6, 8, and under this name
Sarah gives her to Abraham to be his wife, and by her Ishmael
is born unto him, and the condition of Ishmael has no taint of
bondage from the condition of his mother. The Hebrew patriarchs neither held nor sold their own children for slaves.

Some fifteen years after Hagar's first appearance as a שִׁפְחָה,
shiphhah, Sarah, enraged at the mocking of Hagar's son Ishmael, calls her אָמָה, *amah*, rendered by our translators *a bond-
woman*, and her son the *son of a bondwoman*, Genesis, xxi. 10.
But there is no reason for translating this word *bondwoman*
rather than *servant*. God, speaking to Abraham concerning
the whole transaction, calls her אָמָה, *amah*, most generally
translated *handmaid* or *maid-servant*, and says to Abraham,
" Of the son of the *handmaid*, בֶּן־הָאָמָה, *ben-haamah*, will I
make a nation." Now this same word אָמָה, *amah*, is used in
Psalm cxvi. 16, of the mother of David : I am thy servant, and
the *son of thine handmaid*, בֶּן־אֲמָתֶךָ, *ben-amathekha*. It is
also used by Hannah, 1 Samuel, i. 11, addressing the Lord :
Look on the affliction of *thine handmaid*, אֲמָתֶךָ, *amathekha*,
repeated in the same verse three times. Also, addressing Eli,
1 Samuel, i. 16 : Count not *thine handmaid*, אֲמָתֶךָ. This usage
corresponds with that of the word עֶבֶד, *evedh*, under similar
circumstances. But in the eighteenth verse, also addressing
Eli, she says : Let *thine handmaid*, שִׁפְחָתֶךָ, *shiphhathekha*, find
grace in thy sight. It is obvious, therefore, that the words
אָמָה, *amah*, and שִׁפְחָה, *shiphhah*, are synonymous, one being no
more indicative of a state of bondage than the other. Another instance of the use of both interchangeably is in 1 Samuel, xxv. 41, in Abigail's address to David : Behold, let *thine
handmaid*, אֲמָתֶךָ, *amah*, be *for a servant*, לְשִׁפְחָה, *shiphhah*, to
wash the feet *of the servants*, עַבְדֵי, *avdhei*, of my Lord. Here,
then, are these two words, at periods of nearly a thousand

years' distance, employed in the same manner, applied to the same persons. The impossibility of making a distinction between the two, as to dignity, will be further evident by examining the following passages:

Genesis, xx. 14: And Abimelech took sheep and oxen, and *men-servants and women-servants*, וַעֲבָדִים וּשְׁפָחֹת, *evedh* and *shiphhah*, and gave to Abraham.

Genesis, xx. 17: God healed Abimelech, and *his maid-servants*, וְאַמְהֹתָיו, *amah*.

Genesis, xii. 16: Abram had *men-servants and maid-servants*, שְׁפָחֹת, *shiphhah*.

Genesis, xxi. 10: Cast out *this bondwoman*, הָאָמָה, *amah*.

Genesis, xxx. 43: Jacob had *maid-servants*, שְׁפָחֹות, *shiphhah*.

Genesis, xxxi. 33: Jacob's *maid-servants'* tents, אֲמָהֹת, *amah*.

Exodus, xi. 5: The first-born of the *maid-servant*, הַשִּׁפְחָה, *shiphhah*.

Exodus, xx. 10: Man-servant nor *maid-servant*, אֲמָתֶךָ, *amah*.

Exodus, xxiii. 12: The son of thine *handmaid*, בֶּן־אֲמָתֶךָ, *amah*.

Deuteronomy, v. 14: Man-servant or *maid-servant*, אֲמָתֶךָ, *amah;* also xii. 18; xv. 17; xvi. 11, 14.

Exodus, xxi. 7: If a man sell his daughter to be a *maid-servant*, לְאָמָה, *amah*.

Exodus, xxi. 27, 32: Man-servant or *maid-servant*, אָמָה, *amah*.

Judges, ix. 18; Jotham calls Abimlech the son of his father's *maid-servant*, בֶּן־אֲמָתוֹ, *amah*, who was his father's concubine at Shechem.

Ruth, ii. 13, applied by Ruth to herself and the *handmaidens* of Boaz, שִׁפְחָתֶךָ, *shiphhah*.

Ruth, iii. 9, used by Ruth twice, *thy handmaid*, אֲמָתֶךָ, *amah*.

1 Samuel, xxv. 14: Let *thine handmaid*, אֲמָתֶךָ, *amah*.

1 Samuel, xxv. 25: But I *thine handmaid*, אֲמָתֶךָ, *amah*.

1 Samuel, xxv. 27: *Thine handmaid* hath brought, שִׁפְחָתֶךָ, *shiphhah*.

1 Samuel, xxv. 28: Trespass of *thine handmaid*, אֲמָתֶךָ, *amah*.

1 Samuel, xxv. 31: Remember *thine handmaid*, אֲמָתֶךָ, *amah*.

1 Samuel, xxv. 41: Let *thine handmaid*, אֲמָתֶךָ, *be a servant*, לְשִׁפְחָה, *shiphhah*.

2 Samuel, xiv. 15: Thy *handmaid*, שִׁפְחָתֶךָ, *shiphhah*.

2 Samuel, xiv. 15: The request of *his handmaid*, אֲמָתוֹ, *amah*.

2 Samuel, xiv. 16: To deliver *his handmaid*, אֲמָתוֹ, *amah*.

2 Samuel, xiv. 17: Thine *handmaid* said, שִׁפְחָתֶךָ, *shiphhah*.

2 Samuel, xiv. 19: The mouth of thine *handmaid*, שִׁפְחָתֶךָ, *shiphhah*.

2 Samuel, xiv. 6, 7, 12: Thine *handmaid*, שִׁפְחָתֶךָ, *shiphhah*.

2 Samuel, xvi. 20: *Handmaids*, of his servants, אַמְהוֹת עֲבָדָיו, *amah*.

2 Samuel, vi. 22, David calls the same, *maid-servants*, הָאֲמָהוֹת, *amah*.

Job, xxxi. 13: My *maid-servant*, אֲמָתִי, *amah*.

Jeremiah, xxxiv. 9, 10, 11, 16, the same word is used six times, singular and plural, for *maid-servants* of the Hebrews, coupled with *men-servants*, הַשְּׁפָחוֹת שִׁפְחָתוֹ, *shiphhah*.

These instances determine the usage of the words. They are evidently used for precisely the same relation, being each applied, indifferently, to the maid-servant, whether Hebrew or heathen, just as the word עֶבֶד, *evedh*, is applied to the man-servant. Neither word seems to indicate a higher grade than the other, Job using אָמָה, *amah*, Jeremiah שִׁפְחָה, *shiphhah*, and Moses אָמָה, *amah* and שִׁפְחָה, *shiphhah*, indiscriminately, for persons held as maid-servants, both Hebrew and heathen, and the usage in Samuel putting both words indifferently into the mouths of free women, speaking of themselves.

SEPTUAGINT TRANSLATION BY παιδίσκη.

The Septuagint translation uses the word παιδίσκη for both the Hebrew words, אמה, *amah*, and שפחה, *shiphhah*. The same word is used of Ruth, where the Hebrew is the feminine of נַעַר, *naar*, a young man, הַנַּעֲרָה הַזֹּאת, this young woman. So Ruth is the παιδίσκη as well as Hagar. Also, of all the maidens of Boaz the same word is used, as in Ruth, ii. 22 : His *maidens*, נַעֲרוֹתָיו, his *young women*, and ii. 23 : The *maidens* of Boaz, נַעֲרוֹת בֹּעַז, *the young women*. Boaz himself uses the same word, ii. 8 : My *maidens*, נַעֲרֹתַי, my *young women* or damsels. And in ii. 5, 6, Boaz asks concerning Ruth, whose *damsel* she is ? נַעֲרָה, and the servant answers, the Moabitish *damsel*, נַעֲרָה מוֹאֲבִיָּה, *young woman*.

But in the New Testament, the same word, παιδίσκη, is employed in contrast with the word ἐλευθέρας, with reference to the case of Hagar, Galatians, iv. 22, *the servant* in contrast with the *free woman*, the word servant being translated *bond-woman*, though the same is in other places simply translated servant or damsel or maid, as in Matthew, xvi. 69, Mark, xiv. 66 : One of the maids of the high priest, μία τῶν παιδισκῶν τοῦ ᾿Αρχιερέως. If this had been translated one of the bondwomen of the high priest, it would have been an unjustifiable assumption, if by the term bondwoman were signified slave. The ordinary usage in the New Testament may be learned from Matthew, xxvi. 69; Mark, xiv. 66, 69 ; Luke, xii. 45, xxii. 56; John, xviii. 17; Acts, xii. 13, xvi. 16. Only in one of these cases is it clear that the word probably signifies a slave, and that is the case in Acts, xvi. 16, of the damsel possessed of the spirit of divination, who brought much gain to her masters, who were pagans, idolaters. On the other hand, the word δούλη is used only three times, Luke, i. 38, 48, and Acts, ii. 18, in all three, spoken of servants and handmaidens of the Lord.

It is, therefore, impossible to determine, merely from the word παιδίσκη, the exact condition signified : for the term in the New Testament, though it implies service, in a state of servitude, does not imply necessarily bond-service or slavery, but may be used also of a free person hired, a hired servant, as the שָׂכִיר, *sakir*, of the Hebrews, or also a free maiden, in no respect under servitude. As applied to Hagar, the term used by Sarah in the Old Testament, and by Paul in the New, would seem to apply more directly and specifically to her original condition among the Egyptians, and not to her state in the family of Abraham. In Abraham's family, and as his wife, she certainly was not his bond-servant or slave; and the sarcasm of Sarah is directed to her former state, out of which she had been raised, and especially when presented by Sarah to Abraham to be his wife.[*]

---

[*] Two points are to be specially regarded in considering Hagar's condition. 1. The name given to her bears no indication of slavery. Some have derived it from the Hebrew for *stranger*, so that Hagar's name would mean *this stranger*. But Gesenius gives as its definition the word *flight*, from an unused root signifying to flee. Hence, also, the *Hegira*, for the flight of Mahomet. But as Hagar bore this name before her flight from Sarah, it is more likely to have been the name of a *stranger*.

2. Her condition as a servant, whatever it might have been, conveys no taint of servitude or subjection to her offspring. If, therefore, it could be imagined that modern slaveholders are justified in holding slaves, because Abraham held Hagar, they are also bound by the same example to give freedom to the children of their slaves. If they claim a divine permission they must take the whole rule or none. They must strike out from their code the infamous principle, introduced from Pagan slavery, but baptized by Christians (so called) as a rule of justice, piety and divine theology, that *partus sequitur ventrem*. In fine, if Abraham's example with Hagar were followed, the whole system of slavery would come to an end in a moment. It is nothing but the savage brand of Paganism, conveying the act and quality of man-stealing, as a legal right upon the posterity of the stolen parents, and adopted by Christianity (so called) as a right and a missionary virtue, that sustains the system.

CHAPTER XII.

WORD-ANALYSIS THROUGH THE LIFE OF ABRAHAM.—MEANING OF SOULS GOTTEN IN HARAN.—USAGE OF PHRASES FOR DOMESTIC SERVICE.—NO INTIMATIONS OF SLAVERY IN DOMESTIC LIFE.—PRINCIPLES OF JUSTICE AND EQUITY.—ABRAHAM'S SERVANTS NOT BOUND BY COMPULSION.

WE continue now our investigation by tracing the words of service in their usage, renewing thus our analysis of the household of Abraham in a somewhat varied light. The repetition of references, which becomes necessary, may be endured, in consideration of the necessity of confirming every part of our argument, leaving no position at hazard, no citadel unoccupied, or in the hands of the enemy. Following the word-analysis through the life of Abraham, Isaac, and Jacob, the next step is found in Genesis, xiv. 14, 15: Abram armed his *trained ones*, as our translation has it, *born in his own house*, חֲנִיכָיו יְלִידֵי בֵיתוֹ. There were in number three hundred and eighteen; and he divided himself against the enemy, he and *his servants*, עֲבָדָיו.

In this passage, the word חָנִיךְ, *hanikh*, the verbal from חָנַךְ, *instructed ones, experienced, proved*, seems to be used as synonymous with עֶבֶד, *evedh*, servant, and both words are equivalent with יְלִידֵי בֵיתוֹ, *yelidhe betho, the born in his own house, the sons of his house*. In the twenty-fourth verse the same are called young men, הַנְּעָרִים, that which the *young men* have eaten. These young men, though born in Abraham's house, were not slaves, and an examination of the circumstances of the case, and of the phrases יְלִיד בֵית, *yelidh beth*, the born of the house, and בֶּן־בֵּית, *ben-beth*, the son of the house, will show the extreme mistake of defining either of these expressions as signifying necessarily a slave; for Hebrew servants might be *the born of the house*, but could not under any circumstances be *slaves*.

In Genesis, xv. 3, the phrase used is בֶּן־בֵּיתִי, *ben-bethi, the son of my house*, one *born in my house* is mine heir.

But it is clear that at this time Abraham had other servants besides those born in his house; at a previous period he had received such in Egypt, where, as a consequence of Pharaoh's favor, he had *men-servants* and *maid-servants*, or an increasing number of them.

In Genesis, xii. 5, there is mention of the souls that Abram aud Lot had gotten in Haran. Not unfrequently the monstrous assumption has been taken, without one particle of evidence, without even an intimation looking that way, that these *souls* meant *slaves*, that they were such. With just as much authority we might presume and assert that the *cattle* spoken of as Abraham's and Lot's property, meant *souls*, and that when it is affirmed that they increased their *substance*, the word substance means souls. The Chaldee paraphrasts maintain a much more likely assumption, when they insist that the *souls gotten* were proselytes gained by Abraham to the true faith. We might with superior propriety assume that the phrase means persons whom Abraham was able to persuade to go forth with him from his own country to the promised land.* At Bethel they were so rich in cattle and silver and gold, in flocks and herds and tents, that the land was not able to bear them together, and the quarrels among their herdmen led to their separation. At this period they

* Smith's Sacred Annals, Patriarchal Age, page 448: "Many commentators believed that Abram not only worshiped God in his family, but diligently taught his name and his law to those with whom he came in contact. Hence the Chaldee paraphrasts, when rendering the clause as given by Moses, 'the souls that they had gotten in Haran' (verse 5), use these words, 'the souls of those whom they proselyted in Haran.' Abraham was certainly called away from all idolatrous influence, that he might be a witness for the truth to all the nations with which he came in contact." Page 439.

were nomadic chiefs, and those that were born in their tents belonged to their households, and were dependent upon them under the guardianship and care of the patriarchal authority. A patriarchal community that could muster three hundred and eighteen young men to bear arms, born under Abraham's government, and under allegiance of service to him, must have been numerous; and, besides these dependents, he had other servants obtained with money of the stranger; among these his herdmen may have been comprised, for the phrase *bought with money* was applied, as we have seen, to such a purchase or contract as secured the right to their time and labor for a limited period. In regard to the Hebrews, this is clearly demonstrated from the very first law on record in this matter, Exodus, xxi. 2: If *thou buy* a Hebrew *servant*, six years he shall serve, כִּי תִקְנֶה, *if thou buy*, the same word being used as in the description of the portion of Abraham's household designated as *bought with money*. Parents were accustomed sometimes thus to sell the services of their children. It was something like the purchase of apprentices, or the contract of an apprenticeship for a number of years. Hosea bought his wife, Hosea, iii. 2. The term מִקְנַת־כֶּסֶף, *miknath keseph*, *bought with money*, or the *purchase of money*, does not, therefore, necessarily imply an unlimited servile sale; and, as we shall see, a restriction was finally imposed on all such transactions by the laws of jubilee, rendering the system of what we call slavery impossible.

Here, then, are three phrases demanding careful consideration: יְלִיד בֵּית, *yelidh beth*, בֶּן־בֵּית, *ben-beth*, and מִקְנַת־כֶּסֶף, and *miknath-keseph*. In Ecclesiastes, ii. 7, we have the בֶּן־בֵּית, *ben-beth*, thus: I acquired *servants and maidens*, עֲבָדִים וּשְׁפָחוֹת, and *sons of my house* were mine, וּבְנֵי־בַיִת הָיָה לִי. In Genesis, xv. 3, a *son of my house* is mine heir, בֶּן־בֵּיתִי. These two phrases, יְלִיד בֵּית, *yelidh beth*, and בֶּן־בֵּית, *ben-beth*, seem to be nearly synonymous, but the בֶּן־בֵּית, *ben-beth*, *the son of the house*, is descriptive of a class of servants more affectionately attached, and enjoying greater privileges, with greater confidence reposed in them. The whole three hundred and eighteen of Abraham's young men are called יְלִיד בֵּית, *yelidh beth*, born of the house, that is, of the families under his authority and patriarchal government and care; but the בֶּן־בָּיִת, *ben-beth*, the son of his house, who might be his heir, may have been of his own immediate household. In Genesis, xvii. 12, 13, 23, 27, in the detail of the covenant of circumcision, and the execution of that rite on all born in Abraham's house, the phrase used is יְלִיד בֵּית, *yelidh beth*. Elsewhere it is very seldom found, once in Leviticus, xxii. 11, concerning the priest's family, and who in it may, and who may not, eat of the holy things; no stranger, nor any sojourner, nor any mere hired servant of the priest shall eat thereof; but the servant bought with his money, and he that is *born in his house*, וִילִיד בֵּיתוֹ, *yelidh betho*, may eat of it. The hired servant was not regarded as an inseparable part and fixture of the priest's family, in the same manner as the servant born in his house was, and had not the same privileges. A hired servant might be a foreigner, but a servant born in the house was a native of the land, and might be also a native Hebrew.

Neither can this phrase, *born of the house*, with safety or correctness be assumed as always specifically implying servitude of any kind, or a servile state; for it might be right the opposite. It might be used of freemen as well as servants, and of the children of the master and mistress of the house. In Leviticus, xviii. 9, a similar phrase is employed of the daughter of the family, *daughter of thy mother, born of thy house*, בַּת־אִמְּךָ מוֹלֶדֶת בֵּית. In Jeremiah, ii. 14, it has been supposed to be used as synonymous, or nearly so, with עֶבֶד, *evedh*. *Is Israel a servant*, עֶבֶד? *evedh*. *Is he a home-born*, בֵּית אִם־יְלִיד? *yelidh beth*. But these words are not synonymes, and a very different translation of this verse is possible, as may be seen in the note of Blayney, in his translation and commentary on this prophet, a passage which is worthy of consideration. He translates Jeremiah, ii. 14, thus: *Is Israel a slave? Or if a child of the household, wherefore is he exposed to spoil?* And he remarks " that יְלִיד בַּיִת, *yelidh beth*, answers to the Latin word *filius familias*, and stands opposed to a slave. The same distinction is made Galatians, iv. 7, and an inference drawn from it in a similar manner : ' Wherefore thou art no more a servant (a slave), but a son; and if a son, then an heir of God through Christ.' As Christians now, so the Israelites heretofore, were the children of God's household ; and if so, they seemed entitled to his peculiar care and protection."

The passage is susceptible of this rendering. *Is Israel a servant,* עֶבֶד? *evedh ; but if a home-born,* אִם־יְלִיד בַּיִת, *yelidh beth,* why is he yet spoiled? If he were an עֶבֶד, *evedh,* merely, he might be expected to be rigorously treated, to be carried into captivity, and "sold with the selling of a bondman." But if a home-born, then under a care and privilege, which would preserve him from such treatment. The ordinary interpretation is different, grounded on the idea that the question is equivalent to a negation. Israel is *not* a servant, neither עֶבֶד, *evedh,* nor יְלִיד בַּיִת *yelidh beth,* but is God's own son, and free born. Why then is he become a prey ? Because of his own wickedness.

That the phrase יְלִיד בַּיִת, *yelidh beth,* does not necessarily mean a servant, or a bondman in contradistinction from a freeman, appears from Genesis, xvii. 27. After relating the circumcision of Abraham, and Ishmael his son, it is added that *all the men of his house, born in his house, and bought with money of the stranger, were circumcised with him.* It is absurd to suppose that of all Abraham's dependent community or tribe, for such are the households here designated, not one male was accounted a freeman. Every male among the men of Abraham's house was circumcised, and all the men of Abraham's house are divided into these two classes only, *born* *in the house, or bought with money of the stranger.* In the next chapter, xviii. 7, Abraham is described as fetching a calf from the herd, and giving it to a *young man*, הַנַּעַר, to dress it. This young man was in Abraham's service, of Abraham's household, but there is no intimation whatever of his being in the condition of a slave. In fine, we might as well assert that our domestic household animal, the *cat*, was precisely the same animal with the South American *jaguar* or the Bengal *tiger*, as assume that the servants of Abraham's household were what we call slaves. There might be families beneath his patriarchal authority, neither the head nor the children of which, though born in his house, dependent on him, as the יְלִיד בֵּית, *yelidh beth*, were in any condition approximating to that of slaves.*

---

* The history of the word SLAVE is instructive. Gibbon, in his 55th chapter, traces it to the captivity of "the Sclavonian, or more properly Slavonian, race." "From the Euxine to the Adriatic, in the state of captives, or subjects, or allies, or enemies of the Greek empire, they overspread the land; and the national appellation of THE SLAVES has been degraded by chance or malice from the signification of glory to that of servitude."

"This conversion of a national into an appellative name appears to have arisen in the eighth century in the oriental France, where the princes and bishops were rich in Sclavonian captives. From thence the word was extended to general use, to the modern languages, and even to the style of the last Byzantines (see the Greek and Latin glossaries of Ducange.) The confusion of the Σέρβλοι, or SERVIANS, with the Latin *Servi*, was still more fortunate and familiar."—GIBBON'S DECLINE AND FALL, chap. 55.

The only instance in which the word slave has been intruded in our English translation of the Hebrew Scriptures is that of Jeremiah, ii. 14, where the confession that there is no such word in the original was made by the translators themselves, in putting the word *slave* in italics. The original reads, "Is he a *home born?*" The translators added, "Is he a home-born *slave?*" This was a most singularly unauthorized and contradictory assertion. It amounted to an interpolation in the translation, and by means of it, of the falsehood that there was, or might be, under the Hebrew constitution, such a thing as a slave and such a domestic iniquity as that of slavery.

The origin of the word SERVUS is better known, from the custom of preserving for sale the captives taken in war, who were, therefore, from the verb *servare, to preserve,* denominated *servi, the preserved.* "The words *servus* and *mancipium* designated slaves so made; *servus*, as having been preserved by the victor, *à victore servatus,*

From the building of Babel to the time of Terah, Abraham's father, it was but two hundred years, and during this period there is not the slightest intimation of any such vast social inequality in the community as that of slavery on the one hand and freedom on the other; nor is there time and scope, nor are there causes sufficient, in the generations of Shem, to produce such a condition, where the population was sparse, and the whole race, within little more than three generations, on a perfect equality. It is easy to conceive how the habits of patriarchal government and life could arise and be established, but that a state of slavery should become the social state, while Noah and his family were still living, is in-

---

or, according to some etymologists, from the Greek root, ἔρω, or ἐρύω, to drag, to rescue from death; *mancipium*, from *à manu capere*, to take captive with the hand."—FUSS. ROMAN ANTIQ., chap. i., sec. liii.

See, also, EDWARDS' ROMAN SLAVERY, in the sixth volume of the Biblical Repository, 411: "The origin of the word *servus*," says Augustine, de Civit., lib. xix., chap. xv., "is understood to be derived from the fact that prisoners, who, by the laws of war, might have been put to death, were preserved by the victors, and made slaves."

Now, our modern kidnappers and slaveholders, with the new and gracious theory of being the honored instruments of God's missionary providence of salvation to the Africans by means of the merciful reduction of them to slavery, and consequent introduction to Christianity, might take a hint from these etymologies, and establish for themselves and their victims a new nomenclature, commemorative of piety and love. Instead of being named *pirates*, the kidnappers should be called *mission-*

ary pioneers, and their victims, instead of being called *slaves*, should be called *translated ones*, not *servi*, but *salvati*, and the slaveholders should be called *salvatores, saviours*. To designate the subjects of such providential missionary grace, the old word *salvages* might be re-adopted in our language, to signify persons transported from the condition of *savages* to the state of salvation. Or, the kidnappers might be designated as Redemptionists, and the slaveholders as Ministrants and Guardians for them who are the heirs of such a salvation. And inasmuch as the children of those thus providentially redeemed from savage freedom in Africa are appointed for ever to the salvation of slavery in America, from which state of salvation they never can be plucked away, the heirs of this salvation might be named *consecrated ones*, or, better still, *conserved*, and the owners of the conserved race might appropriate to themselves the much-abused term *Conservatives*. Are they not all ministering spirits, sent forth to minister unto them who shall be heirs of such salvation?

credible. There are no intimations of slavery in Bethuel's family, nor in Laban's after him, in Mesopotamia. We find Rachel feeding her father's sheep, and performing servile labor, and all the indications are of a simple social life, in which slavery was unknown. Up to the time of his sojourn in Canaan, Abraham had been engaged in no wars or predatory excursions, so that that which was afterwards so pregnant a source of captivity and slavery, did not in his family exist, and indeed the very first war in which we find him a conqueror, we find him also refusing to hold any of the conquered as his captives. There was no black color as yet to stigmatize a servile race as the legitimate property of the white races. There were no laws by which free persons might be seized and sold for their jail-fees, not being able to prove their freedom. In short, a more gross and gratuitous assumption can hardly be imagined than that the three hundred and eighteen young men born and trained under Abraham's jurisdiction, of his household, were slaves! The tie between him and them was assuredly not of compulsion, or oppression, or legal chattelism, but of service and obedience, at least as justly required, and freely yielded, as that of hereditary clans in Scotland, or tribes and families in Arabia.

The other phrase, מִקְנַת־כֶּסֶף, *miknath keseph*, Genesis, xvii. 12, the *possession of money, the thing bought with money*, is applied to any acquisition gained by purchase, and also to the price paid. In Genesis, xxiii. 9, 18, 20, it is used as synonymous with אֲחֻזָּה, the *possession* of his burying-place. According to the use of the verb קָנָה, *kanah, to buy*, from which it is derived, it would be suitably applied to acquisitions transitory as well as permanent, and to attainments of the mind as well as earthly riches. The same verb קָנָה, *kanah, to buy*, as we have before noted, is applied by Boaz to his purchase of the field that was Elimelech's, and also to his purchase of Ruth herself to be his wife. *I have bought*, קָנִיתִי, *all that was Elimelech's*, moreover, *Ruth have I purchased*, קָנִיתִי, *to be my wife.* It is also applied, Proverbs, iv. 7, to the acquisition of wisdom. Proverbs, xv. 32, to the getting of understanding. So also xvi. 16, and xix. 8. It is applied in Isaiah, xi. 11, to the Lord's *recovering* of people. Cain's name, קַיִן, that is, *gotten* from the Lord, was given because Eve said, Genesis, iv. 1, קָנִיתִי, *I have gotten* a man from the Lord. In Psalm lxxviii. 54, God is said to have *purchased*, קָנְתָה, this mountain with his right hand. And in Proverbs, viii. 22: God is said to have *possessed* wisdom in the beginning, קָנָנִי, *kanani.**

* BARNES' INQUIRY INTO THE SCRIPTURAL VIEWS OF SLAVERY, chap. iii., p. 75. "The word *bought* occurs in a transaction between Joseph and the people of Egypt, in such a way as further to explain its meaning. When, during the famine, the money of the Egyptians had failed, and Joseph had purchased all the land, the people proposed to become his servants. When the contract was closed, Joseph said to them, 'Behold, I have *bought* you— קָנִיתִי, *kanithi*—this day, and your land, for Pharaoh.' Genesis, xlvii. 23. The nature of this contract is immediately specified. They were to be regarded as laboring for Pharaoh. The land belonged to him, and Joseph furnished the people with seed, or stocked the land, and they were to cultivate it on shares for Pharaoh. The fifth part was to be his, and the other four parts were to be theirs. There was a claim on them for labor, but it does not appear that the claim extended further. No farmers, now, who work land on shares, would be willing to have their condition described as one of slavery."

CHAPTER XIII.

It is clear, then, that the circumstance of the servile relation being acquired by money, and called the purchase or possession of money, did not necessarily constitute it slavery, any more than the purchase of a wife constituted her a slave, or the purchase of wisdom constituted *that* a slave. Abraham could acquire a claim upon the service of a man during his life by purchase from himself; he could acquire the allegiance of a man and his family, and of all that should be born in the family, by similar contract, not to be broken but by mutual agreement; and, in this way, in the course of years he might have a vast household under his authority, born in his house and purchased with his money, but not one of them a slave. He might in the same way purchase of the stranger whatever claim the stranger possessed to the service of the person thus sold, and yet the person thus transferred to Abraham's household might be a voluntary party in the transaction, and in no sense a slave. It is not possible to suppose that, if a servant were offered to Abraham for his purchase, who could say, *I was stolen* by my master, as Joseph could say, it is not possible to suppose that Abraham would consider such a purchase as just, or that he could rightfully make such a person his servant, without his own consent. There is no intimation whatever of any such unrighteous or compulsory service in Abraham's household; there is no ground for the supposition that he either bought slaves, or traded in slaves, or held slaves in any way.*

HEBREWS SELLING THEMSELVES.

In Leviticus, xxv. 47, there is mention of two modes in which a poor man might sell himself for a servant, namely, being a Hebrew, he might sell himself to a stranger or sojourner, or, *to the stock of a stranger's family*. Here we have great light cast on these transactions. The poor man sells himself on account of his poverty, but not as a slave. He may sell himself not merely to one master, during that master's life, but to the *stock of the family*, לְעֵקֶר מִשְׁפַּחַת, as a fixture of the household. It is supposable that he might thus sell himself with his children, or make a contract for the service of his children that might be born to him during the time of this stipulation; and the children so born would be the בֵּית יְלִיד, the born of the house of his master, or בְּנֵי בֵית, the sons of the house. But from this contract he might be redeemed by any one of his kin, or he might redeem himself, if he were able, by returning a just proportion of the price of his sale, the price of his services; and whether redeemed or not, the

---

* Kitto's Cyclopædia, p. 774, Servants of Abraham: "In no single instance do we find that the patriarchs either gave away or sold their servants, or purchased them of *third* persons. Abraham had servants bought with money. It has been *assumed* that they were bought of third parties, whereas, there is no proof that this was the case. The probability is that they sold themselves to the patriarch for an equivalent; that is to say, they entered into voluntary engagements to serve him for a longer or shorter period of time, in return for the money advanced them."

The admirable article from which the above paragraph is extracted, stands in marked contrast with the mass of commentators and lexicographers on this subject, by the accuracy with which it marks distinctions, and resists the falsehood of mere assumptions in the place of facts, and the despotism of precedents in the place of principle and just law. It was contributed to the work by Rev. William Wright, M. A. and LL.D., of Trinity College, Dublin, the translator of Seiler's Biblical Hermeneutics.

contract should be binding no longer than up to the period of the jubilee.

In the case of the household of Abraham, the phrase in Genesis, xvii. 12, מִקְנַת כֶּסֶף, *the possession or purchase of money*, is qualified with reference to *a stranger only, which is not of thy seed*.   In the twenty-seventh verse, all the men of Abraham's house are designated as either born in the house or bought with money of the stranger.   They were all circumcised, at the commandment of God.

But Hebrew servants might also be bought with money, as in Exodus, xxi. 2 ; Leviticus, xxv. 47 ; Deuteronomy, xv. 12 ; Jeremiah, xxxiv. 14.

But only for six years ordinarily could such a purchase bind the person bought; the seventh year he was free. Deuteronomy, xv. 12 ; Exodus, xxi. 2.

He might sell himself, that is, sell his own time and labor, for six years.   In such a case, as when a master sold him, he was a servant bought for money, and distinct from the servant born in the house.   The rule was the same for men-servants and maid-servants.

Supposing him to have been a married man, and himself and his wife sold, and that during their six years of servitude they had children born to them, then, in the seventh year, all would go free.   Supposing his master to have given him a wife, if a Hebrew, then his wife could not be retained beyond the period of *her* six years of servitude by law, neither her sons nor daughters.   But yet, on comparison of Exodus, xxi. 2–6, with Leviticus, xxv. 39–41 and 47–54, and Deuteronomy, xv. 12–18, and Jeremiah, xxxiv. 14, it is manifest that Hebrew servants, husbands, wives, and children, might be retained under certain conditions, until the year of jubilee, in servitude. Many of them, in such cases, would be servants born in the house, *sons of the house;* yet, even then and thus, no master could compel them to serve as bond-servants, but they were to be treated as hired servants and sojourners.   If a man with a household already thus composed, should buy a Hebrew servant, and give him a wife from among the number of maidservants that were already, by rightful contract, the fixtures of his family until the jubilee, then he would have no right, if he chose to go out free at the end of his six years, to take away his wife and the children she might have borne him; but they were to remain until the jubilee; and, if he chose not to avail himself of this legal privilege of quitting his master's residence and service, but preferred to remain with his wife and children, the sons of the house, then he, too, must remain till the jubilee. He could not quit, after making this choice, at the expiration of another seven years. But all were free in the year of jubilee, men, women, and children.

It is clear, then, that, while the servants born in the house might, under certain conditions, be born under a claim of continued service till the jubilee, those bought with money could be bound only for a period of six years. On the other hand, the master was obliged by law to treat those who were under servitude until the jubilee as hired servants, giving them their stated and covenanted wages. The question then comes up as to the specific difference between bond, or rather apprenticed, servants and hired servants, and the nature of their respective treatment. This we shall have occasion to examine historically, in considering the successive developments of the law; but much light may be gained from the examination of the words.

ARGUMENT FROM MOSES TO ABRAHAM.

But, before considering this, we have to ask how far it is safe to draw conclusions as to Abraham's household, from the laws made for his posterity more than four hundred years after his age. The gross perversions and mistakes made by commentators taking the state of things in modern Egypt and in pagan Rome, in the horrid prevalence of the lowest and most universal slave-life and manners, and carrying that picture and those ideas back as supposed originals and illustrations of the servitude in the time and even the household of Abraham, may teach us the necessity of caution. Even the words coined out of Roman despotism and slave-customs have been taken by lexicographers to interpret Hebrew words that had no such meaning; and hence the assumption with which עֶבֶד, *evedh*, and אָמָה *amah*, and בְּר־אָמָה *ben-amah*, are sometimes rendered by *mancipium*, *verna*, and *slave*, when there was neither Hebrew word, nor personal chattel answering to any such appellative.

But conclusions and illustrations from the completed theocracy and system of Hebrew law and life, back to Abraham, as chosen and instructed for its beginning, can not be very erroneous. The general principles upon which God would govern and train the Hebrew nation were certainly revealed to Abraham, along with the great covenant that separated them from the heathen world as a peculiar people, and the appointed seal of that covenant, in the rite of circumcision. The application of that rite to servants as well as masters, and to those purchased from the stranger as well as those born in the house, and the admission of all to the privileges of the same national covenant, was a remarkable equalizing interposition, doing away, by itself alone, most of the injustice and evil of the system of slavery as it came to exist in the heathen world. All were to be instructed in religion, and treated with kindness. According to the nature of the Divine law as revealed to Abraham, Abraham could not, if obedient to God, treat his servants, that were hired of the stranger, with his money, or those born in his house, whether obtained in Egypt or elsewhere, according to the principles of idolatry and servitude prevalent in the countries where he traveled and dwelt. When they came into his household, they came on very different principles, and under very different regulations, from those of the system of an irresponsible despotism, or of what we call slavery.

There is really no such thing as slavery discoverable in

Abraham's household, though there were servants that had been given to him by the most despotic slaveholders then in the world, and others whose services were obtained with money, of races of strangers, and others, doubtless, who were in his family as servants for a stipulated time. But, concerning his administration of the whole, God declares, "I know him, that he will command his children and his household after him; and they shall keep the way of the Lord, to do justice and judgment," Genesis, xviii. 19. This is sufficient proof that there never was, in Abraham's household, that thing which the Romans called *mancipium*, nor that iniquitous system which in modern times we call *slavery*. His was a system of paternal and patriarchal kindness, instruction, and well-regulated service, but not of enforced and unpaid servitude. It was a system of generosity and confidence on one side, and of free and affectionate obedience on the other. It was neither power without right, nor submission without willingness. There were no fugitive slave laws, nor any need of them, nor do we find traces of any such custom as that of training hounds to hunt runaways. It is manifest that a confidence almost unlimited was reposed by Abraham in the faithfulness and contentment of those under his authority. The oldest servant of Abraham's house, who ruled over all that he had, and had been trained himself under the influence of the laws and manners of his household, bears witness, by his own character, to the nature of the whole system.

This man was called, Genesis, xxiv. 2, עַבְדּוֹ זְקַן בֵּיתוֹ, *his eldest servant of his house*, or, his servant, the elder of his house, the *major-domo*, the word used being the same employed to designate *the elders of Israel*. In the history of Jacob's burial (Genesis, l. 7), we have the same word applied to the elders of Pharaoh's house, and all the elders of the land of Egypt. "And Joseph went up to bury his father; and with him went up all the servants of Pharaoh, the *elders of his house*, and all the *elders of the land* of Egypt"—

זִקְנֵי בֵיתוֹ, *zikney betho*, and זִקְנֵי אֶרֶץ, *zikney arets*. If the elder of Abraham's household could be assumed to have been a slave, because he is designated as a servant, then were also the elders of Pharaoh's house, and all the elders of Egypt, all the men in authority, the aristocracy and the princes, by the same assumption, slaves, for they are all designated as Pharaoh's servants. In Genesis, xv. 2, this eldest servant of Abraham is called also the steward of his house, בֶּן־מֶשֶׁק בֵּיתִי, *ben-meshek bethi*, the *son of possession of my house*, for so Gesenius renders it, *filius possessionis, possessor of my house*. This steward of Abraham's house was to be his heir. The Septuagint renders it the son of Mesek, υἱος Μέσεκ, as being the name of a tribe or district in Syria, whence Dammesék, or Damascus, *the steward of my house is this Eliezer of Damascus*.

Others again derive the word from a root signifying to wander about, to make excursions in search of something, and so translate it the *son of discursion*, that is, the overseer, or procurator of the house. But any interpretation is less forced and far-fetched than that which assumes this steward and heir of Abraham's house to have been a slave, without a solitary intimation in the text or context on which such a supposition can be built. This elder servant of his house is said to have *ruled over all that he had*, a phrase which answers very well to that of the *son of possession ;* and before a son was born to Abraham, this eldest servant was to have been his heir. In like manner, we find, in Ezekiel, xlvi. 17, an intimation of a prince giving a gift of his inheritance to one of his servants, to be his to the year of jubilee; and it would be a monstrous conclusion to assume from this that this servant was a slave, and that it was the custom for householders in Judea to bestow their inheritance upon their favorite slaves! But what will not prejudice accomplish? Not only has it been assumed, from this one place in the historic record in Genesis, that this servant of Abraham was a slave, but, also, that assumption being settled, another has been drawn from that, namely, that we may gather from this, that in those days it was the custom, if any man died without heirs, his estate descended to the oldest or superior slave of the family! No other proof of any such supposed custom is adverted to; none can be found; there is no ground for any such imagination; the whole is a mere pile of conjecture, built upon an assumption, itself entirely destitute of foundation, entirely false. It, therefore, serves as a remarkable example of the manner in which the idea of slavery and slaves among the Hebrews, and especially in the households of the patriarchs, has got possession of men's minds, has been admitted into books of lexicography and commentary, and passed unquestioned for indisputable fact from generation to generation.*

The arming of the whole multitude of Abraham's servants, and committing to their steadiness and bravery the conduct of a war, argues for them all a participation in the same char-

---

* Havernick's Introduction to the Pentateuch, page 152. And Rosenmueller, in the note. Havernick, following Rosenmueller, observes that the verse describing Abraham's steward " discloses a very ancient custom, that afterwards had nothing corresponding to it. According to that, in case of childlessness, a slave was heir; but the slave here appears under the very peculiar appellation of the son of possession of the house, referring to special nomadic relations." This very ancient custom is inferred by Rosenmueller from the case of the steward; and then from that inference is drawn the conclusion that the steward was a slave, according to the very ancient custom disclosed by his being the heir! What the special nomadic relations are, the learned writer does not state, nor is there any disclosure of them; but the fact of Abraham's steward being his intended heir is said to disclose a very ancient custom, of which there had been no previous trace, nor afterwards any thing corresponding to it, the custom being that of making one's slave his heir!

Even this learned and admirable writer takes it for granted that the eldest servant of Abraham's house could be nothing but a slave, and speaks of him as such: "Rebekah immediately resolved to go with the slave;" "the religious language of the slave;" quite regardless as to any question of morality, indeed, seemingly unconscious of there being any such question in regard to the right or the sinfulness of holding slaves. A great number of just such instances of careless and groundless assumptions might be presented.

acter, and the enjoyment of a freedom among them, and of privileges and blessings so great and valuable under their allegiance to Abraham, that he could repose the utmost confidence in that allegiance, and in their contentment under his authority and service. The only case in which there is any intimation of oppression or severity in the household, is on the part of Sarah, and the subject of it takes an immediate opportunity to flee from such oppression. And such opportunity, in that state of society, was open to all, nor were there, in the sojournings and life of the patriarchs, any of those safeguards of law and State power, to keep down the oppressed, without which a system such as that of Roman or of modern slavery could not be maintained for a single generation.

It is scarcely to be doubted that slavery grew out of idolatry, and in its perfection was one of the last and most perfect fruits of the execrable system of Egyptian and of Roman paganism. The exalting of men of gigantic vice and ability into gods, and the consequent consecration of tyrannic power as a celestial attribute, and the obedience of its instruments to its despotism, the superstitious debasement of the soul before it, and the necessity of slaves as the victims and tools of its ambition and success, very naturally suggest and account for the progress and fixture of slavery in the old heathen social life. Every thing evil and abominable grew, in such society, out of the bestial and oppressive idolatrous systems into which men fell. There were near five hundred years from Abraham to Moses, during which the idolatry of the Egyptians and the Canaanites, and every depraved habit along with it, grew more dreadful and inveterate. It was a prominent article of the divine law: "When the Lord thy God shall cast out the nations from before thee, take heed to thyself that thou inquire not after their gods, saying, How did these nations serve their gods? even so will I do likewise. Thou shalt not do so unto the Lord thy God: for every abomination which he hateth have they done unto their gods: for even their sons and their daughters have they burnt in the fire to their gods."

The consecration of a race to slavery, the adoption of such inhumanity and injustice to be perpetrated from generation to generation, would be worse cruelty by far than the passing of a selected number of children, at stated times, and in idolatrous festivals, through the fire to Moloch. No one of the kingdoms of Satan in our world ever began with the atrocity of slavery as a fundamental law. If this sin and source of misery, this security for the violation of every precept in the decalogue and every principle of righteousness, had been enshrined in the domestic constitution established by Abraham, the scheme would have outdone, in diabolic malignity and ingenuity, any form of evil ever contrived by the father of lies and fastened on posterity. If the problem had been to lay the foundations and provide for the completion of the most depraved possible society on earth, instead of building up a social kingdom through which all the families of mankind might be blessed, this far-reaching, infernal purpose could not have been more certainly accomplished than by the introduction of human slavery, with its atrocious code of law and custom, as the most perfect system of the social state.[*]

---

[*] WARBURTON, Divine Legation, B. I., sec. vi., states what he regarded as a monstrosity almost incredible, but which is renewed among us, in the elaborate defence of slavery as just, and right, and religious, and of the highest benefit to society; that "to the lasting opprobrium of our age and country, we have seen a writer publicly maintain that PRIVATE VICES WERE PUBLIC BENEFITS. An unheard of impiety, wickedly advanced, and impudently avowed, against the universal voice of nature; an impiety in which moral virtue is represented as the invention of knaves, and Christian virtue as the imposition of fools." Compare JAY's Hebrew Servitude, and STROUD, Slave Code, and GOODELL, American Slave Laws, with GROTIUS, COKE, GISBORNE and DYMOND, on the principles of Natural Law and Morality.

CHAPTER XIV.

THE general term for servant, עֶבֶד, *evedh*, is sometimes rendered by our translators *servant* and sometimes *bondman*.
The translation, *bondman*, can not be justified, if the word is
meant to imply slavery. The word is sometimes used with
an emphasis of oppression, determined by reference to the nature of Egyptian bondage, which was the ultimate standard
of rigor, cruelty, and tyranny. Deuteronomy, xv. 15: *Remember that thou wast a servant* (translated in our English
Bible bondman) *in Egypt*, עֶבֶד, an *evedh*, in a bondage without mitigation. Thou shalt not compel thy brother to serve
as such a servant. For they are my servants, which I brought
forth out of the land of Egypt; they shall not be sold as servants. Thou shalt not rule over him with rigor, but shalt fear
thy God. Leviticus, xxv. 39, 42, 43: *They shall not be sold
as servants* (translated in this case *bondmen*), מִמְכֶּרֶת עֶבֶד
לֹא יִמָּכְרוּ, *not with the sale of a servant.* And in verse forty-
four: *Of the heathen shall ye buy bondmen and bondmaids,*
עֶבֶד וְאָמָה, *the servant and the maid-servant.* There was no
separate word for *bond-servant*, no word for *slave.* There
was only the word עֶבֶד, *evedh*, honorable in its origin, and
free in its original meaning, which they had to adopt and
use. But a man might be an עֶבֶד, *a servant*, and yet be a
freeman. It is not the term, therefore, but the context, that

limits and particularizes the signification. In 2 Kings, iv. 1: "The creditor is come to take my two sons to be (in our translation) *bondmen*," that is, לַעֲבָדִים, to be *for servants*, but *not bondmen;* for by law, being Hebrews, they could not be sold as *bondmen*, though they might be taken as *servants*, at a valuation of their time and labor, for the term of six years, for payment of the debt, to work out the debt. But if that did not suffice, but they must be held longer, then it was not lawful to hold them as *bondmen*, but as *hired servants*. See the law, Leviticus, xxv. 39, 40: "If thy brother that dwelleth by thee be waxen poor, and be sold unto thee, thou shalt not compel him to serve as a bond-servant; but *as a hired servant, and a sojourner* he shall be with thee." Not as עֶבֶד, *evedh*, but as שָׂכִיר, *sakir*. *Thou shalt not compel him to serve as a bond-servant,* לֹא־תַעֲבֹד בּוֹ עֲבֹדַת עָבֶד. *Thou shalt not task upon him the tasking of a servant.*

The service of the bond-servant thus designated was frequently compared, for illustration, with the servitude endured by the Israelites in Egypt. This was despotic, and without wages, without stipulated reward; no agreement or bargain between master and servant, but the latter forced into the service and under the rule of the former; a degradation and a yoke, under which no right of a freeman could be asserted. See Leviticus, xxvi. 13; Deuteronomy, xvi. 12; xxiv. 18–22; xxvi. 6; xxviii. 68. It was the bondage endured by the Jews in their captivity, Ezra, ix. 9; Nehemiah, v. 8. It was the bondage into which Joseph was sold, Genesis, xxxvii. 28, 36, and Psalm cv. 17. Various legal privileges, to which even the lowest class of servants among the Hebrews were entitled, and various limitary statutes, controlling the system of servitude, made it impossible for the Hebrews to impose the same despotic slavery upon others. They could not rule over the servants obtained from the heathen with the same unlimited authority with which the heathen ruled over their own slaves. Both the Hebrew servants and the servants "bought

with money of the stranger," were under protection of the
same laws against cruelty, and were in the same relation to
the Church by circumcision, and entitled to their rights in all
the religious festivals and privileges of instruction and of
worship. The Sabbath, and also the Sabbatical year of rest,
was theirs as well as their master's; and, as we shall see, the
recurrence of jubilee was a limit beyond which no form or
period of bondage could in any case be continued.

HEBREW TERM FOR HIRED SERVANT.

The Hebrew term for hired servant, שָׂכִיר, *sakir*, the *hireling*, is from the verb שָׂכַר, *sakar, to hire.* Leviticus, xix. 13,
the wages of him that is hired, שָׂכִיר, *sakir.*—Exodus, xxii. 15,
of a person who has hired himself out with his ox or ass, or im-
plement of husbandry, *if he were a hireling*, אִם־שָׂכִיר. So in
Exodus, xii. 45, a hired servant, שָׂכִיר, *sakir ;* also, Leviticus,
xxii. 16, *a hired servant of the priest;* also Leviticus, xxv. 40,
50, 53. In Isaiah, xvi. 14, we have an illustrative passage:
Within three years, as the years of an hireling כִּשְׁנֵי שָׂכִיר,
sakir; also Isaiah, xxi. 16: *Within a year, according to the years
of an hireling*, כִּשְׁנֵי שָׂכִיר, computed as the years of a servant
hired by the year are computed. But the שָׂכִיר, *sakir, the
hired servant*, might be hired by the day, while the ordinary
servant, the עֶבֶד *evedh*, had no such compensation, having
been apprenticed or hired for six years. Job, vii. 2: As a
servant, עֶבֶד, *evedh*, earnestly desireth the shadow, and as an
hireling, שָׂכִיר, *sakir*, looketh for his wages. Here the contrast between the two words and their respective signification is marked. The עֶבֶד, *evedh*, the ordinary servant, looks
for no wages at the end of the day, but longs for the evening,
and for rest, or for a shadow from the sun, and for some relief
from his toil; but *the hired servant*, שָׂכִיר, *sakir*, looks for the
reward of his work, according to the law in Leviticus, xix. 13.
So, likewise, Job, xiv. 6, *that he may accomplish, as an hireling, his day*, כְּשָׂכִיר,

Now it is to be noted that the word עֶבֶד, *evedh*, is never used in conjunction with any adjective to signify a hired servant; for the עֶבֶד, *evedh*, *the servant*, was one whose whole services were purchased at the outset for a specified time, longer or shorter, as the case might be, from himself, or from some one to whom for such a time he owed those services; it might be for a term of years, it might be till the jubilee. It is quite clear that the distinctive signification of עֶבֶד, *evedh*, excluded the idea of daily wages. In Leviticus, xxv. 39, 49, the particular difference between the ordinary servant and the hired servant is legally drawn out: "If thy brother that dwelleth by thee be waxen poor, and be sold *unto thee*, thou shalt not compel him to serve as עֶבֶד, *evedh;* but as an hired servant and as a sojourner shall he be with thee." The specific word שָׂכִיר, *sakir*, is used; thou shalt not compel him to serve as an עֶבֶד, *evedh;* but as a שָׂכִיר, *sakir*, and a sojourner shall he be with thee. The point in view evidently is this; thou shalt not treat him as a servant of all work, bound to thee irrevocably by his apprenticeship, but as a hireling who can leave at any time, on giving notice. Yet this is spoken *of one who is sold*, one who is *bought with money*. The buying with money did not imply ownership, did not render consequent or extant the condition which we call slavery: this is perfectly clear. All the Hebrew servants so bought were merely servants bound out for a term of years, and if longer than six years, then to be treated as hired servants, not as bond-servants. So in Exodus, xxi. 7, where it is said, *If a man sell his daughter*, the thing signified is merely a six years' contract for her services; her service for six years is sold for so much.

A Hebrew might sell himself to a stranger, sojourner, or alien in Israel, or to the stock of the stranger's family, to the heir, for an unlimited time, that is, for the period of time from the making of the bargain to the jubilee. But this sale had two conditions: first, he was to be with his master "as a yearly hired servant," כִּשְׂכִיר שָׁנָה בְּשָׁנָה, Leviticus, xxv. 53, as a hireling from year to year, or year by year; second, he could at any time be redeemed, that is, could buy back his own time, or have it bought back for him; and his owner was compelled to grant the redemption and take the money. The price of redemption was reckoned from the year that he was sold to the year of jubilee, so much a year, according to the price and time of a yearly hired servant. If more years remained to the jubilee, a greater price, if fewer a less price, was to be paid for his own time. If not redeemed, he and all his family were to be free at any rate in the year of jubilee; and meanwhile he was to receive wages as a yearly hired servant, a שָׂכִיר, sakir, and not an עֶבֶד, evedh. It is added that his master shall not rule with rigor over him. And in Leviticus, xxv. 46, when it is enacted that the servants of the Hebrews may be purchased of the strangers or the families of strangers, the heathen or their descendants in the land, it was added, "but over your brethren, the children of Israel, ye shall not rule, one over another, with rigor." The rigorous rule, as contrasted with the lenient rule over hired servants, consisted partly in the very fact of their being bound to serve the whole six years, or the whole time for which they had apprenticed themselves, for the sum paid for such apprenticeship, without being entitled to receive any other wages, either daily, weekly, or yearly. This was the grand difference between the עֶבֶד and שָׂכִיר.

There were other differences by statute, as described in Exodus, xii. 43–45, and Leviticus, xxii. 10, 11. No uncircumcised stranger or foreigner, nor any man's hired servant, might eat of the passover. But the servant bought for money might eat thereof when circumcised. It was a household ordinance, to be observed by families, as well as national. The home-born servants were regarded in this respect as belonging to the family, but the hired servants not. Yet this could not have been intended to operate to the exclusion of hired servants, under all circumstances, from the passover; it *may*

mean hired servants uncircumcised. Certainly Hebrews themselves were sometimes in the state of hired servants, and could
not have been excluded. But again, in the priest's family,
Leviticus, xxii. 10, 11, while the servant bought with money,
or born in the house, was permitted to partake of the holy
things, the hired servant was forbidden, was not regarded as
belonging to the priest's household.

DIFFERENCE IN VALUE.

In Deuteronomy, xv. 18, there is a computation of the comparative worth of a servant, עֶבֶד, *evedh*, and the hired servant,
שָׂכִיר, *sakir*. "The Hebrew servant, serving thee six years by
sale, *hath been worth a double hired servant to thee in serving
thee six years ;*" or perhaps it means, duplicate the wages of
a hired servant for six years ; that is, if you had kept a hired
servant for six years, by yearly wages, it would have cost you
double the price you have paid for the six years' Hebrew
servant. The servant bought for six years you had no yearly
wages to pay, but the hired servant you must pay by the
year. On this account, when the Hebrew servant was set free
at the end of his six years' service, the master was by law enjoined to give him a parting gift ; was not permitted to send
him away empty, but was " bound to furnish him liberally out
of the flock, the floor, and the wine-press." It was an outfit,
intended in some measure to supply to him the absence of
yearly wages. Deuteronomy, xv. 13, 14.

From all this it appears that, so far as the Hebrew servant
was an עֶבֶד, *evedh*, he was such only for the term of six years,
an עֶבֶד, *evedh*, for the whole term, without daily wages ; but
if in longer servitude, then he was an עֶבֶד שָׂכִיר, *evedh sakir*, a
servant, an hireling, a servant on wages. The mere עֶבֶד was
ordinarily the servant bought for money, and was considered
as bound to pay, by his labor, for the sum of money given as
the purchase of his whole time. If the master had to pay him
yearly or daily wages in addition, then the servant bought

with his money would have cost him much more than the hired laborer. It was the difference between a six years' apprenticeship, and a six years' service on daily, weekly, or yearly wages.

Such were the relations between master and servant in the Hebrew household four or five hundred years after the time of Abraham. Such was the system of servitude as regulated by law, to which God's regulations with Abraham, in the founding of the Hebrew nation and policy, looked forward. Abraham, five hundred years before the operation of the Mosaic statutes, had servants that were born in his house, servants that were given him, and servants that were bought with his money. They were all circumcised and instructed; and his children and his household were to keep the way of the Lord, to do justice and judgment. God's testimony to Isaac concerning Abraham, after his death, was this : " because that Abraham obeyed my voice, and kept my charge, my commandments, my statutes, and my laws." Genesis, xxvi. 5. There were men in Abraham's house, born in his house, and there were those bought with money of the stranger ; they were all circumcised along with Ishmael his son, and formed one and the same religious family.

DESIGNATION OF SERVANTS AS YOUNG MEN.

It is in Abraham's household that we first find mention of servants under the form נַעַר, *naar, a young man*, Genesis, xviii. 7. This designation is repeated in Genesis, xxii. 3, 5, 19, where Abraham's *young men* accompanied himself and Isaac to the mount of the appointed sacrifice. They were employed in menial services, though the word does not necessarily mean servants, and Isaac himself is called by the same designation, rendered in his case *lad*. Indeed, the generic signification is lad, or boy, while it is often applied to designate *servants*, as also is the feminine of נַעַר applied to a *maid-servant*. Thus we find Abraham, on these two important occasions, personally waited on (as also his illustrious guests) by his young men, נְעָרָיו.

There is the same usage in the following instances: 2 Kings, iv. 22, 24, used to designate the servants of the Shunamite, and verse 25, applied to Gehazi, the servant of Elijah. Also, v. 20 and viii. 4. In 2 Kings, vi. 15, it is one of two terms applied to designate the servant of Elisha, the first from the verb שָׁרַת, to serve, to minister, and the second, נַעַר, as also in verse 17. In 1 Kings, xix. 3, Elijah left his servant at Beersheba, נַעֲרוֹ. It is used also in 1 Kings, xx. 14, 15, 17, 19, and in like manner in 2 Kings, xix. 6. The same designation is applied in Nehemiah, iv. 16, 22, 23, and·v. 15, 16, and vi. 5. It is applied to Nehemiah's servants, the people's, Sanballat's, and the former governor's servants. But in the same history, Tobiah, *the servant*, the Ammonite, is designated with intended contempt as the עֶבֶד, probably a runaway slave of the heathen, though he was the son-in-law of Shechaniah, the son of Arah. Nehemiah, ii. 10, 19, and vi. 18, and xiii. 19. In Numbers, xxii. 22, the term נַעַר, is applied to the two servants of Balaam.

After the overthrow of Sodom, Abraham sojourned in Gerar, and there Abimelech took sheep, and oxen, and menservants and women-servants, עֲבָדִים וּשְׁפָחֹת, and gave to Abraham, Genesis, xx. 14. And all that Abraham had, he gave unto Isaac, flocks and herds, and silver and gold, and menservants and maid-servants, and camels and asses, Genesis, xxiv. 35, 36, and xxv. 5. After the death of Abraham we find Isaac dwelling in Gerar, under the divine blessing, so that he had possession of flocks, and possession of herds, and great store of servants, וַעֲבֻדָּה רַבָּה, Genesis, xxvi. 14. Precisely the same words are used of Job, that he had *a very great household*, עֲבֻדָּה רַבָּה, *the whole body of domestics and dependents*, Job, i. 3.

But the servants are here called, as in Genesis, xxii. 3, and other places referred to above, *young men*, הַנְּעָרִים, Job, i. 15—17, three times: first, the servants are slain; second, the sheep and the servants are consumed; third, the camels are carried away and the servants slain by the Chaldeans. These נְעָרִים were certainly a part of the great household, the עֲבֻדָּה, the domestics and servants of Job. But in the nineteenth verse the same word is used to describe Job's own sons as destroyed in the falling of the house; they, too, are called the young men, הַנְּעָרִים. In Job, xli. 5, the feminine plural is used for maidens: Wilt thou bind him for thy maidens? לְנַעֲרוֹתֶיךָ.

This peculiar usage prevails in Judges, Ruth, and the first book of Samuel. Judges, vii. 10, 11: Phurah, the *servant* of Gideon, נַעַר, *naar*. Judges, xix. 3: His *servant* with him, and a couple of asses, נַעֲרוֹ, *naar*. Judges, xix. 9, 11, 13, 19: The master to the servant, and the servant to the master, the distinction being that of אֲדֹנָיו and נַעֲרוֹ, *naar*. Ruth, ii. 5, 6: Boaz to his *servant* over the reapers, his young men, לְנַעֲרוֹ, *naar*. Also ii. 9, 15, 21. The feminine of the same word in this book is used for maidens, as ii. 8, *my maidens*, נַעֲרֹתַי. Ruth, ii. 22, 23, the maidens of Boaz. It is the servants of Boaz that are thus designated, and Ruth calls them, in ii. 13, handmaidens, שִׁפְחָתֶךָ, *shiphhah*. The young men and the maidens, as servants to Boaz, were at work in his fields, and Ruth gleaned among them and after them. In this book, the word עֶבֶד, *evedh*, for servant, is not once employed; an indication that there was no approximation to slavery known in the household of Boaz, though he was a mighty man of wealth of the family of Elimelech.

In 1 Samuel, ix. 3, 5, 8, 7, 22, 27, and x. 14, there is the same usage. Kish said to Saul, take now one of *the servants*, מֵהַנְּעָרִים, *naar*, with thee, and seek the asses. Then said Saul *to his servant*, נַעֲרוֹ, *naar*, and so repeatedly. The same usage in reference to maidens employed in drawing water; in ix. 11, they are called נְעָרוֹת. And so in 1 Samuel, ii. 13, 15, the masculine of the same noun is used for the priest's servant, נַעַר, *naar*.

In 1 Samuel, xxx. 13, the word is used as follows: *a young man* (נַעַר, *naar*) *of Egypt, servant* (עֶבֶד, *evedh*) to an Amalekite. In 2 Samuel, ix. 2, compared with ix. 9, 10, and xvi. 1, and xix. 17, the terms עֶבֶד, *evedh*, and נַעַר, *naar*, are applied to the same person, Ziba, of the house of Saul; and a close examination of the passages indicates the condition signified to be quite different from any thing implied in the appellation of slave. Ziba is first called a servant, עֶבֶד, *evedh*, of the house of Saul, and then he is named the נַעַר, *naar*, of the house of Saul, with twenty servants, עֲבָדִים, *evedh*, under him, in his own house, and all that dwelt in the house of Ziba were servants, עֲבָדִים, *evedh*, unto Mephibosheth. 2 Samuel, ix. 9: "The king called to Ziba, Saul's servant, נַעַר, *naar*, and said unto him, I have given unto thy master's son all that pertained to Saul, and to all his house. Thou, therefore, and thy sons, and thy servants, עֲבָדֶיךָ, *evedh*, shall till the land for him." 2 Samuel, xvi. 1: Ziba is called the servant, נַעַר, *naar*, of Mephibosheth, and meets King David with provisions. 2 Samuel, xix. 17: Again he is called Ziba, the servant of the house of Saul, נַעַר בֵּית שָׁאוּל, *naar*, the *young man* of the house of Saul. Very evidently, Ziba was an officer of some importance in Saul's household, but it is equally clear that he was not a slave, though called both the עֶבֶד, *evedh*, and the נַעַר, *naar* of his master the king. The *naarism* may have been a form of service, more honorable, and of a higher grade, than the *evedhism*. The indication, wherever נַעַר, *naar*, is employed, is certainly that of free service, and not bond-service.

For the present, we stop in our investigation with the Abrahamic period. From the survey of this period, as it lies in the Scriptures, we find no trace whatever of the existence of *slavery*, except among idolatrous and despotic nations. There is no proof that it ever existed in the household of Abraham. There is evidence of the revealed judgment of God against it. God's description to Abraham of the bondage which his seed should be compelled to undergo in Egypt, was a reprobation of involuntary unpaid servitude, as a crime on the part of those who enforced it. *The nation whom they serve will I judge.* Know of a surety that thy seed shall serve them, and they shall afflict them. The sentence is as clearly condemnatory as if God had said, They will be guilty of great and cruel oppression, and for the crime of such oppression I will punish them. Is it possible to conceive that the individual, with an enlightened moral sense, to whom this revelation was made, could himself, as the head and founder of a social race and system, establish in his own family and nation the same reprobated state of enforced, unpaid, involuntary servitude? Could Abraham make *another* seed *his* prey and property, by the same spoliation and affliction denounced of God as a crime to be punished, when inflicted on *his own* seed? The crime of the Egyptians against the Hebrews was the enslaving of them, and treating them as slaves. The enslaving of *others*, and treating *them* as slaves, would be the same crime in Abraham; it would be the founding of the same system of oppression and cruelty, which God plainly informed Abraham was wrong.*

* Antiquities of Egypt. The Future State, 155.

It has been questioned by some writers whether slavery existed in Egypt under what is called the theocracy in that country; and the evidences of slavery, in the laws cited by Diodorus, are referred to a period very much later than that of Abraham. That the Egyptians did not make slaves of their own countrymen, and that the doing of this was regarded as a crime of the greatest magnitude, is manifest from their own records. From the Egyptian ritual pictures in the British Museum there is gathered the following address of the departed soul before Osiris, on entering the Hall of Judgment: "I have defrauded no man; I have not slaughtered the cattle of the gods; I have not prevaricated at the seat of justice; *I have not made slaves of the Egyptians;* I have not defiled my conscience for the sake of my superior; I have not used violence; I have not famished my household; I have not made to weep; I have not smitten privily; I have not changed the measures of Egypt; I have not grieved the spirits of the gods; I have not committed adultery," etc.

The enumeration of slave-making as among the greatest crimes is remarkable. It is hardly to be supposed that the conscience of Abraham, enlightened by divine revelation, would permit him to maintain

Even when, in the execution of God's judgments against
the heathen nations expelled from the promised land, the Hebrews were commanded to put the remnant of those nations
to tribute and service, they were forbidden to treat *them* as
they themselves had been treated in Egypt. The system of
servitude under which they were to be brought, was hemmed
in and restricted by such legal limitations and periodical clos-
ures, that what we call slavery could not grow out of it, but
would, on the contrary, be abolished by it. It is impossible that
the system which God thus predestinated to abhorrence, as a
system of iniquity, could at the same time be set in the household and line of the patriarch as an example and model of social and domestic life. There must be positive proof of the
most unquestionable clearness, before we can admit the existence of such an anomaly; but no proof is found. It is no
proof to take assumptions from the existence and nature of
slavery in ancient Greece and Rome, or in modern ages, and
carry them back to the foundation of the patriarchal society,
and force them there, as a supposititious conclusion in regard
to that society. It is no proof to take from modern times and
languages a name, a term, of which there is no trace in the
Hebrew tongue, and apply it to Hebrew usages that have no
reality corresponding to it, and then, notwithstanding all this,
draw from such application of the term an opinion that the
thing itself existed. Strange to say, this has been the case
with not a few commentators, almost without reflection, with
not the slightest examination of the question; so that we
find the term *slave* most carelessly, incongruously, and
groundlessly applied, even in books and essays assuming to
be critical.

If we could suppose a species of upas-apple to have been
grafted on the antique olive-tree, so that from the time of

as a habit, what even the natural
conscience, and the remnant of religious knowledge among the Egypt-

ians, taught them to consider as an
oppression and a crime.

Julius Cæsar down to this day the most ordinary fruit of the olive should be a bitter, oily, poisonous apple, used for the purpose of intoxication and intemperance, it would certainly be a somewhat serious error to assume the existence and use of this artificial corruption of the olive in the land of Palestine in the time of Joshua and the Judges. If this modern perverted fruit had its own peculiar name, it would be an extraordinary stupidity or willful perversion, for any lexicographer or commentator to call the fruit of the oriental antique olive by that name. And it would be a most disastrous and absurd confusion to carry in our minds the idea of that poisonous and vicious modern invention, when reading of the habitual use of the olive as a native and most precious production of the Holy Land, one of the most gracious gifts of God to its inhabitants. But even this would be not more absurd than for us to carry the name or the idea of *slavery* back to the household life of Abraham.*

---

*SAALSCHUTZ. *Das Mosaische Recht.* Laws of Moses, Vol. II., note on sec. xii., p. 714. SAALSCHUTZ corrects MICHAELIS, and affirms that he had brought in a most pernicious mistake in giving the general title of bondage or slavery to the system of Jewish service. Referring to instances in proof of this error, "With what justice," he asks, "could the appellation of *Leibegenschaft*, servile thraldom, or slavery, be applied to such a system? Servants that were free by law in the seventh year, and universally in the year of jubilee, could not be called slaves; they were in no sense such. With what propriety or justice can any or all these classes of servants be called bondsmen or slaves?"

Compare GRAVES, on the Pentateuch. Moral Principles of the Jewish Law, Part II., sec. iii., and DYMOND, Essays on Morality, with BLACKSTONE and COKE on Natural Law and Right. "As LIBERTY is equally valuable with LIFE," remarks Graves, "the Jewish law, WITH THE STRICTEST EQUITY, ordained that if any man were convicted of attempting to reduce any fellow-citizen to slavery, he should be punished with death." The principle of one and the same law for the stranger and the native applied here, for the death penalty is against STEALING A MAN, and it has been again and again demonstrated that he who holds a man as a slave, against his own will, renews the stealing of him every hour. "Whoever," says GISBORNE, (Slave Trade, 144, 155,) "detains the slave in bondage, directly or indirectly, a moment, commits a flagrant sin against God."

CHAPTER XV.

PATRIARCHAL ESTABLISHMENT OF ISAAC AND JACOB.—THE OUTRAGE AT SHECHEM.—
TRIBUTARY SERVICE.—CAPTIVES IN WAR.—GOD'S REPROBATION ON THE CUSTOM OF
SELLING THEM FOR SLAVES.—THE FIRST INSTANCE OF MAN STEALING.—CONDITION
OF THE ISRAELITES IN EGYPT.

LEPSIUS has noticed the great personality of Abraham, and what he calls the *non-prominent activity of Isaac*. The contrast is indeed striking; and the only interval in which we behold in his circumstances the patriarchal greatness and prosperity of his father, is the period of his sojourn in the land of the Philistines, recorded in the twenty-fifth chapter of Genesis. But Abraham gave all that he had unto Isaac, xxv. 5; and the account given of him some twenty years after Abraham's death, is as follows: "The Lord blessed him, and the man waxed great, and went forward and grew until he became very great; for he had possession of flocks, and possession of herds, and great store of servants," xxvi. 12–14. Here the appellative for the greatness of his household is the Hebrew עֲבֻדָּה, *avudha*, the verbal from עָבַד, *avadh*, signifying the whole body of his domestics, or of those in his employment, including, of course, the herdsmen and well-diggers. Compare Job, i. 3, the description of Job's very great household, מְאֹד עֲבֻדָּה רַבָּה. There is no intimation of slavery, nor any approximation thereto, in Isaac's family or jurisdiction.

From him the same gift of inheritance descended with the right of the first-born to Jacob, in whose family the patriarchal dominion and opulence passed from one person to twelve in the constitution of the Jewish State. During the sojourn of

Jacob with Laban, there is no change of manners, no introduction or appearance of any form of slavery.   Jacob himself
is said to have served Laban for wages ; he was Laban's servant as well as his son-in-law ; and it is said that " the man increased exceedingly, and had much cattle, *and maid-servants
and men-servants,*" וּשְׁפָחוֹת וַעֲבָדִים, Genesis, xxx. 43.   These
went with him, when he fled from Laban : they were his עֲבֻדָּה,
avudha, his patriarchal establishment, when he met Esau, and
sent messengers to his brother, saying : "I have oxen and
asses, flocks, and men-servants, and women-servants," Genesis,
xxxii. 5.   But his two wives, and his two women-servants,
and his eleven sons, are described as his immediate family,
and are set apart by themselves—the handmaidens with their
children, and Leah with hers, and Joseph and Rachel, Genesis,
xxxiii. 6, 7.   After a favorable interview with Esau, he travels
on slowly, with his flocks and herds, to Succoth and Shalem,
and erects an altar.

But here, at Shechem, was perpetrated that murderous outrage, by the sons of Jacob, in the sacking and spoiling of that
city, remembered by the patriarch, with a solemn curse, upon
his dying bed.   After destroying the males of the city, " all
their wealth, and all their little ones, and their wives, took
they captive."   There is no account of the final disposition
made of these unfortunate captives; but in this infamous
transaction we have the first intimation of any possibility of
the possession of servants, by violence and fraud, among the
descendants of Abraham.

WAR AND SLAVERY.—CRIME OUT OF CRIME.

Among the heathen nations, captivity in war was one of the
most common modes by which men became slaves; but in
the history of Abraham we see the patriarch refusing to sanction such a transaction by his example.   When he had conquered those heathen marauders who took Lot captive, the
king of Sodom proposed that Abraham should give him *the*

persons, and take the goods to himself, dividing thus the spoil between them, on grounds easy to be guessed at from our knowledge of the morals of the Sodomites. But Abraham declared that he would enter into no bargain with him, neither for goods nor persons : from a thread to a shoe-latchet, he would take nothing. Aner, Eshcol, and Mamre the Amorite might make what terms they pleased, but he himself would take nothing.

Jacob's abhorrence of the conduct of his sons is marked : he denounced the whole wickedness of the murder and captivity of the Shechemites, and was beyond measure distressed by it. He seems to have made it the occasion of a religious reformation, commanding his household, *and all that were with him*, to put away the strange gods that were among them, and be clean, Genesis, xxxv. 2. Thus Jacob returned to the habitation of Isaac his father, who died in Hebron at the age of one hundred and eighty years, and his sons Esau and Jacob buried him. "And Esau took his wives and his sons and his daughters, *and all the persons of his house*, וְאֶת־כָּל־נַפְשׁוֹת בֵּיתוֹ, and all his substance which he had gotten in the land of Canaan, and went into the country from the face of his brother Jacob; for their riches were more than that they might dwell together, and the land wherein they were strangers could not bear them because of their cattle," Genesis, xxxvi. 6, 7. Here the expression כָּל־נַפְשׁוֹת בֵּיתוֹ *kol naphshoth betho*, is clearly synonymous with עֲבֻדָּה *avudha*, in the description of the households of Isaac and Job; it comprehends domestics and dependents, *the born in the house*, בֵּית יָלִיד, and the hired servants, and all whose time and services, in a limited or definite apprenticeship, were bought with money of the stranger.

The blessing of a birth-right conferred in itself no superior authority upon one brother over the other; but Isaac's peculiar blessing upon Jacob, on the occasion recorded in Genesis, xxvii., made Esau tributary to his brother, as unexpectedly to

Isaac as to himself; for the arrangement had been quite the reverse, but for Rebecca's deceit and Isaac's blindness. "Let people serve thee, and nations bow down to thee: be lord over thy brethren, and let thy mother's sons bow down to thee," Genesis, xxvii. 29. There was the solemnity of a divine inspiration or compulsion in this, for Isaac felt that he could not revoke or change it; yea, and he shall be blessed, in spite of his stratagem and our disappointment. Behold, I have made him thy lord, and all his brethren have I given to him for servants, Genesis, xxvii. 33, 37. The expression *for servants* is לַעֲבָדִים, *laavadhim*, so that an unscrupulous advocate for the divine right of slavery might much more plausibly find it here, in the blessing upon Jacob, than in the curse upon Canaan. But the nature of this domination is instantly defined, and the definition applies to both transactions. "By thy sword shalt thou live, and shalt serve thy brother; and it shall come to pass, when thou shalt have dominion, that thou shalt break his yoke from off thy neck." Here a national subjection was meant, and not a personal servitude.

CAPTIVES IN WAR.—SINFULNESS OF MAKING SLAVES OF THEM.

That the divine reprobation rested upon the custom of making slaves out of captives taken in war, is manifest from many passages. God never permitted it among the Jews themselves, when there were two kingdoms in conflict, and among other nations it is not unfrequently presented as a sin and misery, the result of a marked retributive Providence.

The transaction recorded in 2 Chronicles, xxviii. 8–15, affords a very remarkable proof of God's abhorrence of such a traffic. It is a lucid commentary on the laws against making merchandise of men; and the immediate obedience of the people to the word of the Lord forbidding this crime, shows how deeply their conscience was stirred and struck with remorse under the sense of it, for having intended it: "Deliver the captives again, which ye have taken captive, for the fierce wrath of the Lord is upon you;" "Our trespass is great, and there is fierce wrath against Israel;" "Ye purpose to keep under the children of Judah and Jerusalem for bondmen and bond-women unto you." Such compelled, involuntary bondage would have been slavery, would have been the stealing and holding, and making merchandise of men; would have been, in fact, that very crime, which, by the divine law, was to be punished with death. The number of the captives was two hundred thousand; but so convicted and subdued were the victorious Israelites before the word of God by the prophet Oded, so penetrated with a sense of the magnitude of the crime they were on the brink of committing, that immediately they "rose up and took the captives, and with the spoil clothed all that were naked among them, and arrayed them and shod them, and gave them to eat and to drink, and anointed them, and carried all the feeble of them upon asses, and brought them to Jericho, the city of palm trees, to their brethren." This is a record of immediate obedience to God, in the midst of the rage and flush of victory, and of forbearance and generosity toward the vanquished at God's command, unparalleled in the annals of history.

The account is full of instruction; for of all the modes in which men have ever been made slaves, conquest in war has been supposed to be the least contrary to justice; but here it is denounced as a crime to be visited with the fierce wrath of God. But if so in the case of a war between rival kingdoms, how much more when the war is against a helpless race, such as the natives of Africa; a piratical invasion, and a series, uninterrupted, of savage incursions, entered upon, instigated, and perpetuated, for the sole purpose of seizing and carrying away captive the wretched victims of such cruelty, to sell them as slaves, and to keep them and their posterity as a race of slaves, to be held, bought, and sold, as chattels, and only chattels, for ever. Both the foreign piracy, and the domestic slave trade in the United States, are one and the same crime, but

perpetuated and legalized in this country with greater aggra-
vations; the very legalization and sanctification of it constituting a greater guilt, and working out in it and by it a far more
exceeding and eternal weight of infamy and cruelty.

Among heathen nations it was a custom to dispose of the
captives taken in war by *casting lots* for them. This was the
fate endured by some of the Jews themselves, who were thus
disposed of, in some cases, for the most infamous purposes
conceivable, Joel, iii. 3. " They have *cast lots* for' my people,
and have given a boy for an harlot, and sold a girl for wine,
that they might drink." It was thus that the cities of Egypt
were laid waste, and the inhabitants carried captive. No
Amon is mentioned in Nahum, and it is stated that "they
cast lots for her honorable men, and all her great men were
bound in chains," Nahum, iii. 10. In the prophecy of Obadiah, the Edomites are threatened of God for their violence
against the Israelites, and for standing aloof when the heath-
en carried them away captive, and foreigners entered their
gates and *cast lots* upon Jerusalem, Obadiah, 11. They are
also accused of " standing in the crossway to cut off those
that escaped," and of " delivering up those that remained,"
and it is declared that, as they had done to others, so should
it be done to them, Obadiah, 14, 15.

In the same manner, the tribes and inhabitants of Tyre and
Zidon, and of the coasts of Palestine, are arraigned and assured
of God's vengeance, because they had *sold the children of Judah and the children of Jerusalem to the Grecians*, that they
might be removed far from their border, Joel, iii. 6. For this
iniquity God declares, " I will sell your sons and your daughters into the hand of the children of Judah, and they shall sell
them to the Sabeans, to a people far off, for the Lord hath
spoken it," Joel, iii. 8. As a direct testimony of God in regard to the sinfulness of such a traffic, these passages are very
important. The being sold in bondage is presented as one of
the most terrible judgments of God upon a guilty nation. The

same judgment is threatened against the sinful Hebrews themselves, Deuteronomy, xxviii. 68, as the climax of all the curses
pronounced against them for their sins: "Ye shall be sold
unto your enemies for bondmen and bondwomen, and no man
shall buy you:" ye shall be tossed to and fro for sale, as so
many cattle, with the shame and the misery of being so despised and abhorred that no master will be willing to buy
you.

The despotism of such a dominion, even when it was in
some measure lightened, and God began to redeem them
from it, is graphically set forth in the confession, prayer, and
covenant of Nehemiah and the people, returning from their
captivity.   "Behold we are servants this day in the land thou
gavest to our fathers, and it yieldeth much increase to the
kings whom thou hast set over us because of our sins; also,
they have dominion over our bodies, and over our cattle at
their pleasure, and we are in great distress," Nehemiah, ix.
36, 37.

THE FIRST INSTANCE OF MAN-STEALING.

There needed no law against man-stealing to assure the
conscience of its being a crime; and it has been a subject of
wonder that the sons of Jacob could so deliberately and re-
morselessly plunge themselves into such guilt.   But the steps
in the history are logical forerunners and sequences.   Events
follow upon character, and one act produces another, with a
perfect moral fitness and fatality.   Any thing might have been
expected, any development could not have been surprising,
after the dreadful tragedy at Shechem.   The murderous sacking of that city, and the disposal of the captives, had prepared
the sons of Jacob, "moved with envy," (the former passion
having been revenge), for the crime of kidnapping.   They
took their choice between murdering their brother and selling
him, it being only the providence of God, in the passing of
the Ishmaelites just then, from Gilead toward Egypt, with their
caravan of camels, laden with spices, and balm, and myrrh,

that suggested to them the merchandise as more profitable.
So they sold Joseph to the Ishmaelites for twenty pieces of
silver. And the Midianites sold him into Egypt, Genesis,
xxxvii. 28–36. The word used for this transaction is in both
cases the same, מָכַר, *makar*. And Potiphar bought him,
וַיִּקְנֵהוּ. *vayiknehu*, xxxix. 1. The word *bought* is from קָנָה,
kanah, and the same is applied, Nehemiah, v. 8, to the purchase, for redemption, of the Jews that had been sold unto
the heathen. Joseph is called by Potiphar's wife, xxxix. 17,
the Hebrew servant, הָעֶבֶד, *haevedh*. Joseph describes the
transaction by which he was brought into bondage in Egypt
as *man-stealing;* for indeed *I was stolen away* out of the land
of the Hebrews, גֻּנֹּב גֻּנַּבְתִּי. The chief butler's description or
designation of Joseph is that of a young man, a Hebrew, servant to the captain, נַעַר עִבְרִי עֶבֶד, *naar, ivry, evedh*, Genesis,
xli. 12.

In the course of Joseph's interview with his brethren, the
word עֶבֶד, *evedh*, is very frequently employed; and they and
Joseph use it to signify both the condition of a free servant
and of one condemned to servitude for crime. The variety in
the translation of the same term, sometimes by the word *bondman*, sometimes *servant*, is singularly loose and groundless,
Genesis, xliv. 9, 10, 16, 17, 33 : "With whomsoever of thy
servants (עֶבֶד, *evedh*), it be found, both let him die, and we
also will be my lord's *bondmen*," (עֶבֶד, *evedh*), the same word,
servants. "And he said, He shall be my *servant*" (עֶבֶד, *evedh*).
And again, "Let thy servant (עֶבֶד, *evedh*), abide instead of
the lad, a *bondman*" (עֶבֶד, *evedh*), Genesis, xliv. 33. The bondage here signifies a servitude in punishment of crime—a
slavery into which, without crime, Joseph had been many
years previous most diabolically sold by his own brethren for
twenty pieces of silver. It was a question, then, whether to
sell him or leave him to die; a most extraordinary demonstration of the exactly equivalent nature of the two crimes of murder and man-stealing; showing the diabolism at heart, and

proving that a man capable of making merchandise of his brother man was capable also of murdering him, the latter form of wickedness requiring no greater malignity than the former. And if men, under the light of revelation, can see nothing criminal in slavery, neither would they in murder, if murder, like slavery, should become profitable.

CONDITION OF THE ISRAELITES IN EGYPT.

The question next arises, in the order of the history, whether any of the *great store of servants* spoken of as formerly belonging to Jacob's household, went down with him into Egypt to settle there. No mention is made of them, and only his own posterity are particularized in the census. "And Jacob rose up from Beersheba, and the sons of Israel carried Jacob their father, and their little ones, and their wives, in the wagons which Pharaoh had sent to carry him. And they took their cattle, and their goods, which they had gotten in the land of Canaan, and came into Egypt, Jacob, and all his seed with him. His sons and his sons' sons with him, his daughters and his sons' daughters, and all his seed brought he with him into Egypt," Genesis, xlvi. 5, 7. "All the souls that came with Jacob into Egypt, which came out of his loins, besides Jacob's sons' wives, all the souls threescore and six," xlvi. 26. The enumeration here is simply all that came out of Jacob's loins; it does not prove that none others were with them; and Joseph is said to have "nourished his father, and his brethren, and all his father's household, with bread, according to their families," xlvii. 12, וְאֵת כָּל־בֵּית, *veethkolbeth, all the household.* Joseph's own enumeration to Pharaoh was: "My father, and my brethren, and their flocks, and their herds, and all that they have, are in the land of Goshen." The two years of sore famine must have greatly reduced the עֲבֻדָּה, *avudha,* the household establishment of the patriarch, once so rich and numerous. Servants and dependents would be dismissed, their herds and their flocks would be diminished; nevertheless, we can not certainly conclude that no servants whatever went with them into Egypt. But there we shortly find the testimony, Exodus, i. 7, that "the children of Israel were fruitful, and increased abundantly, and multiplied, and waxed exceeding mighty, and the land was filled with them."

Though they occupied a separate province, yet manifestly at the time of Moses and the Exodus there was much commingling with the Egyptians in social life and in neighborhoods. There was visiting and sojourning between Egyptian and Hebrew families. This is clear from Exodus, xii. 21-23, and Exodus, iii. 21, 22 : " Every woman shall borrow* of her neighbor,

---

* The error in regard to this transaction is very great, if it be supposed that the Hebrews really pretended to borrow with the intention of returning, and that such deception was sanctioned of God. It is a mistranslation, like that of *slave* for *servant.*

" Of those numerous writers who take every opportunity of depreciating the Bible, many have been careful to dilate upon the impropriety of the Israelites borrowing goods of the Egyptians, when about finally to leave the country, and consequently without any intention of repayment. In addition to what is said in the text in explanation of this conduct, and on the justice of this requital, it will be quite sufficient to observe that the idea of *borrowing* arises entirely from the English translation, and has no place in the original, which is, literally, "to ask." So the Septuagint reads: " Every woman shall *ask* of her neighbor," etc. Should any one still contend for rendering the word שאל, *borrow*, let him try to render it so in Psalm cxxii. 6: O borrow the peace of Jerusalem! (KENNICOTT)."— SMITH'S SACRED ANNALS, vol. ii., 62.

Gesenius renders the word, *mutuum petivit*, asked or *sought*, but he also renders it *postulavit*, as a *demand.* But God declared that this was done as a just retribution : "Ye shall spoil the Egyptians;" that is (as in verse 20, where God says, "I will smite Egypt,") "Ye shall spoil Egypt," Exodus, iii. 22. Accordingly, Exodus, xii. 36, it is said, "They spoiled the Egyptians," or, as in the other case, it may be translated, *they spoiled Egypt.* It was a just, retributive process ; for the Egyptians had despoiled the Hebrews, had taken their labor without wages, had made them serve without right and without recompense, so that whatever the Hebrews now took away was no more than belonged to them. God did not propose a compensation to the Egyptians for the loss of so many slaves set free, but in this divine scheme of emancipation he proposed some compensation to the oppressed bondmen, besides their freedom, some compensation for the injustice and robbery they had endured.

If the slaves of the United States were emancipated on these divinely recognized principles, the spoiling of

and *of her that sojourneth in her house.*" A degree of intimacy and familiarity is here intimated, which the oppressive edicts and cruel measures of the Pharaohs had not broken up. Up to the time of the death of Jacob and Joseph and all that generation, their condition in Egypt had been one of honor and prosperity, and their intercourse with the Egyptians was disastrously productive of increasing looseness, luxury, and idolatry in social life, and was full of evil morally, as it was of advantage financially. The system of cruelty at length adopted by the government of Egypt did not find nor create a corresponding cruelty on the part of the Egyptian people, and their friendly communion with the Hebrews was kept up even to the last.

From Exodus, i. 11, it would seem that the avenue or pretense on which their oppressors began to afflict them was the collection of the tribute for the king. Operating by means of officers, tax-gatherers, for the collection of the impost, they seem to have required its payment in labor, and to have increased the severity of that labor at their pleasure : " Let us deal wisely with them. Therefore they did set over them שָׂרֵי מִסִּים, *sarai missim*, *captains for the tribute*, to afflict them with their burdens." Under these exactors, other officers were appointed, called afterwards נֹגְשֵׂי, *nogesai*, *taskmasters*, Exodus, v. 10 ; and under them, from among the Hebrews themselves, were appointed שֹׁטְרֵי, *shoterai*, *overseers*, Exodus, v. 14–19 ;

their oppressors, by compelling them to make some restitution of defrauded wages, would be equally just. The African slaves have as perfect a claim upon their masters as the Hebrews had on theirs ; the borrowing and spoiling would be as just a divine requisition in the one case as in the other. See JOSEPHUS' ANTIQ., book ii., chap. xiv., sec. vi.

See also CALVIN, HARMONY OF THE PENTATEUCH, vol. i., Exodus, iii. 22. Calvin's translation of the word is *postulabit*. HENGSTENBERG supposes the spoil to have been a free gift of the Egyptians to the Hebrews, in consequence of the kindness produced in their hearts towards Israel, by God giving them favor in their sight.

in fact, slave-drivers. How large a proportion of the people were drafted for these burdens, or how many were exempt, we have no means of knowing. It was a servile conscription, but it did not make the whole people, personally, slaves.

The condition of the Hebrews in Egypt was one of kindness, freedom, and comfort, in comparison with the condition of the victims of slavery in America. They were a separate community, with their own institutions, and only tributary to the Egyptians. They possessed large property in flocks and herds, and very much cattle. They had for their abode the land of Goshen, the best part of Egypt. In their neighborhood with the Egyptians, they dwelt in their own houses, which were secure from violation, each family in a house by itself. Their manner of living was, in respect to provisions, abundant and nourishing. There was never any pretense on the part of their oppressors of *owning* them as *chattels ;* they were not treated as merchandise, they could not be sold. It was a governmental oppression, but under which they were as far removed from the condition of that chattel slavery in which four millions of human beings in the United States are trampled and bound, as the subjects of Austrian oppression in Italy. Yet this comparatively light oppression endured by them is reprobated of God as grievous, afflictive, cruel, iniquitous ; a crime deserving of his wrath, a crime demanding, and visited with, the most tremendous retribution. In the light of such a demonstration, what language would be strong enough to describe the divine disapprobation and wrath against American slavery ? And what is the probable future of our country, if we persist in this crime, bold, defiant, impenitent ?

See GRANVILLE SHARPE, Law of Retribution, and WHEWELL, Duty of the State, Vol. II., 1003 ; compared with JEFFERSON, Correspondence, and Notes on Virginia, 39, 40 ; ABBÉ RAYNAL, BURKE and COLERIDGE, Friend, 58, 163. "The only choice left to a vicious government is either to fall *by* the people, if they are suffered to become enlightened, or *with* them, if they are kept enslaved and ignorant."

CHAPTER XVI.

NATURE OF TRIBUTARY SERVITUDE.—CASE OF THE CANAANITES GENERALLY, AND OF THE GIBEONITES PARTICULARLY.

IN the prophetic blessing of Jacob upon his children, it is said of Issachar that "he bowed his shoulder to bear, and became *a servant unto tribute*," לְמַס עֹבֵד, *lemas ovedh*, Genesis, xlix. 16. As our line of induction and of argument is at present historical, taking up the points of statutory law in their regular succession, we propose here to examine the nature of the tributary and personal servitude imposed by the Mosaic laws, and set in practice by Joshua, upon the Canaanitish nations. This phrase, לְמַס-עֹבֵד, *lemas ovedh, a servant unto tribute,* applied by Jacob to Issachar, is the generic expression descriptive of that servitude. Let us carefully trace the principle, the law, and its operation.

THE PRINCIPLE AND LAW.

In Deuteronomy, xx. 11, it was enacted that when any city of the heathen was conquered by the Hebrews, "all the people found therein *shall be tributaries unto thee, and they shall serve thee,*" יִהְיוּ לְךָ לָמַס וַעֲבָדוּךָ. The same expression is found in Joshua, xvi. 10, of the conquered Canaanites serving the Ephraimites under tribute. The form is exactly that used by Jacob in reference to Issachar, וַיְהִי לְמַס-עֹבֵד, *lemas ovedh.* In Judges, i. 28, 30, 33, 35, we have four instances of the same expression applied to the treatment of the Canaanites—by Manasseh, by Zebulon, by Naphtali, and the house of Joseph. They did not drive out nor exterminate the inhabitants, but they *became tributaries unto them*, הָיוּ לָהֶם לָמַס, *hayu lahem lamas;* in verse 28, they put the Canaanites to tribute, לָמַס, וַיִּתְּנוּ אֶת־הַכְּנַעֲנִי, *lamas.* In Joshua, xvii. 13, the same expression, varied only in the use of the verb נָתַן, they set, or appointed, the Canaanites, לָמַס, *lemas*, to tribute. So in Isaiah, xxxi. 8, the young men of the conquered Assyrians *shall be for tribute*, shall serve as tributaries, לְמַס יִהְיוּ, *lamas.* We shall see, from a comparison of 1 Kings, ix. 21, 22, and 2 Chronicles, viii. 8, 9, precisely what this kind of tributaryship was in personal service.

The law in regard to the Hittites, Amorites, Canaanites, Perizzites, Hivites, and Jebusites, was this; that they should be exterminated; nothing should be saved alive "that breatheth," in any of the cities of the people, whose land God had given to the Hebrews for their inheritance, Deuteronomy, xx. 15, 16, 17; also Deuteronomy, vii. 1–4. And the reason was plain, namely, "that they teach you not to do after all their abominations, which they have done unto their gods," Deuteronomy, xx. 18; Exodus, xxiii. 23, 33.

EXCEPTIONS UNDER THE LAW.—TREATY WITH THE GIBEONITES.

Only to the cities of other and distant heathen nations was peace to be proclaimed, and, if accepted, then the people were to be tributaries, as above; but if not accepted, and war was preferred, then all the males were to be destroyed, and the women and the little ones preserved, Deuteronomy, xx. 12–14. See, for an example of the manner in which this law was fulfilled, Numbers, xxxi. 7–18, in the war against the Midianites. The children of Israel took the women of Midian captives, and their little ones. See, also, in regard to the cities of the Canaanites, Joshua, vi. 21, and viii. 26; also, x. 32, 35, 37, 38, and xi. 11–19. And, for example of the different treatment of cities not of the Canaanites, see Joshua, ix. 15, 27, the league that was made with the Gibeonites, under the supposition that they were a distant people; and which was fulfilled, according to the law, as above, by which the distant nations were to be treated. The Gibeonites were made tributaries: "There shall none of you be freed from being bondmen, and hewers of wood and drawers of water for the house of my God," Joshua, ix. 23.

More than four hundred years afterwards, under the reign of David, this treaty was remembered, and a most tremendous judgment came upon the kingdom in consequence of its violation by Saul. The three years' famine mentioned in 1 Samuel, xxi. 1, was declared, of God, to be for Saul and for his bloody house, because he slew the Gibeonites. According to the treaty made with them by Joshua, they were to be always employed in the menial service of God's house. The treaty was kept. The city of Gibeon, with most of its dependencies, fell to the lot of the tribe of Benjamin for an inheritance, Joshua, xviii. 25. It was also, with its suburbs, appointed of God, by lot, to be one of the cities of the Levites, given to them for an inheritance out of Benjamin, Joshua, xxi. 17. But more than this, it became the place of the tabernacle* of the congregation of God, 1 Chronicles, xvi. 39, and xxi. 29, and also 2 Chronicles, i. 3; and the great high place of sacrifice, 1 Kings, iii. 4; and of the brazen altar before the tabernacle, 2 Chronicles, i. 5, where Solomon offered a thousand burnt-offerings at once; and where God appeared to Solomon, and entered into covenant with him, 1 Kings, iii. 5.

There is a remarkable coincidence between this historic fact and the tenor of the treaty with the Gibeonites, Joshua, ix.

---

* "Being brought thither as to the chief residence of the sons of Ithamar, who waited on the sanc-tuary when Shiloh fell."—LIGHTFOOT, vol. ii., p. 198.

27: "For Joshua made them hewers of wood and drawers of water for the congregation, and for the altar of the Lord, even unto this day, in the place which he should choose." No one could have foreseen that he would choose Gibeon; but so it was. Yet not in that city only did the Gibeonites serve the altar; but when the city was passed to the inheritance of the Levites, the Gibeonites and their race must have become the servants of the priests, "for the congregation and for the altar of the Lord," wherever the tabernacle was set up, as at Nob, the city of the priests, where David received the hallowed bread from Ahimelech, 1 Samuel, xxi. 1 and xxii. 19. In his wrath against Ahimelech, and against all that harbored David at that time, Saul not only slew the priests, fourscore and five, but destroyed the whole city of the priests, with all its inhabitants, 1 Samuel, xxii. 18, 19. This was the most atrocious and the hugest crime of all his reign. Nothing is to be found that can be compared with it.

Several points are now determined: 1st, The separation of a particular race to be bondmen of the altar, servants of the priests, for the service of God's house, in a class of labors indicated by the proverbial expression "hewers of wood and drawers of water." There is no intimation of the Gibeonites or their posterity ever being servants in any other way, or in private families. 2d, This service, and their separation and consecration for it as a race, was a boon granted them instead of death, which otherwise, by the Divine law, they must have suffered. They were spared, in consequence of the treaty with them; and the covenant with them was of life and labor as the servants of the sanctuary. The life was pleasant, the service was not over-toilsome; they accepted it with gratitude. 3d, The treaty was kept for hundreds of years; and from generation to generation the Gibeonites and their posterity fulfilled their part of it, continuing, as at first appointed, the servants of the sanctuary. 4th, Saul was the first who broke this treaty; and God's own view of its sacredness may be known by the terrible manner in which he avenged its breach, and continued to protect the Gibeonites. Saul had not only destroyed the city of Nob, but had " devised means by which the Gibeonites should be destroyed from remaining in any of the coasts of Israel," 2 Samuel, xxi. 4.

CASE OF THE NETHINIM.

It has been supposed that the Gibeonites constituted a part of the Nethinim, so often mentioned as the servants of the tabernacle and of the temple. The first trace of this name we meet in Numbers, iii. 9, and viii. 19, where the Levites are said to be given as a gift נְתוּנִים *nethinim*, from God to Aaron and his sons for the service of the tabernacle. Also, Numbers, xviii. 6. The verb from which this word is derived, נָתַן, *nathan*, is used by Joshua in describing the result of the treaty made with the Gibeonites: he gave or granted them to become, he set or established them, hewers of wood, etc., for the altar of the Lord, Joshua, ix. 27; he *nethinized* them for the service of the priests. So, in 1 Chronicles, vi. 48, the Levites are said to have been *appointed*, נְתוּנִים, *nethinized*, unto all manner of service in the tabernacle. In the same manner, for the service of the Levites, others were given, appointed, *nethinized ;* and this class, under the Levites, included the Gibeonites, and came to be designated, at length, apart from them, and from other servants, as the Nethinim, הַנְּתִינִים, 1 Chronicles, ix. 8, where the name first occurs as of a separate class; the people returned from the captivity in Babylon being designated as Israelites, Priests, Levites, and *the Nethinim*. Then the term occurs in Ezra, ii. 43, 58, coupled with the children of Solomon's servants, בְּנֵי עַבְדֵּי, in one and the same classification; all the Nethinim and the children of Solomon's servants, in number, three hundred and ninety-two. "The priests and the Levites, and some of the people, and the singers, and the porters, *and the Nethinim*, dwelt in their cities; and all Israel in their cities," Ezra, ii. 70. Priests, Le-

vites, singers, porters, and Nethinim are again specified in
Ezra, vii. 7; and, in verse 24, the edict of Artaxerxes is specified, forbidding any toll, tribute, or custom from being laid
upon priests, Levites, singers, porters, *Nethinim*, or ministers
of the house of God.

In Ezra, viii. 17–20, a message is sent to Iddo and his brethren *the Nethinim*, at the place Casiphia, for ministers for the
house of God; and in answer to this message, there were
sent, along with a number of Levites, two hundred and twenty Nethinim, of the Nethinim whom David and the princes
had appointed for the service of the Levites. In Nehemiah,
iii. 26, the Nethinim are recorded as having repaired their portion of the wall of Jerusalem, near their quarter in Ophel.
They are also enumerated, as in Ezra, along with *the children
of Solomon's servants*, as having come up from the captivity,
Nehemiah, vii. 60, 73. They are also recorded with the Levites, priests, and others, as parties in the great covenant
which the people renewed with God, to observe his statutes,
x. 28. The particular quarter of Jerusalem where they dwelt
is pointed out, and the names of the overseers that were over
them, Nehemiah, xi. 21. Others of them, as well as of the
priests, Levites, and children of Solomon's servants, dwelt in
other cities, according to their respective possessions and engagements, Nehemiah, xi. 3.

Their return to Jerusalem from the captivity was voluntary: they might have remained abroad. It was not a return
to slavery, but a resumption, of their own accord, of the service of the sanctuary, to which they had been devoted. So it
was, likewise, with "the children of Solomon's servants;" they
resumed their position in their native land, of their own
choice, and by no compulsion. And both the Nethinim and
the descendants of Solomon's servants, had their families and
lineal ancestry preserved in the genealogical register of the
nation. They had "entered into the congregation of the
Lord."

CASE OF THE SERVANTS OF THE CAPTIVE JEWS.

The enumeration given by Ezra of the returned people, is, for the whole congregation, forty-two thousand three hundred and sixty, besides their servants and their maids, עַבְדֵיהֶם וְאַמְהֹתֵיהֶם, of whom there were seven thousand three hundred thirty and seven; and there were among them two hundred singing men and singing women. At first sight it might have been supposed that these singing men and singing women formed a part of the train of servants; but it does not appear so from the corresponding record of Nehemiah: they were an additional class. They, with the servants and the maids, may all have been "bought" by the Jews during their captivity; but the purchase of a servant was no indication of slavery, where this language was customary to describe even the acquisition of a wife, or the buying of a Hebrew servant, who could not be a slave. The case of the free-born Hebrew *selling himself* for money, Leviticus, xxv. 47, is in point; and the same person who has thus voluntarily sold his own time for money is afterward said to have been *bought*, xxv. 51. Such was the common usage of the term, not at all implying slavery.

It seems remarkable that they should return from their captivity in such array: men-servants and maid-servants, עַבְדֵיהֶם וְאַמְהֹתֵיהֶם, seven thousand three hundred and thirty-seven; singing men and singing women two hundred and forty-five, Nehemiah, vii. 67. To account for this, we have to turn to the prophet Isaiah, to the prediction of God, that when he should have mercy upon his captive people, and set them again in their own land, "*the strangers should be joined with them*, and should bring them to their place, and the house of Israel should possess them in the land of the Lord *for servants and handmaids*, לַעֲבָדִים וְלִשְׁפָחוֹת, and they shall take them captives whose captives they were," Isaiah, xiv. 2. Here is a most remarkable fulfillment of prophecy. At the same time it is obvious that the whole arrangement of their servitude must have been of contract, and voluntary—a service for which remuneration was required and given. It must have been in every respect a service contracted and assumed, according to the principles and laws laid down in the Mosaic statutes, and in no respect a slavery such as those statutes were appointed to abolish.

It is to be noted that, in the language of Nehemiah, the term עֶבֶד, *evedh*, is not used in designating servants, but the word נַעַר, *naar, young man ;* as, for example, Nehemiah, v. 16, spoken of the governor's servants, נַעֲרֵיהֶם, having borne rule over the people; also v. 16, all Nehemiah's servants, כָּל־נְעָרַי ; also iv. 22, of the people with their servants, *every one with his servant,* אִישׁ וְנַעֲרוֹ ; also iv. 23, *I, nor my servants,* אֲנִי וּנְעָרַי. The same in v. 10, and other places. The usage is plain, and not to be mistaken. The same usage prevails in the book of Ruth.

On the other hand, when Nehemiah intends to describe what the Jews themselves had been in their captivity, he uses the word עֶבֶד, *evedh.* For example, chapter v. 5, We bring into bondage our sons and our daughters to be servants, כֹּבְשִׁים לַעֲבָדִים ; also ii. 10, Tobiah *the servant,* וְטוֹבִיָּה הָעֶבֶד ; also ix. 36, We are servants, עֲבָדִים ; and xi. 3, The children of Solomon's servants, עֲבָדִים.

There was a "mixed multitude" that came up with the Israelites from the captivity, xiii. 3, and of this multitude the two hundred and forty-five singing men and singing women must have formed a part. The servants belonged to the same class; and there were a large number of strange women of the Moabites, Ammonites, Egyptians, and others, with whom the people had intermarried, and formed families. These would bring their household servants with them; but the class designated by Nehemiah as נְעָרִים, *naarim,* must have been of a different character. They may have been free, and free-born in every respect, making their own contracts of service, and choosing their own masters. And whether עֶבֶד, *evedh*, or נַעַר, *naar*, whether strangers or natives of Palestine, they belonged, when circumcised, to the Jewish nation, and " might enter into the congregation of the Lord." They might have been slaves in Egypt, or Ethiopia, or Assyria, but they could not be such in Judea; on the contrary, however degraded, in whatever country from which they came, the Mosaic Institutes immediately began to elevate and emancipate them.

We find an interesting and important instance in the episode related in 1 Chronicles, ii. 34, 35—the case of the Egyptian Jarha, the servant of Sheshan, and adopted by him as his son, to whom he gave his daughter to wife, and the Jewish genealogy of the family continued uninterrupted in the line of their children. This is an instructive commentary on the laws; and, being a case nearly parallel, in point of time, with the transactions in the book of Ruth (for Sheshan must have been nearly cotemporary with Boaz), it indicates, as well as that history, the admirable contrast between the freedom prevalent in Judea and the despotism in every other country. " I am the Lord your God, which brought you forth out of the land of Egypt, that ye should not be their bondmen; and I have broken the bands of your yoke, and made you go upright," Leviticus, xxvi. 13. The same emancipating power, exerted by God's interposing and protecting providence and discipline upon the Jews themselves, was also exercised by the system of statutes, privileges, and instructions under which the poorest and humblest creature in the land was brought, upon the bond-servants taken from the heathen: the bands of *their* yoke were broken, and they were made to go upright. " Thou shalt not abhor an Edomite, for he is thy brother; thou shalt not abhor an Egyptian, because thou wast a stranger in his land. The children that are begotten of them shall enter into the congregation of the Lord in their third generation," Deuteronomy, xxiii. 7, 8.

The people and the nation were absolutely forbidden to treat any race of strangers in their land as they had themselves been treated in the land of Egypt. Ye shall not oppress the stranger, for ye know the heart of the stranger, for ye were strangers in the land of Egypt; and the stranger in your own land shall not be treated as ye were treated in the land of your bondage. Such was the benevolent tenor, and such the explicit benevolent letter, of the laws of God in regard to the treatment of other races brought into Judea or sojourning in the land. How absurdly incongruous with these statutes is the supposition, which nevertheless many persons entertain, that the Hebrews were at liberty to make slaves of the heathen, the strangers round about. They were expressly interdicted from any such oppression, and warned against it. Their laws made it impossible. The reprobation of God against it is a solemn indication of the exasperated greatness of the sin in his sight, the sin against God and man, when a Christian nation, under so much greater light, distinctly enacts and practices, on a vast scale, the oppressive cruelty which he has forbidden; brands a whole race of human beings as fit stuff only for slavery; assumes the rightful possession of them for such bondage, to make perpetual slaves out of them, to be a supply of chattels from generation to generation.

HYPOCRISY AND CRUELTY OF SLAVE THEOLOGY.

As God is said to have given to Christ the heathen for his inheritance, to save them, so the patrons, theologians, and devout workers and brokers of the slave theology profess to have received the Africans as their inheritance, to bring them through the hell of slavery (which in this case is the highest missionary agency,) to the heaven of a servile piety. It is impossible to regard without horror the diabolic caricature of religion, which has been evoked as from the bottomless pit, in support of this atrocity, and set with anthems in the church of Christ, with a more blasphemous impiety than ever attended the enshrinement of Dagon or of Baal in the temple of the living God. The public solemn excommunication of a race of human beings from all the rights of humanity, and the consecration of them in the name of piety and justice to the perpetual condition of a slavery in many respects the most cruel and unmitigated ever known upon the globe, was a spectacle reserved for the government, judiciary, and people of the United States of America in the nineteenth century of the Christian era. When we behold such a transaction, and read the new enactments and decisions of sweeping and exacerbated cruelty, with which the vast speculative crime is being consummated in practice, we are filled with wonder at the long-suffering of God, that the bolts of divine vengeance do not suddenly break upon such a nation and people.

It has been supposed that this system of iniquity could scarcely be carried to a higher point of juridical impiety than in the decision by the Chief Justice of the United States in the case of Dred Scott—a decision which was, in fact, a decree for the moral assassination of the race. But every step in this sin is onward, none backward, and the States are not to be outdone by the national government in their advancement. It might have been imagined that the slave code was already sufficiently barbarous, but the Dred Scott decision has shown that there was room for improvement, and now it is publicly decreed that negroes, or persons having the least tincture of African blood, are an inferior race, aliens, and not only aliens but enemies, excluded from civilized governments and the family of nations, and doomed to slavery. " It is the policy of this State," says the High Court of Errors and Appeals of the State of Mississippi, " to interdict commerce and comity with this race, and by law expressly provided, we enforce the strictest doctrines of the ancient law as applicable to alien enemies, except as to life and limb, against them. We enslave them for life if they dare set their foot on our soil and omit to leave on notice in ten days, and this not on the prin-

ciple, supposed by some, of enmity, inhumanity or unkindness
to such inferior race, but on the great principles of self-preservation which have induced civilized nations in every age of
the world to regard them as only fit for slaves."

The hypocrisy that, in a Christian State, in the tribunal of
justice, could pretend a necessity of self-preservation as the
motive and the justification for such atrocities, is quite equal
to the malignity of the atrocities themselves. In the lowest
pitch of Jewish or of pagan degradation no ancient people
ever sank so low as this; even when any of the old uncivil-
ized or demon nationalities contemplated a similar crime, they
were not so lost to all truth and decency as to proclaim the
falsehood that their own existence depended on the subjection of a race of slaves, and that therefore they were not
inhumanly, but most righteously, willingly and of necessity
forced into such wickedness as a measure of self-defense. It
was not till they had arrived at such a condition that they
could compass the betrayal and crucifixion of the Saviour of
mankind, their own Messiah, that even the Jews could profess, as a justification of this murder, through the lips of the
high priest of their religion and their justice, that it was
necessary for the welfare of the state that one man should be
sacrificed, "that the whole nation perish not." These two
crimes, the crucifixion of Christ and the consecration of the
African race to slavery, on the same plea of state necessity,
show that nothing but the affinity of the same depravity is
wanting, to make even two such extremes meet in their uttermost corruption, as those of ancient Judaism and modern
Christianity; the same cruel selfishness will convert them, as
with one leaven, into the same putrid mass. The Christianity
that, under the plea of self-preservation, or, still worse, of a
missionary benevolence, can maintain slavery as an element
of justice and humanity, is not a whit behind the religion
that, in the name of a religious state compassion and necessity, could crucify the Saviour of the world.

In addition to the horrible barbarity which, by an act of national piracy, takes possession of a race of strangers and condemns them to be sold as slaves, just as savage wreckers would seize a stranded ship thrown upon the coast and steal both crew and cargo, or destroy the crew to possess the cargo,—in addition to this barbarity, the slave jurisprudence of our country proceeds to an extreme that never disgraced any other, that of excluding the miserable victims of such cruelty from all possibility of an appeal to justice against any violence or wrong, however diabolical. The laws of the Jews commended the stranger to the protection of the same statutes by which the people of the land were secured from cruelty and fraud. The laws even of the Romans provided *some* appeals to religion, if not justice, for the lowest slaves.* Our Christian system denies all possibility of any rights belonging to this persecuted, tortured, colored race, that their white persecutors, their missionary saviours, are bound to respect. We cast them out as mere things, chattels, and not persons, from all possibility of any appearance or *status* in a court of justice, or any claim upon the laws of the coun-

---

* A fugitive slave, who entered a temple, or embraced a statue of a god, or of an emperor, could not be restored to his own master, but could claim from the magistrate the privilege of being sold at auction, the privilege, at least, of a change of masters. The slaves were also allowed a *peculium* of their own, which might increase, by industry, to a small patrimony, enabling them to buy their own liberty. But the slave in America finds mercy neither from religion nor the law. The state of perpetual slavery is impudently proclaimed to be, for him, the highest happiness of which he is capable on earth, and the surest pathway to the happiness of heaven. The laws against emancipation, and in favor of slavery, are every year more rigid, and every new decision is made more unalterably against freedom. Mr. Baker Woodruff, a slave owner in New Orleans, who died in May, 1857, ordered in his will that his slaves, sixty-two in number, should be liberated and sent to Pennsylvania, providing also for their passage thither and their support during the first year. The permission to apply any portion of the estate for the execution of this will was denied by the court, on the ground that the slaves could not be liberated. The Supreme Court of Appeals, in April, 1859, decided in the same way, and the slaves have been sold.

try, save the security of being oppressed by those laws. They are subjects of law for oppression only, for use and abuse at the will of their so-called owners. It is not possible to convey in human language an adequate idea of the complication of cruelty and wrong, impiety toward God, inhumanity toward man, defiance and violation of all just law, human and divine, and of every sentiment of benevolence and justice in the law of nature engraven on the common heart and conscience of mankind, with which, in this Christian country, and by a professedly Christian people, the miserable race of outcasts and yet natives, subjected to the state of slavery, are treated on the plea of having a skin not colored like our own.

But the very worst feature of the crime is this, that the popular religion of the country accepts, defends and sanctions it; and those persons are held to be bad citizens, agitators, disturbers, dangerous to the peace and good order of the state, suspicious and afflictive members of the church, not who defend slavery, but who oppose it, and demand its abolition as a sin against God and man! It hurts no man's character or popularity to be a slaveholder; it does not exclude him from membership even in missionary churches, nor from the station of corporate membership or directorship in missionary or Bible associations; on the contrary, the ownership of slaves, or a known fellowship with the owners of them as Christians of unspotted piety, and a defense of the propriety and expediency of such continued ownership, make up an element of conservatism, that rather increases than diminishes the influence of such a member of society. And Christian preachers can, without losing caste, declare, that if by a single prayer they could emancipate the slaves they would not do it; that under Christian masters no condition can be conceived more favorable to salvation than that of the slaves; that slavery possesses the divine sanction; that nevertheless it is "a sore social evil, but was entailed upon us by God, that freedom might be established and Christianity spread over Africa!" Such monstrous wens and excrescences of moral pestilence men can carry about with them, and not be shunned by a sane and healthful society, nor quarantined in it; while they who lift up their voices against this iniquity, and denounce it in the name of God, especially from his Word, from the pulpit on the Sabbath day, are marked for avoidance and suspicion, and wherever it is possible, ejected from their parishes, and shut out from the opportunity of ministering God's truth.

What an amazing and portentous phase of the Christian religion, what judicial blindness it would seem to intimate, and a state like that of the idolaters under the light of divine revelation, as described by the prophet Isaiah; men who, with their eyes open, could carve out their own gods for themselves, as schoolboys might cut a whistle or an image from a poplar branch, and burn the remainder of the stick in the fire; could carry their gods under their girdles or in their trowsers' pockets, and yet not be able even to suspect the folly of such idiotic debasement; not so much unclouded reason left as to be capable of asking, "Is there not a lie in my right hand?" It is an equally strange inconsistency, when men in one and the same breath proclaim, to the honor of Christianity, that its prevalence abolished Roman slavery, when almost universal through the world, and that the very same Christianity, better known, reinstates a worse slavery in religious and enlightened America, and inaugurates it as God's last, chosen and most effective system of social, civil, and missionary progress and refinement!

CHAPTER XVII.

CASE OF THE CHILDREN OF SOLOMON'S SERVANTS, AND OF THE STRANGERS APPOINTED TO LABOR.

The children of Solomon's servants, as well as the Nethinim, have the honor of being registered, according to their genealogy by families, as in Nehemiah, vii. 57–60. Ten individuals, or heads of families, are named; and their children are the children of Solomon's servants, numbering, together with the Nethinim, only three hundred and ninety-two. From the context it would appear that their fathers' house was considered of Israel; and they, being able to show their genealogy, were honorably distinguished from others, who could not show their fathers' house, nor their pedigree, whether they were of Israel, Nehemiah, vii. 61. On the whole, it would seem that they were a favored class, and honorably distinguished by their service, which was to them an hereditary privilege worthy of being retained, and not an ignoble or a toilsome separation, nor a mark of bondage.

We must, however, consider their state and probable employment, in connection with the following passages and proofs in regard to the tributary service levied by Solomon upon them and similar classes. In 2 Chronicles, ii. 17, 18, we find it recorded that Solomon numbered all the strangers that were in the land of Israel, after the numbering wherewith

used in 2 Chronicles, viii. 9, and 1 Kings, ix. 21, of the tribute
of bond-service levied by Solomon.   See Joshua, xv. 63 and
xvii. 12, 13; also Judges, i. 21, 27, 28, 30, 33, 35; also iii. 3, 5.
This tributary service did not make them all hereditary bondmen; but was a tax of service to a certain amount, levied
according to fixed rules, so that these foreign races must supply a sufficient number of laborers to work out that tax.   The
tax was a perpetual tribute; consequently, the bond-service
by which it must be paid, was perpetual, unless there had been
a system of commutation, of which, however, we find no direct
evidence.   It was only the races of the land of Canaan, such
as are mentioned in 1 Kings, ix. 20, 21, and 2 Chronicles, viii.
7, that could by law be thus treated; and such treatment was
itself, in reality, a merciful commutation, instead of that destruction to which they had originally been devoted.

The numbering of these strangers for the work of building
the temple, was begun by David; that work was a public,
national, and religious service, such as that to which the Gibeonites, more especially, from the outset had been consecrated,
at a time when it was supposed that they only, of all the inhabitants of Canaan, would have been spared.   But a great
many others were spared also; so that, in the general numbering of the people by Joab, at David's command, 2 Samuel,
xxiv. 2, and 1 Chronicles, xxi. 2, the cities of the Hivites and
of the Canaanites are particularly designated, 2 Samuel, xxiv.
7; and comparing this with Joshua, xvii. 12, and Judges, i. 27
–33, there is reason to suppose that the particular designation
is with reference to the class of inhabitants.   In this general
census of the people, Joab seems to have noted these "strangers" by themselves; and after this census "David commanded to gather together *the strangers* that were in the land
of Israel, and he set masons to hew wrought stones to build
the house of God," 1 Chronicles, xxii. 2.   It is doubtless to this
that the reference is made in 2 Chronicles, ii. 17, "Solomon
numbered *all the strangers* that were in the land of Israel,

after the numbering wherewith David his father had numbered them."

That the strangers numbered and appointed for their work by David, and those numbered and appointed by Solomon, were of the same class, and that this class comprised the races named in Solomon's catalogue of tribes from whom he levied his tribute of bond-service, is rendered more certain by an examination of the number of foreigners or strangers of all classes that must have been, at this time, under the royal government of Israel. In 1 Chronicles, v. 10, 19, 20, 21, there is an account of a battle between the Reubenites and a very numerous tribe of Hagarites, in which the children of Israel gained a great victory, insomuch that they captured a hundred thousand souls. This was in the days of Saul. Besides these Hagarites, it is evident that the number of tributaries must have greatly increased from David's own wars, as is proved in 2 Samuel, viii. 4, 14. We should have a census of more than a hundred and fifty thousand "strangers," from these transactions alone; so that the number recorded in 2 Chronicles, ii. 17 (a hundred and fifty-three thousand and six hundred) as being all the strangers in the land of Israel, must be taken as rated for legal bond-service, from the nations or remaining races of the Canaanites only.

In this connection we must remember the law in regard to all heathen nations conquered in war, (except the Hittites, Amorites, Canaanites, Hivites, Perizzites, and Jebusites, devoted to extermination,) which was as follows, Deuteronomy, xx. 10, 11: "When thou comest nigh to a city to fight against it, then proclaim peace unto it; and it shall be, if it make thee answer of peace, and open unto thee, then it shall be that all the people that is found therein *shall be tributaries unto thee, and they shall serve thee*." Between these and the races of the Canaanites there seems to have been a distinction as to treatment always maintained. It would seem that Leviticus, xxv. 45, "Of the children of the strangers that do sojourn

among you, of them shall ye buy," must refer particularly to
the Canaanitish races, as we shall see more particularly in the
examination of that passage. These nations and their descendants were to be made to pay a tribute of bond-service, such
as the Hebrews could not exact from all the heathen, and
were forbidden to impose on one another. Accordingly, in
the account of such bond-service, as laid by Solomon on the
descendants of these races, it is expressly stated in contrast,
that " of the children of Israel did Solomon make no bondmen." A levy was raised at the same time, from all Israel,
of thirty thousand men who labored in Lebanon, ten thousand
a month, by courses, 1 Kings, v. 13, 14 ; but this was very
different from the tribute of bond-service levied, which comprised the threescore and ten thousand that bare burdens, and
fourscore thousand hewers in the mountains. Along with
these tributary and hereditary laborers, there were united the
laborers obtained from Hiram, king of Tyre, for whose service
Solomon paid Hiram, but not them : " unto thee will I give
hire for thy servants, according to all that thou shalt appoint,"
1 Kings, v. 6.

That the condition of the races under this law of tributary
service was not one of general or oppressive bondage, is clear
from the position in which Araunah, the Jebusite, appears before us in the interview between him and David, 2 Samuel,
xxiv. Araunah, although of the tributary race, is a substan-
tial householder and farmer, dwelling amidst his own possessions, and making a bargain with king David, as in every respect a freeman. Uriah, also, though high in the service of
David, and having his house at Jerusalem, was a Hittite. The
tributary service was evidently a very different thing from
universal personal servitude. In the same way, from the
transaction recorded in Exodus, ii. 9, we learn that the servitude of the Hebrews in Egypt was not so universal as that all
were slaves, or treated as such. Pharaoh's daughter makes a
bargain with the mother of Moses, for a nurse's service, and

gives her her wages. The woman is free to make such a bargain, and to receive such wages on her own account. There is no master over her, notwithstanding that the tyranny of Pharaoh is so terrible that she dare not acknowledge her own child, lest he be put to death.

In our own country there is a service of tribute, called the highway tax. Those who do not choose to pay this tax in money, may work it out, if they please, in person, or may hire laborers to work it out for them. The service of tribute levied upon the strangers in Judea, must have been something such a service. It is possible that David's sin against God in numbering the people, may have consisted in some purposed odious distinction, oppressive and illegal, by which it was intended to set apart the descendants of the strange or foreign races, and to exact from them a tribute or impose upon them a bondage, in connection with the building of the temple, displeasing to God, and manifesting the style of a conqueror, a despot, rather than a constitutional king. Joab's expostulation on the occasion, intimates some such difficulty; for he takes pains to remind David that all the inhabitants of the land are equally the king's servants; why then doth my Lord require this thing? why will he be a cause of trespass to Israel? Any such bondage of service as the Israelites had endured in Egypt, if laid upon the strangers in Israel, would have been contrary to the divine law. They were to be tributaries to the government, but not personal servants, except at their own pleasure. To treat them with cruelty, or make them the subjects of oppression such as the people of God had endured in Egypt, was explicitly and many times forbidden. They could not be treated as the king's or any man's property, they could not be made slaves; no service was ever to be laid upon them, which would take away their rights as freemen.

Michaelis, in his Commentaries on the Laws of Moses, (vol. ii., page 185,) presents a Jewish Rabbinical story, illustrative of the oppression of taking men's labor without wages. The Egyptians (so the Jews relate,) sued the Jews for the, gold and silver vessels carried off by their ancestors at their departure from Egypt, (the transaction of borrowing,) and insisted on their making restitution. One should suppose that the Jews would have pleaded the law of prescription. But they did no such thing. They readily admitted the claim, and offered restitution; but they at the same time preferred a counter-claim of their own. For two hundred and ten years, said they, we were in Egypt, to the number of 600,000 men. We therefore, demand days' wages for that period, at the rate of a *denarius* for each man; and our account stands thus: $365 \times 210 = 76,650$ days, the time of each man. This multiplied by 600,000 men, gives of *denarii*, 45,990,000,000, that is, of our money, two thousand eight hundred and seventy-four millions of ducats. On this the Egyptians began to wax warm, and dropped their suit.

If a bill of this nature were made out by the four millions of slaves in our country, who could compute the amount of our robbery of their just wages? But God has calculated it, and in good time will send in his bill for settlement.*

---

* GRANVILLE SHARPE. Law of Retribution against Tyrants, Slaveholders, and Oppressors. Compare SIR JAMES MACKINTOSH'S speech in the case of the Missionary Smith, Works, Vol. III., p. 405. Compare, also, WHEWELL, Elements of Morality, and DYMOND, Essays, ch. xviii. "Every hour of every day the present possessor is guilty of injustice." The guilt of rendering the crime hereditary no man has attempted to compute. God only can measure it. The necessity of its abolition by the State becomes more and more urgent, because of the future, and WHEWELL (Vol. II., 1003, Duty of Abolition by the State) notes that "a State cannot neglect this, without divesting itself, to an extent shocking to all good men, of its moral character, and renouncing its hope of that moral progress which is (ought to be) its highest purpose." Compare GOODELL, American Slave Code. Ownership and use without wages. Part L, ch. v., 10, 12

CHAPTER XVIII.

THE first moral judgment of God concerning the slavery of
Egypt was impressed upon the mind of Abraham in the covenant which God made with him : "Know of a surety that thy
seed shall be a stranger in a land that is not theirs, and
they shall serve them, וַעֲבָדוּם; and they shall afflict them, וְעִנּוּ;
and also that nation whom they shall serve will I judge." The
moral sense of Abraham was sufficiently enlightened to know
that not simply because the subjects of oppression were of his
seed, was such oppression sinful, but that the bondage, unless
inflicted of God as a punishment for sin, was itself sinful. The
slavery prevalent in Egypt is here condemned as a crime
worthy to be punished.

The first historical description of it, after this prophetic
judgment, is in Exodus, i. 11 : "They did set over them taskmasters, to afflict them with their burdens," שָׂרֵי מִסִּים לְמַעַן עַנֹּתוֹ,
בְּסִבְלֹתָם, overseers of tribute, on purpose for their oppression in
their burdens. "And the Egyptians made the children of Israel to serve with rigor, and they made their lives bitter with
hard bondage, בַּעֲבֹדָה קָשָׁה, hard labor, in mortar and in brick,
and in all manner of service in the field; all their service
wherein they made them serve was with rigor," Exodus, i. 13,
14. Now therefore behold the cry of the children of Israel is
come unto me : and I have also seen the oppression, לַחַץ, wherewith the Egyptians oppress them, Exodus, iii. 9. The same

word is used in Exodus, xxiii. 9: "Thou shalt not oppress a stranger." This dreadful bondage was a type of the slavery of sin; as also the passover, in memory of their deliverance, was a most affecting and powerfully significant type of redemption by the blood of Christ.

This bondage, continued, would have become a *Helotism*, and was fast verging to a system of perpetuated oppression and cruelty, like that described by historians as having been endured by the unhappy conquered victims of despotism in the Spartan state. It might have been all that, and still at a great remove from the dehumanizing cruelty of American slavery.*

---

* GROTE'S HISTORY OF GREECE, vol. ii., pp. 372-379. Helots in the Villages.

The condition of the Helots under the tyranny of Sparta, treated like slaves, yet never sold out of the country, and, probably, never sold at all; beaten, down-trodden, put to death without punishment of their murderers, yet belonging not so much to the master as to the State; "living in the rural villages as *adscripti glebæ*, cultivating their lands, and paying over their rent to the master at Sparta, but enjoying their homes, wives, families and mutual neighborly feelings apart from the master's view;"—this condition would represent much more nearly the state of the Hebrews under their Egyptian bondage, and would give a fairer idea of their oppression, than can be drawn from modern slavery. The Helots were a conquered race. The word, according to some etymologists, is synonymous with *captive*; according to others, derived from the town of Helos, " which the Spartans are said to have taken after a resistance so obstinate as to provoke them to deal very rigorously with the captives." They were a part of the State, "having their domestic and social sympathies developed, a certain power of acquiring property, and the consciousness of Grecian lineage and dialect."

Deprived of their liberty, oppressed and maltreated, they were dreaded by their tyrants, who adopted measures against them, to prevent their increase and insurrection, singularly reminding us of the policy of Pharaoh and the princes of Egypt towards the Hebrews. The terror of Helotic revolt sharpened the cruelty of the Spartans, and led them to " combinations of cunning and atrocity, which even yet stand without parallel in the long list of precautions for fortifying unjust dominion." On the authority of Thucydides we learn that on one occasion two thousand of the bravest among the Helots were entrapped by promises of liberty, and assassinated at once. On the authority of Plutarch, from Aristotle, it was an institution of the State, that every year war should be declared against the Helots, " in order that the murder of them might be rendered innocent;" and that " active young Spartans should be armed with daggers and

Out of this bondage, when God delivered them, they went up, "about six hundred thousand men, on foot, besides children; and a mixed multitude went up also with them, and flocks, and herds, very much cattle," Exodus, xii. 37, 38. The

sent about Laconia, either in solitude or at night, to assassinate such of the Helots as were considered formidable."

How long it may be before the incomparably more atrocious and criminal system of American slavery, with the frightful increase and intelligence of its victims, may lead to similar horrible combinations on the part of masters and of the government, and similar assassinations, sanctioned by law, under pretense of the necessity of self-defense from the apprehended horrors of a servile insurrection, is only known to that God whose own vengeance merely waits the justest and most perfect time. Meanwhile, the proposed reduction of the free blacks into slavery, the doctrine practiced as an edict, that black men have no rights that white men are bound to respect, the renewal and intended sanction of the foreign slave-trade by law, the proposed establishment of slavery in free territories, and enactment by the government of a special code of slave laws for the protection and perpetuity of slave-property, in addition to the savage barbarity of existing State slave codes, make the crime and guilt of this Christian people incomparably greater than any ever committed by the government or people of Sparta, or any other pagan nation in the world. What we think to sanction, and defend from Heaven's reprobation, and commend as duty to Christian families and churches by human law, is a far greater outrage of the conscience, and

defiance against God and nature, than the law of war against the Helots on purpose for the sanction of their murder.

The *manumitted* Helots, those who had gained their liberty by signal bravery, and those whose superior beauty or stature placed them above the visible stamp of their condition, were regarded in the Lacedemonian community with peculiar apprehension, and if not put to death, were employed on foreign service, *or planted on some foreign soil as settlers.* The intervention of colonization societies as safety valves for the security of slave property in this country, had not been suggested, neither does it seem to have been the custom to imprison the subjects of such tyranny and jealousy, and then sell them for their jail fees. But it is stated that the Helots "were beaten every year, without any special fault, in order to put them in mind of their slavery; while such masters as neglected to keep down the spirit of their vigorous Helots were punished."

Slave-breeding does not seem to have been an element of the Spartan chivalry, nor an employment of the first families, or oldest and most aristocratic class of the State. The selling of slaves not being customary, the breeding of them for high prices never came to be a profitable business. Indeed, in this quality of glory, this feat of mammon and of morals, the Christian slave States of America surpass the accomplishments of any other age or nation in the world.

mixed multitude, עֵרֶב רַב, are nowhere definitely described. The question whether they had bond-servants of their own, whom they carried away with them from Egypt, might possibly be settled could we have a classification of that *mixed multitude*. On the whole, it seems not probable that any Egyptians were under bond-service to them, and their own race were certainly not slaves to one another, though they might be servants. If they had foreign servants, not of their own race, we judge (from the manner of the enumeration in a similar case, namely, the return of the Jews from the captivity in Babylon), it would have been distinctly stated. In Ezra, ii. 64, 65, and Nehemiah, vii. 66, 67, as already noted, the number of the whole congregation of Israel, is first given, as in Exodus, and then it is added, "besides their men-servants and their maid-servants, of whom there were seven thousand three hundred and thirty-seven." The whole number of the people to be cared for and to be fed, are again mentioned by Moses in Numbers, xi. 21, as six hundred thousand footmen, no reference being made to any others than those named in the first census. The mixed multitude, also, are again referred to in the same chapter by themselves: "The mixed multitude that was among them fell a lusting," Numbers, xi. 4; but no reference is found to the servants among them.

In regard to this point, it is impossible to determine absolutely from the law of the passover, because that law looked to the future condition of the congregation, providing for future emergencies. No uncircumcised stranger might eat of the passover; but every man's servant, bought for money and circumcised, might eat of it. The uncircumcised foreigner and hired servant might not eat of it; and both the home-born and the stranger were under one and the same law in regard to it, Exodus, xii. 43–49; Numbers, ix.14. The servant bought for money was bought into the Lord's family; he was, in point of fact, redeemed from bondage into comparative freedom, taken under God's especial care, and from a system of lawless slavery, passed into a system of responsibility to God, both on the part of the master and on his own part. It was a change of amazing mercy, from hopeless heathenish bondage to the dignity of citizenship in the commonwealth of Israel.

RELIGIOUS PRIVILEGES OF SERVANTS.—LAW OF THE SABBATH.

After the law of the passover, the first indication looking to the condition of servants is in the law of the Sabbath, Exodus, xx. 10: "Thou shalt not do any work; thou, nor thy son, nor thy daughter, *thy man-servant, nor thy maid-servant,* וַאֲמָתְךָ עַבְדְּךָ." This was a provision unheard of in the world, a provision necessary for the religious privileges and freedom of those under servitude, a provision which alone, if there had been no other, would have separated the condition of servants and the system of menial service, among the Hebrews, from that among any other people on earth, raising it to a participation in the care and sanction of God, and transfiguring it with social dignity and liberty. Such would be the effect of the Sabbath, fully observed according to its intent and precept, upon the system of labor and the condition of the laboring man, all the world over; for the Sabbath is the master-key to all forms and means of social regeneration, freedom, and happiness. But it was a new thing in the world for the leading, governing gift, privilege, and institution of instruction, refinement, and piety to be conferred upon the poor as well as the rich; upon the serving and laboring classes equally with the ruling; and appointed as directly and on purpose for the enjoyment and benefit of the one class as of the other. The work of the transfiguration of the toil and bondage into a system of free and voluntary service, carefully defined, protected, and rewarded, adopted and adorned of God with all the equalizing religious rights flowing from a theocracy to the whole people; this work, thus begun in the appointment of the Sabbath, was carried on, as we shall see, in the same spirit, and with the same purpose, in all additional regulations, till society, in this its normal form, became (as it would have continued, in reality, if the appointed form had been carried out) a fit type of the Christian dispensation to come, "where there is neither Jew nor Greek, circumcision nor uncircumcision, barbarian, Scythian, bond nor free; but Christ all and in all," Colossians, iii. 11, and Galatians, iii. 28. Such an institution of free and willing service, guarded by the law as an integral portion of a free and happy state, was preparing and molding, by divine command, and in form was perfected, as should not need to be put away or unclothed, at Christ's coming, but was fitted to be clothed upon with his Spirit, and sanctioned by his benediction. This was to take the place of slavery, was to put slavery out of existence; and, wherever and whenever the oppressed of other communities should be gathered beneath its operation, was to make freemen of slaves.

There is a striking particularity in one of the repetitions of the law of the Sabbath, Exodus, xxiii. 12, where the servile classes specified in the first normal form are omitted, and the purpose of the Sabbath's rest is stated to be "*that the son of thine handmaid, and the stranger, may be refreshed.*" Here the expression, "son of thine handmaid," is בֶּן־אֲמָתְךָ, the same as used in Psalm cxvi. 16, of David: "I am thy servant, and *the son of thine handmaid.*" I am not *a* servant, but *thy* servant, and the son of thine handmaid. The son of the handmaid, in Exodus, xxiii. 12, is catalogued in the same class and standing with the free stranger; and the passage is certainly, in some measure, a key to the interpretation of the expressions, בֶּן־בֵּיתִי and יְלִיד־בַּיִת, Genesis, xv. 3; xvii. 12, 13; Leviticus, xxiii. 11; Ecclesiastes, ii. 7; and Jeremiah, ii. 14. These expressions, so far from indicating *slaves*, as the assumptions and perverse interpretations of some lexicographers and translators might lead the English reader to suppose, do not necessarily even mean *servants*, but are a form of expression purposely separate and different from the generic appellation for servants, because they intimated a relation to the master, and the family which was *not* that of servants. The condition of the child did *not* follow that of the parent; but, after the period of natural dependence and minority, the בְּנֵי־בָיִת and the יְלִידֵי בָיִת, the *sons of the house*, and the *born of the house*, or *home-born*, were their own masters, free to choose for themselves the master whom they would serve, and the terms on which they would serve him. This is susceptible of demonstration beyond possibility of denial in regard to children of Hebrew descent, because not even the parents could, by law, be kept as servants longer than six years; and, of course, the children, being Hebrews equally with the parents, and coming under the same law, could no more be so held than the parents themselves.

This shows how monstrous is the assumption and perversion of the lexicons, beginning with the *fons et origo* of modern interpretation, that of Gesenius, when they deliberately, and without one particle of proof, render these expressions by the Latin word, *verna*, followed by English translators with the word *slave*. Neither by periphrasis, nor literal signification, can these expressions be so interpreted; never, in any case, in which they are used. And if the literal interpretation had, in every case, been adhered to, *sons of the house* and *born of the house*, instead of the word *slave*, employed in the lexicons, or *servant*, which is mostly used in our translation, no one could have connected the idea of servitude with these expressions, much less the idea of slavery. For example, the literal translation of Ecclesiastes, ii. 7, is thus: "I obtained servants and maidens, *and there were to me sons of the house*," וּבְנֵי־בָיִת הָיָה לִי, a relationship of dependence, certainly, and showing wealth and perpetuity in the family, whose servants were not hirelings merely, but voluntary domestic fixtures, of choice as well as dependence; but not a relationship of compulsory servitude, or slavery, or of servants considered as property. Now the transfer of the degrading and infamous chattelism signified in the Latin word *verna* and the English word *slave* to such a relationship, and to the phrase *son of the house*, or *born of the house*, as its true meaning among the Hebrews, is one of the most unauthorized and outrageous perversions ever inflicted upon human language. It is almost blasphemous, as designed to fix the blot and infamy of slavery upon what was and is the noblest, most benevolent, most carefully guarded, freest, and most affectionate system of domestic service in the world.

It is a system of such freedom and benevolence, and so ingeniously designed and adapted to conquer every surrounding and prevailing form of slavery, and subdue it to itself, that its infinite superiority to the selfish law and oppressed condition of the world, and its enthronement of benevolence instead of power as the ruling impulse and object (in that part of social legislation especially, where the law and custom of mankind have made selfishness not only supreme, but just, expedient, and even necessary,) are something supernatural. The contrast and opposition of this system over against the creed and habit of power, luxury, oppressive selfishness, and slavery, so long prevalent without question of its right, is, by itself, an impregnable proof of the divine inspiration of the Pentateuch. It is a proof, the shining and the glory of which have been clouded and darkened by the anachronisms, prejudices, and misinterpretations of Biblical archæologists and translators, but which is destined to be yet cleared, and acknowledged by the Christian world with gratitude to God. We shall at length cease to look to Arab or Egyptian sheikhs and pashas for illustrations of the life of Abraham, and to Roman or American slaves for pictures of the Hebrew households.

THE YEAR SABBATH AND THE ANNUAL FEASTS.

But besides the weekly Sabbath of devotion, every seven years the land should keep a Sabbath of a whole year unto the Lord, the seventh year, a Sabbath of rest for the land,

and, in consequence, for all classes of servants: " And the Sabbath of the land shall be meat for you; for thee, and for thy servant, and for thy maid, and for thy hired servant, and for thy stranger that sojourneth with thee," Leviticus, xxv. 27. Here the עֶבֶד, the servant of all work, the אָמָה, the maid-servant, and the שָׂכִיר, the hired servant, are all specified ; the seventh year belongs to them as well as to their masters. In Exodus, xxiii. 11, 12, these two institutions of the year-sab-bath and the seventh-day Sabbath are coupled, and the pur-pose specified is that of rest and refreshment " for the son of thine handmaid and the stranger," בֶּן־אֲמָתְךָ וְהַגֵּר. Here are already two sevenths of the time of life guarantied to the serv-ants for rest and sacred discipline. The injunction of a cir-cumspect piety is added to the enactment of both these or-dinances.

Then in the same chapter, the three great annual feasts fol-low, enacted in order, Exodus, xxiii. 14–17, these enactments being drawn out with minute detail and precision in Deuter-onomy, xvi. 2–16, and they are designated as the Feast of Unleavened Bread, the Feast of Weeks, and the Feast of Tab-ernacles. In Exodus, xxxiv. 21–23, the weekly Sabbath and these three annual festivals are coupled in the same manner as the Sabbath and the seventh year of rest in Exodus, xxiii. The spirit of these festivals and their duration are described in Deuteronomy, xvi., and Leviticus, xxiii. 34–43. And the equalizing benevolence of these institutions is the more marked by the repetition of the rule: " Thou shalt rejoice in thy feast, before the Lord thy God; thou, and thy son, and thy daugh-ter, and thy man-servant, and thy maid-servant, and the Le-vite that is within thy gates, and the stranger, and the father-less, and the widow that are among you," Deuteronomy, xvi. 11. Taking into consideration the time necessary for going and returning to and from each of these great festivals, to-gether with their duration, we have in their observance some six weeks, or nearly another seventh of the whole time devoted, for the servants as well as the masters, to religious joy, and rest and refreshment.

Then, in addition, are to be reckoned the Feast of Trumpets, Leviticus, xxiii. 24, the Day of Atonement, xxiii. 27–34, and xvi. 29, the Feast of the New Moon, Numbers, xxviii. 11. Hosea, ii. 11 ; Ezekiel, xlvi. 1, 3. If to these we add the Feasts of Purim and the Dedication, and the oft-recurring joyous family festivals, 1 Samuel, xx. 6, Genesis, xxi. 8, we have more than three sevenths, or nearly one half the time of the servants given to them for their own disposal and enjoyment, instruction and piety, unvexed by servile labors, on a footing of almost absolute equality and affectionate familiarity and kindness with the whole household: father, mother, son, daughter, man-servant and maid-servant, all having the same religious rights and privileges—" They go from strength to strength, every one of them in Zion appearing before God." How beautiful, how elevating, how joyous was such a national religion, and how adapted to produce and renew continually that spirit of humility and love, in the exercise of which the whole law was concentrated and fulfilled.*

---

* SAALSCHUTZ. *Das Mosaische Recht.* Laws of Moses, Vol. II., 715, refers to the appellation of the Oak of Weeping, Gen. xxxv., 8, given on occasion of the death of Rebecca's nurse, as a proof of the intimacy and affectionate equality with which the servants entered among the family relationships of the Hebrews. SAALSCHUTZ remarks very truly that nothing more felicitous could have happened to a heathen slave than to have been sold into Judea, where a law prevailed, leading, central, fundamental, by which he was released from his master, if he choose to quit the service, for he could escape from him, and the whole Hebrew world were forbidden to do anything towards bringing him back, but were bound of God to shelter the fugitive. In all the earth there never has been such an expression of kindness in human law towards the oppressed and persecuted. Compare GRAVES on the Pentateuch, P. II., L. iii. Also, LELAND'S Divine Authority O. and N. T., 75. Also, Judge JAY on Hebrew Servitude.

CHAPTER XIX.

WE have seen what a transfiguration would be produced
by a religious and legal system, that gave to the servants
nearly one half their time for their own disposal, in the observance of the rites, and enjoyment of the privileges of the national religion. We are now to consider the times of service,
and the manner of treatment, both for Hebrew and heathen
servants, on engagements or contracts, always voluntary, and
arranged with legal exactness.

TIME AND TREATMENT OF THE HEBREW SERVANT.—THE SIX YEARS' CONTRACT.

The section in Exodus, xxi. 2–11, prescribing the time and
treatment for the Hebrew servant, is full of instruction : "If
thou buy a Hebrew servant, תִּקְנֶה עֶבֶד עִבְרִי, six years he shall
serve, יַעֲבֹד; and in the seventh he shall go out free for nothing," יֵצֵא לַחָפְשִׁי חִנָּם; his term of service expires, and he is free
without cost. He had himself sold his own time and labor to
his master, by contract, for six years—no longer; and this was
called buying a Hebrew servant. Such a servant was not the
master's property, nor is ever called such, although he might
have been described as "his money;" that is, he had paid in
money for his services, for so long a time, and, in that sense,

he was his money, but in no other. We have already noted the usage of the word קָנָה, to buy; and its application in describing the purchase of persons in such relations as to forbid the idea of property or slavery. This is one of those instances. The Hebrew servant was bought with money, yet he was in no sense a slave, or the property of his master. In entering into a six years' contract of service, he was said to have sold himself; yet he was not a slave. He might extend this contract to the longest period ever allowed by law, that is, to the Jubilee; yet still he was not property, he was not a slave; his service was the fulfillment of a voluntary contract, for which a stipulated equivalent was required, and given to himself. The reason for the adoption or appointment of six years for the ordinary legal contract of Hebrew servitude is not given; but doubtless the arrangement was based upon some previous custom or statute; perhaps some social law like that which must have led Jacob to propose a service of seven years to Laban for his wife, Genesis, xxix. 18, and six years for his cattle, Genesis, xxxii. 41. "Twenty years have I been in thy house; I served thee fourteen years for thy·two daughters, and six years for thy cattle." The period of service with the year of release, thus made a *septennium*, a week of years, the multiplication of which seven times brought them to the great Jubilee of universal national freedom, equality and joy.*

This section is to be compared with Deuteronomy, xv. 12–18 : *If thy brother be sold*, that is, *if he have hired himself*

---

* It is worthy of note, as indicating the general moral sense of the social circle in which Abraham, Isaac, and Jacob moved as patriarchal legislators, that even in Laban's mind, the idea of any man serving another without wages was absurd, not to say, immoral. Even a brother, a near kinsman was not expected to do this, much more a stranger; and if service without wages could not be imposed upon a member of a family, much more could not a stranger be compelled into such service. Laban's manner of speaking is an intimation that involuntary and unpaid servitude was, in their society, a thing unknown, an enormity. "Because thou art my brother, shouldst thou serve me for nought? Tell me, what shall thy wages be?" Genesis, xxix. 15.

to thee, and serve thee six years; or if a Hebrew woman do the same; then, when this period of service is ended, not only is he free, as above, but thou shalt not let him go away empty. Thou shalt furnish him liberally out of thy flock, and out of thy floor, and out of thy wine-press. This extraordinary provision of an outfit was some offset, and was intended to be such, for the comparatively low wages of a six years' עֶבֶד, *evedh,* or servant, as compared with the wages of a hired servant, by the year or by the day. It was a great inducement to continue the engagement to the end of the contract, and not be seeking another master. And at the same time it is enjoined as a reason why the master should be liberal in this outfit, that he has gained so much more from the labor of the servant in six years, than he could have done if he had contracted with him as a שָׂכִיר or hired servant. The computation is made as follows: *He hath been worth a double hired servant, in serving thee six years;* מִשְׁנֶה שְׂכַר שָׂכִיר עֲבָדְךָ, *double the wages of a hireling serving thee;* that is, if thou hadst hired a servant by the year, and kept him six years, he would have cost thee twice as much as a servant whom thou buyest or contractest with, for six years at a time.

AVERAGE OF WAGES.

Suppose that for a six years' term a man could be engaged for eighteen shekels; then a yearly hired servant could not be got for less than six shekels the year; it would, therefore, in most cases, be more desirable to engage a six years' עֶבֶד, *evedh,* than to hire by the year; and, notwithstanding the difference in price, it might, in many cases, be more desirable for the servant also. Micah, in the case recorded in Judges, xvii., hired a young Levite from Bethlehem Judah, to dwell with him as his priest, for wages; and he gave him ten shekels of silver, and a suit of apparel, and his victuals, *by the year.* There are no such examples of specific contracts with ordinary servants recorded; but the price of Joseph's sale to the merchant-men of the Midianites, was twenty skekels of silver. The sum to be paid when a man-servant or maid-servant was gored to death by an ox was thirty shekels of silver to the master, Exodus, xxi. 32, the price, perhaps, of a six years' contract. The price of the prophet, in Zechariah, xi. 12, or the hire or wages, (שְׂכָרִי is the word used,) at which he and his services were valued, and paid, was thirty shekels of silver. The redemption-price for a man who had vowed himself to the Lord, was fifty shekels of silver from twenty years of age till sixty; and for a woman, thirty shekels; from five years to twenty, twenty shekels for a man, ten for a woman; from a month to five years old, five shekels for the man-child, three for the girl. And it is added, from sixty years old and above, fifteen for the man, ten for the woman. This was the priest's estimation of the persons for the Lord, Leviticus, xxvii. 2–7. Now this seems an estimate adopted from the value of labor or service at these different periods, the value of a man's time and labor.

ARGUMENT FROM WAGES.

Now, the *wages* of a man as a servant are often the subject of consideration in the Scriptures, but the *price* of a man never. There is no such idea recognized as the price of a servant considered as property, or as if he were a thing of barter and sale: his owner is never spoken of; there is no such thing as the owner of a man, and no such quality is ever recognized as that of such ownership. When the recompense is appointed for the master whose servant has been killed by another's ox, it is the master, not the owner, to whom the recompense is to be made, *as* master, not as owner. The words employed are strikingly different, Exodus, xxi. 32: If the ox shall push a man-servant or maid-servant, he shall give unto their *master*, לַאדֹנָיו, *adhonai*, the word applied to Jehovah as Lord. But Exodus, xxi. 29, 34, 36, if the ox hath been used to push, or if a pit have been digged and not covered, their *owner*, בַּעַל, *baal*, shall make it good. The selection and appplication of the words are emphatic.*

There was no servant without wages, either paid beforehand, for a term of years, or paid daily, if hired by the day, or annually, as the case might be. The three kinds of contract or service, and of corresponding wages, are specified; first, generally, Leviticus, xix. 13, the wages of him that is hired shall not abide with thee all night until morning, פְּעֻלַּת שָׂכִיר, the *reward* of the hired servant; second, Job, vii. 1, his *days* like the *days of an hireling;* third, Leviticus, xxv. 53, *as a yearly hired servant;* fourth, Exodus, xxi. 2, where the rule seems referred to as most common, of a six years' service and contract. There was no indefiniteness in any of the legal provisions, no difficulty in ascertaining each servant's rights; and they were not only secured by law, but such tremendous denunciations were added in the prophets, as that in Jeremiah, xxii. 13 : Woe unto him that useth his neighbor's service without wages, and giveth him not for his work; and Malachi, iii. 5 : I will be a swift witness against those who defraud the hireling in his wages, and keep the stranger from his right. The *stranger* comprehended *servants*, as well as *sojourners*, of heathen extraction.

Now when the recompense of thirty skekels was ordained for the master, whose servant had been gored by another man's ox, they were to be paid, not because the servant was his, as property, or as being worth that price, as if he were a slave, a chattel, belonging to an owner, but because the mas-

---

* JOSEPHUS' ANTIQUITIES, book iv., chap. viii. sec. 36. The discrimination of Josephus in referring to these laws is emphatic. He applies a different word to the owner of the cattle and the master of the servant; although the difference in the Greek can not be so strikingly illustrative of the distinction in the original between the owner of property and the master of a household with the servants. The goods were *owned*, the men were *governed;* the goods, the cattle, were *chattels, property;* the servants were *persons, men*, their own only owners, with freedom to dispose of their services for a proper and just equivalent in wages. The description in Josephus is very properly, *owner* of the cattle, *master* of the servants.

ter *had paid to him* the price of a certain number of years of
labor, which years the servant owed; and therefore the recompense was for the loss of that part of the service which had
been paid for, but, by reason of death, could not be fulfilled.
The master did not and could not own *him*, in any case, but
only had a claim to his time and labor, so far as it had been
contracted and paid for. It must have been paid for beforehand, because, otherwise, if the servant's pay had not been
promised till after the time of the contract, the master would
have been owing the servant at his death, and could have no
claim, but the nearest of the family of the servant would have
had the claim. But the case being that of the עֶבֶד, the six
years' hired servant, or perhaps the servant obtained from
among the heathen, the master has the claim for services which
were paid for, but not fulfilled.

The legal term of service for six years could not be length-
ened, *except at the pleasure of the servant.* The man-servant
and the maid-servant were equally free in making their contracts; neither of them could be held at the pleasure of the
master, nor could be disposed of, but at their own pleasure.
They were perfectly free, except so far as by their own act
and free will they had bound themselves for an equivalent to
a term of service. Under certain contingencies they could, by
law, compel their master to keep them, but he could never use
them as property, never make merchandise of them, never
transfer them over to another. If a maid-servant chose to
contract herself to her master's family, in such manner that he
on his part could keep her till the jubilee, and she on her part
could forbid his sending her away, then both herself and her
children were to remain till that time. The covenant was
legal and explicit. They were bound to him, in his service,
and could not quit, but with his consent, till that time. On
the other hand, he was bound to them, and could not transfer
them to another family, country, or household, nor any one
of them, nor convey their service to any other person.

ONLY CONDITION ON WHICH THE SERVANT COULD BE KEPT TILL JUBILEE.

This is to be regarded, in examining the next clause, which states the *one only condition* on which the servant could be retained by the master until the jubilee. If, during his period of six years' service, his master had given him a wife, and she had borne him children, then, at the end of the six years, he could not, in quitting his master's service, compel the master to relinquish the contract, whatever it was, which had given him a right to the service of the maid-servant, his wife, for a still longer period, or to the jubilee. It was optional with him to leave his wife and children with his master, and go out from his service by himself alone, or he could stay, and with his wife and children engage with his master anew until the jubilee; and his master could never separate the family, nor send any one of them away, nor violate any of the terms of the contract; and both for time and for wages, the covenant was at the pleasure of the servant, as well as the master, and by law the master was compelled to treat him as a שָׂנָה מָשְׂכָה שָׂכִיר, as a yearly hired servant, and not as an עֶבֶד, or servant of all times and all work; as a servant on stipulated monthly or yearly wages, and not as one whose whole time of service until the jubilee had been bargained for and paid for in the lump. The whole covenant was determined and ratified in court, before the judges, with the greatest care and solemnity, on the affirmation of the servant that he loved not only his wife and children, but his master also, and his house, and was well with him, (compare Deuteronomy, xv. 16,) and would not go away from him. The sign of the covenant, and its proof positive and incontrovertible, so that neither master nor servant could by fraud have broken it, was the boring of the ear, both of man-servant and maid-servant.

This transaction was entered into by the servant, notwithstanding the claim of a liberal outfit from his master, from the

flock, and the floor, and the wine-press, to which he was entitled by law, if he chose to leave his service. The receiving a
wife from his master, during any time of his six years' service,
was also at the servant's own pleasure; all the conditions of
such marriage being perfectly well known to him, the dowry
which he would have to pay for his wife, if he remained with
her, being in part the assuming of a new contract of service with
the master, as long as hers had been assumed, or to the jubilee.
And then, they and their children would go from his service,
with all the property they had been able to acquire by their
wages and privileges in his household. This, if they had been
provident and sagacious in the use of lawful means and opportunities, might at length amount to an important sum. The
servant might become possessor of a competency, during a
twenty-five or thirty years' sojourn in his master's family.
And the servant born in the house, his son, יְלִיד בָּיִת, the home-
born, וּבְנֵי־בַיִת, or of the *sons of the house*, might become his
master's heir, as in the household of Abraham; or he himself
might be his master's steward, with all the wealth of the establishment under his hand.

The position of such an עֶבֶד, or Hebrew servant, or even
heathen servant, as in the case of Eliezer of Damascus, might
be more desirable than that of the hired servant not belonging to the family. It was only households of comparatively
considerable wealth that could afford to enter into such contracts with their servants, or to keep a retinue of retainers
born in the house. Hence the fact of having such a class of
servants is referred to in such a manner as proves it to have
been esteemed a mark of greatness and prosperity, Ecclesiastes, ii. 7. And these domestic servants, born in the family
and holding by law such a claim upon it, were attached to it,
and its members to them, with an affection and kindness like
that of its sons and daughters, one toward another. Perhaps
the passage in Jeremiah, ii. 14, may be rendered with reference to this fact: "Is Israel a servant, עֶבֶד? If a home-born,

אִם־יְלִיד, why is he a spoil?" How should he be carried away and made a prey, if he belongs to the household, if he is the home-born of his God? These home-born servants, and those whose contract of service lasted beyond the six years' term of ordinary legal indenture, were at the same time to be treated on the same footing with the hired servants and so-journers, with the same careful regard to all their rights and privileges.

In connection with the case of the master giving his servant a wife, the instance of Sheshan is illustrative, 1 Chronicles, iii. 34, 35. Sheshan had no sons, and he gave one of his daughters as a wife to one of his household servants named Jarha, an Egyptian. This Egyptian servant, beyond all doubt, was received into Sheshan's service on the legal conditions laid down in Leviticus, xxv., on a contract voluntary and for a stipulated equivalent. There is not the slightest indication of his ever having been a slave. Egyptian strangers and so-journers among the Hebrews, as well as those from other nations, often sold themselves to service in this manner in the Holy Land. Yet with such reckless confidence and mistake, characterizing the assertions of too many commentators on this whole subject, it is asserted in Kitto's Cyclopædia, article Sheshan, that Jarha was not only a slave, but that his marriage took place while the children of Israel were themselves in bondage in Egypt! This is said, notwithstanding the fact that the recorded genealogy of Sheshan demonstrates that he and his family were cotemporary with Boaz, Obed, and Jesse, being in the seventh generation in direct descent from Hezron, the grandson of Judah.

CONDITION OF MARRIED SERVANTS AND THEIR CHILDREN.

There is no other instance, save this in Exodus, xxi. 4, (which is plainly mentioned as an exception to a general rule,) in which any claim of the master to the children of his servants is ever intimated. The home born, יְלִיד־בָּיִת, and the sons of

the house, בְּנֵי־בַיִת—though in subjection to him, as the father
of the family, and lord of the household, were not his property, in any sense; and because he had a servant-maid, her
children were not on that account his servants, except by a
separate specific contract. No child, whether Hebrew or
heathen, in the land of Judea, was born to involuntary servitude, because the father, or mother, or both were servants;
but every child of the house was born a member of the family, dependent on the master for education and subsistence.
If married persons engaged themselves as servants, or *sold
themselves*, according to Hebrew phraseology, then, when the
six years' time of their service expired, they went forth free,
and their children with them; there was never any claim
upon the children to retain them merely because they were
בְּנֵי־בַיִת, sons of the house; but their parents had authority
over them, and possession of them. The phraseology in the
case before us, *the wife and her children shall be her master's*,
הָאִשָּׁה וִילָדֶיהָ תִּהְיֶה לַאדֹנֶיהָ, conveys no meaning of possession, but
simply of *remaining with* the master, as long as the contract
specified, as long as he had a right by law to her services.
Inasmuch as she herself was not, and could not be, *her master's*, except only by voluntary contract, for a price paid to
herself, and for a time specified, neither could the children be
her masters.

The only way in which he could give her to her husband
to be his wife was, (1) either by paying to her father the dowry required, and so purchasing her for a wife for his servant,
in which case he would have a claim upon his or her services
or both, additional to the amount of that dowry; or (2) she
was his maid-servant already according to the ordinary or extraordinary legal contract, for the six years, Deuteronomy,
xvi. 12, or for the time from the making of a new contract,
till the jubilee, Deuteronomy, xvi. 17, and as such he gives
her in marriage. In either case, she being bound to him for a
longer time than her husband, her children would, of right,

and by law, remain with her, under subjection in her master's household, and could not be taken away by the father, if he chose to quit. The children could not be taken from their parents, but after a certain age they were at liberty to choose their own masters, and to make their own terms of service. This resulted inevitably from the law limiting and defining the period of service in every case; even when until the jubilee, still, most absolutely and certainly defined and limited by that. There was nothing left indefinite, and no room for the assumption of arbitrary power, so long as the provisions of the law were complied with. And it was the breaking of those provisions, and the attempt on the part of the masters to force their servants into involuntary servitude, and so change the whole domestic system of the state from freedom to slavery, that, by the immediate wrath of God in consequence, swept the whole country into a foreign captivity, and consigned the people to the sword, the pestilence, and the famine, Jeremiah, xxxiv. 17. The horror with which any approximation again towards any infraction of the great law of liberty, was regarded, after the return of the Jews from that retributive captivity, is manifested in Nehemiah, v. 5, and is instructive and illustrative.

AVERAGE TIME OF THE LONGEST SERVICE.

Let us now see what would be the actual operation of the exceptional contract in Exodus, xxi. 4–6, running on to the jubilee. That this is the meaning of the term *for ever*, in the terms of this contract, is not disputed, and is incontrovertible from Leviticus, xxv. 39, 40, the law of the jubilee overriding all others and repressing all personal contracts within itself. At the recurrence of the jubilee, all were free. Then, after the year of jubilee, when every family had returned to its original possessions, new engagements were necessarily entered into with servants, new contracts were made. It does not seem likely that, at the outset, any indenture of service for the next forty-nine years would be deemed desirable, either by masters or servants. Almost all contracts would be the ordinary legal ones of six years. But after the expiration of one or two *septenniums*, there might be cases of contracts looking to the jubilee. On a probable computation, the instances would be rare of such engagements beginning before the middle, or near the middle of the period. In that case, if a master gave a wife to his servant, and the covenant was assumed by boring the ear, the children, as בְּנֵי־בָיִת, home-born, the sons of the house, would be under subjection to the master, at the very farthest, not longer than our ordinary period of the minority of children. For example, take the contract of a maid-servant as occurring in the fourth *septennium*, or say in the twenty-fifth year, an agreement to serve in the family for twenty-three years, or until the jubilee, and according to the Hebrew idiom for contracts till that time, *for ever*. During the first *septennium* of this maiden's service, a Hebrew servant is engaged for six years, and soon forming an attachment, asks of his master the maid-servant for a wife. She is given to him by his master, and they have children; and, at the expiration of his six years, he avails himself of his legal privilege, and enters into a new contract with his master till the jubilee. At that time the oldest of his children would be about twenty-one years of age, and the youngest might be five or ten; they are all free by the operation of the law of jubilee. From twenty to twenty-five years would ordinarily be the utmost limit of any contract of service, whether for parents or children.

PENALTY AGAINST CRUELTY TO SERVANTS.

The penalties against the master for cruel or oppressive treatment of his servants were the same, whether the servants were Hebrew or of heathen extraction. Whatever injury was committed against any servant, was to be avenged; for loss of an eye or a tooth the servant should have his freedom, whatever might have been his contract with his master, whatever sum his master might have paid him beforehand, no matter how many years of unfulfilled service might remain, Exodus, xxi. 26, 27. In connection with a similar section it is added, " Ye shall have one manner of law, as well for the stranger as for one of your own country, for I am the Lord your God," Leviticus, xxiv. 22. The application of this principle is beautifully and pointedly illustrated in Job, xxxi. 13–15 ; and the reason given is the same, namely, that the same God and Creator is the God both of master and servant : " If I did despise the cause of my man-servant or of my maid-servant, when they contended with me, what shall I do when God riseth up ? and when he visiteth, what shall I answer him ? Did not he that made me in the womb make him ? and did not one fashion us in the womb ?" If a servant were killed by his master, the punishment was death; if the servant died after some days, Exodus, xxi. 20, 21, in consequence of blows inflicted by the master, then, in mitigation of the punishment, the presumption was admitted in law that the killing was not intentional; because, the master having paid the servant beforehand for his services up to a certain time, " he was his money," and he could not be supposed to have intended to kill him, unless he did kill him outright; and then the penalty was death.*

* In regard to the possession, acquisition, and merchandise of property, and the increase of personal riches, by servants, such being their privileges as freemen, see SAALSCHUTZ on the Laws of Moses, page 719. · Saalschutz again refers to a mistaken conclusion by Michaelis, and remarks, in illustration of the subject, that Jacob's possession of flocks and herds, with servants to take care of them for him, while he himself stood in the relation of servant to Laban, shows the nature of such service. It was the service of freemen by contract, for wages. "Mit welchem Rechte können diese Alle Leibeigene genannt werden?" See note on page 714. "With what propriety can any of these be called slaves?" Compare, on the meaning of the jubilee contract (forever), STILLINGFLEET, Origines Sacræ, Vol. I., p. 263.

CHAPTER XX.

WE have illustrated the position of the *buyer*, and the meaning of the word used for the *purchase* of servants. Let us now examine the usage of the word which is applied to designate this transaction on the part of the *seller*. We take the first example from the law of contracts with servants, Exodus, xxi. 7, 8, *if a man sell his daughter to be a maid-servant*. Here the subject of the sale, so called, is a Hebrew daughter. Her sale as a servant could not possibly be any thing more than an engagement for six years' service, at the end of which she was again free. The person who purchased her had no property in her, for she was as free as he was, except in the engagement of service for a limited time. But in the case before us she is sold for a wife, and is purchased as such; and the law defines and secures her rights with her master, who has betrothed her to himself. He buys her for his wife and must treat her as such, and can not transfer her to another. If he put her away, she is free without money. She is described as being sold at one and the same time, to be a maid-servant and a wife. She is at once the אָמָה and the אִשָּׁה of the husband. Her master may be the husband himself, or he may marry her to his son; but the section shows that her father has engaged her in the service of the master on condition of her marriage either to one or the other; and if this engagement is not fulfilled, she returns to her father free without money.

1. The word here used for this transaction is the verb מָכַר, to sell. It is used of contracts with free persons, both as servants and wives. The first instance is in Genesis, xxxi. 15, where Rachel and Leah declare that their father *had sold them*, מְכָרָנוּ, merely the concise description of his giving them in marriage to Jacob, who had paid for them to Laban, seven years' personal service for each. The instances in Exodus, xxi. 7, 8, Genesis, xxxi. 15, and Deuteronomy, xxi. 14, are the only cases in which the word is employed in reference to a wife. These cases form a class by themselves.

2. Then there is the class of passages in which the same word is applied to the ordinary legal contract of a Hebrew servant with his master or employer. Deuteronomy, xv. 12, if a Hebrew man or woman be sold unto thee, כִּי־יִמָּכֵר לְךָ. Jeremiah, xxxiv. 14, hath been sold unto thee, יִמָּכֵר. Leviticus, xxv. 39, 42, 47, 48, 50, different forms of the same word, מָכַר. To these cases we add the instance of a similar purchase, but forced beyond what the law admits, that is, an arbitrary contract, forbidden in regard to the Hebrew servant. *Will ye sell your brethren? or shall they be sold unto us?* תִּמְכְּרוּ, יִמָּכְרוּ. Both the sale and the purchase are forbidden, except on the conditions in Exodus, xxi. 2–11.

3. The same word is used to designate the crime of *man-selling*, the idea of contract for service being excluded. It is the sale of persons as of chattels, by way of merchandise. The first instance is in Genesis, xxxvii. 27, the selling of Joseph by his brethren, וְנִמְכְּרֶנּוּ, *let us sell him;* also, xxxvii. 28, וַיִּמְכְּרוּ, *they sold him.* The same, Genesis, xlv. 4, 5, and Psalm cv. 17. This crime of selling a man is described by the same word, and forbidden under penalty of death, Exodus, xxi. 16, and Deuteronomy, xxiv. 7.

4. A fourth class describes selling as the penalty for theft, Exodus, xxii. 3. But here the sale is not indefinite; it is in case of the thief not being able to make restitution, in which case he must be sold, that is, put to compulsory service, for

such a period as would make up the sum by the customary
wages for labor. In this class of passages we include the cases
of selling for debt. Isaiah, l. 1 : To which of your creditors
have I sold you? Compare Matthew, xviii. 25. The selling
for debt is simply an engagement of service for so long time
as would be sufficient, by the ordinary legal wages, to pay
the legal claim. It was not slavery, nor any selling as of
slaves.*

5. A fifth class of passages, in which God is described as
selling his people for their sins, or causing them to be sold to
the heathen. Deuteronomy, xxviii. 68, sold unto their enemies for bondsmen, *ye shall be sold*, הִתְמַכַּרְתֶּם. Deuteronomy,
xxxii. 30, *except their rock had sold them*, אִם־לֹא כִּי צוּרָם מְכָרָם.
Judges, ii. 14 ; iii. 8 ; iv. 2 ; x. 7. 1 Samuel, xii. 9. Psalm
xliv. 13. Joel, iii. 8. The sense in these cases is that of delivering up into the power of another. Of this meaning is
Judges, iv. 9, *the Lord shall sell Sisera.* To this class must
be added, Isaiah, l. 1, and lii. 3, where the Jews are described
as selling themselves for their transgressions ; that is, they
did, *by* their sins, what God did, *for* their sins, delivered
themselves over into the power of their enemies.

6. A sixth class comprehends, 1 Kings, xxi. 20, 25, Ahab
selling himself to work wickedness, and 2 Kings, xvii. 17, the
people selling themselves to do evil ; that is, giving themselves

---

* JOSEPHUS, ANTIQ., book xvi.,
chap. i., sec. ii. The great mistake
of imagining the selling for theft or
debt to have been a selling into slavery, or a species of slavery, would
have been prevented, even by consulting Josephus alone. This historian refers to an instance of such oppression committed by Herod, and
remarks : "This slavery to foreigners
was an offense against our religious
settlement [or constitution], such a
punishment being avoided in our
original laws; for those laws ordain
that the thief shall restore fourfold,
and that if he have not so much, he
shall be sold indeed, but not to foreigners, nor so that he be under perpetual slavery, for he must have been
released after six years." If so with
the criminal, how much more with
the mere debtor, who also might be
taken for service to work out the
debt, but must be released within the
septennium.

up unrestrainedly, in consideration of the wages of sin for a season.

7. In a seventh class of passages, the word is employed to describe the bondage of the Jews in their captivity, Nehemiah, v. 8, הַנִּמְכָּרִים לַגּוֹיִם.   Add instances in Esther, vii. 4, where the word is used to signify delivering or betraying into the power of another, first, for destruction, second, for bondage.

8. In another class still, the heathen are arraigned for the crime of selling Hebrew captives.   Joel, iv. 3, 6, 7, *sold a girl for wine,* מָכְרוּ ; *sold the children to the Grecians,* מְכַרְתֶּם. Here the meaning obviously is that of traffic, as in merchandise, and the denunciation of God's wrath follows accordingly.

The crime of selling one another is also described by the same word in Amos, ii. 6 : " *They sell the righteous for silver* (those that have committed no crime, they sell), *and the needy for a pair of shoes.*" Compare Amos, viii. 6, where the oppression of buying the poor with silver is denounced along with the crime of perjury and false balances in traffic. The *getting,* or in Hebrew phraseology, the *buying,* of servants, *as provided by law,* was a just transaction, *voluntary* on both sides; but in the cases before us, the thing forbidden is the buying and selling of persons against their own consent, who are compelled by their poverty to be thus passed as merchandise; and this is denounced as crime.   So in Zechariah, xi. 5 : *They that sell them say, Blessed be the Lord, for I am rich ;* adding to this monstrous crime the iniquity and hypocrisy of invoking and asserting God's blessing upon it.

MAKING MERCHANDISE OF MEN OR WOMEN UTTERLY FORBIDDEN.

From all these cases it is clear, that in law the word מָכַר, to sell, when applied to persons, signified a voluntary contract, such as ours of hiring workmen, or the contract between a master and his apprentices; and that in any other cases, ex-

cept as making restitution for theft, or to work out a just
debt, the buying and selling of persons was a criminal transaction. The buying as well as the selling, in such a transaction, is denounced as criminal. It was making merchandise
of men, a thing expressly forbidden in the divine law, on penalty of death. Accordingly, even in anticipation of the law,
its principles were already acted on. There is not one particle
of indication that Abraham, Isaac or Jacob ever sold one of
their servants, nor any supposition of the power or right to do
so. Nor ever, from the patriarchs down, is there any instance
of any man or master•selling a servant. The history of the
world fails to disclose one single case of such merchandise. On
the contrary, it proves that it was forbidden, and was regarded as sinful; and that either the holding, or selling, or both,
of a servant for gain, and against his will, or without his voluntary contract, was an oppression threatened with the wrath
of God.

And here belongs the consideration of Deuteronomy, xxi.
14, the case of the captive woman taken from the heathen for
a wife, but afterwards rejected. Two things are forbidden in
the treatment of her; 1. *Thou shalt not sell her at all for
money;* וּמָכֹר לֹא־תִמְכְּרֶנָּה בַּכָּסֶף. Compare Exodus, xxi. 8.

2. *Thou shalt not make merchandise of her.* Thou shalt
not bind her over to another, thou shalt not transfer her to
the power of another. She shall not so be subject unto thee,
that thou canst deal with her as merchandise or property.
The word in this second prohibition is תִתְעַמֵּר, from עָמַר, *to
bind.* Our English translation seems to make it exegetical
of the preceding prohibition; but it is not a synonyme with
מָכַר, neither was intended as paraphrastic of that. It is the
same word employed in Psalm cxxix. 7, of the mower binding
sheaves to be carried away for use or traffic, לֹא־יִתְעַמֵּר בֵּהּ, thou
shalt not play the master or oppressor over her.

A comparison of this with Exodus, xxi. 8, where the English
translation speaks of *selling a Hebrew woman to a strange na-*

tion, which is forbidden, will show that in that passage the translation does not convey the proper meaning; for it was *never* permitted on *any* ground, or for any reason whatever, to bind a Hebrew woman to a heathen, or to deliver over to a foreign nation any Hebrew man or woman as servant or wife. In the case before us, Deuteronomy, xxi. 14, this is forbidden in regard to the captive taken from the heathen in war; how much more in regard to any Hebrew! The expression in Exodus, xxi. 8, לְעַם נָכְרִי לֹא־יִמְשֹׁל לְמָכְרָהּ, *to a strange nation he shall have no power to sell her*, should be rendered, to sell her to *a strange tribe*, or to *a strange family ;* and the meaning evidently is, that she shall not be transferred from her master to *any other* family, but is wholly free. For the usage of נָכְרִי, compare Leviticus, xxi. 1, 4, Ecclesiastes, vi. 2. It might mean, *to a family of strangers*, sojourning in the land, and joined to the congregation by circumcision. The hiring, selling, apprenticing, or disposing of her *in any way at all for money*, is strictly forbidden. She is perfectly free.

RESULT OF THE EXAMINATION.

The result of the examination of the phrase *to sell*, in the word מָכַר, *makar*, and in the passages in which it is employed with reference to servants or captives, is perfectly conclusive against the existence of slavery, and triumphant in demonstration of its guilt, as reprobated and forbidden of Jehovah. The *buying* being proved to have been a bargain free and voluntary with the servant himself, and not the purchase, as of property, from any third party, and the *selling* being absolutely forbidden, in the sense of merchandise, as property, the making merchandise of a man being forbidden on pain of death ;— between these two lines of argument the demonstration of the guilt and crime of slavery is perfect.

Now it is interesting to bring together the two prohibitions, in each of which precisely the same terms are made use of, but the one relating to the treatment of captive women, strangers, the other to the treatment of Israelites, and in each case the treatment of man or woman as property forbidden. In the first case, Thou shalt not sell her at all for money: thou shalt not make merchandise of her. In the second case, If a man be found stealing any of his brethren of the children of Israel, and maketh merchandise of him, or selleth him, then that thief shall die; and thou shalt put evil away from among you, Deuteronomy, xxiv. 7. The repetition of the prohibition by separate phrases, as if one were not explicit enough, though ever so plain, in reprobation of the crime of treating human beings as property, is exceedingly emphatic: Thou shalt *not sell her at all ;* thou shalt *not make merchandise* of her. If thou *make merchandise of him,* or *if thou sell him,* thou shalt die. It would be difficult to reprobate more explicitly the infamous supposition that man can hold property in man, or to guard more carefully against the infamous crime of treating man as property; converting human beings into merchandise, buying, holding, transferring, selling them as chattels.

In forbidding this traffic in human beings on pain of death, having already sealed up the original crime of man-stealing, in which the traffic began, under the same condemnation and penalty, the Divine Being brands slavery, slaveholding, and the slave traffic, so incontrovertibly, so palpably, as the subject of divine hatred and wrath, and forbids it, so unquestionably, for all mankind, that the reader of these statutes stands amazed at the hardihood and impiety of any nation or people, professing any regard to the authority of God, any belief in divine revelation, that can permit the crime within its borders, much more can sanction, legalize, protect it; can raise it to the dignity of a domestic institution, perpetuate it to other generations by laws for its entailment, set apart a race for its enormities of oppression and of cruelty to be exercised upon, and make the breeding of that race, and the domestic trade in human stock, thus propagated, the object of State and National protection, as the most sacred and valuable of all the rights of property under heaven.

It is a fit climax of such infinite rascality and impiety to select, as the qualifying direction of this crime, as the mark denoting the consecrated subjects of such ineffable atrocity, a seal of God's own providence, the tincture of the skin, the hue it has pleased him to impart in the organization of a portion of his creatures. Had the race of men-stealers in the United States, and of judicial tyrants and impostors, thought good to set forth and establish as the guidance of their detestable villainy, the reason of their slave-law, and the security and ground of its execution, some infernal or atrocious discovered quality of character, some combination of moral and physical depravity, so that it might seem as if the very will of God, in his providential retributive justice, were being carried out in the reduction of such a race to slavery, the crime had not reached such a height of impudent malignity, such a depth of meanness, such a consummation of intense, causeless, irreligious cruelty. But to take the divine providence, in the hue of the African race of human beings, as a guide and sanction for the violation of the divine law, in the commission against that race of the one crime which God has branded, because of its guilt, in co-equality with murder; and to make that providential color of the skin, the reason of an announcement from the highest tribunal of national justice, that BLACK MEN HAVE NO RIGHTS THAT WHITE MEN ARE BOUND TO RESPECT—this, certainly, is to have reached at once an impious sublimity and deformity of wickedness, such as no other nation under heaven ever yet attained.*

---

* This opinion is the concentrated essence of the current of slave legislation, down to the present time. Compare, for proof, the volume of Judge STROUD, Laws relating to Slavery, the twelve propositions of the nature of the system, with cases and decisions, a demonstration not to be questioned. Also, the volume of Rev. W. GOODELL, equally demonstrative, with a more particular and powerful moral application. The history of the world contains nothing, as a system of outrage, wrong and cruelty, so dreadful as the reality in these volumes, viewed under the gospel.

CHAPTER XXI.

THE LAW AGAINST MAN-STEALING.—WHAT IT PROVES.

IMMEDIATELY after the laws determining the nature and time of contracts with servants, the legislator passes to the crime of murder and the death penalty against it. Then follows the great fundamental statute, which demonstrates the criminality of slavery in the sight of God: HE THAT STEALETH A MAN AND SELLETH HIM, OR IF HE BE FOUND IN HIS HAND, HE SHALL SURELY BE PUT TO DEATH, Exodus, xxi. 16. As the stealing of men is the foundation of slavery in most cases, and especially of modern slavery, this statute condemns it as sinful, intrinsically, absolutely. The stealing, the selling, the holding, of a man in slavery, is death; either form of the crime shall be so punished. Whether the kidnapper keep or sell his victim, the crime is death.

But the purchaser, with knowledge of the theft, is equally guilty, and would be treated as conspirator and principal in the same crime. On the principles of common law, as well as common justice, this is inevitable. Common law and justice, as well as common sense and piety, pronounce the slaves and their descendants in our own country a stolen race, their progenitors having been stolen at the outset, and there being no possibility, by transmission, of changing the original theft into a just possession, the original man-stealing into a just claim of property in man. On the same principles of simple incontrovertible justice, every receiver and buyer of the stolen race, or of any individual slave, with the claim of property in him, is the man-stealer, an accomplice in the crime; for the maxim at common law holds, above all, in such a case, that *the receiver is as bad as the thief.* He that buys and holds a man, knowing him to have been stolen, steals him; and his having been bought and sold forty times, before the last trafficker in human flesh bought him, could make no difference. He remains, and must remain, a stolen man, no matter through how many hands he passes. All the hands that hold him as property are red with this crime of stealing him, this murder of his personal freedom. The same principle on which the buyer of a stolen horse, knowing him to have been stolen, is a horse-thief, makes the slave buyer and the slaveholder a man-stealer. The slaveholder in withholding the slave from his freedom, steals him. The continuing to withhold him from his freedom, and to hold him as property, is the renewed stealing of him. It is as truly the stealing of him, as the buying of a stolen horse from a horse thief, while the owner was bound, and gagged, and helpless, would be the stealing of the horse, even though the thief was paid for him.

In connection with the other provisions in the Hebrew system, this law against man-stealing rendered slavery absolutely impossible. The limitation of legal servitude to six years, and the law of universal freedom on the recurrence of the jubilee, would alone have prevented it; but the law of death against man-stealing made the practice of slavery as criminal a system as an organized system of murder would have been. The stealing of a man is the stealing of him from himself; the buying of him is the receiving of stolen property; the enslaving of his children is the stealing of them both from themselves and from him, so that the crime is incomparably exasperated in its descent; by transmission, the crime is at once increased in extent, and undiminished as to the original iniquity.

ANY TRAFFIC IN HUMAN BEINGS IMPOSSIBLE UNDER THIS LAW.
—PROPERTY IN MAN IMPOSSIBLE.

This law must effectually and for ever have prevented any traffic in human beings. It denies the principle of property in man. The stealing of a man is the stealing of him from himself, and the converting of him into property; and that is to be punished with death. No matter if the thief merely kept him as a captive for his own use, and did not intend to sell him; the being found in his hands was enough; he should surely be put to death. He might say that he captured him in Africa, among savages, and brought him to Judea as one of God's missionaries, on benevolent grounds and with justificatory circumstances. The pretense would avail nothing; he should surely be put to death for the stealing of a man. The stealing alone should be punished by death; and the holding would be sufficient evidence of the stealing; the holding of him as a slave would be itself the stealing; the being found in his hands, under constraint, against his own will, would be enough.

Then comes the selling, equally to be punished by death, because the selling is not only the converting of him into property, but it is the transfer of that property, under such circumstances as to make the stolen man a more hopeless victim still of such cruelty. It is the transfer of that property under the pretense of a just claim. It is putting the counterfeit bill in circulation, with a voucher; it is giving the forgery a currency by endorsement. The selling is the assumption of property in the stolen person, and the selling is punishable by death. The stealing *alone*, if the thief did not sell, might not be the *assertion* of property, or of the *principle* of property in man; but the *selling* of him would be; and either stealing *and* holding, or stealing *and* selling, or stealing, holding, or selling, the crime is put on a level with murder.

THE POWER OF THIS DIVINE LOGIC.—DAMNING NATURE OF THE TRAFFIC IN HUMAN BEINGS.

There is no escaping from this logic. It holds the slave-holder with a grip more inexorable than his own remorseless and infernal claim of property in man. He commits the original iniquity of man-stealing comfortably and innocently, as he thinks, without either the guilt, or the trouble, or the danger of the original piracy; but God will hold him to an inexorable account under his own explicit law, and on the principles of common justice, as to fraud and cruelty between man and man. God will not hold him guiltless, though man may; God will never hold his own truth in unrighteousness, though the church of God on earth may do it, and may sacrifice both truth and righteousness in the compromise with crime; God's judgment remains, and is unalterable, and by that, and not by human compromises, or adjustment of expediencies, must men be tried, when they violate God's law, and proclaim such violations innocent, by framing a human law for its protection.

The stealing of human beings *as* property, and the converting of them *into* property, is worse, by the divine law, than the stealing *of* property; as much worse as murder is than stealing. Such is the distinction which God makes between this and a common theft, between the stealing of a *man* and the stealing of *property*. The theft of property was punished by fine; but the stealing of a man, by death: "If a man shall steal an ox, or a sheep, and kill it or sell it, he shall restore five oxen for an ox, and four sheep for a sheep," Exodus, xxii. 1. "If the theft be certainly found in his hand alive, whether it be ox, or ass, or sheep, he shall restore double," Exodus, xxii. 4. Compare Exodus, xxii. 9. If slavery had had any existence among the Hebrews, any toleration, if man had been considered as property, then the penalty for such theft could not have been death, but the restoration of five slaves for a slave, or the payment of five times as much as the stolen man would bring in the market.   And the near and striking contrast between these crimes and the respective penalties attached to them, must have made men feel that the assertion of property in man was itself a crime.

Accordingly, there is no indication of any traffic in human beings except where it is indicated as a crime, with the wrath of God pointed against it.   There was such traffic among other nations, but no approach to it in Judea.   The trade in human beings is set down by the prophet Ezekiel as among the commercial transactions in the market place of Tyre; but no Hebrew had any thing to do with it, Ezekiel, xxvii. 13.   It is set down by Joel as a damning trade of Tyre and Zidon, of the heathen, and the Grecians, Joel, iii. 2–8, and every approximation to it, on the part of Israel, is marked for divine vengeance. But no such traffic was allowed, or existed, under the law of God ; no such thing as slavery was either recognized or tolerated.   There is no instance of the purchase even of servants from a third person, as if they were articles of possession that could be passed from hand to hand, from master to master, without their own agreement.   There is no instance of the *sale* of any servant *to* a third person.   There is no indication that masters ever had any power to sell their servants to others, or to put them away from their own families, except in perfect freedom.   Our English translators, and the lexicographers, have indeed, in most cases, *assumed* slavery and the slave trade as existing in Judea ; but the Mosaic laws and the Jewish history demonstrate the contrary.   A single assumption, by Gesenius, that the word for souls in Genesis, xii. 5, נֶפֶשׁ, *souls that Abraham and Lot had gotten in Haran*, means *slaves*, shall be followed, without examination, by other lexicographers, and shall set the tide of opinion to run on without questioning.

HUMAN BEINGS CAN NOT BE TREATED AS PROPERTY.

But the statute under consideration shines like a sun upon such an investigation, and throws its light backwards as wel' as forwards in history and law, as a light of supreme defining and controlling principle. *Human beings can not be treated as property.* There is no restriction: the universality of the law is unquestionable; the subject of it being a man, not a Hebrew man exclusive of a stranger, but a man, whosoever he might be. The universality of this law is as evident as that law in verse 12 : *He that smiteth a man so that he die, shall surely be put to death.* There is no more ground for restricting the application of the statute against stealing a man to the Hebrew stolen, than that against killing a man. So with the statute against killing a servant; there is no restriction. A comparison of this with Leviticus, xxiv. 17, 21, 22, makes it still clearer. In this place the statute is also concerning the death-penalty, and the form is as follows : He that killeth any man shall surely be put to death; and it is added, Ye shall have one manner of law, as well for the stranger as for one of your own country; for I am the Lord your God. So with the laws concerning the treatment of one's neighbor; if any man ask, But who is my neighbor? willing to restrict their application to a countryman, the commentary of our Lord, in Luke, x. 30, settles the matter. But if so in a smaller injury committed, or benefit required, much more in the greater. Along with this statute is placed the law, Thou shalt not vex a stranger, nor oppress him, Exodus, xxii. 21, and again xxiii. 9. But finally the matter is settled by Paul, in 1 Timothy, i. 10 : " The law is made for man-slayers, *men-stealers,*" and others named, without restriction as to lineage or land. The reference is unquestionable ; the application equally so.

He that stealeth A MAN. If it had been (as some modern supporters of the system of slavery affirm) a statute for the support, sanction, and better protection of slavery and slave property, a statute against stealing *slaves* or servants, the distinguishing word would have been used (had there been a word in the Hebrew tongue signifying slave); and for want of such a word, the nearest approximation to it would have been taken. The statute must have read, *He that stealeth a servant*, גֹּנֵב, not he that stealeth אִישׁ, *a man*. So gross a blunder could never have been committed by the lawgiver as the introduction of the *genus* instead of the *species*, in a case involving the penalty of death; so gross a blunder as that by which the *slaveholder* instead of the *slave-stealer* might have been obnoxious to the penalty. If it had been a law against the stealing of another man's *slaves*, then the slaveholder might have stolen *a man* and *made* him a slave, with perfect impunity; and only the thief who should dare to steal from *him* the slave so *made* would be subject to the penalty. The law would have been not against the stealing of a man, *as man*, and making him property, but against the stealing of him as property, *after he is so made*. The assumption of those who would maintain that Moses promulgated this law for the protection of slavery, is just this; that man, *as man*, is not sacred against kidnapping; but man as kidnapped and made property, *man as property*, is so sacred and inviolable a possession, that the theft of him *as a slave* must be punished with death.

DETESTABLENESS OF THE ATTEMPT TO FALSIFY THIS STATUTE.

Did the history of crime, or of impudent wickedness in justifying it, ever record an endeavor so brazen to falsify fact, to distort the laws of the Almighty, to pervert their meaning, to change good into evil, and put darkness for light? The trick is too barefaced and palpable even to be dignified with the name of sophistry; it is a downright and deliberate falsification of God's word, in order to shield from his reprobation that which, along with murder, and equally as that, constitutes the greatest of human villainies. These deliberate falsifiers of God's truth endeavor to shield from condemnation the crime of stealing a freeman, and making him a slave, because the condemnation of that crime, as a crime worthy of death, includes inevitably, and necessitates, the equal condemnation of slavery, as the result and essence of that crime. If it be a crime to steal a man, it is an equal crime to hold him when stolen; for the holding of him is the renewal of the stealing every day. If he is passed over to a second thief for a consideration, then that thief, holding the stolen man, does himself steal him, does himself renew the theft of a man. The fact that he paid for him does not make it any less the stealing of him.

These falsifiers of God's word endeavor to shield this crime of stealing A MAN from condemnation, and to throw the whole reprobation against the imaginary crime of stealing a slave. There is no such crime; for the stealing of a slave would be criminal, merely because it is the stealing of a man from himself, and not a slave from his master; merely because God has denounced the stealing of a man as being a crime as great as that of murder. Therefore, the stealing of a slave would be criminal, because it is the stealing of a man, but not because the slave can be any man's property, not because he belongs, or can belong, to his master, which God forbids, but to himself only; and his master, in claiming and holding him as property, steals him; in making a slave of him, steals him.

But these apologists for slavery maintain that it is a greater crime to steal a stolen man than it is to steal a freeman. They hold that it is no crime at all to steal that which is not property, namely, a freeman; but the moment the man is stolen, and converted into property, then he becomes sacred, as another's possession, and the stealing of him becomes robbery, because it is the stealing of a slave! The stealing of a freeman from himself and from God is to be protected, because it is a mode of creating the most valuable of all property; but the stealing of the stolen man, when thus once created a slave, once transformed into property by the original stealing of a freeman, is the worst kind of theft, because it is the stealing of a stolen man from his owner, after he has been laboriously, and at great cost of cruelty and wickedness, transfigured into a slave! A slave, by God's law, according to these "doctrines of devils," is sacred from theft, but a freeman is not! A MAN may be stolen with impunity, but the stealing of a *slave* is to be punished with death! A slave is to be protected as *property*, but not as a MAN. A man, as a man, and a freeman, can not be shielded from being stolen, and there is no law against the man-stealer; but as a *slave*, God interposes and makes it death to steal him, not, however, on his own account, or for his own protection as a MAN, but for the protection of his master's sacred right of property in him as a *stolen* man!

With what sublimated essence of cruelty and compound wickedness these moral chemists charge the word of God! Passing it through the manipulations of such complicated power of lying, the retorts and crucibles of their own diabolism, it comes forth glaring like a demon, filled, in this thing, with their own murder, debate, deceit, malignity. The glory of the incorruptible God is changed into the image of a devil, when that unrighteousness of men against which the wrath of God is revealed from heaven, is, by their dreadful ingenuity, enthroned as the object of Heaven's sanction and protection; it is the all-deceivableness of unrighteousness in them that perish, when the truth is thus held by them in unrighteousness, and the unrighteousness is presented as the truth.

UNIVERSALITY AND PARTICULARITY OF THE STATUTE.

An attempt has been made to deny the universality of the first grand enactment against stealing A MAN, by an appeal to the other and second statute in Deuteronomy, xxiv. 7, where the application is directly to the *Hebrew man*. "If a man be found stealing any of his brethren of the children of Israel, and maketh merchandise of him, or selleth him, then that thief shall die, and thou shalt put evil from among you." As if Jehovah could have taught that it was evil to steal a Hebrew, but not evil to steal a man! As if, in the sight of God, the stealing of a Hebrew was a crime worthy of death, while the stealing of a man might be permitted with impunity! This attempted evasion is almost as detestable as the other, that the only thing criminal is the stealing of a slave from his master, while the stealing of a man from himself, being only the making of a slave, is not only no sin and no evil, but a benefit to society, and an act of missionary intelligence and mercy.

This statute, which was passed concerning the *Hebrew* forty years after the other concerning the MAN, and without any connection with or reference to the first, as we have already noted, had a special object, which confirms and strengthens the principle. It can not possibly be regarded as a statute of limitation or interpretation merely, much less of abrogation, as if the specific abrogated the general. Rather, if any such reference were supposed, might it be contended that it having been found in the course of forty years that the first and general law might have been claimed as applying only to the stranger or the heathen, and not to the stealing of a Hebrew, whose servitude, even if stolen, could not last more than six years (so carefully by law was this adjusted), it was found necessary, for greater security and definiteness, to add the second enactment, specifying also the Hebrew. But here again, any limitation of the first statute by the second is forbidden in the same chapter, by the application of verse 14: "Thou shalt not oppress a hired servant that is poor and needy, whether he be of thy brethren, or of thy strangers that are in thy land within thy gate." Now if a hired servant that was not a Hebrew could not be oppressed, any more than a native, much more could not such a one be stolen with impunity, or the thief escape the penalty. He would not be

permitted to plead that, because there was a law against stealing *a Hebrew*, therefore the law against stealing *a man* was
null and void.

Whether of thy brethren or of strangers, the oppression was
alike sinful, alike forbidden. But the greatest of all oppression was that of stealing a man and making a slave of him;
and if this was forbidden on pain of death in regard to a Hebrew, it was equally criminal and forbidden in regard to the
stranger ; if a crime worthy of death when committed against
a servant, then not less a crime when perpetrated against a
freeman. The stealing of an African was as sinful as the stealing of a Jew. The stealing of an Egyptian would have come
under this penalty of death for punishment as certainly as the
stealing of a son of Abraham. Ye shall have one manner of
law, as well for the stranger as for your own countryman—a
most humane, merciful, and wise provision of a large and impartial benevolence and justice, which, if our own enlightened
country and government had followed, we should not now
have been laden with the iniquity of an accursed jurisprudence,
of the most infamous injustice and cruelty, for keeping four
millions of human beings in perpetual slavery.

If this law had been against stealing Jews, instead of men,
then the apostle, in transferring it, must have said the law was
made for Jew-stealers, not *men-stealers*, for Ἰουδαιονποδισταῖς,
not ἀνδραποδισταῖς. And so, if the law had been against
stealing *slaves*, not *men*, for the protection and sanction of
slave-property, not to declare God's protection of men as human beings, against theft, or for the security of slave-owners,
and not for the sacredness of men as created in God's image ;
then the apostle, in translating that law into the wider dispensation, and defining its application, must have said, the law
was made for *slave-stealers*, δουλοποδισταῖς, or δουλοπατιαῖς,
not men-stealers. The context in Exodus, and context in
Timothy, nail the passages as beyond all disputation referring
to the same law. In Exodus it lies alongside with statutes

against man-slayers, cursers, and murderers of father and mother; in 1 Timothy the conjunction is the same: " Knowing this, that the law is not made for a righteous man, but for the lawless and disobedient, for the ungodly and for sinners, for unholy and profane, for murderers of fathers and murderers of mothers, for man-slayers, for whoremongers, for them that defile themselves with mankind, for MEN-STEALERS, for liars, for perjured persons; and if there be any other thing that is contrary to sound doctrine, according to the glorious gospel of the blessed God, which was committed to my trust."

This reference is as clear as the noon. No man can for one moment doubt the precise law in Exodus, which is referred to by Paul, in writing to Timothy.* Paul could not, therefore, in referring to it, have wholly distorted either its meaning or its application. He could not have made so great a mistake as that of leveling against the very foundations of slavery and the slave-trade, a law published originally, and intended of God for the protection of slave property. He could not have interpreted, in behalf of the rights of man against slaveholders, a law intended of God to secure the rights of slaveholders

* JOSEPHUS, ANTIQ., book iv., chap. viii., sec. 27.

There is no question as to the interpretation given to this law by the Jews of Paul's time. Indeed, a man must be almost an idiot to believe, or quite a villain to maintain, that the law against stealing a man recognizes the lawfulness and justice of slavery, and forbids merely the stealing of a slave. But to this extreme will the defense of this iniquity carry even a professed Christian, though against common sense as well as common piety. Josephus quotes the law: "Let death be the punishment for stealing a man; but he that hath purloined gold or silver, let him pay double."

Josephus must have used the word *slave* instead of A MAN, had the interpretation of the law been imagined as against slave-stealing instead of man-stealing. The late Judge Jay, an eminent jurist, philanthropist, and Christian, speaks, in his admirable ESSAY ON THE MOSAIC LAWS OF SERVITUDE, with just severity and contempt of the "intense baseness to which northern apologists for slavery will sometimes descend, as strikingly illustrated in a pro-slavery article of the American Quarterly Review, for June, 1833," in which the impious evasion and falsification above noted are resorted to.

against men. To this extent of infamy and blasphemy against God the clerical Christian and theological defenders of slavery, as under God's sanction, are compelled to drive their argument. The fountains of the great deep of wickedness are broken up in the defense of this national crime, and the tops of the highest mountains are so covered by the deluge, that we have had Christian ministers declaring, in the zeal of their celestial enthusiasm in the slave theology, that if by a single prayer they could emancipate all the slaves in the country, they would not offer it.

APPLICATION OF THIS STATUTE TO AMERICAN SLAVERY.

The application of this statute to the condemnation of American slavery and slaveholding, as man-stealing, is inevitable. It brings not only the whole system, though sanctioned by human law, under the curse and wrath of God, but those who, personally and individually, practice it with God's pretended sanction. The taking, the holding, or the selling of human beings as property, constitutes the very crime which God himself has set apart, along with the crime of murder, for the punishment of death. The act of slaveholding is this very crime; the act of slave-selling is this very crime. It is not the *system* merely or generally, but *the very act*, that God's wrath is leveled against; it is not the system of slavery, but the individual act and practice of *slaveholding* and *selling*, that God has sealed with such terrible reprobation unto death. It is the personal, individual act and practice of the crime, and the repetition of it, that makes it a custom; and it is the framing of laws protecting and sustaining it that organizes it into what is called an organic sin, an institution, and a system. The wickedness of the system lies in the continued perpetration of the act, the crime, by the individual slaveholder. The act of the crime came before its enactment, in stealing, in holding, in selling men as slaves. The act of slaveholding is the act of sin. Without the individual slaveholding there could be no system of slavery; the slaveholding goes before the system, prepares for it, and makes it up.

The slaveholding constitutes that oppression which is the subject of God's wrath. The slave-stealing, holding, and selling came before any laws, and against all law, both of God and man; afterwards came the passage of laws to sanctify, protect, and establish the crime. Thus legalized and systematized, men think its guilt is canceled, and that God no longer looks upon the crime through the medium of his own law and righteousness, but through the medium of human law, which thus becomes a vicarious redeemer, to bear the guilt of the violation of his own law. God's statute, "Thou shalt not follow a multitude to do evil," is annuled, and the combination of the multitude, with the consolidation of their crime into an institution, by means of a body of human enactments defending it, divests it of the quality of guilt, and puts it beyond God's reach, secure from his reprobation!

NO SLAVEHOLDER CAN ESCAPE.

But no slaveholder can thus escape the reprobation of the Almighty. The fact that the crime is erected into a system, and legalized, so far from removing or diminishing the guilt of the act of slaveholding, is a terrible increase of the wickedness, over and above that of the individual crime. The crime of slaveholding still stands by itself under God's wrath; the crime of enacting laws in justification and defense of it, the crime of enthroning it in the place of justice, is also another and a gigantic guilt by itself, for which God will hold the nation to account, as he holds the individual slaveholder for the guilt of man-stealing. Human law can not possibly make that an article of just property, which God has declared to be a robbery punishable with death. The man who perpetrates that robbery, in holding a fellow-creature as property, as a slave, and then justifies it by human law, commits two crimes instead of one; the crime of man-stealing first, unaltered by human enactments in its favor; the crime of preferring man's law above God's, second, which is deliberate defiance of the Almighty, and adds to the sin of disobedience that of teaching it as righteousness; that of teaching that man's law is obligatory above God's, and that man's law is capable of transfiguring into innocence and duty, what God's law has most explicitly forbidden, as the highest crime.

But there is a still greater exasperation of this wickedness, that of justifying it in the name of Christianity, that of sealing with the pretended sanction of the cross, under the New Testament, and as a missionary providence and virtue, that very crime which God has branded under the Old Testament by his own law as the highest guilt. The crime of slaveholding received into the church, baptized in the name of Christ, sanctioned as not inconsistent with the Christian profession, is such a confusion and chaos of impiety with holy things, that the incongruous monstrosities against which the Levitical enactments were leveled, are but a type of the blasphemy. A church is corrupted, its conscience defiled, and its piety must soon become putrid, that can admit and endure the discord of such abominable profanations, such abominations of desolations set in the holy place. Men might as well talk of Christian murder as Christian slaveholding, and of receiving the Christian murderer into sacramental and celestial fellowship, as well as the Christian slaveholder.

This conclusion is inevitable the moment the definition of slaveholding in the Word of God, and in the bare reality of the crime, is admitted, and the letter and spirit of the Christian law are applied to it. The language of reprobation, such as has been employed by Adam Clarke, John Wesley, Dymond, and others, seems strong and terrible, but who can deny its justice, admitting the sin to be such a crime as it is described to be in the book of divine revelation? The survey of the system in the slave laws, (see STROUD and GOODELL, with decisions,) in the light of the Word of God, is all that is needed.

CHAPTER XXII.

STATUTE FOR THE PROTECTION OF OPPRESSED FUGITIVES.

THE Mosaic legislation, the more it is examined, is seen to be a system of supernatural, divine wisdom. Amidst a congeries of particulars, sometimes seemingly disconnected, great underlying and controlling principles break out. The principle revealed in the statute against man-stealing, is the same developed in the next statute which we are to consider, in the order of the logical and historical argument from the Old Testament Scriptures against slavery. The principle is that of the sacredness of the human personality, which can not be made an article of traffic, can not be bought and sold, without a degree of criminality in the action like the criminality of murder. As the sacredness of human life is guarded by the penalty of death for the crime of maliciously *killing* a man, so the sacredness of human liberty, the property of a man's personality, as residing solely in himself, is guarded by the same penalty against the crime of *stealing* a man. The theft is that of himself *from* himself, and from God his Maker. As murder is the destruction of the life, so man-stealing and selling is the destruction of the personality, the degradation of a man into a thing, a chattel, an article of property, transferred, bartered for a price, as if there were no immortal soul nor personal will in existence.

The statute in Deuteronomy, xxiii. 15, 16, is properly to be

examined next after that in Exodus, xxi. 16, and Deuteronomy, xxiv. 7. The whole form of the statute is as follows:
"Thou shalt not deliver unto his master the servant which is
escaped from his master unto thee. He shall dwell with thee,
even among you, in that place which he shall choose in one of
thy gates, where it liketh him best: thou shalt not oppress
him." Of the *interpretation* of this statute, there can not be
the least doubt; as to its *application* only can there remain,
in any mind, some little question.

1. THE LANGUAGE. THE SERVANT TO HIS MASTER; NOT, THE SLAVE TO HIS OWNER.

The first thing to be considered is the language: "Thou
shalt not deliver up the servant to his master, which is escaped unto thee from his master." *The servant to his master*,
עֶבֶד אֶל־אֲדֹנָיו. It is not, *the slave to his owner*, or the *heathen*
slave to his *owner*, which would have been the proper form
of expression, if either *slaves* at any rate were under consideration, or *heathen* slaves alone. The word for servant is the
ordinary עֶבֶד, and the word for his master is אֲדֹנָיו, which is
to be compared and contrasted with the word for owner, בַּעַל,
the latter word being used when a beast or an article of
property instead of a human being is spoken of. The contrast
may be fairly and fully seen, and the usage demonstrated, by
comparing Exodus, xxi. 4, 5, 6, 8, with Exodus, xxi. 28, 29,
32, 34, and 36, and likewise Exodus, xxii. 11, 12, 14, 15.
Here, in the first case, where the subject is a human being,
(the servant), the *master*, אָדֹן, is spoken of, but never the
owner. The relations and responsibilities are brought to view
between master and servant, but never between owner and
slave. But in the other cases, where the subject is property,
as an ox, ass, sheep, or article of raiment or furniture, the
owner, בַּעַל, is spoken of, not the master. The distinction is
one of purpose and care, and not accidental; and in no case
is any such relation between human beings brought to view

as of the one being owner of the other, with sanction of such relation. The history of such relationship is the history of crime, and the selling of human beings is always a criminal transaction. The whole transaction of the selling of Joseph is described as the crime of stealing; and no person in Judea could ever have sold any human being, no matter by what means in his power, without the conviction of doing what was forbidden of God. Man-selling was no more permitted than man-stealing. Accordingly, there are no instances of its being practiced.

Now if there had been in Jndea, from Abraham downwards, the system of what we call slavery, the system of chattelism, the purchase, ownership, and sale of human beings as articles of property, there must have been some traces of such purchase, ownership, and sale, in the history of the people. Their domestic life is so fully set before us, that if this system were a fixture of it, the evidence could not fail to have leaked out; nay, the proof would have been glaring. If this fixture, with all its concomitant transactions and habits, had existed, had been maintained, as a national institute, *against* the divine law, we should as certainly have found it in the history and the books of the prophets as idolatry itself; we do find it instantly recorded, in the only case in which it was attempted; and the case in which the crime was completed occasioned the instant vengeance of God, in the destruction of the Jewish State. But if it had existed by *appointment* of the divine law, under the sanction and favor of God, then much more should we have found some traces of it not only in the law itself, but in the manners and customs of the people, and in their historical and commercial records.

2. THE WHOLE HISTORY AN ACCOUNT OF SERVANTS, NOT SLAVES.

But in the whole history, from that of Abraham, Isaac, and Jacob, down through the whole line of their descendants, not one instance is to be found of the sale of a man, a servant, or a slave. The only approximations to such a thing are treated and denounced as criminal; as, for example, in Amos, ii. 6, thus saith the Lord, "For three transgressions of Israel and for four, I will not turn away the punishment thereof, because they sold the righteous for silver, and the poor for a pair of shoes." When they obtained servants, or purchased them, as the phrase was, they purchased their time and labor from themselves; but if they attempted to sell them, it could not be done without stealing them; it was making articles of property out of them; it was asserting and violently assuming ownership in them; it was man-stealing. But if slavery had been a legal institution appointed of God, a righteous policy and habit of the domestic life, we should have found somewhere some traces of the transactions by which always it is attended and maintained. We should have found mention not only of obtaining servants by contracts made *with* them, but of buying *them* as slaves from others, and of ownership in them, and of the sale of them; and if they were considered in law as chattels, as articles of property, we should have found legal provisions for reclaiming and securing them when lost, fugitive, or stolen; just as we do in the cases of oxen, asses, sheep, or property of any kind, lost, strayed, or stolen. It would not be possible, for example, to write the history of laws and customs in the United States for a single century without such traces of slavery and of slave-laws coming out.

3. HEATHEN SERVANTS AS WELL AS HEBREW COMPREHENDED IN THIS LAW.

When, therefore, we search for such traces in the Mosaic legislation, what do we stumble upon? The first thing in regard to fugitives is this law before us, a law made *for their protection against their masters,* and not in behalf of the masters, or to recover their lost property. The judgment gathered from this law in regard to slavery is in condemnation of the whole system, and remains in full, to whatever class of inhabitants the passage be applied. The question is, whether its operation was intended to comprehend Hebrew servants, or heathen servants only; whether it was a law for Judea at home, or for the nations abroad, or equally for both.

1. There is no restriction or limitation expressed; it would have to be supposed, and a construction forced upon the passage, which the terms do not indicate, and will hardly permit. It would be unfortunate to have to treat any passage in this manner, to make out a case, unless the context required it, or the history and some more comprehensive laws enforced it. Compare, for illustration, the command in Isaiah, lviii. 6, 9, where it is enjoined: "To loose the bands of wickedness, to undo the heavy burdens, to let the oppressed go free, and that ye break every yoke." And again: "If thou take away from the midst of thee the yoke." We might assert concerning these passages that they referred only to the heathen, whereas it is notorious that they applied to abuses and oppressions committed not among the heathen, but in Judea itself, by the Hebrews themselves, and not against strangers only, but against their own countrymen, as in Amos, ii. 6, and viii. 6, Jeremiah, xxii. 13–17, and Habakkuk, i. 14–16, and other places. But when it is said, *that ye break every yoke*, it is not meant that the lawful and appointed contracts with Hebrew servants or others were to be broken up, for those were not yokes, nor regarded as such; and it only needed the application of common sense to know perfectly the application of the passage to unjust and illegal oppressions.

But, again, if a stranger or a heathen was thus oppressed and subjected to the yoke, it applied to him, as well as to the Hebrew; and the distinction was well known between oppressive and involuntary servitude, which was forbidden of God, and the voluntary service for paid wages or purchase money, as appointed by the law. The command, *to take away the yoke from the midst of thee,* applies to every form of bondage imposed upon any persons whatsoever in the land, contrary to the divine law, and without agreement on the part of the servant. The fugitive from such oppression was to be relieved and protected, and not delivered back to bondage. The Hebrew is emphatic, אִם־תָּסִיר מִתּוֹכְךָ מוֹטָה, if thou remove *from the midst of thee* the yoke; the yoke in thine own country, not in a heathen country. And so, in the statute before us, the oppression, the escape, and the protection are neither, nor all, exclusive of Hebrews.

2. But, second, it is contended by some that this is merely a law to prevent heathen slaves that were escaping into the land of Judea from being sent back to their heathen masters. It certainly comprehends this class of persons, and this would be an inevitable result of its operation, at any rate, whether Hebrew servants were excluded or not. But no intimation can be found, either in the text, the context, or the whole history, of its application being restricted to the heathen. The word in this statute used for *servant* is עֶבֶד. It is not a statute concerning the *hired servant,* the שָׂכִיר, nor the six years' hired servant, who could not be compelled to remain at service any longer than that period, but was free as soon as his engagement was over. It certainly could not apply to him, for he received his pay from his master beforehand, and the law would have been an incentive to dishonesty and villainy, if he could have received his six years' wages, on entering into covenant of service, and the next week could have decamped from his master with the money in his pocket, secure against being retaken. Such a person was not the עֶבֶד contemplated in this law, nor could there have been any danger of its being so perverted. At the same time, the proofs are numerous that in the land of Judea, among the Hebrews themselves, there were, and would be, persons unjustly held as servants beyond their time of service, as contracted for, persons oppressed in such bondage, and for whose protection such a statute as the fugi-

tive law before us, might be more necessary than for persons fleeing from idolatrous masters in heathen lands.

3. In the third place, then, we must remember that there were servants in Judea, both of the Hebrews and the heathen, whose term of service was not limited to six years, but extended, with somewhat more undefined dominion of the master, to the jubilee. There were servants of all work, indentured servants, bound, by their own contract, for the whole number of years intervening between the time of the contract and the jubilee. These were mostly of heathen families, though also of Hebrew, and were much more in the power of their masters for ill treatment and oppression, if they were cruelly disposed. Now it is most likely that the statute in question was interposed for the protection of just this class of servants from the cruelty of their masters; servants, the nature and the term of whose service was, to such a degree, undefined and unlimited. There certainly was such a kind of service, and such a class of servants, to which and to whom the expression עֶבֶד, and *service of an* עֶבֶד peculiarly applied. See, for example, Leviticus, xxv. 39, 40 : The Hebrew servant, contracting till the jubilee, shall not be compelled to serve with the service of an עֶבֶד, the servant of all work, but as a hired servant and a sojourner. But the *term* of service was unlimited, except by the jubilee; and so, in some respects, was the power of the master.

The statute before us seems to have been passed for the protection of such servants from the possible cruelty of their masters. Although it was not deemed best entirely to abolish that kind and tenure of servitude, but to lay it mainly upon the idolatrous nations who were to be conquered by the Jews; yet God imposed such protective safeguards in respect to it as would keep it from being a cruel and unjust treatment, even of them; such safeguards that the masters should find kindness toward their servants not only commanded by the letter and spirit of the law, but the only safe and profitable policy. Therefore it was enacted that, if any servant chose to flee from a tyrannical and cruel master, and could succeed in getting away, the master should not be able by law to recover him, should not be able to force him back; or, at all events, that none should be obliged to return him to his master; on the contrary, that those to whom he might flee from the oppression of a cruel master, should be bound to protect him, should not be permitted to deliver him up, but should give him shelter, and suffer him to dwell in safety, wherever he chose, without oppressing him.

BENEFICENCE OF THIS STATUTE.—A SECURITY OF UNIVERSAL FREEDOM.

This beneficent statute was, in this view, a keystone for the arch of freedom, which the Jewish legislation was appointed to rear in the midst of universal despotism and slavery; it formed a security for the keeping of all the other many provisions in favor of those held to labor or domestic service; it opened a gate of refuge for the oppressed, and operated as a powerful restraint against the cruelty of the tyrannical master. There might be cruelty and tyranny in the land of Judea, but there was a legal escape from it; the servant, the עֶבֶד, if men attempted to treat him as a slave, could quit and choose his master, was not compelled to abide in bondage, was not hunted as a fugitive, nay, by law, was protected from being so hunted, and everywhere, on his escape, found friends in every dwelling, and a friend and protector in the law.

It is impossible that such a provision as this should be made only in regard to the heathen slaves of the Canaanites, or of the nations around Judea, since the Jews were forbidden to enter into any treaties with the Canaanites, and were commanded to bring under tribute of service as many of them as were spared. Their whole legislation, in regard to all the heathen, was by no means that of amity with masters or kings, but of opposition and of jealousy against them. They were forbidden to enter into covenant with them. Nor was there any more need of a statute for not restoring heathen slaves that had fled into the country of the Hebrews, than there would be of a law in Great Britain for not restoring the slaves of Egypt, or of the South Sea islanders, or of the cannibals or savages in New Zealand, that had got away from their masters. But there might be need of such a law among the Hebrews, to mitigate the evils of servitude, to preserve the עֶבֶד, the indentured servant of all work, from cruelty and oppression, to prevent his service from passing into slavery, and to render it for the master's interest to treat him well and kindly, as knowing that, if he did not, the injured servant could escape from him, and seek another master, with impunity. So, if he would not lose him altogether, he was compelled to treat him kindly.

There was no such law as this, no such humane statute, among the heathen; and hence the heathen masters were ferocious despots and were accustomed to restore fugitive slaves, even for the support of the system of slavery, that there might be neither relief nor release from their own authority, nor restraint nor check upon their own cruelty. Accordingly we see the terror of the Egyptian slave whom David encountered after the foray upon Ziklag, lest he should be sent back to his master, 1 Samuel, xxx. 15. The slave called himself a *young man* of Egypt, נַעַר מִצְרִי, *the servant* עֶבֶד, to an Amalekite, 1 Samuel, xxx. 11, and his master had left him to die, because he fell sick. He made David swear that he would not send him back into that slavery. There was no such system of slavery among the Hebrews, and, with this humane law, there could be none. The operation of this law, in connection with other statutes, was certain, at length, to destroy all remains of slavery among the people, and to make all within the limits of the Hebrew nation wholly free. To bring about this desirable end, God so surrounded the system of servitude with wholesome checks, and entangled and crippled it with such meshes of benevolent legislation, such careful protection of the servants, such guardianship of their rights, such admission of them to all the privileges of the covenant, such instruction of them, and such adoption of them at length as Hebrews, even when they were foreigners at first, that, in that land, among that people, there could be no such thing as that system of injustice, cruelty, and robbery, which we call slavery. It did not, and it could not, exist.

FORCE OF THE DEMONSTRATION FROM THIS STATUTE AGAINST THE POSSIBILITY OF PROPERTY IN MAN.

This law, like the grand statute against man-stealing, strikes at the principle of property in man. It shows that God would not permit human beings to be regarded as property, as slaves in our day are considered property. Even if they had been *called* slaves, it is clear that their masters were not considered to be their *owners*, for they could take themselves off at pleasure, if oppressed, and nevertheless no wrong was charged upon them for thus escaping from bondage. They did not belong to the master in such manner that wherever found he had a claim upon them, and they must be given back. When they fled away, they were not considered as having stolen themselves; and the man who found them neither acquired any claim over them himself, nor was under any obligation to the master to return them or to inform against them. The master, in such a case, was not the owner.*

---

* SAALSCHUTZ, *Das Mos. Recht,* Laws of Moses, Vol. II., ch. ci., p. 697. He remarks that as the laws were successively published, they took under their protection, in every relation, the manly worth and feeling of those who served; and the people were forbidden from delivering up the fugitive, on any consideration, or from doing according to the customs and laws of other ancient and modern States, where bondage and slavery have prevailed at the absolute will of the master. Slavery, in the sense of opposition to freedom, he says is not found in the Mosaic polity, nor has the Hebrew language any word for slave. Compare, for the system and its details, STROUD, Slave Code, and GOODELL, American Slave Laws.

CHAPTER XXIII.

DEMONSTRATION AGAINST PROPERTY IN MAN.

THE prodigious power of demonstration in this statute against the possibility of property in man can not be seen but on a close comparison of it with the divine laws concerning the restoration of lost or stolen articles of property. The statute in regard to a MAN escaping from thralldom was explicit: THOU SHALT NOT RESTORE HIM TO HIS MASTER. Owner there was none; no such possibility was admitted.

But in regard to A THING, the statute was equally explicit, the contrary way: THOU SHALT RESTORE ALL MANNER OF LOST THINGS, whether found or stolen. All manner of property was to be restored; but no human being, for a man could not be property. Examining these statutes, it will be seen at once what a difference is made between the *mastership* of a man over his servants, and *ownership* over his cattle, his lands, his houses, and all riches. Exodus, xxiii. 4: "If thou meet thine enemy's ox or his ass going astray, thou shalt surely bring it back to him again." So in Deuteronomy: "Thou shalt not see thy brother's ox or his sheep go astray, and hide thyself from them; thou shalt in any case bring them again unto thy brother. And if thy brother be not nigh unto thee, or if thou know him not, then thou shalt bring it unto thine own house, and it shall be with thee until thy brother seek after it, and thou shalt restore it to him again. In like manner shalt thou do with his ass ; and so shalt thou do with his raiment ; and with all lost things of thy brother's, which he has lost and thou hast found, shalt thou do likewise ; thou mayest not hide thyself." Deuteronomy, xxii. 1–3.

Now as to the force of this demonstration that men can not be property, that men-servants and maid-servants were not and could not be the property of their masters, it makes no difference whether this statute be restricted to the heathen or not. It was incumbent on the Jew, if he saw the ox or the ass, even of his enemy, even of a heathen, or a stranger, going astray, to inform him of it, or bring the animal back : it *belonged* to the man who had lost it, from whose power it had escaped.   But if the servant of the same man, worth to him fourfold, escaped from him, and the Jew knew it, there was not only no obligation to let the master know, or to help return the fugitive, but a direct command from God *not* to do this, but on the contrary to aid and protect the fugitive. It is impossible to deny or condemn more forcibly the assumption of property in man. Yet that is the assumption on which slavery is grounded, and if God condemns the one, he does the other.

It is plain that if a slave were a thing, or if there had been such a thing as a slave recognized, such a possibility as that of property in man, there would have been no withdrawing that kind of thing, that kind of property, from under the operation of these laws ; the obligation was universal, of restoring all lost things, and the law would inevitably have read, Thou shalt especially restore unto his owner his lost slave. Instead of that, it reads, Thou shalt *not* restore him, nor oppress him. If he could have been property, then he would have been the most valuable of all property, and the men detaining him from his owner would have been the greatest of all thieves. If he could have been property, as an ox or a sheep is property, then the obligation to restore him to his owner would have been as much greater as a man is more valuable than a sheep.

But he could not be; the claim of property in man was inadmissible, it was piracy, it was man-stealing; and he that stole, sold, or held a human being as a slave, was inevitably to be put to death. The claim of property in man was such a crime that any connivance with it was worthy of death; and any legal toleration or establishment of its possibility, would be a wrong against man so immeasurable, and a sin against God so infinite, that to admit it even by implication in a just code was impossible. God forbade the very supposition of property in man.

GRANDEUR AND BENEVOLENCE OF THIS STATUTE.

This glorious fugitive law, enshrining this majestic impossibility of property in man, stands by itself in the divine code, terse, whole, angular and perfect, as well defined and indisputable as a diamond in its setting. It is a suitable companion for the law against man-stealing, completing the demonstration against slavery, and with the running fiery commentary of the prophets, denouncing this and every form of oppression, will for ever remain among the most convincing proofs of a divine revelation. What enmity and treachery towards God, what wanton malignity towards man, are involved in the attempt to prevent and falsify the meaning, or to deny the application and authority of these sacred statutes! He that labors to hide or strike away such radiant seals of divinity in the Scriptures is worse than an infidel.

VIOLATION OF THIS STATUTE BY THE FUGITIVE SLAVE BILL OF THE UNITED STATES.

It might have been supposed that every Christian State would rejoice in such legislation, and copy the same in its own jurisprudence. For the Hebrew statute, as revealed and enjoined directly from Jehovah, must inevitably contain, it can not be denied, the exposition and concentration of perfect justice and benevolence; an example of the will of God and the way of righteousness in this thing, for all generations and all nations. It is a fountain star, an orb of light divine, hung in the firmament of God's own legislation for his own people, the object of all that legislation being to train them more and more perfectly for his service, to bring them more completely away from the example and the power of human depravity, and to prepare them to reflect, as in a mirror, the glory of his truth, righteousness, and goodness in the world.

Now, in the place of that orb of light, the United States government and people have hung up, in the fugitive slave bill, in the firmament of their legislation, a perfect orb of cruelty and darkness. It is one of the most complete and finished examples ever known on earth of a Christian nation deliberately ignoring and defying the instructions vouchsafed from heaven, and in the very face of those divine teachings on a subject of universal and fundamental morality between man and man, proceeding on principles contrary to the divine benevolence, and enacting laws contrary to the divine law; just as absolutely contrary as they possibly could be made. If the intention had been absolute, to contradict Heaven, and thwart the purposes of God, the statute could not have been more cunningly contrived.

The divinely revealed statute was enacted by command of God to shield the weaker party from cruelty and oppression. The statute of this Christian country was enacted by inspiration and command of the oppressor, to secure and establish him more completely in his oppression, and to render it impossible for the victims of such oppression to escape.

God's statute was framed that if the victim should escape, he should not be recaptured. The statute of this Christian republic was passed, that if the victim should escape, Christian men should be forbidden to aid him, and compelled to bring him back again to bondage.

God's statute sympathizes with the oppressed. This Christian statute sympathizes with the oppressor. It was rightly declared by a slave commissioner and judge, in the act of sentencing a fugitive under this law, that there being no principle of Christian charity in it, no appeal could be taken to Christian charity against it.

God's statute was framed to prevent the possibility of a covenanted and voluntary service passing into the enforced and involuntary servitude of slavery. The statute of this Christian nation was framed to prevent slavery from the possibility of any alleviation, or transformation into free, voluntary, just and righteous service.

God's statute was framed to prevent the possibility of building upon the service of a freeman a claim to the service of a slave, or upon a contract with the parent a claim to the service of the child. The statute of this Christian country was framed to subject the man, once stolen, to hopeless bondage, and the parent to the operation of a compound oppression, that, through him, descends with aggravated power upon his children and his children's children.

This hereditary cruelty is the most infernal feature of its infamy and wickedness. For this law, by the most infamous fraud and robbery ever perpetrated under heaven, taking advantage of the wrong, that in acknowledged defiance of natural right, and common justice and humanity, gave possession of the parent, fastens, through him, and without shadow of law, whether in letter or in spirit, nay, against both the spirit and letter of the Constitution, its teeth upon his offspring.

Under cover of the phrase, persons owing service and escaping shall be returned to the party to whom such service is due, the parents themselves are not only returned to the oppressor from whom they had escaped, but the torture of this oppression, the complicated fangs of this viper-knotted scourge of law, strike and are riveted within the sacred vail of unborn life. The pincers and forceps of the demon of slavery are the instruments by which, under this Christian legalized surgery of hell, the pledges of the slave-mother's love are born into the world. The brand of this cruelty is burned in before the chattel-babe has seen the light, and the Constitution, perverted for this purpose, descends upon that stamp, under forgery of service due (! ! !) under seal and sanction of the Supreme Court of Justice; and the whole power of the government is flung down upon it, to send the image and superscription through all generations. Under forgery of *service due*, the Constitution is distorted into a vast piracy; and under such torture and perversion, the government and people have concocted a law diabolically contrary to the divine law, and subversive of every principle of Christian morals, every instinct of natural humanity, and every obligation of Christian charity. It is a law affirming that slavery is service due, and that the returning of stolen property to the thief becomes, when the article stolen is a human being, a national obligation!

With the infamous crime of child-stealing foisted into it, the Constitution itself becomes a kidnapping instrument; and if there were anywhere on earth a constitution made for such villainy, a constitution concentrating, justifying, and perpetuating such a crime, it would be the enemy of the human race, and ought to be outlawed from human society, broken up and destroyed, as you would a den of pirates. There is no such iniquity in our Constitution, there never was designed to be, there never can be; and yet the slaveocracy have succeeded in boring a place for it, and laying the eggs of the monster; and the Fugitive Slave Bill hatches it into life, full grown. By this perversion of the Constitution, and this enactment fostering and securing it, we have become, not so much a nation of man-stealers as of child-stealers, infant-thieves. When the Roman Church commit this sin against a single Jewish child, it is an outrage on the moral sense of the world; but when the church of the slaveocracy practice it on the children of millions, then it is God's grand providential missionary institute!

ILLUSTRATIONS AND PROOFS OF GOD'S STATUTE FROM THE HISTORY.

We may add that, if the servant in any class, either the עֶבֶד, or the שָׂכִיר, *had* been regarded as property, and if the law against the recapture or restoration of fugitive servants was intended only with reference to foreigners, and did not apply to the Hebrews, then must the exception necessarily have been made clear in such a statute as Deuteronomy, xxii. 1–3. "All lost things" of his brother's, a Hebrew was bound to restore; and if slaves were property, and the Hebrews had held slaves, then inevitably must lost or escaped slaves have been enumerated as among the things to be restored. Compare Exodus, xxii. 9: "For all manner of trespass, whether it be for ox, for ass, for sheep, for raiment, or for any manner of lost thing, which another challengeth to be his, the cause of both parties shall come before the judges, and whom the judges shall condemn, he shall pay double unto his neighbor." If men had not been forbidden thus to challenge the fugitive, עֶבֶד, the escaping *servant*, as their property, a like provision must inevitably have been made for trying *this* claim also before the judges. But in the whole history of the Hebrews, there are no instances on record of the reclamation of fugitive slaves in their country, under their laws. There are cases mentioned of servants escaping; and the statute itself was the supposition that they *would* escape, and formed a protection and a safeguard for them; but there is never a case named, nor any intimation of any such event, of a master hunting for slaves, going in search of, or reclaiming, his runaway property, in the country of the Hebrews. There are instances of men going from Dan to Beersheba to hunt up and reclaim an ox or an ass, but never a hint of any such thing as a man hunting, or reclaiming, or recapturing, a fugitive servant.

And yet, from incidental testimony, the more striking because it falls out naturally in the course of the history of David, we said that it was no uncommon thing for servants to escape, and to be going at large, unmolested. Nabal's complaint to the messengers of David proves this: "There be many servants, עֲבָדִים, nowadays, that break away every man from his master," 1 Samuel, xxv. 10 ; and the manner of the complaint argues the anger of Nabal because such a thing could be, and the servants get off with impunity. But no instance can be found of any man undertaking, with marshals, or otherwise, to recapture them. There is no hint of any *posse comitatus* at the disposal of the master for this purpose. Had there been such a thing as a Fugitive Slave Law *against* the slave, instead of one for his protection, Nabal's language would rather have been that of threatening, than complaint. "You rogues, if you do not take yourselves off, I will have you arrested as fugitive slaves, such as you doubtless are, you vagrant rascals. I will have you lodged in the county jail, and, if your master does not appear, you shall be sold to pay the jail fees." But Nabal's language is that of " a son of Belial," who is furious because there is no help for such insubordination against tyranny.

THE CASE OF SHIMEI, CURSING AND SLAVE-HUNTING.

The case of Shimei must be considered in illustration, because, at first thought, it might seem to be an exception, and might appear as an instance of reclamation. 1 Kings, ii. 39, 40. Two of the servants, שְׁנֵי־עֲבָדִים, of Shimei ran away to Achish, king of Gath, son of Maachah, and from thence information came to Shimei ; and in his blind haste to recapture these runaways, forgetting or despising his oath to Solomon, he saddled his ass and went to Gath, and found his servants, and brought them back to Jerusalem. It is no wonder, from the description given of Shimei's cursed manners and disposition, that his servants, even purchased, as they may have been, from the heathen, could not endure his service, but preferred to run away even into a heathen country; and it is not a little singular that the first and only instance of a slave-hunter figuring in sacred history is that of this condemned liar, hypocrite, and blasphemer. But he captures his servants in the country of the Philistines, and not in a land under Hebrew law. Doubtless, they were foreigners and heathen, not Hebrews, or they would not have fled away to Achish, king of Gath; they would have been secure against Shimei's claim in their own country, but there was no law for the protection of slaves in the land of the Philistines; and, although they imagined themselves more secure from pursuit there, especially as they must have known that their master himself was a prisoner of state within certain limits in Jerusalem, yet the rage of Shimei defeated their calculations, and they were brought back. It may have been by some friendship of Achish with Shimei, and a spite against king Solomon, that this was accomplished, which made king Solomon the more ready to inflict upon Shimei, without any further reprieve, the sentence he had brought upon himself.

The history in 2 Chronicles, xxviii. 8–15, has an important bearing in illustration of this and other statutes, especially those for the protection of the Hebrews from becoming slaves. The kingdoms of Judah and Israel were at war, and the latter had taken captive of the former two hundred thousand, whom they proposed to keep for bondmen and bondwomen, the ordinary fate of those taken captive in war. But the fierce wrath of God was instantly threatened, if they carried this intended crime into execution; and some able and patriotic leaders of the tribe of Ephraim resisted the proposition with such effectual energy, that the men of the army left the captives to their disposal; whereupon they generously clothed and fed them, and carried them back free to their own country. The intention had been, contrary to the divine law, to bring them into bondage in a manner expressly forbidden. It is to be feared that in some instances the legal prohibitions against such slavery had already been set at defiance both by rulers and people in the two kingdoms; but never yet had the attempt been made in so bold and public a manner, and on so huge a scale, to override the laws.

VIOLATIONS OF THE LAWS BY OPPRESSION.

There are very decisive intimations, however, that look as if this iniquity of a forced and continued bondage, by which the Jewish masters retained their servants contrary to law, had become, at a later period, one of the great outstanding crimes of the nation. After the divulsion of the kingdom into two, those persons unjustly held in bondage would be likely to take refuge from cruel taskmasters in one kingdom by fleeing into the other; and the law in Deuteronomy was unquestionable and explicit: "Thou shalt not deliver unto his master the servant which is escaped from his master unto thee. He shall dwell with thee where it liketh him best. Thou shalt not oppress him." Contrary to this great statute of Jehovah, there may have been compacts or compromises between the two kingdoms for the delivering up of such fugitive; or if not between the kingdoms, at least between confederacies of masters. But whatever fugitive slave laws might be passed, or compacts entered into, they were all as so many condemned statutes, judged and condemned beforehand by the law of God, and to be held null and void by those who would keep his commandments. Nevertheless, with the example once set, first in one kingdom then in the other, of such unrighteous statutes, it might become comparatively easy, through powerful interests, by the combination of large holders, or of those who could profitably become slave-masters by trading with the heathen, not only to evade the divine law, but at length to get statutes passed, though manifestly and directly contrary to it, for the protection of slave property, or to assist in retaining or recovering such property.   There might be enactments for the interests of the masters, s tting at naught all the provisions of the divine law for the limitation of servitude, the preventing of slavery, and the protection and emancipation of indentured servants.

That some such form of oppression began to be prevalent soon after the separation of the kingdoms of Judah and Israel, the tenor of the Prophets and the Psalms, from Joel to Malachi, leads us to suppose.   It is probable that this legislation for the masters, this care for their interests and their favor, this oppression of those whom they held in bondage, and this disregard of the divine law in their behalf, are referred to by the prophet Amos, especially in the fourth chapter of his prophecy, where God rebukes the princes, the rulers, and the wealthy and great men, for oppressing the poor and crushing the needy, but saying to their *masters*, Bring business and wealth, and let us trade and drink together, Amos, iv. 1. Compare also Amos, ii. 6 : "They sold the righteous for silver, and the poor for a pair of shoes."   Scott's note on the first of these passages presents the case in a manner not improbable : "They crushed and trampled on their unresisting brethren, and sold them for slaves.   Having made the iniquitous bargain, perhaps, on low terms, they required from the purchaser in this *slave-trade* to be treated with wine."   It may have been partly in reference to such sins as these, that the rebuke of God by the prophet Micah was directed, that "the statutes of Omri were kept, and all the counsels of the house of Ahab," Micah, vi. 16.   For, immediately after that indictment, it is asserted that "men are hunting, every man his brother, with a net ; and the prince asketh, and the judge asketh, for a reward, and the great man uttereth his mischievous desire ; and so they wrap it up, the best of them being as a briar, and

the most upright sharper than a thorn-hedge," Micah, vii.
2, 3, 4.

It was in reference to such iniquity, this great and glaring
guilt of oppression especially, that many passages in the
Prophets and the Psalms were written. "Woe unto them
that decree unrighteous decrees, and that write grievousness
which they have prescribed, to turn aside the needy from
judgment, and to take away the right from the poor of my
people," Isaiah, x. 10. "He looked for judgment, but behold
oppression," Isaiah, v. 7. "Hear the word of the Lord, ye
rulers of Sodom; give ear unto the law of our God, ye people
of Gomorrah. Your hands are full of blood. When ye make
many prayers, I will not hear. Put away the evil of your doings. Seek judgment; relieve the oppressed," Isaiah, i. 10–
17. "Woe unto them which justify the wicked for reward,
and take away the righteousness of the righteous from him.
Therefore as the fire devoureth the stubble, and the flame
consumeth the chaff, so their root shall be as rottenness, and
their blossom shall go up as dust, because they have cast
away the law of the Lord of Hosts, and despised the word of
the Holy one of Israel," Isaiah, v. 23, 24. Compare Jeremiah,
vi. 6, and vii. 5, 6, and xxii. 17.

THE GREAT ILLUSTRATIVE RECORD IN JEREMIAH.

It is in the light of such historic references, showing to
what a degree the Jews had corrupted justice, and set up oppression, in a system of precedent and law, in contempt of
the divine law, that we come to the consideration of the great
illustrative record in Jeremiah, xxxiv. The progress of the
iniquity and the ruin therein recorded had been gradual, from
father to son, from generation to generation, Jeremiah, xxxiv.
14; but at length it arose to the crisis of an open, combined,
and positive rebellion against God, in entirely trampling under
foot the great ordinance against Hebrew slavery, contained in
Exodus, xxi. 2, and confirmed and guarded by other statutes.

The crime of injustice and rebellion was the more marked and daring, because it had been preceded by a fitful penitence and acknowledgment of the oppression, and acceptance of the law as righteous, and a return to its observance, with a new covenant to that effect. So the whole people, princes and people, loosed their grasp upon the servants they had been unjustly retaining in bondage, and for a season, at the word of the Lord, let them go. But, on reflection, they felt that it was too great a sacrifice of power, and relinquishment of property, to which they would not submit. " So they turned, and caused the servants and the handmaids, whom they had let go free, to return, and brought them into subjection for servants and for handmaids," Jeremiah, xxxiv. 11. Then came the word of the Lord, and its execution followed, as the lightning doth the thunder: " Because ye have not hearkened unto me, in proclaiming liberty, every one to his brother, and every one to his neighbor, behold I proclaim a liberty for you, saith the Lord, to the sword, to the pestilence, and to the famine ; and I will make you to be removed into all the kingdoms of the earth," Jeremiah, xxxiv. 17.

It throws a solemn light of additional warning upon this transaction, to compare with this chapter of Jeremiah, the cotemporary prophecy of Ezekiel, in the twenty-second chapter of that prophet. As men gather silver, brass, iron, lead, and tin, into the midst of the furnace, to blow the fire upon it, to melt it, so God informed Ezekiel that he was now gathering the whole house of Israel, that had become dross, priests, princes, prophets, and people in the midst of Jerusalem, to pour out his fury upon them, and melt them as refuse metals in the midst of the fire. The indictment of their wickedness in this chapter, issued just three years before the prediction of Jeremiah, in the thirty-fourth of his prophecy, closes with these words: " *The people of the land have used oppression, and exercised robbery, and have vexed the poor and needy ; yea, they have oppressed the stranger wrongfully.* And I sought for a man among them that should make up the hedge, and stand in the gap before me for the land, that I should not destroy it, but I found none. Therefore have I poured out mine indignation upon them ; I have consumed them with the fire of my wrath; their own way have I recompensed upon their heads, said the Lord God."

Almost at the same moment, and in view of the same predicted event, though residing at so wide a distance from each other, these two prophets were charged with God's denunciation against the same sin of oppression, as the one climacteric occasion and cause of the destruction of the nation. God refers the people back to the first covenant of freedom in Exodus, xxii., abolishing and forbidding slavery for ever ; and the violation of that covenant, in the attempt to establish the forbidden sin, is distinctly and with sublime and awful emphasis, marked by Jehovah in his one, final, conclusive reason for giving over the nation into the hand of their enemies, and sweeping the whole community into bondage. It would not be possible to transmit, in historic form, a more tremendous reprobation of the sin of slavery, and of slavery as a sin. From Ezekiel, xxii., and Jeremiah, xxxiv., this lesson stands out as the one grand lesson of God's vengeance in the captivity.

TESTIMONY OF COTEMPORARY PROPHETS.

MICHAELIS, on this historic passage, supposes that for some considerable time this oppression, this violation of God's covenant in depriving the servants of their freedom, had been going on; but that king Zedekiah, terrified by Jeremiah's preaching, and by the armies of Nebuchadnezzar, had agreed with the princes and people to repent of this their wickedness, and had accordingly, for a little season, set their servants free, as God had commanded. But then, reflecting on the profitableness of such property, and the vastness of the sacrifice of power and gain in relinquishing it, they concluded that they would not do it, and accordingly reënslaved their servants as their property for ever. For this renewed crime, against which Jeremiah, Ezekiel, and other prophets had been thundering the word of the Lord, God's wrath arose without remedy, and he swept the whole race away.

With this view of the case, the prophets all agree, and many passages become plainer in the light of the closing development of the great tragedy. For example, Jeremiah, v. 26–31, manifestly refers to the progress of this iniquity: " For among my people are found wicked men; they lay wait as he that setteth snares; they set a trap, they catch men. They judge not the cause of the fatherless nor the right of the needy. The prophets prophesy falsely, and the priests bear rule by their means." Also, Jeremiah, vi. 6: "The city is wholly oppression in the midst of her; cast a mound against Jerusalem, the city to be visited." Also, Jeremiah, vii. 4–17: " If ye oppress not the stranger, the fatherless and the widow, then may ye dwell in the land; but otherwise, I will cast you out of my sight." Also, xxi. 12: "Execute judgment in the morning, and deliver the spoiled out of the hand of the oppressor, let my fury go out like fire and burn that none can quench it, because of the evil of your doings." Also, xxii. 3–13–17: " Execute ye judgment and righteousness, and deliver the spoiled out of the hand of the oppressor; and do no wrong, do no violence to the stranger. Woe unto him that buildeth his house by unrighteousness, and his chambers by wrong; that useth his neighbor's service without wages, and giveth him not for his work. Did not thy father do judgment and justice, and then it was well with him? He judged the cause of the poor and needy; then it was well with him; was not this to know me, saith the Lord? But thine eyes and thy heart are not but for thy covetousness, and for oppression and violence. Therefore are they cast out into a land which they know not."

The particular sin, and the particular punishment, oppression and the retribution, are here developed.

On a comparison of Ezekiel, xviii. and xxii. the same great facts are manifest. One of the characteristics of a man of true piety, a just man before God, is repeatedly stated as being the hatred and avoidance of oppression; "hath not oppressed any, hath spoiled none by violence, hath executed true judgment between man and man." But on the other hand, the characteristics of a wicked man, and the sure conditions of God's wrath, are, "if he have oppressed the poor and needy, spoiled his brother, cruelly oppressed any." In the twenty-second chapter, the princes and the people are arraigned as having done this, among other wickedness: "In the midst of thee have they dealt by oppression with the stranger; in thee have they vexed the fatherless and widow; in thee have they set light by father and mother; in thee are men that have carried tales and taken gifts to shed blood, and thou hast greedily gained by extortion. The priests have violated my law. The princes are like wolves ravening the prey, to get dishonest gain. And her prophets have daubed them with untempered mortar, divining lies. The people of the land have used oppression and exercised robbery, and have vexed the poor and needy; yea, they have oppressed the stranger wrongfully : therefore have I consumed them with the fire of my wrath."

On a comparison with other cotemporary prophets, Zechariah, Zephaniah, Habakkuk, and, somewhat later, Malachi, we meet with astonishing illustrations; as, for example, where God reminds Zechariah of his former commandment: "Execute true judgment, and show mercy and compassion every man to his brother; and oppress not the widow nor the fatherless, the stranger nor the poor; and let none of you imagine evil against your brother in his heart. But they refused to hearken, and made their hearts as adamant against the law, lest they should hear; therefore came a great wrath from the Lord of hosts, and he scattered them with a whirlwind among the nations," Zechariah, vii. 7–14.

The testimony of Zephaniah is to the same point: "Woe to the oppressing city! Her princes within her are roaring lions; her judges are evening wolves; they gnaw not the bones till the morrow." The same terrible facts of oppression and cruelty, unjust judgment, violence, and compulsory servitude without wages, are disclosed in Habakkuk; the violence of the land, the city, and all that dwell therein.

It is the iniquity of oppression, in the shape of unrequited and unjustly compelled servitude, the oppression of the stranger in the same way; the defrauding him of his rights, the perversion of law and of just judgment in regard to him, and the trampling upon him and his children with hereditary cruelty, that are distinctly described as having brought down the wrath of God without remedy. *And these are precisely our sins;* and there are some expressions in these indictments and catalogues of crime fearfully descriptive of the state of jurisprudence and of social manners in the United States.*

---

* For example, HER JUDGES ARE EVENING WOLVES. One needs only to read the published account of the atrocious injustice and cruelty perpetrated by one of the judges of Maryland. under the Fugitive Slave Bill, against a mother and her child, remanding them both into slavery, *refusing the introduction of proof*, that even if the mother had been a slave, the child was not a runaway, and was free! Condemning them both to slavery, on the ground of pretended *service due*, when it could be proved that the child was not only in no sense a fugitive, but had never been a slave! A hyena should be set in bronze as the image of such American justice; and the statue of an evening wolf would be a fitting monument for a man capable of a decision so mean, so detestable, so superfluously cruel and barbarous.

CHAPTER XXIV.

WE have now to consider the institution and the law of the jubilee, as the completion of the system of social benevolence and freedom embodied in the Mosaic statutes.

Meantime we have before us, even if we stopped short of that, a body of laws embracing, as thus far traced, beyond all comparison, the most benign, protective, and generous system of domestic servitude, the kindest to the servants, and the fairest for the masters, ever framed in any country or in any age. The rights of the servants are defined and guaranteed as strictly, and with as much care, as those of the employers or masters. Human beings could not be degraded into slaves or chattels, or bound for involuntary service, or seized and worked for profit, and no wages paid. The defenses against these outrages, the denouncement and prohibition of them, are among the clearest legal and historical judgments of God against slavery. The system of slavery in our own country, even in the light only of these provisions, holds its power by laws most manifestly conflicting with the divine law, and stands indisputably under the divine reprobation.

FOUR FORMS OF STATUTE LAW RENDERING SLAVERY IMPOSSIBLE.

Four forms of statute law combined, in this divinely-ordered social arrangement, to render slavery for ever impossible among a people regardful of justice and obedient to God. First.

The law of religious equality and dignity, gathering all classes as brethren and children of one family before God. Instruction, recreation and rest were secured in the institution of the Sabbath, and its cognate sacred seasons, following the same law; and freedom, not slavery, was inevitable.

Second, by the same system, the original act of oppression and violence, which has been the grand and almost only source of all the slavery in our own country, was branded and placed in the catalogue of crime, on a level with that of murder, to be punished by death. It requires no particular acuteness of vision to perceive that what was an injustice to the parents, worthy of death, can not be transformed, in the next generation, or the next after, to a righteous institution, sacred by the grace of God. By covenant, the curse of the Almighty is upon it.

Third, the right of possession to himself, is recognized as resting, by the nature of humanity and the authority of God's law, in each individual; and the sacredness of the human personality is demonstrated by the same law to be such, that a human being can not, but by the highest violence and crime, be degraded into an article of property and merchandise. From the Mosaic statutes, it is indisputable that such is the judgment of God; and the successive history, which takes its course and coloring from them, or from their violation, confirms the demonstration. From the statutes and the history together it is as clear that slavery is a moral abomination in the sight of God, as it is from the history in Genesis that the iniquity of Sodom and Gomorrah was a sin. The destruction of Judah and Jerusalem for the iniquity of oppression, *in this particular form, of a forced involuntary bondage,* was a more stupendous and enlightening judgment by far, all things considered, than the overwhelming of the cities of the plain with fire. How can it be possible for any unprejudiced reader of the word of God to avoid acknowledging our own condemnation in this light?

Fourth, the protection, by statute, of the servant escaping from his master, instead of any provision for the master's regaining possession of the servant, was another interposition in behalf of the weaker party, in the same design of rendering slavery impossible, and is another plain indication of the judgment of God as to the iniquity of American slavery, and of the laws for the support of it. The Hebrew system was so absolute and effective a safeguard against oppression, and rendered any form of slavery so impracticable, and in its legitimate working would have so inevitably subdued the slavery of all surrounding nations to its own freedom, that it stands out as a superhuman production, the gift of God, The wisdom and benevolence of the Almighty appear in it to such a degree, in comparison and contrast with the habits and morals of the world, that the claim of the Pentateuch to a divine inspiration might, in no small measure, be permitted to rest upon it.

THE LAW OF JUBILEE.—UNIVERSALITY OF ITS APPLICATION DEMONSTRATED.

We come now to the consideration of the law of the jubilee, in Leviticus, xxv. 10, 35–55. This great statute of personal freedom was as follows: " Ye shall hallow the fiftieth year, and proclaim liberty throughout the land unto all the inhabitants thereof: it shall be a jubilee unto you, and ye shall return every man unto his possession, and ye shall return every man unto his family." LIBERTY THROUGHOUT THE LAND UNTO ALL THE INHABITANTS THEREOF. The expression is chosen on purpose for its comprehensiveness. It is not said to all the inhabitants of the land, *being Hebrews*, or such as are Hebrews, which restriction would have been made, had it been intended ; as is manifest from the case in Jeremiah, xxxiv., where the restriction is carefully and repeatedly announced. But the phrase *all the inhabitants of the land*, seems to have an intensity of meaning, comprehending, purposely, all, whether

Hebrews or not; it being well known that many of the inhabitants of the land were *not* Hebrews. This phrase, the inhabitants of the land, had been frequently used to describe its old heathen possessors, the Canaanites, and others, as Exodus, xxiii. 31, xxxiv. 12, and Numbers, xxxii. 17, xxxiii. 52. It is used, Joshua, ii. 9, vii. 9, ix. 24, in the same way. It is never used restrictively for Hebrews alone; not an instance can be found of such usage in the Mosaic books. It is used in Jeremiah, i. 14, *an evil on all the inhabitants of the land*, and in Joel, i. 2, and ii. 1, *let all the inhabitants of the land tremble*. In this statute in Leviticus, it is the whole number of inhabitants of the land, *held in servitude*, that are included. Ye people of Israel shall do this, shall proclaim liberty to all the inhabitants of the land.

And proclaim liberty throughout the land to all the inhabitants thereof. The Hebrew is as follows: וּקְרָאתֶם דְּרוֹר בָּאָרֶץ לְכָל־יֹשְׁבֶיהָ, *and preach freedom in the land to all the dwellers thereof.* The expression is emphatic: the proclamation to be made throughout the length and breadth of the land, not to those only who inhabited it as Hebrews by descent, but to all that dwelt in it. Had it been intended to restrict the application of this statute, the class excluded from its application would have been named; another form of expression would have been used. Had it been intended to make a law broad, universal, exceptional in its application, no other phraseology could be used than that which is used. If it had been a form of *class-legislation*, it must necessarily have been so worded as to admit of no mistake. But the expression employed is found, without exception, in all cases, with an unlimited, universal meaning. It is *never* used where a particular class alone are intended. The proof of its usage, and the demonstration from its usage may be seen by examination of the following passages.

Isaiah, xviii. 3: *All ye inhabitants of the world, and dwellers on the earth.* כָּל־יֹשְׁבֵי תֵבֵל וְשֹׁכְנֵי אָרֶץ. Here are two words used as synonymous. The first is the word employed in the law under consideration, from the verb יָשַׁב, with the meaning to *continue*, to *dwell*, to *inhabit ;* and this is the word ordinarily employed to designated the whole people inhabiting a country. The second is from the verb שָׁכֵן, to *encamp*, to *rest*, to *dwell*, employed much less frequently, as in Job, xxvi. 5, the waters and the inhabitants thereof, מַיִם וְשֹׁכְנֵיהֶם. Also, Proverbs, i. 33 ; viii. 12 ; x. 30. Psalm xxxvii. 29 ; cii. 28. In Isaiah, xxxii. 16 ; xxxiii. 24, and in Joel, iii. 20, and some other places, as in Psalm lxix. 35, both these verbs are used interchangably. But the verb שָׁכֵן is used exclusively in a number of passages which speak of God as dwelling among his people, or in his temple. And hence the use of the word Shechinah, שְׁכִינָה, the tabernacle of God's presence. In Isaiah, xxxiii. 24, we have the noun שָׁכֵן for *inhabitant*, and the verb יָשַׁב for the *people that dwell*. But the noun שָׁכֵן is very seldom used, while the participle from יָשַׁב is employed in more than seventy passages to signify the inhabitants of the land, or of the world, without any restriction. For example :

Leviticus, xviii. 25 : The land vomiteth out *her inhabitants*, וּשְׁבֶיהָ.

Judges, ii. 2 : Make no league with *the inhabitants of the land*, לְיוֹשְׁבֵי הָאָרֶץ.

Psalm xxxiii. 8 : All the inhabitants of the world, כָּל־יֹשְׁבֵי תֵבֵל.

Psalm xxxiii. 14 : All the inhabitants of the earth, הָאָרֶץ כָּל־יֹשְׁבֵי.

Isaiah, xxiv. 1, 5, 6, 17 : Inhabitants of the earth ; also, xxvi. 9, inhabitants of the world, יֹשְׁבֵי תֵבֵל.

Jeremiah, xxv. 29, 30 : *Inhabitants of the earth*, and Lamentations, iv. 12, *of the world.*

Joel, ii. 1 : Let all the inhabitants of the land tremble, כָּל־יֹשְׁבֵי הָאָרֶץ.

And so in multiplied instances. There is no case to be found in which this expression signifies only a portion of the inhabitants, or a particular class. Of the two words to which we have referred, the form שָׁכֵן would most probably have been employed, if only a portion of the inhabitants, and not all classes had been intended. There would be just as good reason to restrict the denunciation in Joel, ii. 1, or i. 2: *Give ear all the inhabitants of the land,* to a particular and limited class, as to restrict the expression in which the law of jubilee is framed.

IF ANY EXCEPTION, IT MUST HAVE BEEN STATED.

Indeed, according to the universal reason of language, and especially according to the necessity of precise and accurate phraseology in the framing of laws, had the blessings and privileges of the jubilee been intended only for native-born Hebrews, or guaranteed only to such, the expression universally employed on other occasions when that particular portion of the inhabitants alone are concerned, would have been employed on this. There being such a well-known phrase, capable of no misunderstanding, the law would have been conveyed by it. The phrase must have been the common one, of which one of the earliest examples is in Exodus, xii. 19, עֲדַת יִשְׂרָאֵל בָּאֶזְרָח: *The congregation of Israel born in the land.* In Exodus, xii. 48, the distinctive expression, to particularize the native Hebrew, is used along with אֶרֶץ, thus, אֶזְרַח הָאָרֶץ *the born in the land,* the native of the land of Hebrew birth or origin.

Whenever there was danger of misinterpretation, misapplication, or confusion, as to the class intended by a law, this phrase was employed, and the distinction, whatever it was, which the law intended, was made plain ; or, if there was danger of making a distinction where none ought to be made, *that* was equally plain. For example, Leviticus, xvi. 29, the fast and Sabbath of the day of atonement being appointed, its observance is made obligatory on the stranger as well as the native Hebrew, by the following words: הָאֶזְרָח וְהַגֵּר הַגָּר בְּתוֹכְכֶם: *Both the native born and the stranger that sojourneth among you.* So in Leviticus, xviii. 26: " Ye shall not commit any of these abominations, *neither any of your own nation, nor any stranger,*" הָאֶזְרָח וְהַגֵּר. Again, Leviticus, xix. 34: *As one born among you shall the stranger be that dwelleth with you,* הָאֶזְרָח מִכֶּם יִהְיֶה לָכֶם הַגֵּר; and it is added, *Thou shalt love him as thyself,* for ye were strangers in the land of Egypt. Again, Leviticus, xxiv. 16: He that blasphemeth the name of the Lord, *as well the stranger as he that is born in the land,* כַּגֵּר כָּאֶזְרָח. And Leviticus, xxiv. 22: Ye shall have one manner of law, *as well for the stranger as for one of your own country,* כַּגֵּר כָּאֶזְרָח.

So in regard to the passover, Numbers, ix. 14: Ye shall have one ordinance, *both for the stranger and for him that was born in the land,* וְלַגֵּר וּלְאֶזְרַח הָאָרֶץ. The same in regard to atonement for sins of ignorance, and punishment for sins of presumption, Numbers, xv. 29, 30, two instances of the same expression, employed where there was any danger of a misapplication or insufficient application of the law.   In the first instance, the expression, *Him that is born among the children of Israel,* הָאֶזְרָח בִּבְנֵי יִשְׂרָאֵל, is set over against *the stranger that sojourneth among them.*   In the second instance, the comparison is more concise: *Whether the born in the land or the stranger,* מִן־הָאֶזְרָח וּמִן־הַגֵּר.   Joshua, viii. 33, affords a striking example, where, to prevent the expression *all Israel* from being restricted so as to exclude the stranger, it is added, *As well the stranger as he that was born among them,* כַּגֵּר כָּאֶזְרָח.   The expression *all Israel* not being necessarily so universal as the expression *all the inhabitants of the land,* its *enlarged* meaning is defined; and just so if the expression, *all the inhabitants of the land,* had been used in any case where *not* all the inhabitants of the land, but only all the native Israelites were meant, the *restrictive* meaning must have been defined; otherwise, it would inevitably include both the native and the stranger, both the אֶזְרָח and the גֵּר.

This word אֶזְרָח, used to designate the native Hebrew in

distinction from the stranger or any foreigner, is a very striking one, from the verb זָרַח, *to rise, to grow, or sprout forth*,
as a tree growing out of its own soil. It is used in Psalm
xxxvii. 35, to signify a tree in full verdure and freshness; in
the common version, *a green bay-tree,* אֶזְרָח רַעֲנָן. It is thus a
very idiomatic and beautiful word for particularizing the Israel-
ite of home descent, the child of Abraham. There can not be
a doubt that this expression must have been used in framing
the law of jubilee, had it been intended to restrict its privileges as belonging *not* to the stranger, but to the home-born.

IF NOT FOR ALL, THEN A PREMIUM ON SLAVERY.

Moreover, it is obvious that, if this comprehensive and admirable law meant that only Hebrew servants were to be set
free, but that others might be retained in servitude at the
pleasure of the masters, or, in other words, might be made
slaves, the law would have acted as a direct premium upon
slavery, offering a very strong inducement to have none but
such servants as could be kept as long as any one chose, such
as were absolutely and for ever in the power of the master.
So far from being a benevolent law, it would thus become a
very cruel and oppressive law, the source of infinite mischief
and misery. If the choice had been offered to the Hebrews,
by law, between servants whom they could compel to remain
with them as slaves, and servants whom they would have to
dismiss, at whatever inconvenience, every sixth year, and also
at the jubilee, it would have been neither in Jewish nor in
human nature, to have refused the bribe that would thus have
been held out in the law itself for the establishment of slavery.
Even in regard to Hebrew apprentices, it was so much more
profitable to contract with them for the legal six years' service, than to hire by the day, or month, or year, that we are
informed, Deuteronomy, xv. 18, that the עֶבֶד, the servant of
six years' apprenticeship, was worth double the price of the
שָׂכִיר, *the hired servant.* This difference at length came to be

felt so strongly, and operated with such intensity upon the growing greed of power and gain, that the Jewish masters attempted a radical revolution in the law. And what they would have done, had the law allowed, is proved by what they did attempt to do *against* the law, when they forced even Hebrew servants to remain with them as slaves; and because of this glaring iniquity and oppression, in defiance of the statute ordaining freedom for ever, they were given over of God to the sword, the famine, and the pestilence. The intention and attempt to establish slavery in the land constituted the crime for which, and the occasion on which, God's wrath became inexorable. There is no possibility of a mistake here. God's indictment was absolute, and we have already examined and compared the passages.

The motive for this crime was profit and power; and now it is clearly demonstrable that, if the people of Judea had had a race of human beings at their disposal, whom, by their own law, they could possess and use as slaves, chattels, property; and if the law had marked off such a race for that purpose, and established such an element of superiority and of despotism in the native Hebrew nation, over such a race, consecrated for their profit to such slavery—it is demonstrable that the Hebrews would not have degraded any of their own to such a state. It would have been quite a needless wickedness to set up slavery as a crime, if they had it already legalized as a necessary virtue. Their attempt to make slaves of the Hebrews, is a demonstration that they were not permitted, by law, to make slaves of the heathen.

ANALOGY OF OTHER STATUTES.

The analogy of other statutes is in favor of this interpretation, nay, requires it. This statute is a statute of liberty going seven-fold beyond any other; intended to be as extraordinary in its jubilee of privileges, as a half century is extraordinary above a period of seven years. But already, by the force of other statutes, a septennial jubilee was assured to the Hebrews; the law would never permit a Hebrew to be held as an apprenticed servant more than six years; in the seventh he should go free. Every seventh year was already a year of release to most of the inhabitants of the land, so that the fiftieth year, if that jubilee was restricted to the Hebrews, would have been little more to them than the ordinary recurrence of the septennial jubilee. What need or reason for signalizing it, if it brought no greater joy, no greater gift of freedom, than every seventh year of release must necessarily bring? But it was a jubilee of seven-fold greater comprehensiveness and blessing than all the rest; and whereas the others were *not* designated or bestowed for all the inhabitants of the land, this *was ;* and in this circumstance lay its emphasis and largeness of importance and of joy.

This constituted its especial fitness as a prefiguration of the comprehensiveness and unconditional fullness of our deliverance and redemption by the gift of God's grace in Christ Jesus. It was a jubilee, not for those favored classes only, who already had seven such jubilees secured to them by law during every fifty years, but for those also, who, otherwise, had no such gift bestowed upon them, and could look forward to no such termination of their servitude. It was a jubilee of personal deliverance to all the inhabitants of the land, Hebrews or strangers, whatever might have been the tenure of their service. The servants apprenticed or hired, were all free to seek new masters, or to make new engagements, or none at all, according to their pleasure. The Hebrew land-owners were to return to the possessions of their fathers, "every man unto his possession, every man unto his family," Leviticus, xxv. 10. But no man could carry his apprenticed servants, his עֲבָדִים, with him, or his hired servants, except on a new voluntary contract; for all the inhabitants of the land were free.

The clause preceding this statute is an enactment concerning every seventh year, to be observed as a Sabbath of rest

for the land, but not necessarily of release for the servants;
consequently, provision is made in the promise of sustenance
through that year, "for thee, and for thy servant, וּלְעַבְדְּךָ, and
for thy maid, וְלַאֲמָתֶךָ, and for thy hired servant, וְלִשְׂכִירְךָ," all
of each class, being supposed still with the family. But when
the enactment of the fiftieth year as a year of rest is announced, it being announced as a year of liberty for all the inhabitants of the land, nothing is again said of the servants of
the family; neither in regulations as to buying and selling,
with reference to the proximity of the jubilee, is there any exception made in regard to servants, as though they were not
included in the freedom of the jubilee. But in regard to some
things there *are* such exceptions stated, as in Leviticus, xv.
30, of a house in a walled city, and verse 34, of the field of
the Levites; showing that, if any exception had been intended in regard to servants, it must have been named.

PROCLAMATION OF LIBERTY.—PROOF FROM THE PROPHETS.

We come, next, to consider the phrase וּקְרָאתֶם דְּרוֹר, *proclaim
liberty*, announce deliverance. The strongest corresponding
passage is Isaiah, lxi. 1, to proclaim liberty to the captives,
and the opening of the prison to them that are bound; to
proclaim the acceptable year of the Lord. In this passage, it
is called שְׁנַת־רָצוֹן, *the year of acceptance*, or of benefits, or, as
it might be rendered, *of discharge*. In Ezekiel, xlvi. 17, it is
called by the word with which the law is framed in Leviticus,
שְׁנַת הַדְּרוֹר, *the year of liberty*. And the passage in Ezekiel is
emphatic in more respects than one. 1. It is a recognition
of the year of jubilee at a late period in the history of the Hebrews; it is also a notice of a prince giving an inheritance *to
one of his servants*, לְאַחַד מֵעֲבָדָיו, who *might* be, not a Hebrew;
but in the year of liberty, the servants were free, and the inheritance returned to the original owner, or to one of his
sons. 2. It is an incidental argument against the existence
of slavery, when we find the servants made co-heirs with the

sons. It can not be slaves who would be so treated. 3. Ezekiel's designation of the year of liberty corresponds with that
of Isaiah, at a period more than a hundred years earlier. The
allusion, in both prophets, to the jubilee, is unquestionable;
and, in both, the grand designation of the year is that of a
period of universal freedom. In Isaiah it is *deliverance to captives and prisoners,* לִשְׁבוּיִם דְּרוֹר וְלַאֲסוּרִים. *Those that are
bound,* includes those under any servile apprenticeship; but if
any one should contend that it means slaves, then it is very
clear that the jubilee was a year of deliverance to such, and
therefore certainly applied to the heathen, inasmuch as among
the Hebrews there were no slaves, and by law could be none.
But if it was a year of freedom for heathen slaves, admitting
they could be called such, then it was the complete extinction
of slavery; it was such a periodical emancipation as abolished
slavery utterly and entirely, and rendered its establishment in
the land impossible.

Here we see the inconsistency of lexicographers and commentators between their own conclusions, when they assume
that the jubilee was a year of deliverance to *slaves,* and at the
same time restrict its emancipating operation to the Hebrews.
For example, under the word דְּרוֹר, we read in Gesenius the
definition of *the year of liberty,* שְׁנַת הַדְּרוֹר, as " *the year of deliverance to* SLAVES, *namely, the year of jubilee.*" This is
either assuming the Hebrews to be slaves, contrary to the
well-known law which made this impossible, or, of necessity, it
assumes and asserts the application of the law of jubilee to
other classes, namely, of strangers and of the heathen; and
interprets that law (as, beyond all question, its phraseology
demands) as applying to all the inhabitants of the land. The
Septuagint version of the proclamation is, ἄφεσιν ἐπὶ τῆς γῆς
πᾶσι τοῖς κατοικοῦσιν αὐτήν, *deliverance to all the inhabitants;*
and the Septuagint version of Ezekiel, xlvi. 17, is, ἔτους τῆς
ἀφέσεως, the year of *discharge* or *deliverance;* and the Hebrew for *the year of jubilee,* שְׁנַת הַיּוֹבֵל, is translated, in the

same version, by ἔτος τῆς ἀφέσεως and ἐνιαντὸς ἀφέσεως, *the year of freeing, of discharging, of letting go.*

It is of little consequence whether the Hebrew appellation was adopted from the *instrument*, the species of trumpet, used in making the proclamation of the jubilee, or from the meaning of the root-word, from which the name of that instrument itself was derived. The Jubel-horn may have been a ram's horn, or a metallic trumpet. But the name, יוֹבֵל, to designate, repeatedly, *a jubilee*, and הַיּוֹבֵל, *the jubilee*, and בַּיוֹבֵל, *in jubilee*, and שְׁנַת הַיּוֹבֵל, *the year of jubilee*, besides the expression, שְׁנַת הַיּוֹבֵל הַזֹּאת, *the year of this jubilee*, would lead us more naturally to the verb, יָבַל, *to go, to flow, to run*, as the origin of the appellation, by its peculiar meaning of *deliverance, freedom, remission, a flowing forth as a river.* This is the more probable, because the appellation יוֹבֵל, *jubilee*, is not first given in connection with the blowing of the trumpet, but with the proclamation of liberty. When the forty-nine years are passed, "then shalt thou cause the trumpet of rejoicing to sound—in the day of atonement ye shall make the trumpet to sound," Leviticus, xxv. 9. The Hebrew, here, is not the trumpet, יוֹבֵל, *of jubilee*, as might be supposed from our version, but, שׁוֹפַר תְּרוּעָה, *the trumpet of rejoicing* or of *shouting for joy.* After this trumpet-sounding, comes the proclamation of liberty; and then, first, we have the name *jubilee.*

The Hebrew, in its connection, is full of meaning: וּקְרָאתֶם דְּרוֹר בָּאָרֶץ לְכָל־יֹשְׁבֶיהָ יוֹבֵל הִוא תִּהְיֶה לָכֶם, *and proclaim liberty throughout the land unto all the inhabitants thereof: a jubilee it shall be unto you.*

The leading idea in the law is that of freedom from servitude, and the *proclaiming clause* is the proclamation of liberty; and *from that proclamation*, and not from the *enacting clauses* immediately following, in regard to restitution of property and the return to patrimonial possessions, is the name of the jubilee taken. The trumpet of rejoicing shall sound, and ye shall hallow the fiftieth year, and shall proclaim liberty to all the inhabitants of the land, AND THIS SHALL BE YOUR JUBILEE. And in the year of this jubilee ye shall return, every man, unto his possession. And so on with the detailed enactments of the law. It is manifest that this great year is called the jubilee *from its ruling transaction of liberty* : that joyful announcement in the proclamation gives it its reigning character : it would have been worth little or nothing without that. It was the breaking of every yoke, and the letting of every man go free.*

* KITTO'S CYCLOPEDIA, Article JUBILEE. The law of jubilee was a continual recognition of God's sovereign rights, and of the equality of the people one with another, in their dependence on him. These laws continually did, what is needed to be done at intervals in the best constituted States, brought back the people and their constitution to the first principles of liberty and equality. If, every fifty years, we could return where our fathers set out in the Revolution, there would be no more slavery. "These laws prevented vast accumulations, restrained cupidity, precluded domestic tyranny, and constantly reminded rich and poor of their essential equality in themselves, in the State, and before God. Equally benevolent in its aim and tendency does this institution appear, showing how thoroughly the great Hebrew legislator cared and provided for individuals, instead of favoring classes." WARBURTON adduced this law in proof of the divine legation of Moses.

CHAPTER XXV

LAW OF JUBILEE.—SPECIFIC ENACTMENTS OF THE LAW.

THE enacting clauses from Leviticus, xxv. 39–46, are occupied with the regulation of the treatment of such Hebrew and heathen servants respectively, as were bound to servitude until the jubilee. The Hebrew servants so bound were to be treated as hired servants, not as apprenticed servants; but the heathen servants so bound might be employed as apprenticed servants, and not as hired servants, up to the period of the jubilee. And always there was to be maintained this distinction; for ever the quality of apprenticeship to the jubilee was to belong to the heathen, not to the Hebrews; the heathen were to be the possession of the Hebrews and their posterity, as an inheritance or stock, from whom, and not ordinarily from the Hebrews, they might provide themselves for such a length of time with apprenticed servants, as well as hired Subject always to the law of freedom every fifty years, during that interval all their apprentices for longer than six years, all their servants obtained as apprentices till the jubilee, and to be treated as apprentices up to that time, and not as hired servants, were to be of the heathen, or the stranger, for ever, and not of the Hebrew. But every fiftieth year was a year of jubilee throughout the land for all the inhabitants thereof, Hebrew or heathen, all the inhabitants, of whatever class or station. The heathen apprenticed servant was not regarded, because obtained of the heathen, as on that account not an inhabitant of the land ; on the contrary, this grand statute was evidently made additional to all the other statutes of relief and release, for the special benefit of all those whose case the other statutes would not cover.

The chapter of laws in regard to the jubilee is occupied, first, with specific enactments as to the operation of the jubilee on the distribution or restoration of personal possessions; secondly, with similar specific enactments as to personal liberty. It is necessary to separate the respective clauses in regard to liberty, and to analyze them with great care.

CLAUSE FIRST, OF PERSONAL LIBERTY.

The first clause is from verse 39 to 43 inclusive. We quote it in our common version, because it is essential at this point to remark the false sense put upon the law by the use of the English word *bondmen*, assumed as meaning *slaves*. The effect of this construction is like that of loading dice, or of forging an additional cipher to a ten pound note, making it worth, apparently, instead of 10 a 100. The clause is as follows : "If thy brother that dwelleth by thee be waxen poor, and be sold unto thee, thou shalt not compel him to serve as a bond-servant, but as an hired servant, and as a sojourner he shall be with thee, and shall serve thee unto the year of jubilee ; and then shall he depart from thee, he and his children with him, and shall return unto his own family, and unto the possessions of his fathers shall he return. For they are my servants, which I brought forth out of the land of Egypt ; they shall not be sold as bondmen. Thou shalt not rule over him with rigor, but shalt fear thy God."

We must examine the Hebrew, phrase by phrase. In the first verse, *be waxen poor, and be sold unto thee,* וְנִמְכַּר־לָךְ יָמִיךְ, *wax poor, and sell himself unto thee.* Beyond all question, the translation of נִמְכַּר, Niphal, of מָכַר (the word here used for *selling*), should be, *sell himself*. 1. *Niphal*, as reflexive of *Kal*, admits it; 2. The context requires it; 3. In the 47th verse the translators have so rendered it, *if thy brother sell himself unto the stranger*, the Hebrew word and form being precisely the same, נִמְכַּר. The context requires it, because, being a Hebrew, he could not *be sold* by another; it is poverty on account of which he sells himself, and he is not sold for debt or for crime; and if any master *had* possessed the power to sell him, his waxing poor would not have been the reason. His waxing poor is the reason for selling himself, or, in other words, *apprenticing* himself, until the year of jubilee; and by law, no being but himself had this power over him, or could make such a contract. And it was perfectly voluntary on his part, a transaction which he entered into for his own convenience and relief.

MANNER OF TREATMENT.

The next Hebrew phrase respects the manner in which the master to whom he had thus hired himself was to treat him; it was a proviso guarding and protecting the poor servant from a despotic and cruel exercise of authority. It is translated, *Thou shalt not compel him to serve as a bond-servant;* but the Hebrew is simply as follows : לֹא־תַעֲבֹד בּוֹ עֲבֹדַת עָבֶד, *thou shalt not impose upon him the service of a servant*, that is, the hard work of a servant, who, not being engaged כִּשְׂכִיר, *as a hired servant*, by the day or the year, for a particular service, could be set to any work without any new contract or additional wages. As we have clearly seen, there is no term nor phrase in the Hebrew language to signify what we mean by the words slave, bondman, or bond-servant; and there was no law in the Hebrew legislation which permitted any Hebrew to be, or to be treated as, slave, bondman, or bond-servant. But a poor man, making a general contract of his services till the jubilee, might be cruelly treated by his

when there is no reference whatever in the passage or the chapter to any such law, or to any sale for debt, nor any intimation that any such thing was possible! The references to the passages in illustration are instances of mistakes equally gross; but, as we have before considered those passages, we shall revert to only one, that in 2 Kings, iv. 1, because it is often perverted. There is, in that passage, no mention of any sale, nor any intimation of it; but it is said, "The creditor has come to take unto him my two sons to be servants (לַעֲבָדִים)." That is, has come demanding that my two sons be put to service till they work out the debt; further than this there is no demand; and as to any law for the sale of the debtor, it exists only in the imagination of the writer; there was no such law nor permission. But thus carelessly and frequently have assertions been made and reiterated, of which, if any student wishes to be convinced, let him turn to Horne's Introduction, to the chapter on the condition of slaves and servants, and the customs relating to them. He will find, on a single page, almost as many mistakes and misstatements as there are lines; all proceeding from the first false assumption, taken up without investigation, that all the servitude in the Old Testament was slavery, and that, wherever the word servant occurs, it means slave. These statements have been repeated so often, that they have come to be regarded as truisms, and, by possession and reiteration, are in many minds impregnable.

The *implicit statement* Mr. Trench might have found to be, on comparing verse 42 with verse 39, that they shall *not* be sold with the selling of bondmen: "Thou shalt not compel him to serve as a bond-servant;" and, in the original, he might have found that it is the sale of the man by himself which is referred to, and under such circumstances as would put him in a condition, from being entirely poor, of so great improvement as to be able himself to buy back his contract in a short time. The making of the contract of his services, for a specified time, was said to be the selling of himself; and the securing a right, by contract, to those services, was the buying of a servant.

PROOF AND CORRECTION OF THE ERROR.

Even Michaelis, who applies the word *slave* to the Hebrew six years' servant, thereby showing that he does not mean slave, but a voluntary hired laborer, admits that he can point out no such law in the Mosaic institutes as a law authorizing the sale of men, women or children for debt.* On the contrary, this was an outrage against law, against both the spirit and letter of the law. This is proved from Nehemiah, v. 5, 8, where the nobles and the rulers are accused by Nehemiah of having sanctioned and committed this very oppression; and he sets a great assembly against them, and arraigns them for the crime. His argument plainly is, that their procedure is contrary to the law of God, for he says, It is not good that ye do; ought ye not to walk in the fear of our God? And it is added, that they did not attempt to excuse or justify themselves. Then they held their peace, and found nothing to answer. The exaction of usury was put along with this crime.

Now if it had been enjoined in the divine law, or permitted, that a man's children could be sold as slaves for the parent's debt, then nobles, rulers and usurers would not have remained quiet under this accusation, would not have failed to justify

---

* Michaelis, Commentaries, Article 148, vol. ii. This celebrated scholar was one of the earliest writers on the Old Testament who used the word slave to indicate the nature of the domestic service among the Hebrews; but after him there was a deluge, and to this day, professedly critical writers reiterate the assertion that the Hebrews held slaves, and refer to Michaelis for their proof, but not to the Scriptures. They are also in the habit of asserting the existence of slavery, and referring to passages as proofs, which, on examination, incontrovertibly prove the contrary. In the Bibliotheca Sacra for 1856, in an article on "Aliens in Israel," the writer declares that one of the kinds of service among the Hebrews was "absolute and hereditary slavery," and that "foreigners could purchase Hebrew slaves," and "Hebrews foreign slaves," and among other authorities, appeals to Michaelis and the Mishna! This amazing carelessness has become a habit. But see, for its correction SAALSCHUTZ, *Das Mosaische Recht* Vol. II., 714, etc.

themselves by law. But they did no such thing, simply because they could not; they knew that their oppressive procedures were contrary to the divine law. Moreover, it is singularly in point, and interesting to note, that certain articles of property were forbidden to be taken for debt, under any circumstances, Exodus, xxii. 26, Deuteronomy, xxiv. 6, among which were a man's outer garment or coat, and the upper and nether millstones; articles of such necessity to personal comfort and the subsistence of the household, that it was not permitted on any account to take them away or sell them. Now it is impossible that a man's coat should be regarded as dearer to him or more sacredly in his possession than his children; that a law should be framed forbidding his garments and his household furniture from being attached by the sheriff, but at the same time permitting the creditor to take his children; a law permitting a poor widow to keep in her house the upper and nether millstones, and a change of raiment, but not her own children; a law preventing the creditor from taking away her household utensils, but allowing him to sell her children, for whose sake alone her furniture was valuable to her, and by whose help alone she could obtain corn to grind between the millstones. She could have pounded corn on an emergency with common stones, but nothing could supply the place of her children; and to suppose that a divine law could, at one and the same time, allow her children to be sold by an oppressive creditor as slaves, while under the plea of kindness it would not permit the same oppressor to take her household furniture from her, is to suppose an absurdity, is to fasten an inconsistency and reproach upon a divine revelation too crude and monstrous to be entertained for a moment.

A man that supposed he was commenting upon a divine revelation would be restrained from such heedless assertions; but when the Scriptures fall into the hands of men that have no more belief in their divine inspiration than they have in that of the laws of Lycurgus or the poems of Homer, and the

commentaries and theological decisions of such men are allowed
to direct the opinions of the church, and set the style and
current of theological literature, there is no error or contradiction, the prevalence of which can be a subject of astonishment. Mistakes, absurdities, and even injustice and impiety,
may come to be installed and maintained as articles of divine
inspiration. Where would be the vaunted benevolence and
wisdom of the Mosaic laws, where the proof of their having
come from God, if such monstrous abominations of cruelty
as those necessary for the support and sanction of the system of human slavery were found, permitted, or enjoined in
them ?

Now let it be remembered, in connection with the case before us, how explicit and benevolent was the divine statute in
Exodus, xxii. 22, 23, also Deuteronomy, xxiv. 16, 17: "Ye
shall not afflict any WIDOW, or FATHERLESS CHILD. If thou
afflict them in any wise, and they cry unto me at all, I will
surely hear their cry. Thou shalt not pervert the judgment
of the stranger nor the fatherless, nor take the widow's raiment to pledge." It is not to be imagined for a moment that
though the usurer or the creditor was forbidden from taking
the widow's raiment, he might take her children and sell them
for slaves, leaving her hopeless and desolate. If children were
not permitted to be punished for the father's sins, much more,
most certainly, would they not be permitted to be sold as
slaves, as merchandise, for their father's debts.

But the thing was impossible on still another ground. At
the end of every seven years, the creditor was compelled to
make a release, and could not exact the bond, but it was null
and void. At the same time, in that seventh year, every servant was released and free, on whatever grounds apprenticed.
This was the universal, fundamental law, interwoven in the
very texture of the Jewish constitution, and no custom or procedure was permitted contrary to it. How then can any man
imagine that such a cruelty as the selling of a widow's children

by the creditor into slavery for debt could be permissible under this law? It could be possible only by the direct violation of it. Deuteronomy, xv. 1, 2, 9, 12. The statutes of Omri and Ahab, the express subjects of the divine reprobation, and forbidden to be obeyed, may have included such wickedness. It was under the dominion of their tyranny that the incident in 2 Kings, iv. 1, is reported as having taken place. But whatever the transaction there intended, there was nothing of slavery in it, nor, by the Jewish law, could there possibly be any approximation thereto. The woman, by direction of Elisha, sold the oil, and paid the creditor, but she was not permitted to sell her children, nor indeed is there in the original any intimation of any such possibility, the utmost of the danger there stated being just this, namely, that her dead husband's creditor had come to take her two sons *to be to him for servants,* that is, to work out, by their service, the amount of debt, but not to be sold in any way. But even for this there was no law; it is wholly a conjecture of the commentators, and can nowhere be pointed out.

On the contrary, in Job, xxiv. 9, *the taking of the fatherless child from the mother,* and, as Michaelis translates it, *the child of the needy for a pledge,* is set down as an act of monstrous wickedness, along with other similar piratical crimes, as the removing of land-marks, stealing of sheep, killing the poor and needy, and rebelling against the light. The crime of child-stealing is here catalogued along with that of compelling men to labor without wages, and that also of murder and adultery, and the whole description is of the character and habits of kidnappers and slaveholders in defiance of God's law.

NO MAN PERMITTED TO BE ENSLAVED, OR TO ENSLAVE HIMSELF.

Here again, Leviticus, xxv. 42, the common version translates as follows: *They shall not be sold as bondmen,* although the verb is the same, and the form is the same (Niphal of מָכַר)

as in verse 39, and afterward 47, where it is rendered *sell him-self*. But the Hebrew is simple and clear, לֹא יִמָּכְרוּ מִמְכֶּרֶת עָבֶד, *they shall not sell themselves the selling of a servant*, that is, an עָבֶד of unlimited contract, and of all work. This phrase, מִמְכֶּרֶת עָבֶד, is nowhere else employed. It seems to denote a venal transaction, as in regard to a piece of goods, or a thing over which the buyer and the seller have the supreme power. Such a transaction would have been, in reference to a human being, a slave trade ; and such a transaction in regard to a hu-man being, was absolutely and expressly forbidden. The He-brew people were God's property, and God's servants, and they should never sell themselves, nor be sold, as the prop-erty of others. Not only was this transaction forbidden to any one for another, and to any two for any third party, but to every one for himself. No man was permitted or had the right, to enslave himself. The voluntary hiring of himself to a Hebrew master, or even to a stranger, as we shall see, to the year of jubilee, was not slavery, nor any approximation thereto. And to prevent the possibility of its ever passing into slavery, the proviso was inserted, making it a crime to apprentice themselves, or to be apprenticed beyond a limited time.

It is very plain, therefore, that the words *bond-servant* and *bondman* are a wrong and very unfortunate translation, be-cause they convey inevitably, to an English ear, a meaning wholly different from that of the original. They seem to recognize slavery, where no such thing is to be found. By the central, fundamental law, which we have already exam-ined, no Hebrew could be made to serve as a bond-servant or bondman, under any circumstances, but only as an appren-ticed servant for six years. The object, therefore, of the en-acting clause which we have now examined was simply this, namely, that if he became so poor as to be obliged to enter into a contract for service till the year of jubilee, he should not be held, even during that time, as an apprenticed servant merely, but as a hired servant and sojourner. And if the question recurs, In what particular as a hired servant and a sojourner? the answer is plain: First, in respect to specific labor, in contradistinction from the obligation of the servant of all work. The hired servant and the sojourner could contract for themselves in some particular service, and could not be commanded to any other without a new agreement; the servant of all work was of an inferior condition, employed for any labor whatever of which his master might have need, or for which he might require him. Secondly, in respect to appointed wages at specific times, which wages must be continued, although the contract of service was till the year of jubilee; and this in contradistinction from the condition of the servant whose purchase-money, or the payment of his services and time, for whatever period engaged, was all given to himself at the outset, and who could, consequently, afterwards have no claim for any thing more. We have already illustrated this distinction in the consideration of Job, vii. 2, where the *servant*, the עֶבֶד, who had already received his money for his time and services, beforehand, according to the ordinary six years' contract, *earnestly desireth the shadow*, but the *hired servant*, the שָׂכִיר, *looks for his wages*, desires his wages, which are the result of his accomplishing as an hireling his day. No servant, or עֶבֶד, served without payment for his work; but the ordinary עֶבֶד had received his payment beforehand, or when the contract was made; and the *distinctive* meaning of that word excluded the idea· of periodical wages after the work was done.

Once more, we must remark on this clause the provision in regard to the Hebrew servant, *for himself and his children.* It presents a case in which, being hired until the jubilee, he might have children born to him during his period of service as contracted for. These children were born in his master's house, in his master's family, but they belonged ·to himself, not to his master. They were not slaves, and could not be, any more than himself. Yet they were examples of the יְלִיד בַּיִת, *the born in the house*, as in Abraham's family, and *the trained ones*, as in his household, and בְּנֵי־בָיִת, *the sons of the house*, as in Ecclesiastes, ii. 7. They were not bondmen, and could not be made such, or held as such, but by law were free. The fact of their being born in the house of their master while their father was in his service did not give the master the least claim upon *them* as his servants, without a separate voluntary contract, or payment for their services. All were born free, and their freedom could not be taken from them, neither could they be made servants at the will of the master alone; nor could the father sell them, though he might apprentice them for a season, yet never beyond the period assigned by law.*

UNAUTHORIZED TRANSLATION OF TERMS.

This being the case, it is greatly to be regretted that our translators, for want of an English word which would express the difference between a hired servant, the שָׂכִיר, and an apprenticed servant of all work, the עֶבֶד; and also for want of a word answering to the extremest meaning of the same word עֶבֶד, which *never* meant among the Hebrews *a slave*, should have taken the words *bond-servant* and *bondman*, as well as the word *servant*, to translate the *same* Hebrew word for servant, giving it thus a meaning which it can not bear in the original, and at different times meanings directly opposite.

* BLACKSTONE'S COMMENTARIES ON THE LAWS OF ENGLAND, vol. i., p. 425. —This great writer describes three classes of servants, acknowledged by the laws of England. First *menial servants*, so called from being *intra mœnia*, or domestics; second, *apprentices*, so called from *apprendre*, to learn, usually bound for a term of years; third, *laborers*, who are hired by the day or the week, and do not live *intra mœnia*, as part of the family.

The classification here is very striking for its similarity with that of servants among the Hebrews. It might with just as much propriety be asserted that the *intra mœnia* servants in England were slaves, as that the *sons of the household* in Judea were slaves. The domestics in Judge Blackstone's own family could be proved to have been slaves by the same method in which those in the family of Abraham have been assumed as such.

We have before noted some of the reasons why they took this course; as, for example, because the unpaid servitude into which the Hebrews were compelled in Egypt is designated by עֲבֹדַת עֶבֶד; and it is said, *Remember that thou wast an* עֶבֶד *in Egypt.* Our translators said, Remember that thou wast a *bondman* in Egypt; but truly the word would have been more fully rendered by the phrase *an oppressed servant*, because, as we have seen, the Hebrews were not *slaves* in Egypt, were not held as such; a fact which makes God's prohibiting of the Hebrews from laying the same oppressive servitude upon others much more significant. This *bond-service* they were forbidden by law from imposing upon their own servants, who never were, and never could be, what in common usage we understand by the word *bondmen*.

But seeing the word repeatedly used to describe a class of servants among the Hebrews, what other conclusion can the mere English reader adopt, unless he goes into a very critical comparison of passages, than that such servants were slaves? Yet the very word thus translated is the word used for native Hebrew servants, who sometimes, as this law of jubilee under consideration proves, were held in servitude just as long as any servants of the heathen or of strangers could be, that is, *until* the jubilee, but could not, under any circumstances, be slaves. We have sometimes admitted the word *bondman* as the translation of עֶבֶד, in our argument, to describe the rigorous rule which the Hebrews were forbidden from using in regard to their servants; but it is inapplicable as the true translation of the word, whether the servants designated are Hebrew or adopted heathen.

We might suppose that our translators had followed the Septuagint translation; but the Septuagint frequently uses παῖς where the English version uses *bondman*, for the same word עֶבֶד; as, for example, Deuteronomy, xxviii. 68: Ye shall be sold for *bondmen and bondwomen*, Septuagint, παῖδας καὶ παιδίσκας, Hebrew, עֲבָדִים וְלִשְׁפָחֹ֖ת. In Deuteronomy, xxiii. 15:

Thou shalt not deliver unto his master the servant who hath escaped, the English version and the Septuagint agree, and the word is translated *servant* and παῖδα, for the Hebrew עֶבֶד. But in Deuteronomy, xv. 15 : "Remember that thou wast a bondman in Egypt," the same Hebrew word is translated *bondman*, and Septuagint οἰκέτης. The same in Deuteronomy, vi. 21. But now in Leviticus, xxv. 55, the same Hebrew word is translated by the Septuagint, in the same verse, both οἰκέται, and παῖδες, but in our English version, *servants*, not bondmen. Singular then it is, that in Leviticus, xxv. 44, *Both thy bondmen and thy bondmaids*, וַאֲמָתְךָ עַבְדְּךָ, is translated by the Septuagint Καὶ παῖς καὶ παιδίσκη, and precisely the same words at the close of the same verse are translated δοῦλον καὶ δούλην.

This use of terms by the Septuagint translators proves, as we shall see in the argument from the New Testament, that the occurrence of the Greek words for *slave* does not necessarily indicate slavery, they having been applied, by very common usage, to describe *servants*, of whom it is known positively that they were free, and never had been, and could not possibly be, at any time, *slaves*. Just so the Greek term for *slavery* is applied to a *service* which is known to have been a free service, proving that no argument can be instituted for the existence of *slavery*, merely from the use of that term. The person called a δοῦλος may have been a free servant, and the service called δουλεία may have been a voluntary, free, paid contract.*

---

* JOSEPHUS, Antiq., B. 3, Ch. xii., Sect. 3, and B. 16, Ch. i., furnish instances of the usage of δουλευω and δουλειαν for free service. In the first of these cases Josephus uses the phrase employed in Lev. xxv., 47, *though of the same stock*, that is, the native Hebrew stock. It illustrates the meaning of what is described as the sale of a Hebrew to the stock of the stranger's family. For an example of the unauthorized use of terms, and of error thereby perpetuated, see MICHAELIS, Laws of Moses, Vol. II., Art. 145. "Whoever devoted himself to God became a SLAVE of the sanctuary!"

CHAPTER XXVI.

CLAUSE SECOND, OF PERSONAL LIBERTY.

This verse, Leviticus, xxv. 44, constitutes the second clause, as to personal liberty, in the law of jubilee. The English translation is, *Both thy bondmen and thy bondmaids, which thou shalt have, shall be of the heathen that are round about you; of them shall ye buy bondmen and bondmaids.* We must compare this with the Hebrew in full, and the Hebrew with the Septuagint, and we shall see an important difference from the true meaning of the original. The Hebrew is as follows: וְעַבְדְּךָ וַאֲמָתְךָ אֲשֶׁר יִהְיוּ־לָךְ מֵאֵת הַגּוֹיִם אֲשֶׁר סְבִיבֹתֵיכֶם מֵהֶם תִּקְנוּ עֶבֶד וְאָמָה, literally, *And thy man-servants, and thy maid-servants, which shall be to you from among the nations that are round about you, of them shall ye obtain man-servant and maid-servant.*

The meaning of this, at first sight, would seem to be: he shall be permitted to obtain (or *purchase*, according to the Hebrew idiom for a contract made with a servant), from as many servants as may be with you, from among the nations round about you, men-servants, and maid-servants, or, the man-servant and the maid-servant. The Hebrew construction does not read, that "ye shall purchase of the nations that are round about you," but, "of the servants that have come to you from among those nations." Ye may take such as your servants, making with them such contracts of service as you choose.

But this being a proviso under the law of jubilee, the reference naturally is to contracts of service until the year of jubilee. It might possibly have been argued or imagined, from such laws as that in Deuteronomy, xxiii. 15, 16, concerning servants that had escaped from their masters, that it was not permitted to take the heathen servants for apprentices, or to put them under contract until the year of jubilee. This law gives such a permission. It can not mean that your men-servants and your maid-servants thus legally bound, shall be only of the heathen; for the preceding clause is an enactment respecting the treatment of the *Hebrew* servants so bound; nor is it imperative, as if it had been said, " Of them *only*, *ye shall* buy bondmen and bondmaids," or, " Ye shall have your bondmen and bondmaids (using our version) only from the heathen." But the statute is permissive—ye *may;* it is allowed you by law to make what contracts of service you please, with servants from the heathen, or the nations round about you, limited only by the law of jubilee.

Now, that this is the meaning of this clause, is rendered somewhat clearer by the Septuagint translation of this 44th verse: Καὶ παῖς καὶ παιδισκη ὅσοι ἂν γένωνταί σοι, ἀπὸ των ἐθνῶν ὅσοι κύκλῳ σου εἰσὶν ἀπ' αὐτῶν κτησεσθε δοῦλον καὶ δούλην, literally, "And servant, and maid-servant, as many as there may be to you from the nations round about you, from them shall you procure bondman and bondwoman." We use the words *bondman* and *bondwoman*, not because δοῦλον, and δούλην, necessarily mean that and that only, but to preserve the contrast manifest in the Septuagint translation of this verse. Now it seems clear that the Septuagint translators have conveyed the literal construction of the Hebrew, except only in the use of these latter words, more truly than our English translators. But we do not insist upon this, as if it were in the least degree essential to the argument; for it makes very little difference whether the law says, "Ye may procure from the nations round about you, servants and men-servants," or, "Ye may procure from as many servants as may come to your country from the nations, your men-servants and maid-servants." The contract in either case was of voluntary service, and not involuntary servitude or slavery.

This law gave no Hebrew citizen the power or the privilege (even if it could have been considered a privilege, which it was not), of going forth into a heathen country and buying slaves, or of laying hold on any heathen servants and compell-ing them to pass from heathen into Hebrew bondage. But it did give permission to obtain servants, on a fair and volun-tary contract, from among them, limiting, at the same time, the longest term of such service by the recurrence of the ju-bilee. Such permission by statute was not only expedient, and for the sake of the heathen, benevolent, but circumstances made it necessary.

MANNER OF OBTAINING SERVANTS.

The heathen round about Judea were idolatrous nations. Now the Hebrews were so defended and forbidden by law from entering, with the Canaanitish tribes especially, into any treaties of fellowship and commerce, of relationship and inter-course, socially or otherwise, that there seemed a necessity of inserting this article in regard to servants, as an exception. The Hebrews might obtain servants of the heathen, might employ them as servants of all work, and by the longest con-tract. They were thus prepared for freedom, and made free. But as to making slaves of them, there could be no such thing; there was no such sufferance or permission. There were no slave-marts in Israel, nor any slave-traders, nor slave-procur-ers, nor *go-betweens* of traffic in human flesh. The land of Canaan itself was given to the Hebrews for a possession, but never the inhabitants, nor the inhabitants of heathen nations round about them.

How then should Hebrew householders or families get possession of heathen servants as slaves? Who, at liberty to choose, would bind himself and his posterity to interminable slavery? Even supposing it possible for Hebrew masters to make such a foray into a heathen neighborhood, and bind a heathen bondman as their slave, and bring him into Judea for that purpose; at the moment of his transfer into Judea, he came under all the protective and liberating provisions of the Hebrew law; he was encircled with the safeguards and privileges of religion, and was brought into the household and congregation of the Lord; he could flee from an unjust master; and no tribe, city, or house in Judea was permitted to arrest or bring him back as a fugitive, or to oppress him, but all were commanded to give him shelter and to protect his rights.

The whole body of the Hebrew laws, as we have examined them, demonstrates the impossibility of importing slavery into Judea from the heathen nations round about the Hebrews. It is monstrous to attempt to put such a construction as the establishment of perpetual bondage upon the clause in the law of jubilee under consideration. The respective position of the Jews and the nations round about them, renders this construction impossible. But the language itself forbids it. It is not said, "The heathen are given to you for slaves, and ye may take them and make bondmen of them;" which is the construction put by the advocates and defenders of slavery upon this passage; but, "Ye may procure for yourselves servants, from among the servants that may be with you from the nations round about you," מֵהֶם תִּקְנוּ, *from them ye may obtain,* not, *them ye may take.* If the word be translated *purchase,* or *buy,* then, as we have clearly demonstrated, it means no more than an equivalent paid for services to be rendered during a period specified in the contract. Nothing more than this can possibly be drawn from this clause.

CLAUSE THIRD, OF PERSONAL LIBERTY.

We pass then to the third clause, contained in the 45th and 46th verses, in our common version rendered as follows: "Moreover, of the children of the strangers that do sojourn among you, of them shall ye buy, and of their families that are with you, which they begat in your land; and they shall be your possession. And ye shall take them as an inheritance for your children after you, to inherit them for a possession; they shall be your bondmen for ever." Here this clause, in the original, stops, and the next passes to a wholly different subject, the treatment of *Hebrew* servants bound to service till the year of jubilee. But in our version this clause is made to take up what seems, more accurately, to be a part of the next, and verse 46 is completed with the following paragraph, as if it belonged to the preceding and not the succeeding clause: "But over your brethren, the children of Israel, ye shall not rule one over another with rigor." There is nothing in the construction that forbids this connection, but the context, as we shall see, would seem rather to appropriate this to the next following clause.

The class here marked as the recruiting class for servants for the Hebrews, consists of the children of descendants of sojourning strangers, and of their families begotten in Judea. The Hebrews might obtain of them servants, whose service was purchased on such a contract that, up to the year of jubilee, it lasted from generation to generation as a fixture of the household; the claim upon such service, by the original agreement or terms of purchase, constituted a possession and inheritance, from the parents who had made the bargain to the children for whom, until the jubilee, it was made. That this was a voluntary contract on the part of the servants, and that it did not and could not involve any approximation to what we call slavery, nor constitute them *bondmen*, an examination of their condition by law, as a class of inhabitants, will clearly show.

RECRUITING CLASSES FOR SERVANTS.

Two classes are clearly defined in the two clauses of the law now under consideration, the second clause contained in verse 44, and the third clause in verses 45 and 46. The first class was of the nations surrounding the Hebrew territory, in our translation, *the heathen round about*. But because they were heathen, they were not therefore the selected and appointed objects and subjects of oppression; the Hebrews were not, on that account, at liberty to treat them with injustice and cruelty, or to make them articles of merchandise. Nay, they were commanded to treat them kindly. The fact that many of them were hired servants, proves incontestably that they were never given to the Hebrews as slaves, and that no Hebrew master could go forth and purchase any of them as such. They could not possibly be bought without their own consent; and, in thus selling their services, they could make their own terms of contract. The 44th verse can not possibly mean a purchase of slaves from third parties, but only the purchase of the labor of free servants, that is, the acquisition of service rendered by voluntary contract, for a specified consideration paid to the person thus selling his services for a particular time. There is no definition of the time. There is no qualification in this clause giving the right to hold heathen servants in any longer term of bondage or servitude than Hebrew servants; there is no permission of this kind in regard to *the heathen that were round about them*, there is no line of distinction, making slaves of the heathen, and free servants of the Hebrews.

How could there be? The fugitive slaves from heathen masters were free by Hebrew law, the moment they touched the Hebrew soil. The heathen households, or families that remained among the Hebrews, or came over into their land, were to be received into the congregation of the Lord, after the process of an appointed naturalization law, and, when so received, were in every respect on a footing of equality with the natives as to freedom and religious privileges. How then could such families, or their servants, be a possession of slaves? The children begotten of the Edomites and Egyptians, for example, were to enter into the congregation of the Lord in the third generation.

The children of Jarha, the Egyptian, the servant of Sheshan a Hebrew, were immediately reckoned in the course of Sheshan's genealogy, 1 Chronicles, ii. 34, 35. Ruth, the Moabitess, was immediately received as one of God's people, and Boaz purchased her to be his wife. He could not, because she was a heathen, have taken her to be his slave. Nor could any heathen families, coming into the Hebrew country, engage in a slave-traffic, or set up a mart for the supply of slaves to the Hebrews. In the Hebrew land they could no longer have slaves of their own; for by the law of God, as plain and incontrovertible as any of the ten commandments thundered upon Sinai, a heathen slave was free, if he chose to quit his master: no master could retain him a moment, but by his own consent. Much less, then, could such families have had slaves for sale. The Hebrews could have no heathen servant, but by contract with the servants themselves; and that renders what we call slavery impossible.

IMPOSSIBLE TO MAKE THEM SLAVES.

But if this were impossible in regard to servants coming to the Hebrews from the heathen round about Judea, much more in regard to the second class, namely, the children and families of the stranger sojourning in Israel, and their posterity. This sojourning was a voluntary and an honorable thing. And their condition was better ascertained, defined, and secured than that of the class named in verse 44. They were families of proselytes. They could not be tolerated in the country at all, except on condition of renouncing their idolatry, and entering into covenant to keep the law of God. They had entered into the congregation of the Lord, or would have done so before a single jubilee could be half way in progress. In regard to this class, as also the other, express laws were passed in their favor, protecting and defending them. Their rights were guaranteed by statute. They were as free as the Hebrews, and were to be treated as freemen. They had the same appeal to the laws, and the judges were commanded, Deuteronomy, i. 16 : "Hear the causes between your brethren, and judge righteously between man and his brother, and the stranger that is with him," בֵּין־אִישׁ וּבֵין גֵּרוֹ בֵּין־אָחִיו, *between man, and his brother, and his stranger.* They entered into the same covenant with God at the outset, Deuteronomy, xxix. 10–13 : "All the men of Israel, your little ones, your wives, and *thy stranger* (וְגֵרְךָ) that is in thy camp, from the hewer of thy wood unto the drawer of thy water, that thou shouldest enter into covenant," etc.,—"that he may establish thee for a people unto himself." And again, Deuteronomy, xxxi. 12, 13 : "Gather the people, men, women, and children, and *thy stranger* (וְגֵרְךָ), that is within thy gates, that they, and their children may hear, and learn, and fear."

The Sabbath, and all the many and joyful religious festivals, with all the privileges of the people of God in them, were theirs to observe and enjoy. The greatest and most careful benevolence was enjoined toward them. "Thou shalt neither vex a stranger nor oppress him, for ye were strangers in the land of Egypt," Exodus, xxii. 21. "Cursed be he that perverteth the judgment of the stranger," was one among the twelve curses, Deuteronomy, xxvii. 19. In the very chapter next preceding this chapter of the law of jubilee, it is enacted, that "ye shall have one manner of law, as well for the stranger as for one of your own country; for I am the Lord your God," Leviticus, xxiv. 22. These injunctions were enforced in various forms, and with much emphasis and repetition. "The Lord your God loveth the stranger; love ye therefore the stranger, for ye were strangers in the land of

Egypt," Deuteronomy, x. 17, 18, 19. "Thus saith the Lord, execute ye judgment and righteousness, and deliver the spoiled out of the hand of the oppressor, and do no wrong, do no violence to the stranger," Jeremiah, xxii. 3. If, in defiance of these statutes and precepts, they had attempted to bring the strangers into subjection as slaves and articles of property, on the ground that they were heathen, it would have been regarded as man-stealing, and any single case of such crime would have been punished with death.

OPPRESSION OF THE STRANGER FORBIDDEN.

In Isaiah, lxvi. 6, 7, the sons of the stranger are brought under a special covenant of blessing from Jehovah, to make them joyful in his house of prayer—"the sons of the stranger, that join themselves to the Lord, to serve him, and to love the name of the Lord, and to be his servants." Moreover, in the last indictment of God against the Hebrews, in which Ezekiel just before the captivity of Judah and the destruction of Jerusalem, enumerated the reasons why God finally poured out his wrath upon them, the last crime mentioned, as if it were the one that filled up the measure of their iniquities, was *the oppression of the stranger*, Ezekiel, xxii. 29. "The people of the land have used oppression, and exercised robbery, and have vexed the poor and needy, *yea, they have oppressed the stranger wrongfully*." Also, in the prophecy of Zechariah, *after* the captivity and destruction of the city, "the word of the Lord came to all the people of the land," referring to God's former commands, "to execute true judgment, and show mercy, and *oppress not the stranger*," and declaring that for such oppression, and for not executing judgment and mercy, God had "scattered them as with a whirlwind among the nations," Zechariah, vii. 9, 10, 14. Finally, in the nineteenth chapter of Leviticus, the same chapter that contains the precept, *thou shalt love thy neighbor as thyself*, there stands out this conclusive, emphatic, comprehensive law: "If a stranger

sojourn with you in your land, ye shall not oppress him; but
the stranger that dwelleth with you shall be unto you as one
born amongst you; and thou shalt love him as thyself, for ye
were strangers in the land of Egypt. I am the Lord your
God," Leviticus, xix 34.

Now it is incredible, impossible, that this very class of persons, thus protected and favored of God, and commended to
the favor and love of the Hebrew people, could have been at
the same time selected as the subjects of bondage, and appointed as a class on whom the Hebrew masters might exercise the tyranny of perpetual slavery. It is impossible that
they could have been doomed and treated as an inheritance
of human chattels. Yet this is the argument, and this the
monstrous conclusion of those who would restrict the application of the free law of the jubilee to persons of Hebrew birth,
and who contend that in the 45th and 46th verses of this
chapter, there is a wholesale consignment of the heathen to
the Hebrews as their chattels, their slaves.

Let us examine the Hebrew of this clause. The first phrase
essential to be marked, is the designation of the class from
whom servants may be taken, *of the children of the strangers
that do sojourn among you,* מִבְּנֵי הַתּוֹשָׁבִים הַגָּרִים עִמָּכֶם. The
same expression is used in Leviticus, xxv. 23: *Ye are strangers and sojourners with me,* גֵּרִים וְתוֹשָׁבִים. Job uses a word
derived from the same verb, גּוּר, from which this noun, גֵּרִים,
is derived, to signify a dweller in the house: *They that dwell
in my house, and my maids,* גָּרֵי בֵיתִי וְאַמְהֹתַי, Job, xix. 15. So
in Exodus, iii. 22: Every woman shall borrow *of her that sojourneth in her house,* מִגָּרַת בֵּיתָהּ. So also in Genesis, xxiii. 4,
the words גֵּר, *stranger,* and תּוֹשָׁב, *sojourner,* are almost synonymous. They are thus used, Psalm xxxix., "I am a stranger
and a sojourner with thee," גֵּר אָנֹכִי עִמָּךְ תּוֹשָׁב. The same words
are used, Leviticus, xxv. 47, in the next clause of the law
under consideration, *if a sojourner or stranger,* גֵּר וְתוֹשָׁב,
(*stranger and sojourner*). One might be merely a stranger

passing through the land, but not a sojourner, because not making any stay in the land; but the sojourners, settling in the country, were called the strangers of the land, and their children are the class designated in the verse before us, their descendants generally.

Of them shall ye buy, and of their families that are with you, which they begat in your land. This is an additional description. *Their families that are with you,* מִשְׁפַּחְתָּם אֲשֶׁר עִמָּכֶם, *i. e.,* separate and independent families, living by themselves, settled in the land under protection of its laws, and in the enjoyment of its privileges; not families in bondage, nor in any way under tribute, but free families, under protection of Jehovah. Of these, *begotten in the land,* and consequently citizens, proselytes, covenanters, with all the Hebrews, a naturalized part and parcel of the nation, might the Hebrews *buy,* (תִּקְנוּ is the word used), *obtain,* by purchasing their services, servants for themselves, as in the verse preceding, עֶבֶד, וְאָמָה *the serving man and serving woman, the servant and maid-servant.*

MEANING OF THE PHRASE, THEY SHALL BE YOUR POSSESSION.

Then it is added, *and they shall be your possession,* וְהָיוּ לָכֶם לַאֲחֻזָּה, *they shall be to you for a possession;* that is, the servants so obtained by purchase of their services on contract for time, shall be your possession; not the families, not the race of sojourners, but such of the children or descendants of the sojourners, or members of their families, as might enter into such contract of service for money; as, in Ezekiel, xliv. 28, God says of himself, that he is the possession of the priests, the Levites, אֲנִי אֲחֻזָּתָם, *I am their possession.* Still it is not absolute; they shall be to you *for* a possession, not absolutely *your possession.* Nor is it any stronger than where it is said in Exodus, xxi. 21, of the servant purchased, that is, apprenticed according to the legal contract, for money paid beforehand to the servant for his services, that he is his master's money, *for he is his money*, כִּי כַסְפוֹ הוּא. He might be a Hebrew servant, and yet be called, in this sense, his master's money, his master's possession, his services belonging to his master for so long a time as might have been specified in the terms of the contract. But the servant himself was never, and could not be, the property of the master, though he might be bound for a term of service, extending from master to son, as would be the case, if bound until the jubilee. It would be regarded in the light of a long lease, conveyed for an equivalent, in consideration of which, though the servant making the contract was not the master's property, yet the *service*, promised and paid for *was*. And this claim, up to its legal expiration, would with propriety be spoken of, be described, as conveyable from the master to his children, for any period within the limit of its legal conclusion at the jubilee. If the master who made the contract with the servant died, while any part of the contract remained unfulfilled, the claim belonged as an inheritance, or family possession, to his children after him.

For example, if, during the first year after the year of jubilee, when many new contracts would be made, and householders would be looking out for servants on the most profitable terms, a master could agree with a servant, could hire or apprentice him, could *buy* him, as the Hebrew phrase is ordinarly translated, from a family of strangers or sojourners, to serve in his household till the next jubilee, this would be an engagement for at least forty-seven years. Now suppose such a master to be of the age of fifty, and at the head of a family, the contract would bind this servant, in effect, as a servant to the children of the household; and supposing the master to die at the age of seventy-five, the claim upon his services would descend as a possession, as an inheritance to the children for some twenty-two years longer. The servant might be said to belong to the family still, for that period of the unfulfilled engagement. It was an engagement which had bound the servant, in Hebrew phrase, for ever.

But this phrase, in respect to legal servitude, is absolutely and beyond dispute, demonstrated to mean a period no longer than to the jubilee. Two prominent instances, in the case of Hebrew servants, put this beyond possibility of controversy, showing that the *for ever*-contract, לְעֹלָם, had always its termination, by the law of jubilee, at that period; nor could any contract override that law; nor was there ever a pretense, because the servant was bound to his master, technically, for ever, that therefore he was bound to him beyond the jubilee, or was not to be free at the coming of the jubilee. One of these cases is that of the Hebrew servant renewing his contract with his master to the longest period, Exodus, xxi. 6: His master shall bore his ear through with an awl, *and he shall serve him for ever*, וַעֲבָדוֹ לְעֹלָם. But at the jubilee, on the sound of the trumpet, he was free, and must return to his own family, he and his children with him.

The second instance of this illustration of the usage and meaning of the word and the law, is in Deuteronomy, xv. 17, comprehending the Hebrew men-servants and maid-servants under the same rule. At his own agreement and desire, the Hebrew servant has his ear bored, and is bound until the longest period ever admitted by the law: *And he shall be thy servant for ever*, וְהָיָה לְךָ עֶבֶד לְעֹלָם. *And also unto thy maid-servant thou shalt do likewise.* Nevertheless, at the jubilee they were to be free; this contract, which was said to be for ever, terminated by a law that lay at the foundation of the whole system of Hebrew jurisprudence and polity, at the jubilee; it could not be made to run across that limit; no one could be held in servitude, no matter what were the terms of his contract, beyond that illustrious year of liberty.

A similar usage and illustration are found in 1 Samuel, xxvii. 12: "And Achish believed David, saying, He hath made his people Israel utterly to abhor him; *therefore he shall be my servant for ever*, וְהָיָה לִי לְעֶבֶד עוֹלָם, he shall be to me *for a servant for ever.*"

In the book of Job there is another illustration, xl. 28—in our translation, xli. 4: "Will he make a covenant with thee? wilt thou take him for a servant for ever?" The phraseology here is strikingly illustrative; for it seems to be drawn from the very contract made with servants who were willing to enter into the longest apprenticeship, and the manner of sealing it, that is, by boring the ear of the voluntary bondman. "Can any man bore the nose of leviathan with a gin, and take him in his sight? Canst thou bore his jaw through with a thorn? Will he speak soft words unto thee? *Will he make a covenant with thee,* הֲיִכְרֹת בְּרִית עִמָּךְ? *Wilt thou take him for a servant for ever,* תִּקָּחֶנּוּ לְעֶבֶד עוֹלָם?" It is to be marked that the word here translated *take,* is a synonyme of that for purchasing or buying the contract with a servant: "Wilt thou buy him for a servant for ever?" In buying a servant, the covenant or contract was made with himself, not with a third party. Hence the condition here referred to, for the possibility of taking leviathan for a servant—"will he enter into covenant with thee?" Thou canst take him for thy servant in no other way. Will he agree with thee to be thine, עַבְדּ, thy bounden servant of all work, for thyself and thy family? Wilt thou bind him for thy maidens? Will he consent to be a fixture in thine household?

COMPLETENESS OF THE DEMONSTRATION.

Nothing is requisite, nothing needed, to strengthen this demonstration. It is as clear as the noon that the longest period of servitude among the Hebrews was entered into by voluntary contract, and was terminated by the jubilee. Hebrew servants were apprenticed for ever, and so were a possession, an inheritance, until the jubilee, but never slaves. The children of strangers and sojourners, in like manner, were apprenticed for ever; and in like manner were a possession, but never slaves. With Hebrew servants the long term was the exception, and the ordinary term was six years ; and even during the long term, they were to be treated as hired servants, rather than as apprentices, though they were legally bound. With servants from the heathen, or from the families of strangers, the long term of apprenticeship would seem to have been the ordinary term, and the six years, or less, the exception ; and during the long term there was no such legal provisions for them as for the Hebrews, requiring that they should be treated as hired servants. But the advent of the jubilee put an end to both periods and both kinds of servitude, and all were free, all the inhabitants of the land. We shall advert to some of the reasons for the difference that was made between the Hebrew servants and those from the families of sojourners, or of proselytes, or from the heathen. But we are now prepared to consider the 46th verse, the remainder of the third clause of the jubilee-enactment, in its true meaning. In our version it runs thus : *And ye shall take them as an inheritance for your children after you, to inherit a possession : they shall be your bondmen for ever.*

Taking the Hebrew, phrase by phrase, it is as follows : *And ye shall take them as an inheritance,* וְהִתְנַחַלְתֶּם אֹתָם. The verb is Hithpael of נָחַל, *to receive, or to inherit,* and with לְ following it, is rather transitive than active ; so that instead of meaning, "Ye shall take them for an inheritance," it rather means, "Ye shall leave them behind as an inheritance," Ye shall bequeath them as an inheritance ; or, Ye shall possess them to be bequeathed. Gesenius renders the phrase thus : *Eosque possidebitis relinquendos filiis vestris post vos, Ye shall possess them to be left to your children after you*—to your children after you, *to inherit a possession ;* not *them for* a possession, but, simply, *to inherit a possession ;* that is, the right to their services during the legal, contracted period. The Hebrew phrase is, לָרֶשֶׁת אֲחֻזָּה, *to occupy a possession, to receive as heir a possession.* Compare Genesis, xv. 3, 4 ; xxi. 10 ; Jeremiah, xlix. 1, 2 ; Numbers, xxvii. 11 ; xxxvi. 8.

The next phrase, translated, *they shall be your bondmen for ever*, contains no word for " bondmen," but is as follows in the original : לְעֹלָם בָּהֶם תַּעֲבֹדוּ, *for ever on them ye shall lay service,* or *from them ye shall take service ;* or, as in similar passages it is sometimes translated, *shall serve yourselves of them.* Compare Jeremiah, xxx. 8 ; xxv. 14 ; xxii. 13. In this last passage in Jeremiah, this form of phraseology is applied to the serving one's self of his neighbor without wages. And so, Exodus, i. 14, *all their services which they served upon them,* כָּל־עֲבֹדָתָם אֲשֶׁר־עָבְדוּ בָהֶם. The same phrase would be applied to designate the employment of a Hebrew servant, the ordinary six years' servant, so that there is no meaning of a bondman, or of bond-service, connected with it. It means, " Ye may have them for your servants for ever ;" that is, as we have seen, for the longest permissible and legal time of contract.

Or, the qualifying epithet of duration may belong to the previous phrase, *to inherit a possession for ever ;* and then the phrase of service would stand alone, *of them ye shall serve yourselves.* It makes little or no difference with whichsoever member the word of duration, עֹלָם, be coupled. Whether applied to the individuals, as a class, or to the service contracted for, as a possession, it is clearly limited by the statute itself, as in Deuteronomy, xv. 17, and in Exodus, xxi. 6. It is simply the permission to engage, and keep until the jubilee, servants from among the heathen and from the families of sojourners in the land. Such contracts should be binding in law, and in fact they served to incorporate the strangers and sojourners more immediately and closely with the people, and constituted a process of naturalization eminently wise and favorable, considering the character and habits which those born and bred in heathenism, and but recently come to sojourn in the Hebrew country, must have assumed. This would seem to be one of the reasons for the difference put by law between the nature and extent of the lease by which Hebrew servants might be hired, and that by which the heathen might be bound ; the former being by law always treated as hired servants, even when bound till the jubilee, but the latter subjected according to the letter of the contract.

RESULTANT POINTS CONCLUSIVE AND DEMONSTRATIVE.

Two points in this examination deserve a most emphatic regard. First, the unfortunate, unauthorized introduction of the word *bondmen* in our English translation, without any word corresponding to it in the original, can not but lead the mere English reader to a false conclusion. This is one of the sources of error on this subject. The difference between the phrases, *they shall be your bondmen* and *of them ye shall obtain your service*, or *from them ye shall serve yourselves*, might be all the difference between slavery and freedom. The phraseology indicating slavery produces a most deplorable falsehood; and when the effect is to load a divine revelation with the reproach of a wicked institution, or to provide the slaveholder with an anodyne for his conscience, preventing a conviction of the greatness of his crime in holding his fellow-creatures in bondage, and the apologists for slavery with the argument of its being appointed and sanctioned of God, no reprobation is sufficiently severe for such perversion of the word of God. If it be deliberate, the whole curse at the close of the New Testament comes down upon the person who is guilty of it; if it be carelessness, the sin is little less: the result, every way, is beyond measure injurious.

Second: the reference in Job to the bargain with leviathan, as entering into a contract or covenant of service, the contract being with leviathan himself, and not with any third party, supposed to have any ownership or authority for such a transfer or sale; the contract being voluntary, and no supposition of its being attainable or customary in any other way; is one of the most important of the illustrations of truth concerning this subject in all the current of the Scriptures. It is the more forcible, because incidental. It is like a

clear, transparent window, through which the light floods the
whole apartment. There could have been no such illustration as this employed concerning *slavery*, in which there is no
bargain even with the slave; no agreement, no persuasion,
nor any attempt at persuasion, nor any need of it; but a bargain and sale over the head of the slave, without any consultation of his will or wishes; and with no more possibility of his
interposing any obstacle or opposition against being so bound,
so transferred, so bought and sold, than if he were a stick of
wood or a wheelbarrow; no more will of his own, no more
consultation with him as to the bargain; no more supposition
of any obstacle or difficulty to be overcome on his part than
if he were the skeleton of a mastodon or a whale, to be transferred from Judea to the British museum.

The illustration is of a man endeavoring to persuade another
to be his servant, to enter into a contract of service for the uses
of his household; it is a household servant himself, with whom
the contract is supposed to be made, and not a slave-dealer, or
an owner or master of the man. It is the servant himself, who is
supposed to have the whole and sole power and right of making the contract; and the possibility of referring to a third
party, or a party that has the power of compelling the servant
into such contract, or of making it for him, or against his will,
or without his voluntary permission and engagement, is not
mooted. It is not supposed that there exists any such possibility. It is supposed that the only mode of getting a servant
is by applying for his services to himself, and making the contract or covenant with him, persuading him to enter into it;
and if that persuasion be not successful, there is no other mode
of effecting the bargain, no power that can compel the servant
into it.

The freedom and naturalness of this illustration make it very
powerful; it is a most convincing refutation of those who say
that Job and the patriarchs bought their household servants
as property; for men never use persuasion with an article of

property, nor solicit of a chattel the favor of entering into an agreement of service. It is clear and convincing against the supposition of property in man, showing, most conclusively, that that was not the ground nor tenure of domestic servitude, but that such service was a voluntary thing on the part of the servant; just as voluntary with him, as the agreement to take him for a servant was on the part of the master. As an illustration of the freedom of the social state, and its separation from the oppressive despotism of slavery, it corresponds perfectly with every reference to the same subject in the book of Job, showing a domestic constitution, and style and spirit of social equality and kindness, incompatible with the existence of slavery, and not admitting its supposition.

The language employed in regard to this voluntary contract, this persuasion of the servant himself to enter into a covenant of service, is similar to that used in regard to Abraham's getting his servants, and the Hebrews generally theirs. The word is somewhat different from that in Exodus, xxi. 2, in regard to obtaining a servant, but there translated, *If thou buy* a servant, and also in Ecclesiastes, ii. 7, *I got me servants* and maid-servants, and also in Genesis, xvii. 23, and other places, where the souls or servants of Abraham or others are spoken of as gotten with money, or *bought with money*, that is, gotten by the same persuasion and contract with the servants themselves as is here described as a voluntary contract with the servant alone, and not with any third party. The phraseology here used, Wilt thou take leviathan for a servant? will he make a covenant of service with thee? might have been applied, for example, to the contract of Abraham with his head servant, the *major domo* of his house: Wilt thou take this Eliezer of Damascus to be the steward of thine house? Will he enter into covenant with thee? Thou canst get him only by a bargain with himself; thou canst buy him for thy servant in no other way; only by persuading him canst thou take him, for he is his own master, and free to engage with whomsoever he pleases. And so of every one of Abraham's servants, as well as Job's; and so of all the servants ever described as employed among the Hebrews, whether native or of strangers; the " possession" of them was a possession of their services merely as an equivalent for money paid to themselves.

The culminating and conquering point in this illustration is that of its being employed with reference to the longest period of service pòssible, that is, the period to the jubilee, and styled *for ever.* This kind of service also, this, which was to be for an inheritance of a possession for the children of the family, is proved to have been as voluntary on the part of the servant, whose services were thus engaged as a family heritage,· as on the part of the master or householder engaging them. Wilt thou take him for a servant for ever ? Will he make this covenant with thee? Canst thou buy him, canst thou persuade him by money to be such a fixture in thine household, bound, for so long a time, to thee and to thy children? Nothing can exceed, nor can any thing evade, the demonstrative power of this illustration against slavery, and in proof of freedom.*

---

* Compare ROSENMUELLER on Job xl., 28, the *pactum* or covenant, as in Deut. xv., 17; also SAALSCHUTZ, Laws of Moses, Vol. II., devotes a paragraph to the consideration of the impossibility of slavery, in the sense of that word in modern times, and among other people, prevailing among the Hebrews, and the impropriety of the word slavery, as applied to their system of domestic service. Every element of injustice and oppression inhering in slavery was most carefully and distinctly forbidden, and instead of being at the disposal of the master, to be used by him as his property, to be maltreated and put to death at his pleasure, to be tasked, tortured, bought and sold, as a brute beast, the servant was protected by law from all injustice, was shielded from the tyranny of the master, and from every one of the abuses of which slavery, and especially American slavery, is the monstrous accumulation. There could consequently be no slaves among the Hebrews. Compare JAY on Hebrew servitude.

CHAPTER XXVII.

WE are not left to conjecture in regard to the meaning of the phrase *inherit a possession*, or receive *an inheritance for your children after you*. We have it most happily demonstrated as not indicating any such thing as slavery or involuntary service, by the case of Hebrews themselves engaging to become just such an inheritance for the children of the stranger, in the family of the stranger. But they could not be slaves; they were neither permitted to enslave themselves nor others. Yet they could engage their services, in a voluntary contract, for so long a period, that the contract, the time, the service engaged, might legally and justly belong to the children of the master engaging and paying for them, till the whole contract was fulfilled.

FOURTH CLAUSE, OF PERSONAL LIBERTY.

The meaning of the verse before us is settled entirely beyond question by the next clause in the enactment, where the phrase, *a possession and inheritance for your children after you*, is defined and explained by a phrase in the 47th verse, where the case is supposed of a native Hebrew selling himself to a stranger or sojourner, to be taken in the same manner as an inheritance for their children after them; the Hebrew selling himself for a servant TO THE STOCK OF THE STRANGER'S FAMILY. Here is the whole meaning of the preceding con-

selling himself on this long lease of his services, limited only
by the jubilee, to the family of some rich stranger.   He is
said to have sold himself, in this transaction, to the stock of
the family; that is, he has made a contract to abide in the
family and serve them, and their children after them, until
the jubilee.   This is precisely what the strangers were supposed to do, when they were taken as an inheritance for the
Hebrews and their children after them.   They sold themselves
to the stock of the Hebrew family, that is, they made a lasting contract for service, not to be interrupted till the jubilee,
unless they were redeemed, brought back again before the
conclusion of the contract.   A relative might redeem the
Hebrews thus sold, or, if they were able, they might redeem
themselves, that is, might buy back the right to their own
services, for which they had been paid beforehand.

For they had received the money for the whole number of
years remaining, when the contract was made, before the next
jubilee.   This is proved by verse 51, and by the provisions of
the enactment regulating the manner of the repurchase.   The
servant redeeming himself was to reckon with his master, and
pay back part of the money for which he had sold himself, according to the number of years remaining of his unfulfilled
contract up to the jubilee.   If more years remained, he would
have to pay more, if less, less, as the price of his redemption.
And the reckoning was to be year by year, according to the
reckoning by which the yearly hired servant was paid for his
services; for the peculiarity of the treatment of a Hebrew
servant bound to his master's family until the jubilee, was just
this, that he should be treated as a yearly hired servant would
have to be treated; this is apparent from verses 50 and 53,
compared with verse 40.   It seems to have been considered a
generous and gentle treatment of the servant on this long
contract, if he were treated as a hired servant, a שָׂכִיר, but if
not, then this long contract was a rigorous rule.   It was enacted in behalf of every Hebrew servant that during this long

contract he should be with his master as a yearly hired servant, כִּשְׂכִיר שָׁנָה בְּשָׁנָה, and that his master should not rule with
rigor over him. But no such specification was made in behalf of the heathen servant, or the servant from the families
of the sojourners and strangers, and in this important respect
the native Hebrew was preferred before the foreigner, and
greater privileges were secured to him by law. Indeed, the
specific clauses of enactment in this jubilee chapter, from verse
38 to the close, are occupied mainly with establishing these
distinctions between one and the same class of Hebrew and
heathen servants, namely, those whose lease of service extended to the jubilee.

In this view, it is not important whether the latter half of
the 46th verse, which we have preferred to read as the opening or preamble of the fourth clause, be joined to what follows
or to what precedes. In our translation it belongs to what
precedes, and the Hebrew conjunction has been translated
but instead of *and;* so giving the force of contrast, as if the
families of strangers might be subjected to a more rigorous
service than of native Hebrews. In the respect which we
have pointed out, this is true ; but the word *bondmen* in the
preceding part of the verse so translated, not being in the
original, nor any thing to justify it, a wrong impression is
produced ; it is made to appear as if the heathen might be
used as bondmen or slaves, but the Hebrews not ; whereas,
there is no consideration of the state of a bondman or slave
at all, nor any possibility of such state admitted, but only a
specification of the respective manner in which the Hebrew
and heathen servant, under the same contract as to time,
should be treated during that time. Over such servants of
the children of strangers as the Hebrews might buy, they
might rule for the whole period of the contract, without being obliged to treat them during that time as hired servants
must be treated ; " but over your brethren, the children of
Israel, ye shall not rule one over another with rigor." That

this is the only point of contrast is proved by the 53d verse :
" As a yearly hired servant shall he be with him, and his master shall not rule over him with rigor in thy sight."

MEANING OF THE PHRASE, RULE WITH RIGOR.

This phrase, *rule over him with rigor*, as in verses 53, 46,
and 43, *thou shalt not rule over him with rigor*, לֹא־תִרְדֶּה בּ
בְּפָרֶךְ, is found only in this chapter of Leviticus, and in connection with this law of jubilee. But in the first chapter of
Exodus a *similar* phrase is employed, descriptive of the rigorous service imposed by the Egyptians on the children of
Israel in the time of their oppression : They made the children of Israel *to serve with rigor. All their service, wherein
they made them serve, was with rigor*, כָּל־עֲבֹדָתָם אֲשֶׁר עָבְדוּ בָהֶם
בְּפָרֶךְ. Any such oppressive rule was forbidden ; it was a
crushing oppression, from which God had delivered *them*, and
they were defended by special edict, from ever exercising the
same upon others. It only needs to repeat, in this connection,
the benevolent command in the nineteenth chapter of Leviticus : " If a stranger sojourn with thee in your land, ye shall
not oppress him, but the stranger that dwelleth with you shall
be unto you as one born amongst you, and thou shalt love
him as thyself, for ye were strangers in the land of Egypt,"
and to connect with this the statute in Leviticus xxiv. : " Ye
shall have one manner of law, as well for the stranger, as for
one of your own country," and we shall feel it to be impossible that, in one and the same breath of divine legislation, an
oppressive treatment, forbidden for the Hebrews, was permitted and appointed for the strangers.

If it had been plainly said, Ye shall not oppress the children
of the Hebrews, but ye may oppress the children of strangers,
what must have been thought, what would have been said, of
such legislation, so contradictory in itself, and so glaringly inconsistent with previous legislation in regard to the same class?
Yet this is the very inconsistency, and contradiction, and moral

obliqaity, implied and involved in the assertion of those who contend that the forbidding of a rigorous treatment of the Hebrew servants, licenses and authorizes, and was intended so to do, an oppressive treatment of the heathen servants, even as slaves. Never was a more monstrous argument instituted, subversive of the very first ideas of the divine benevolence and justice taught in the Mosaic books themselves, as well as in all the other Scriptures. The argument could hardly have been proposed, had it not been for the use of the word *bondmen* in our English version, in the 46th verse of this chapter, where there is no such word, nor any thing answering to it, in the original Hebrew. And even in the margin our translators have put the more literal and truthful rendering, so that a careful English reader may see that there is no such word as *bondmen* in the text.

THE CROWNING STATUTE OF PERSONAL LIBERTY IN THE JUBILEE LAW.

The jubilee statute, the great crowning statute of universal personal liberty, was passed for all the inhabitants of the land, and no statute of limitation or exception was, at any time, afterwards added; but only statutes were added specifying the manner of treatment *up to the time of release*. But if there is nothing in the great jubilee statute itself that limits it, expressly and undeniably, then it must be interpreted in accordance with the humane and free spirit of other Hebrew legislation on the same subject. It should be our desire not to give to despotism, but freedom, the benefit of any doubt. Were it not for a desire to interpret the statute as against universal freedom; and were it not for the careless assumption that slavery existed among the Hebrews, it could never have been so interpreted. Men have looked through the glass of modern slavery, and the history of ancient, to find the same system among the Hebrews. But, in reality, there is found a set of laws and causes to prevent and render it impossible, and at length to break it up, all over the world. The system of Hebrew common law would, by itself, have put an end to slavery everywhere. The Hebrew laws elevated and dignified free labor, and converted slave labor into free.

Slavery could not be utterly abolished in any other way than by a system of such laws. A people must be trained for freedom. The heathen slaves could not be admitted to dwell among the Hebrews, except in such subjection, preparatory to complete emancipation. The subjection itself was a voluntary apprenticeship, and not involuntary servitude; and by reason of the privileges secured, and the instruction enjoined by law, it was a constant preparation for entire emancipation, a constant elevation of character; and then, every fifty years, the safety of complete emancipation was demonstrated. The jubilee statute can not be understood in any other light. But when the vail of prejudice is taken away, it is especially by the tenor of the Hebrew laws in regard to slavery, that the beauty and glory of the Hebrew legislation, its justice, wisdom, and beneficence become more apparent than ever.

This law of heathen servitude until the jubilee, was a naturalization law of as many years' duration as would elapse before the next jubilee. It was so many years' probation of those who had previously been idolaters and slaves, for freedom. It was a contrivance to drain heathenism of its feculence. The heathen slaves were in no condition to be admitted at once to the privileges of freedom and of citizenship among the Hebrews. They needed to be under restraint, law, and service. They were put under such a system as made them familiar with all the religious privileges and observances which God had bestowed and ordered, a system that admitted them to instruction and kindness, and prepared them to pass into integral elements of the nation. It was a system of emancipation and of moral transfiguration, going on through ages; the taking up of ·an element of foreign ignorance, depravity, and misery, and converting it into an element of native comfort, knowledge, and piety. And the statute of the jubilee, the statute of liberty to all the inhabitants of the land every fifty years, was the climax of all the beneficent statutes by which the sting was extracted from slavery, the fang drawn; and by this statute, in conjunction with all the rest, the Hebrew republic was to hold to the world the glory of an example of freedom and equality, in marvelous and delightful contrast with the system of horrible oppression, cruelty, and bondage, everywhere else prevailing.

The distinction between the tenure and the treatment of Hebrew servants and foreign, was not arbitrary. It grew naturally out of God's whole revealed and providential system, as well as being in conformity with the necessity of the case. But if there had been no necessity, it was only in keeping with the favor of God toward his own chosen people, that the servants from among the heathen might, if they were willing, be held for a period much longer than the servants from among the Hebrews, and in a less exalted and more general service than their own. A Hebrew servant was free every seventh year; a heathen servant might be held by a contract for a much longer time, for the whole time remaining to the jubilee. It would have been a strange thing, a solecism, if there had not been some such distinction. Yet the distinction itself was voluntary; that is, it was at any heathen servant's option to make a contract for the whole period to the next jubilee, or not. If, rather than make such a contract, he chose to return to the heathen country, he was at perfect liberty to go; and if he staid, and could find any master to take him as a hired servant, and not as a servant of all work, till the jubilee, there was no law against that: he was at liberty to hire himself out on the best terms, and to the best master that he could find. So much is indisputable, and so much is absolutely and entirely inconsistent with slavery.

GENERAL ARGUMENT FROM THE AFTER-HISTORY.

The argument and evidence from the after-history of the Jews, in regard to the unlimited application of the law of jubilee to the strangers as well as native Hebrews, is nearly as demonstrative and irresistible as that from the statute itself. It is clear that if the heathen had been given and appointed of Jehovah to be taken as perpetual slaves by the Hebrews, a race of slaves must have been constituted, who would have increased, in the course of a few centuries, to the number of hundreds of thousands, even to millions. But that no such race was ever in existence is equally clear, not the least trace of them being found in the sacred records. Had there been such a race in the time of Jeremiah, the Jewish masters would not have been so eager to convert their Hebrew servants into slaves. That conspiracy against the law indicates that they had, at that time, very few heathen servants. Indeed, by the natural process of the law of jubilee, in connection with other statutes, each generation of heathen servants, instead of being perpetuated and increased, passed into free and integral elements of the Hebrew State; so that, after the lapse of no very long period, the supply of heathen servants must have been greatly diminished, and almost the only prevailing form of service must have been the six years' period, as appointed in the twenty-first chapter of Exodus.

If the Hebrew families and masters could, by law, have held as many heathen as they chose for slaves, and the children born of such slaves followed the condition of their parents, then nothing could have prevented such a set of men as were ready to undertake and carry through a revolution from freedom to slavery in respect to their own countrymen, from buying and breeding heathen slaves without limit, especially if God's law for the land had absolutely given and bequeathed the heathen to them for that express purpose. This would have been such an establishment of slavery by the

divine law, as would have rendered inevitable and permanent
the most diabolical and venal licentiousness and cruelty that
ever, in any systematic shape, has cursed the earth. But, by
the law of the land, after an appointed time, the strangers and
sojourners, and children of strangers from among the heathen,
all became denizens, citizens, proselytes, and could claim the
privileges of Hebrews. By the time one season of jubilee had
been run through, they would " enter into the congregation
of the Lord ;" and thus slavery was effectually and for ever
prevented, both by law, and the practical working of the institutions of society. Hence the grasping avarice of the Jews
turned at length against their own native servants ; and
hence their daring and cruel attempt to change, by violence,
those fundamental and far-reaching statutes of freedom and
a free policy, appointed for them by Jehovah.

To those who have not examined the subject, it seems
strange that not the sin of idolatry, but the sin of slavery,
the violation of the law of freedom, should have been marked
of God, among the catalogue of Jewish crimes, as the one
decisive act of wickedness that filled up the measure of their
iniquities, and brought down the wrath of God upon them
without remedy or repeal. But the wonder ceases, when the
nature of the crime is taken into consideration. Being a
crime concocted and determined by all the princes, priests,
and people, together with the king, it was really making the
whole nation a nation of men-stealers ; and man-stealing was a
crime appointed in the law of God to the punishment of death ;
so that the adopting of it by the government and the people,
was an enshrining of the iniquity in public and most glaring
defiance of God's authority, in the form of their state policy.
They had thus contrived, as they imagined, a security even
in the midst of their oppression, against punishment. It was
doing that, as a corporation of usurpers, in safety, which they
could not have done as individuals without exposure to the
penalty of death. But though hand join in hand, God's ven-

geance is but the surer and more terrible. And the sword of God came down upon them in the very midst of this appalling crime, as swift, almost, as the lightning.

Beyond all question there were many who lent themselves to this iniquity for the sake of gain and power, who never were guilty of the sin of idolatry; they would have abhorred that wickedness, as worse than any sacrilege; and the sin of idolatry was not, at that time, adopted by the government and the nation, in open defiance of Almighty God. But the sin of bringing free servants into a forced, involuntary servitude, the sin of changing freemen into articles of property, the sin of stealing men from themselves, and *chattelizing* them in perpetual slavery, *was* so chosen and adopted; and God's extremest wrath came upon the whole nation in consequence. Many at that time were strenuous for rites, but not for righteousness; for the law as to religious ceremonies, but not for humanity and justice; for sacrifice towards God, but not mercy nor common honesty towards man. They would kill an ox for worship, and steal their neighbor's wages, and slay his freedom, in the same breath. They "trusted in oppression and perverseness, and staid themselves thereon;" and these are crimes, the lurid light of which burns in the pages of the prophets Isaiah, Jeremiah, Hosea, and others, in such a manner, that we see how the nation went into the establishment of slavery against the repeated warnings and denunciations of God's messengers, in every faithful, free pulpit all over the land. Amazement at God's wrath, as if slavery were, in his sight, a guilt greater than idolatry, passes, under these circumstances, under a true knowledge of the case, into amazement at God's forbearance, and at the infatuation of the Jewish people.

They were deliberately inaugurating a crime, as their chosen state policy, which they knew would increase in a numerical ratio from generation to generation. If it could have been restricted to the first persons stolen and deprived of their liberty, the iniquity would have been comparatively small. But for two immortal beings forced into this chattelism, there would be five others stolen and forced, in like manner, by the next generation; the guilt of oppression on the one side, and the sufferance of cruelty on the other, enlarging as it ran on into posterity. Now to set agoing such a system of injustice, which was to branch out like the hereditary perdition from the depraved head of a race, increasing as the Rio de la Plata or the Amazon; to set a central spring of thousand other springs of domestic and state tyranny coiled, and coiling on, in geometrical progression; and a central fountain of thousand other fountains of inhumanity and misery; and to do this in opposition to the light of freedom and religion, and of laws in protection of liberty, given from God, and maintained by him for a thousand years, was so extreme and aggravated a pitch of wickedness, that it is not wonderful that God put an instant stop to it, by wiping Jerusalem and Judea of their inhabitants, as a man wipeth a dish and turneth it upside down; it is not wonderful that we find the king and the nation cut off at once, by this enormous crime, from all possiblity of God's further forbearance.

The evil of such a crime was the greater, because, while it is enlarging every year, both in guilt and hopelessness, it *seems* lessened in intensity, as it passes down into posterity. Posterity are content to receive and uphold that slavery as a comfortable domestic institution, which, at the beginning, was acknowledged as a glaring crime. The sons of the first men-stealers would, with comparatively easy consciences, take the children of those whom their parents had stolen, and claim *them* as their *property*, being slaves born. But, in fact, in a nice adjustment of the moral question, we find that the guilt is doubled; because, while the parents may have been stolen only from themselves, the children are stolen both from the parents and from themselves. The stealing and enslaving of the parents could create no claim upon the children as property, nor produce any mitigation or extenuation of the sin of stealing the children also and holding them as slaves. And so the guilt runs on, nor could the progress of whole ages diminish it, or change its character.

Now, although never a word should have been found bearing on this subject in the New Testament, it is manifest that a large space is given to it in the Divine revelation, and if there is any silence in the New Testament, it is because so much and so plainly was spoken in the Old. It may be said, If ye hear not Moses and the prophets, neither will ye be persuaded though one rose from the dead. If the Pentateuch and prophets be received as the word of God, we need no further testimonial or expression of God's judgment against slavery. And it is a fearful thing for any man to endeavor to distort the tenor of this revelation from justice to injustice, from kindness to oppression, from the advocacy of freedom to the sanction of slavery. Let no man, because slavery is the sin of his own country, therefore seek to defend it from the Scriptures, handling the word of God deceitfully, acting with it as a dishonest dealer with a pack of cards, or a gambler with loaded dice. Strangely intense must be the prejudice that, for the sake of shielding slavery from being reprobated as a sin, would rather rejoice to have found it commended and commanded in the word of God, than admit the demonstration that it stands in the condemnation of the Almighty.

The word of God is as an electric or galvanic battery, composed of many parts, all of them being directed to the object of overcoming and removing sin, and establishing love to God and man as the rule and habit on earth as in heaven. Then what a piece of villainy it is towards mankind as sinners, to draw off, as it were, over night, the power from any part of this battery, its power to rouse the conscience, its power to startle the moral sense into the noting and abhorring of moral abominations long practiced as forms of social expediency and luxury. Both historical and preceptive, the word of God is a warning against sin; many things in it are light-houses on dangerous reefs. Therefore, no greater treachery is possible, nor more malignant treason against mankind, than to creep into one of these light-houses, and under pretense of being its keeper, to put out its light; or, still worse, to put up the signal of its being a safe harbor, when the man or the nation that makes for it will inevitably be dashed in pieces.

In the face of danger and death, God's ministers were commanded to speak all the words of the Lord to the guilty people, to the nation, the cities, the king, the princes, the prophets, and the priests. "Diminish not a word; if so be they will hearken, and turn every man from his evil way, that I may repent me of the evil which I purpose to do unto them, because of the evil of their doings." And again: "It may be that they will hear, and return, that I may forgive their iniquity and their sin." And again, in regard to the prophets that withheld the truth, "They walk in lies; they strengthen also the hands of evil doers, that none doth return from his wickedness. But if they had stood in my counsel, and had caused my people to hear my words, then they should have turned them from their evil way, and from the evil of their doings."

What could be more impressive than these warnings, in regard to the guilt of concealing God's word because of the fear of man, and on account of the popularity of sin? The very purpose for which a divine revelation was given is prevented, and its accomplishment made impossible, by such treachery; and therefore our blessed Lord, in the very opening of his own ministry, declared, in regard to all the commands in the Old Testament, in the law and the prophets, that whosoever should break the least of them, AND TEACH MEN SO, which he would do by denying, perverting, or concealing them, should be excluded from the kingdom of heaven.

CHAPTER XXVIII.

Comparison of Roman and American Slavery.—The Climax of Immorality in the Sanction of Slavery under the Gospel.—The Laws of God in the Old Testament in full force in Judea under the New.—Oppression Sinful in itself.—What is Sinful under the Old Testament, Sinful also under the New.—Impiety of Making the Gospel the Minister of Sin.

It is wonderful and fearful to see how the persistent indulgence of any sin, under the light of the gospel, conducts back the soul at length, as it were blindfold, into a worse darkness than that of heathenism; worse by contrast with light, and worse because committed against light, and without the excuse of darkness. The practice of slavery, under the light of the gospel, has at length carried a whole Christian community, with the sanction of the church of God, to the maintenance of a system, as divine, which reproduces the most atrocious features of Roman slavery. The product of a corrupt Christianity, the result of the truths held in unrighteousness, and of that judicial blindness which follows, is much worse than the product of heathenism, even in being only the same; for it is accompanied with a conscience seared as with a hot iron. The old Greeks and Romans, in the absence of a divine revelation, did not see the cruelty and wickedness of slavery, but they never attributed the system to the benevolence of God, never dreamed of asserting that it was one of the activities of the divine attributes, or proofs of a preëminent piety. In the United States, a Christian people, under the light of a divine revelation, explicit in regard to this very form of oppression, adopt, cherish, applaud and pray over it, yea, give thanks to God for it, not only as the most perfect state of human society, and not antagonistic with the divine will, but as of direct divine appointment and support, as being the completest and most comprehensive providential missionary institute.

And what is this INSTITUTE? What is the *gehenna* of discipline on earth, by the passing of the soul through which, God's providence is impiously affirmed to have appointed the African race to salvation, and constituted the kidnappers and slaveholders of the United States his ordained and sanctified missionaries? It is the reproduction of the most barbarous system of slavery ever endured in the pagan world. The reader has but to consult the customary authorities, and he will be appalled at the exactitude of the sameness of Roman and American slavery.*

Whether we take the definition of slavery from the essence of the crime of man-stealing, the claim of PROPERTY IN

---

* See STROUD and others on the laws relating to slavery. Among the Romans, more particularly, slaves were held, *pro nullis, pro mortuis, pro quadrupedibus, for no men, for dead men, for beasts*, nay, were in a much worse state than any cattle whatever. They had no *head* in the state, no *name*, no tribe, or register. They were not capable of being injured, nor could they take aught by purchase or descent; they had no heirs, and could make no will. Exclusive of what was called their *peculium*, whatever they acquired was their master's; they could neither plead nor be pleaded for, but were entirely excluded from all civil concerns; were not entitled to the rights of matrimony, and therefore had no relief in case of adultery; nor were they proper objects of cognation or affinity. They might be sold, transferred, or pawned, like other goods or personal estate; for goods they were, and as such they were esteemed. — Compare FUSS, TAYLOR, BECKER, ESCHENBERG, HORNE, and others.

Compare the accounts of these authorities with the slave laws of the Southern States, or with the elaborate reports of State trials, revealing the nature of slavery, as, for example, the striking case of Bayley *versus* Poindexter, in Virginia. Compare also the modes of punishment, the constituted scourgers and torturers. The burning of slaves to death is certainly worse than the feeding of fishes with their flesh, which is the climax of horror. in the judgment of Seneca, on the cruelty of Vedius Pollio. But in the Roman Pandects burning alive is also mentioned as a punishment. Compare, on the point of the negation of marital rights, and the impossibility of relief in the case of adultery, the judgment of the court in the trial of Sickles, in Washington, and the opposite conclusion of a similar trial of a black man at the same time in Baltimore.

MAN, which, wherever assumed and enforced, though under sanction of law, constitutes the pretended owner of such pretended property a MANSTEALER; or from the elementary crimes against God and man involved in it and resulting from it, but dignified by some with the nomenclature of abuses of slavery; or from the rigid terms of the slave code itself; we find it alike incompatible with Christianity, and reprobated and forbidden by it. There is no such oppression or sin admitted or tolerated in the Bible. There is no term for it in the Hebrew Scriptures; but the reality of it, as described by its elements, is forbidden on pain of death.

We have seen the proof of all this in the Mosaic laws, illustrated and enforced in the Prophets. Now in entering upon the New Testament, we come directly from the latest utterances of divine inspiration in the Old, not to find those utterances disregarded, or denied, or repealed, not to find ourselves confounded by a system of social wickedness received into Christ's church, and taught by his apostles, against which every attribute of God had been pointed from the beginning. We find the divine law in full force, with all its precepts of benevolence, and all its penalties. The laws against stealing and making merchandise of men, the laws against oppression, the commands to love thy neighbor and the stranger as thyself, to break every yoke, to deliver the oppressed, to betray not the outcast, to shelter the fugitive, were familiar to the Jews, were read in the synagogues.* Our blessed

---

* PRIDEAUX'S CONNEXION, vol. i., p. 309.—"If it be examined into," says Prideaux, "how it came to pass that the Jews were so prone to idolatry before the Babylonish captivity, and so strongly and cautiously, even to superstition, fixed against it after that captivity, the true reason hereof will appear to be, that they had the law and the prophets every week read unto them after that captivity, which they had not before. After that captivity, and the return of the Jews from it, synagogues being erected among them in every city, to which they constantly resorted for public worship, and where every week they had the law and the prophets read unto them, and were instructed in their duty, this kept them in a thorough knowledge of God and his laws. The threats which they found in the

Lord, in the very first public announcement of his Messiah-ship, robed himself in these very Scriptures, and placed upon his own head this crown; himself the promised Deliverer, the Consoler and Redeemer, to break every yoke, and fulfill the "acceptable year," the jubilee year, of the Lord.

There was no slavery in Judea; there could not have been, except by the renewal and successful accomplishment of a crime, the very attempt at which had been followed of God with the captivity of the whole people, accompanied by sword, famine and the pestilence. There was now no more need of mentioning slavery by name than there had been in the Old Testament; but it was anew forbidden in its ele-ments, and finally rendered impossible all over the world, by the injunctions of divine inspiration upon masters. RENDER UNTO YOUR SERVANTS THAT WHICH IS JUST AND EQUAL, is the great law of Christian abolitionism.

Now what could be thought of a Christian man's mind or piety if such a man were asked whether *oppression* was to be regarded as a sin against God, and should make answer that it could not be regarded as sinful *in itself*, but only *in its cir-cumstances*, only in its abuses? What *are* the abuses of oppression? It will be acknowledged that oppression is for-bidden in the word of God. We are instructed to pray for deliverance from oppression, because it is a state so hostile to a life of piety, so unfavorable to the keeping of God's com-mands. What is true of oppression in any of its forms must be true of the highest degree of oppression. If it is oppres-

---

prophets against the breakers of the laws deterred them from transgres-sing against them."

The same may be said of the en-tire ceasing of any violation of the laws against slavery. James informs us that Moses had of old in every city those that preached him; and it was not on the Sabbath merely, but three days in the week, that they had stated reading services. And Paul disputed and taught incessantly in their synagogues, and afterwards dai-ly in the school of Tyrannus. The di-rect testimony of God against slavery could neither have been unknown nor passed by in silence, neither could the rights of servants, as protected in the Old Testament, have been ignored in the New.

sion to compel a man to serve without wages, it is certainly a still greater oppression to sell him for money. If it is oppression to take away a man's property, it is still greater oppression to use the man himself *as* property, to convert him into merchandise for another's profit, and to make it impossible for him to possess any thing in his own right. If oppression is forbidden at all in the word of God, then this highest kind of oppression is forbidden. And if it be a sin in itself, a sin *per se*, to take away a man's wages, or to deprive him of any of his rights, it is not less a sin *per se* to take away *all* his rights, to reduce him to such a condition that by law he has no rights, can plead none, but is a mere thing, a chattel, at the disposal and for the profit of his owner.

Now, by what defiance of God and his truth and righteousness, or by what moral insanity, or by what judicial blindness of depravity, dare men aver, or can they aver, that while oppression is forbidden of God, slavery is not; that while the oppression of a man is sinful, the holding of him as a slave is not sinful? How can any man, not an idiot, affirm that while oppression is denounced of God, slavery is commanded? or that while in the Old Testament slavery is forbidden, and every one of its elements reprobated as under God's hatred and wrath, in the New Testament it is sanctioned and legalized as under God's favor? If this extreme slander were true, then would the old dispensation, under the law, be proved more benevolent and kind, more loving and merciful, more just and righteous, than the new, under the gospel.

Under the Old Testament dispensation men were forbidden, on pain of death, to take, hold, or sell human beings as property. The taking of a man as a slave, against his own consent, was the stealing of him, not from another person, but from himself. Under the new dispensation it is affirmed by some that all this crime is not only not forbidden, but sanctioned, and that those who committed it, instead of being arraigned as criminals, were permitted to continue in it, to hold slaves, and, of course, to do every thing with them that by the law of slavery may be done, to hold them or to sell them as property at the master's sole will and pleasure ; and that such stealers, holders and sellers of men as property were received into the Christian church, this their wickedness not being forbidden, but received and sanctioned along with them.

Under the Old Testament dispensation the right of servants to escape from bondage was admitted, and men were forbidden to return them into bondage when so escaped, but were commanded to aid and to shelter them, and not to oppress them. It would be oppressing them in the highest degree to return them into bondage; and the law of God that they should not be so returned proved that no creature had any right of ownership in them, but that they themselves had the most perfect right of ownership in themselves, and the right to take themselves away, to assert and take their own freedom. To take this right away from them, and deliver them up into slavery, would be again the crime of stealing them.

Under the new dispensation it is asserted by the apologists for slavery under the gospel, that slaves must not escape from their masters, that they have no right to their freedom, that if they do escape they must be captured and sent back into slavery, especially if their owners were members of the Christian church. It is asserted that both they, as slaves, and their masters as their owners, were together members of Christian churches, and being such, having been admitted as such, the law of Christianity sanctions slavery as right, and forbids the slave from escaping and the Christian from sheltering him if he escapes.

The amount of this is, that while, under Moses, under the law of God as given by Moses, oppression was forbidden as sinful, under Christ oppression is baptized and sanctioned as a Christian grace. Under Moses the worst kind of oppression, that of slavery and the MAN-STEALING, by which slavery is created and maintained, was branded as a crime to be punished by death.

Under Christ and the gospel the injunction against it is removed, and it is not only consecrated by the Christian sacraments, the seal of the church's sanction being put upon it, but it becomes sinful for Christian men to speak against it as sin. The gospel of Christ becomes, in fact, a deliverance to do those very abominations which the law of God punished with death; a license of selfishness and cruelty, a freedom to sin, and to violate the law of love. The slaveholders in the Christian church, and they who sanction this crime as consistent with the gospel, as a crime admitted without rebuke into the churches of the New Testament, do really declare that the law was imperfect, but that Jesus was made a surety of a better testament, a high priest of good things to come, of a temple of liberty for the enslaving of men, into which we have boldness to enter as into the holiest, and to take our slaves with us, Christ having brought in this better hope, this diviner freedom, blotting out the hand-writing of ordinances that was against us, which was contrary to us, and took it out of the way, nailing it to his cross.

It is claimed now, that whatever might be the meaning, or necessity of the Mosaic laws against slavery, or in behalf of escaping servants, and against any claim of their masters for their restoration; and whatever might be the inspiration of the Prophets and the Psalms against kidnapping and catching men, or holding and selling them as merchandise, or the commands of God to give liberty to the enslaved, to break every yoke, and let the oppressed go free; that, nevertheless, under the new law of love in the New Testament, Christ and the gospel, replace and sanctify the bonds, and forbid them to be broken; admitting into the Christian church those very oppressors that under the law were excommunicated from it, and those very realities of oppression that under the law were branded as crimes worthy of death.

It is averred that Christ's own silence on the subject of this sin gives consent to it. Christ was silent in regard to the

sin of sodomy, in regard to infanticide, in regard to idolatry;
and by this method of reasoning, not only is the law of God
against these crimes abolished, and the crimes themselves
made innocent by such silence, but he that speaks against
them, when Christ did not, is himself guilty of a presumptuous sin, and may think himself happy if he is not struck with
some divine judgment.

Now, dreadful as the blasphemy against the divine inspiration of the Old Testament has been, in asserting that slavery
was sanctioned of God there, the blasphemy against Christ is
worse, in asserting that the cast off vices under God's reprobation in the laws of Moses and the prophets have been taken
up, endorsed, patronized and received to Christian communion
and credit, in the teachings of Christ and the apostles.   What
a signal and an execrable impiety, to contend that he who announced the great rule of life, Whatsoever ye would that man
should do to you, do ye even so to them; and declared concerning the law, Thou shalt love thy neighbor as thyself, that
upon this, along with the law of supreme love to God, hang
all the law and the prophets, would and did at the same time
admit into the Christian church, and sanction by his gospel,
and establish as a custom of Christian life, the greatest violation of that law!

To maintain that Christ and his apostles would set up as a
Christian institution, what Moses and the prophets had forbidden on pain of death, what they had put in the same category of sin with the worship of Moloch, of Baal, of Dagon,
what they had classified with sodomy and matricide, is to
introduce into divine revelation a profaneness and confusion
worse than that which is denounced of God in the 18th of
Leviticus and the 27th of Deuteronomy.   As the land itself
vomiteth out her inhabitants guilty of such defilement, so the
unsophisticated moral sense, in the least degree enlightened
above the ignorance and darkness of savage life, would reject
a revelation burdened with such enormities, especially a gospel

that pretending to remove men's sins, introduces a system of avarice and cruelty, and admits iniquities as elements of Christian grace and fellowship, that even a previous, imperfect and preparatory system of religion cast out as abominable in God's sight. In truth, the gospel could not be received as of God, could not but be rejected, under such burdens of impiety, if the moral sense of men did not assure them that the leprosies thus foisted into the authority of God's word are a corruption of its purity.

In the first preaching of the gospel, the word of God in the Old Testament was the standard of Christ and the apostles. It was their storehouse of proofs, texts, doctrines, arguments. Our blessed Lord himself was wont to answer questions of conscience and of casuistry by a direct appeal to the Old Testament Scriptures. What is written in the law? How readest thou?

Furthermore, the apostle informed Timothy that he must take the law in its particulars, and apply it to MEN-STEALERS, and to any other thing contrary to sound doctrine, according to the gospel. Nothing could be plainer. True gospel preaching was that which applied the law to the consciences of men to bring them to Christ.

The disciples everywhere were commanded to search the word of God, and to hold fast what they found there. The oracles of God were to be consulted, that they might know his will, and approve the things that were more excellent, being instructed out of the law, and able to reprove the darkness of the world and the sins by which it was filled with unrighteousness.

It was the prayer of our Lord Jesus, Sanctify them by thy truth; thy word is truth. "The Spirit of the Lord is upon me, because he hath anointed me to preach the gospel to the poor; he hath sent me to heal the broken-hearted, to preach deliverance to the captives, and recovering of sight to the blind; to set at liberty them that are bruised, to preach the acceptable year of the Lord." It is impossible that he should habitually, in the synagogues, expound such passages as the 61st chapter of Isaiah, and instruct his disciples to preserve a politic silence as to the sins which those passages rebuke, as to the oppressions which they forbid, since it was plain to all that the 58th and 59th chapters particularized the very sins of which the 61st proclaimed the remedy. He never taught his disciples to be afraid of announcing to the whole world under the gospel any thing that the prophets were command-ed to communicate under the law. On the contrary, "What I tell you in darkness, that speak ye in light, and what ye hear in the ear, that preach ye upon the housetops. And fear not them which kill the body, but are not able to kill the soul."

He would not permit his preachers to consult human preju-dices, or to take human laws or customs for their guide in preaching. He would not suffer the word of God to be made of none effect by human precept or tradition. "In vain do they worship me, teaching for doctrines the commandments of men." The teaching of human slavery, the admission of it into the church of God, the implication of its just authority, would have set the gospel against the law, the morality of the New Testament against that of the Old, the conscience in-structed by the apostles against that instructed of God in his word. The admission of human slavery, the wickedest crea-tion of human law, is one of the most dreadful examples on record of making the word of God of none effect, not merely by the power of tradition, but the licensing of crime ; one of the most sweeping and destructive instances ever known of the corruption of piety and the debasement of God's wor-ship, by teaching for doctrines the commandments of men ; nay, it is the doctrines of devils set in the place of God's teachings ; for human slavery, in its perfection, defiles and destroys all the commandments of the decalogue. If there were this fatal incongruity and opposition between the Old and New Testaments on so vital a question as that of the nature of sin or its treatment; if the Old were distinguished by the fear of offending God, but the New by the fear of offending man; if the Old spoke out fearlessly against men's sins, while the New took up the line of a cautious policy, making the great rule of preaching the truth to be the rule of giving none offense to any man, and carefully concealing such truths as might produce disturbance; then would the proof of a divine inspiration be greatly weakened, if not wholly destroyed, and one half of God's word would be effectually neutralized by the other. But there is no such imperfection, no such contradiction.

On the contrary, Paul expressly denounces all such carnal, fearful, dishonest policy, abhorring either the concealment or corruption of the word of God, by flattering words and the cloak of covetousness. "We have renounced the hidden things of dishonesty; not walking in craftiness, nor handling the word of God deceitfully, but by manifestation of the truth commending ourselves to every man's conscience in the sight of God." It was the very object of God, by the power of the truth, with the Holy Spirit, to produce a fearless, holy, testifying church; and he committed the truth to his people, with the assurance of the Holy Spirit to accompany it, that they might conquer the world in righteousness. What a monstrous conclusion, therefore, to suppose that through the fear of persecution or disturbance God would have the preachers of the gospel keep back or veil the righteousness of his word! How absurd to suppose that the work of the new inspiration would be to make men afraid of the old! that the work of the Comforter would be to teach men to hide what God had revealed, and to keep back, from a cunning expediency, through fear of trouble, what he had instructed the old prophets to proclaim in the face of death!

CHAPTER XXIX.

The Argument of Silence Considered.—The Same Argument as to other Monstrosities Under Roman Law.—Infanticide.—Wives as Property.—New Testament Reprobation of Slavery from the Old.—The Divine Reprobation of American Slavery, and Light as to our Duty.

From the large space given to the denunciation of the sin of oppression in the Old Testament, and from the fact of the crime of slavery having been extirpated from the land of Judea, we should not expect to find it often referred to, or by name prohibited, in the New Testament. If we should find a perfect silence in regard to it, this silence could not be pleaded in its favor. If the Saviour never encountered it, there would be no occasion for him to denounce it by name. It would be a monstrous conclusion to aver, on this account, that he did not agree in the reprobation of it by the word of God in the Old Testament. If the mere absence of a prohibition of any sin by the Saviour and his apostles is to be taken for a justification of it, there is almost no crime that in some form may not be justified. When John was beheaded by Herod, the disciples of the murdered prophet took up his body and buried it, and went and told Jesus. Not a word did he say in condemnation of that murder. Are we therefore to conclude that an oath to commit murder, and a murder committed for the keeping of such an oath, are right, or that in a ruler they are excusable or acceptable before God, or that, when we see such crimes committed, we are to keep silence in regard to them, and on no account to rebuke them? Or would it be proper to conclude that Christ and his apostles never taught any thing against particular sins but what is recorded in the New Testament?

The three great relations in private life, says Blackstone,
are, 1. That of master and servant; 2. That of husband and
wife; 3. That of parent and child. He then goes on to consider the responsibilities and duties, the rights and obligations
of all these parties.*

Under the Roman law, slavery being legitimate, the slave
had no rights, and the master could treat him as a thing or a
brute beast at pleasure. Under the same law the husband
had almost unlimited control over the wife, exercising the authority of an absolute despot, even in the matter of life and
death. By the same system the power of the father over his
children was that of the master over his slaves; he could sell
his children, could imprison, scourge or punish them in any
manner, however atrocious, even after they were grown up.†
He might decree them to death when born, if he preferred
not to rear them, infanticide being thus as legitimate an element of paternal authority as the breeding of slaves is of the
domestic slavery in the United States. The children were
considered, like slaves, part and parcel of the goods of their
father, so that they might be disposed of by him just like
slaves or cattle. With respect to the right of sale, they were
in a worse position than even slaves, in that they were released from his power only after a thrice repeated act of selling. Likewise, "as any thing became a person's property, by
being possessed by him for a certain space of time, so a wife
became the lawful property of her husband." He could re-
pudiate her at pleasure.‡

Now, in every one of these relations, the Roman laws and
customs stood point blank opposed against the divine law.
In neither of them could any other rule be right than that of
a divine revelation. In every one of them there is clear and
explicit instruction in the Old Testament. If now, in the New

* BLACKSTONE's Comm., ch. iv.
† GIBBON's Decline and Fall, ch. xliv.
‡ FUSS' Roman Antiquities. Sec. 82, 476, 481.

Testament, the filial relation or the marriage relation is recognized as of God, and its duties are enjoined under his authority, while, nevertheless, the sacred writers are perfectly silent as to the abuses of those relations, and the crimes committed against them under the law of the Romans, will such silence answer for the allowance and sanctification of such abuses?   Can an argument be sustained that because neither our Lord nor the apostles denounced the despotism of the father over the child, and of the husband over the wife, therefore the divinely appointed paternal and marital authority included and sanctioned that despotism?   Could it be argued, because wives are commanded to obey their husbands, that therefore the Roman institution of marriage was ordained of God? or because children are to obey their parents, therefore the fathers have the right to sell or put to death their children?   No more can an argument be sustained that because our Lord and his apostles taught servants to obey their masters, therefore they were the property of their masters; or because our Lord and his apostles did not say that Roman slavery was wrong, therefore both it and American slavery are right, and have the sanction of the Almighty.

Yet this very argument of silence is relied upon for the defense of slavery, as being a system not inconsistent with Christianity! It is affirmed that the Lord Jesus Christ did not rebuke slavery, and therefore it is presumption in any human being to denounce it as sin.   Neither did the Lord Jesus rebuke idolatry.   These apologists for slavery probably are not aware that never in one of the evangelists is to be found a word against idolatry, no testimony of Christ against it, nor any direction to preach his gospel against it.   Does this prove that therefore idolatry is not inconsistent with Christianity, or that because Christ did not denounce idolaters, therefore it is presumption in us to proclaim the gospel against them? Does this prove that true piety includes idolatry as one of its elements?   Just as clearly it proves this, as our Lord's

that the holding of them as slaves, as property, was forbidden on pain of death.

Men say, " Show us some instances of dealing with slave-holders in the apostolic churches. If we only had one such case it would be a guide."

The epistle to Philemon is precisely such a case. It was given for that very purpose. If Onesimus were once a slave, then it is incontrovertibly a declaration that he could no longer be held as such. If Philemon had been a slaveholder while a Pagan, it is plain that he could not be such as a Christian.

If men will resist such evidence, or distrust it, in support of a practice known to be wrong, stronger evidence would be of little avail. It is one of the qualities of divine light not to force itself upon the soul; but if, having eyes, men see not, and ears, they hear not, neither will they be persuaded though one rose from the dead.

God did rebuke and forbid this iniquity plainly enough. And now for men to say, It is not set down by name, therefore it is not sinful, argues not doubt, but obstinate blindness.

When the crime of slavery disappears from the world it will not be imagined that the Bible ever sanctioned it in any way. It is not named by name in the New Testament, neither is it in the Old Testament; but the *act* in the Old Testament is denounced, and this edict against it is referred to in the New. One whole epistle on this subject is enough; and if in any previous epistles it had not been referred to, it would be because the divine Spirit knew that that epistle was to be added. The principles laid down forbade slavery utterly, and rendered it impossible. What need of any thing more? In the first churches not a slaveholder was to be found. Jewish masters were not slaveholders, and they certainly did not become such on becoming Christians.

To teach a sin as expedient, or to leave a gross iniquity doubtful, would be to destroy the possibility of holiness.

God will bear with a small amount of piety; but he will **not** endure a corrupted piety, a perversion of it. He can save by a little truth; but he will not endure error in the place of truth. He can endure with much long suffering the vessels of wrath fitted for destruction; but when sin comes to be vaunted as holiness, when it is taken into the church, it is death. If a wickedness be fallen into, but admitted, confessed, it may be pardoned; but when it is taught as of God, when doctrines of devils are boasted to have the sanction of the Saviour, then indeed it is time for God to work. If the foundations be destroyed what can the righteous do?

Here then, in the Old and New Testaments, we find, on this subject, the leading elementary statutes laid down, the necessary result of God's own justice, and the determination of what is just and right among men. It is impossible that these principles can be just and righteous in one age, and unjust, unrighteous and impracticable in another, or just and righteous for the government of a nation of two millions of people, but unjust and unrighteous for a nation of thirty millions. It is impossible that what in God's view was just and benevolent between man and man eighteen hundred years before the coming of Christ, can be unjust and unbenevolent, or its obligation nullified, eighteen hundred years after Christ. But if there were any doubt, the matter is decided by distinct reference to these very laws as our rule of duty under the gospel; and the Old Testament Scriptures, in all their parts and detail, are said to have been given and written for our instruction, and to be profitable for our discovery and application of God's righteousness.

And when an apostle by divine inspiration commands masters everywhere to give unto their servants that which is just and equal, it is not merely that which the natural conscience, uninstructed by the divine word, affirms or intimates to be just and equal, which would be a rule unreliable, uncertain and variable in the extreme, differing according to every man's moral character and notions of expediency, but that which the word of God declares and defines to be just and equal, that which the Old Testament Scriptures reveal and enjoin on this very subject as the will of God. And the very first article of that justice and equality or equity is, *that no man shall hold or treat any other man as property*, that no human being shall make merchandise of man. And a second great ruling article of justice and equality from masters to servants is, that no man shall use his servant's service without wages, stipulated wages, according to mutual bargain and agreement, on grounds of equality and justice on both sides.

It is beyond question that the minuteness and particularity of detail in the statutes and commentaries of the Old Testament, on this great commanding subject of human economy and morals, were intended for all future time, and not for the Jews or the Jewish dispensation merely. Not more certain is it that the profound and inexhaustible mines of coal, now being wrought for the wants of the world's inhabitants, were laid up by creative and forseeing wisdom for the supply of those wants, and were designed to be used, as men are now using them, for the progress of civilization and social comfort, than that the instructive, comprehensive, far-reaching principles and laws in reference to domestic service, inwrought in the revelation of the Old Testament, were set there for the instruction and guidance of this present age. And they are as much more important for our instruction and guidance now, and as much more obligatory on us for examination and obedience, than upon the Jews merely, as the character and welfare of a hundred millions of people are more important than of two millions. And the great obligation of righteousness resting now upon the church of God and the ministry is that of promulgating anew and enforcing in all their spiritual and universal authority these denied and impiously violated principles and laws of common morality and justice from man to man.

We have among us a people branded as a *strange race,* a race set apart by our laws, prejudices, judicial decisions, for moral assassination and destruction ; a race crushed beneath the most horrible, hopeless, galling system of perpetual slavery the world ever knew ; a race consigned by our very religion —perverted for the purpose—as the subjects of avarice and profitable lust ; a race dehumanized, disfranchised of the very personality of manhood, for the purposes of uttermost and unimpeded oppression; branded by law as *things,* that they may not have the rights and protection of persons, but admitted by a fiction as *persons,* that they may be the subjects of such punishment and injury as mere things could not be ; persons when their owners can be benefited by the fiction, things when themselves could have any defence against their owners, by being considered as persons.

We have this race of strangers, stolen at first, flung by piracy upon our shores, as smuggled goods might be thrown upon the beach by smugglers, to be snatched up and sold by shore thieves, complex in the crime ; stolen at first, propagated afterwards, and the race a stolen race ; every babe new born, new stolen, branded from the birth as property. We have this race, from whom we tear by human law the divine seals of marriage, and of parental and filial love and obligations ; burning and searing from out even the mother's soul, by the sacrament of property, by the hot iron of that conviction from the birth of belonging to another, even the maternal instinct, so as to reduce it to the level of the mere animal impulse " of the hen or the partridge."* We have this race, whom we have so unnaturally defrauded even of the intelligence in which brutes might be nurtured, and so violently and perfectly divorced from that which belongs to their very nature by the ordinance of God as his children, that when they grow

---

* See the testimony in the South Side View of Slavery, by Rev. Dr. Adams.

up under our nurture and admonition, under the training of the slave system, they are not able to conceive the nature of the parental or the filial relation, or the meaning of the sacred word father !*

We have this race, concerning which, the sentiment of perverted justice, the instruction issued from the highest tribunal of justice in our country, is just this, *that black men have no rights that white men are bound to respect ;* and the social despotism and practice growing out of this judicial instruction, the practical treatment of this devoted race, is the carrying into demonstration of the theory that they are stuff only for slaves, the lineal, legitimate subjects of interminable, unalleviated, remorseless cruelty, hopeless because hereditary, and remorseless by the very aid of the church and its ministers sanctifying it with unction, in the name of the Lord; pacifying and stupifying men's consciences with lies, daubing the walls and palaces of this iniquity with their untempered

---

* ADAMS' South Side View.—The infamous maxim, *partus sequitur ventrem*, is a manufacture of heathen slave law, adopted from Paganism, and baptized by slaveholding churches in the name of Christ. It is asserted by Christian theologians to be a maxim of nature, justice, religion and divine providence! Yet the very code of Roman law, out of which this diabolic doctrine is drawn, to be transfigured with the sacredness of the Christian religion, contained also the admission that "all men by the law of nature are born in freedom;" and slavery was defined as being "contrary to natural right," and capable of being constituted only by positive law *against* the law of nature and of right. Moreover, "in order to determine the question of a child's freedom or servitude, the whole period of gestation was taken into view by the Roman jurists; and if at any time between conception and birth the mother had been for one instant free, the law, by a humane fiction, supposed the birth to have taken place then, and held the infant to be free born." From all such mixtures of humanity, the slave laws of Rome, as adopted by a Christian people, are purified, and no instinct of benevolence is suffered to co-exist with them; and that which even the natural conscience of a Pagan condemned as against nature and right, is declared to be the perfection of righteousness both natural and divine.—REPORT of Synod of North Carolina on Slavery, 1851; SOUTHERN PRESBYTERIAN REVIEW, 1857; GIBBON'S Decline and Fall, chapter xliv.; EDWARDS on Roman Slavery, Bib. Rep., vol. 6, p. 419; BECKER, Rom. Ant., Slavery, Bib. Sacra, vol. 2. POTTER, Gr. Ant.

mortar, and promising peace and prosperity in such wickedness.

We have this race, a race of strangers, and it is inevitable that we ask what are the principles and rules of conduct which God would have us adopt towards them. What is our duty to them in God's sight? We turn to the Old Testament for light, and we find it written, "The stranger that dwelleth with you shall be unto you as one born among you; AND THOU SHALT LOVE HIM AS THYSELF. Cursed be he that perverteth the judgment of the stranger."

We then say, by the logic of the gospel, by the inevitable enlargement, advance and comprehension of love from the Old Testament to the New, that whatever obligations of tenderness, charity and kindness were imposed of God in reference to strangers upon the Hebrews, are double upon ourselves; for all are one in Christ, and all brethren, neither Barbarian nor Scythian, nor bond, nor free, being any other than brethren, to be loved and treated alike as we, in similar cases, would be treated ourselves. Would we be held ourselves as slaves? Would we, under any circumstances, consent or be willing to be the property of other men, as our owners? If not, the logic of the gospel, the logic of love, declares our condemnation, if we hold others in slavery. Out of thine own mouth will I judge thee, thou wicked servant.*

---

* On the wickedness of the maxim, *partus sequitur ventrem*, See STROUD, Laws relating to Slavery, ch. i., and Prop. 12, p. 99; also GOODELL'S American Slave Code, 83 and 248. Compare a passage on the atrocity of slave legislation, in the diary of SIR SAMUEL ROMILLY (Memoirs, vol. iii., pp. 337–343). "No pains have been spared to raise a cry against Mr. Wilberforce and the other friends of the slaves in this country. It has become extremely difficult to counteract the effects of this powerful combination. No man can venture to write in defence of the negroes without exposing himself to a prosecution." This was written as late as 1818.

CHAPTER XXX.

With the Old Testament in Existence, any new Command against Slavery Un-
necessary.—The Absence of Slavery the Natural Result of the Old Testament
Laws.—But if Slavery Had Been Sanctioned of God, it Would Have Filled
the Land.—The Jurisprudence of the Land Would Have Been Occupied with
it.—The Gospels Would Have Been Filled with Proofs and Pictures of it.—
A State of Morals Would Have Been Found Such as Grows Out of it.

WE shall show that no argument can be set up in behalf
of slavery from the Greek words used to describe the customary domestic service, as it was encountered by our Lord
and his disciples in Judea. With the Mosaic laws and the
prophets as the rule of faith and practice for the nation, and
with the instructive record in Jeremiah xxxiv., slavery could
not be tolerated. It can not be denied that the laws against
man-stealing, holding and selling, were in full force. The laws
against making merchandise of man prevented every possibility of the slave traffic, which certainly did not exist. The law
forbidding the restoration of fugitives was equally sacred,
equally binding, and there is no proof of its having been disregarded or obsolete. The laws for the benevolent treatment
of strangers were the same as at the beginning ; precepts as
well known as any in the decalogue, and very distinctly referred to by our Saviour.

It was therefore not necessary in the Gospels to issue any
new commands against the crime of slavery, with the pages
of the prophets and the law blazing with denunciations against
every one of its elements, and the original crime of *slave-
making* condemned, along with the crime of murder, to the
punishment of death. The possible existence of slavery
under the Gospel, among those who admitted the authority

of the Scriptures, was not even supposed; and the instructions given to masters in the New Testament rendered such an enormity as a Christian slaveholder, a man claiming property in man, and yet pretending to be a Christian, impossible.

From the latest utterances of Jeremiah, Zephaniah, Zechariah, Nehemiah and Malachi, under the solemn impression produced by their assurances of vengeance from the living God against an oppressing nation and people, we should expect to find just what we do find in Judea, under our Lord's ministry, an entire absence of any indication of the existence or the practice of slaveholding. We should expect to find the very system of hired labor, and of voluntary domestic service, which we do find. Our Saviour no more encounters slavery than he does idolatry in the land. And the fact of its absence from Judea, the fact of the singular freedom of this people from this one sin, with all its train of abominations, while the whole Roman world was filled with it, and groaning under its oppressions, would of itself go far to prove that it must have been forbidden in the Jewish law. Nothing less than the strictest divine prohibition could have kept it out, could have kept the avaricious nobles and landholders from a traffic so lucrative as that in slaves, from a claim so infernally attractive as that of property in man.

If God had, by divine revelation, given over a race of human beings into the possession of another race, to be enslaved by them, and their posterity converted into chattels, stamped and used as property, bought, sold, conveyed as merchandise, put into social pens, or *contuberniums*, and propagated as the most valuable of all stock; the stock, its increase, and the privilege and the right of breeding, being constituted and transmitted as an inheritance for the children and children's children, of the dominant race, to the latest generation, thus appointed as slaveholders by the Almighty; if such had been the will of a pretended divine revelation, accepted as such,

there would have been some trace left of the operation of such
an edict, such a will; there must have been some remnant of
an estate so vast, so inalienable, so multiplying.

A property thus sacred and self-propagating, devised and
appointed of God as a legacy to his own chosen people, could
not be, or become, like other riches, which take to themselves
wings; they could no more fly away and disappear, or evap-
orate, than the landed estates of Judea could go off in ele-
mental smoke, or the mountain ranges of Horeb and Sinai
could soar away on wings as eagles. The land would have
been full of this heaven-sanctioned human wealth; for of all
kinds of wealth and modes of money making, this would have
constituted the sole exception to the great and terrible
rule, that it is easier for a camel to go through the eye of
a needle than for a rich man to enter into the kingdom of
heaven.

Although a merchant with his camel could not, yet a drove
of slaves, a procession reaching from the open door of the
ark on Ararat to the river of Egypt and the last day, would
be " bound for the kingdom," and the owner would drive in,
as God's under shepherd, in the care of a property more sacred than the cattle on a thousand hills.   The love of money
in this shape—an inheritance devised of God and sent down
to posterity, and his own people constituted his trustees and
owners for themselves and for their children—so far from
being the root of all evil, would be the spring perennial of
ever growing good.

It is impossible, under these circumstances, but that such a
vine, so planted of God, and cultivated under his command
and blessing, must have filled the land with its fruit, must
have been like the vine which he brought out of Egypt, sending her boughs unto the sea, and her branches unto the river.
The hills would have been covered with the shadow of it, and
the boughs thereof would have been like the goodly cedars.
For God himself, having prepared room before it, and issued

orders for its treatment, would have caused it to take deep root, and to fill the land. And every owner, every heritor of such consecrated property, every trustee for his children of such investments in the merchandise of immortality, would have been seized and inspired with a holy greed of gain, a sanctified and sanctifying avarice of such possessions.

It is impossible that under such securities and safeguards, such insurances not only of the property in perpetuity, but such guarantees for its demand, such provisions for a never-failing ambition after it, such pledges for a perpetual high rate of such stock in the market, such a commanding high price, and contrary to the rule of money among the Hebrews, such a living inalienable usury reverting to the owner; it is impossible that this species of property, of all others, should have ceased out of existence.

And if it had not ceased, but, according to the pretended sanction and command of God, had gone on increasing from generation to generation, then there would have been some evidence of its existence. A continually increasing body of jurisprudence would have been requisite in regard to it; just as, in our own country, the growth of such jurisprudence has filled the land, and overtopped and borne down all other laws as inferior, till in the short space of less than a century it asserts and holds supremacy in the United States Supreme Court of Justice, and interprets and commands the Constitution. A system of legislation for it, not against it, would have been seen, not only at its foundation, but growing up from it, springing out of it, necessitated by it, every step of the way.

There never yet was a nation in which slavery was a fundamental institution, sanctioned, admired, venerated and profitable, and boasting of the seal of heaven, where it did not enlarge and increase; never one, where its patronage and care did not constitute and occupy the ruling policy; never one where its laws did not stand out unmistakable and severe;

never one where its existence and its progress were not palpable, as a matter of undeniable history.

But in the Jewish state there is no such race, nor any trace of its existence ; there is no such legislation, but the contrary ; there is no such history, nor any appearance or action of the institution or element of slavery, or the propagation or increase of a slave population.   There are none of the inevitable and unmistakable signs, concomitants and consequences of such an institution ; no markets for human beings, nor merchandise in them, nor any traces of the existence or acknowledgment of such property, in any transactions of wills, investments, exchanges, appraisements, mortgages, sheriffs' sales, settlements of estates ; not to speak again of what in the very constitution of the Jewish State was rendered impossible, the hunting for fugitives, the provisions against their escape, the securities for their recapture, trial, and return into slavery.

Much use has been attempted of the argument of silence, alleged especially in the New Testament.   But this argument, in view of the certainty that if slavery had been a thing sanctioned of God it must, by the fifteen hundredth year of the Jewish State, by the process of patronage and propagation through fifteen centuries from Moses to Christ, have filled the land, comes to be of prodigious power against the possibility of its existence.   There would be no possibility of writing five books of Greek, Roman, or Egyptian history, so frank, unelaborate, unaffected, so full of pictures of every-day life, such a series of photographs of customs, laws, social, domestic and civil manners, institutions and observances, so artless, so without concealment, so self-evidencing in reality and truth, and so full of knowledge and instruction as the Gospels, and the Acts of the Apostles, without the omnipresent and prominent institution and customs of slavery in those countries coming out, and the sentiments, morals and manners produced by it, as well as the laws governing it, and keeping down the victims of its cruelty. There would be no possibility, if it had been an ordinance appointed of God, and existing fifteen hundred years, of having it left in doubt, or capable of being brought in question, whether it was a reality in the land, or whether Christ and his apostles approved or disapproved of it. Silence in regard to it, and the exclusion of its evience from the pages of such historic volumes, could only be effected by stratagem, by art, and maintained for a purpose, by a violence of concealment contrary to historic truth.

Before the Grecian and Roman empires have attained one half the duration of the kingdom of the Jews, the germ of slavery has grown among them from a seed to a forest.- Without being divinely planted or appointed, without any assertion or pretence on the part of historians or commentators on the laws and institutions of those States, of its ever having been revealed from heaven as a divine inheritance, or a social oppression agreeable to the divine will, slavery runs on as if it were indeed divine, and it only takes a few centuries to absorb nearly all forms of domestic service in the unpaid, enforced, unmitigated condition and institution of absolute chattelism. Slavery characterizes and fills the country, through the enforced ignorance and immorality of the slaves, and inevitable pride, luxury and cruelty of their owners, with all its peculiarities of law, licentiousness, despotism, and every abomination. Its presence can not be concealed, and its progress is as the slow consuming stream of lava down garden slopes and vineyards to the sea.

According to Gibbon, the number of slaves in the Roman empire had increased, under the reign of Claudius, till it equalled the number of free inhabitants. From the time of Augustus to Justinian there may be reckoned three slaves to one freeman, so that, out of a whole population of twenty-eight millions in Italy, twenty-one millions may be set down as slaves. The prodigality of wealth in this single species of property (revealed from heaven as an abomination worthy of death) came to be, where a divine revelation was unknown, almost incredible. Ten and twenty thousand slaves were sometimes owned by one person.

Out of all this there grew what might have been expected, under the darkness of Paganism, but what must have been still worse had the sin been perpetrated along with Judaism, and what must be worse than either, if it be maintained under the light of Christianity, a state of society unexampled since the deluge, for its revelry, abandonment and wantonness of depravity. Inhumanity and cruelty in sentiment and on principle carried to an art; the tenderness even of woman's nature changed into a fiendlike insensibility, or even delight, in the infliction of pain on others; inventions of new atrocities, subtle and devilish, cruelties practiced for mere variety of recreation; man-stealing, sodomy, *pederasty*, all those iniquities and abominable hideous caricatures and deliriums of depravity hinted at in the Epistle to the Romans; fornication and adultery established in a system of law, in the forbidding of the matrimonial contract among slaves, just as at the South; all the tempests and fermentations in the State, and in social life, consequent on such abominations, and developed in history; rebellions, insurrections, devastations, servile wars, vast massacres, tortures, crucifixions, amphitheatrical butcheries, gladiatorial wholesale murders for the people's sports; luxury, idleness, dissolution, along with the malignity and cruelty of fiends, taught and fostered both in the higher and lower classes; barbarity and licentiousness perfected into a science, but the victims of such ferocity and lust unconsciously revenging themselves, as a dead body sometimes does upon its dissectors; fatal diseases fostered and festering, pestilences raging in the body, as well as sins gangrening in the soul, and making society a mass of moral putridity and misery. Such was the result of slavery in Rome; such would have been its result in Judea, had it ever been established and perpetuated there.*

* Consult, for proof in detail, SMITH'S Roman and Grecian Antiquities, ed. Anthon; GIBBON'S Decline and Fall; BECKER, Roman Antiquities; FUSS, Roman Antiquities, Part I; EDWARDS, Roman Slavery; ESCHENBERG, Greek and Roman Antiquities; GROTE, History of Greece; ARCHB. POTTER, Archæologia. When any master was murdered by a slave, it was a law in Rome that all the slaves who were under the roof of the deceased at the time of the murder should be put to death, and all who had received their freedom. An instance of the execution of this decree to the letter occurred in the year 61, the very year, it is supposed, of Paul's arrival at Rome. The whole body of slaves belonging to Pedanius, amounting to at least four hundred, and including many women and children, were sacrificed, though confessedly innocent; a most frightful example of the atrocity of the laws which regulated the relations of slave to master, and, it may be added, of the wickedness and atrocity of the relation itself, of which all cruelties and depravities of life and morals are but the natural result.

The law under which they were put to death was passed by the Senate (see TACITUS, Ann. B., 13, 33) some three years previous. The populace opposed the execution, but the majority of the Senate maintained it, and Nero lined the streets with troops to keep down the mob. Tacitus gives the speech of Caius Cassius, one of the senators, against repealing or suspending the decree, His arguments were worthy of the slave democracy of modern times. "At present," said he, "we have in our service whole nations of slaves; the scum of mankind, collected from all quarters of the globe. Who can hope to live in security among his slaves, when so large a number as four hundred could not defend Pedanius Secundus?" The argument was that the four hundred innocent should be put to death, to strike terror among the millions. TACITUS, Annals, B., xiv., 42, 45. Compare THOLUCK, Nature and Moral Influence of Heathenism; STROUD'S SLAVE LAWS, ch. ii., Of the Incidents of Slavery; BECKER, in Bib. Sacra. vol. 2; KITTO, Cyclop. Bib. Lit. Art., SLAVE. NEANDER, Ch. Hist., v. i.

CHAPTER XXXI.

EXAMINATION OF GREEK USAGE IN THE NEW TESTAMENT.—TERMS OF SERVICE AND SERVANTS DERIVED FROM THE HEBREW, WITH THE OLD FREE HEBREW MEANING, AND NOT THE MEANING OF SLAVERY.—USAGE IN THE GOSPEL OF MATTHEW.

IN the examination of passages in the New Testament bearing on this subject, especially those in which the Greek terms for *servants, servitude, slaves* or *slavery* occur, we have to bear in mind that, while the *language* of these terms was Greek, the *signification* was to a great degree Hebrew. The ideas for those terms, as they lay in the Hebrew mind, were different from the same in the Greek mind, so that the Hebrew law and idea govern the Greek words, not the words the idea. It was an inevitable result of the discipline of the Mosaic laws, with the instructions of the Prophets, that the conceptions of the Jews, as to social life and liberty, were so far raised above those of the whole world beside, that neither the language of the Greeks nor of the Romans was adequate fully to convey them. Neither the Greek nor Roman term for *wife* could convey the sacredness of its meaning in God's Word.

The signification of such terms inevitably comes from the Hebrew through the Greek of the Septuagint translation, and is to be corrected by the Hebrew. "All the world," remarks Lightfoot, "that used the Old Testament at those times (unless it were such as had gained the Hebrew tongue by study) used it in the translation of the LXX., or the Greek—the quotations of the penmen of the New Testament out of the Old Testament might be examined by the Greek Bible."* The

* LIGHTFOOT, vol. xii., 587, vol, iii., 62, 310. CONYBEARE and HOWSON, i., pp. 11, 32, 43. HUG., Intr. N. Test. ALFORD, N. T. int.

terms for *servants, servitude, bondage, et cetera*, were the old Hebrew terms, drawn through the medium of the Septuagint translation, and possessing the old Hebrew signification. The The Septuagint translators sometimes used δουλος for עֶבֶד, sometimes παις, sometimes οικετης. But there was no Greek word for servant answering to the Hebrew עֶבֶד, free from the possible signification of bondage, in the way of chattelism, or human beings held as property. The Septuagint translators having applied δουλος so freely as the rending of עֶבֶד, which is the word for a free Hebrew servnnt, δουλος mnst have come to be as common a usage in Judea to signify free Hebrew servants, as it was in classic Greek to signify slaves. The ordinary meaning of it, therefore, in the New Testament, is not a slave, but a laborer for wages on a voluntary agreement. The comparison of passages proves this.

"Besides the writers of the New Testament," says Professor Planck, "the Alexandrian interpreters have also transferred from the Hebrew *usus loquendi* new significations to many Greek words. The cause of this some have supposed (and not without a semblance of truth) to lie in the poverty of the Hebrew; whence it has happened that since one word in that language often serves to express several ideas, the same variety of signification has been transferred to a Greek word, which perhaps properly corresponds to it only in one signification."* It is not so much a proof of poverty in the Hebrew tongue as of freedom and nobleness in the people, and righteousness in their laws, that the language had no word for *slavery*. The Greek word for *slave* and *slavery*, being used by the Septuagint interpreters to translate the Hebrew words for *servant* and *service*, received thenceforward from the Hebrew a meaning of freedom, which they did not bear in what is called classic Greek. Consequently, the same Greek words which, outside the New Testament, might mean *slave* and *slavery*, can not be proved to possess that meaning

* PLANCK. Greek Style of the New Testament. Bib. Rep., vol. i, p. 686.

in it, but are rather proved to possess the Hebrew idea, which they must have been used to convey. The general presumption in regard to the word δουλος, in the New Testament, is that it means a free servant, such as the Jews were accustomed to, such only as the law of God permitted, such as was familiar in the social life and households of the country. For it is taken from the Hebrew vocabulary, with the Hebrew meaning, and the meaning of slavery can not be supposed or admitted, without positive proof in the context, or in the nature of the particular case. General instructions to servants, and to masters in regard to the treatment of servants, must inevitably mean such kind of servants as the law of God permitted, and not slaves, which the law of God forbade. It would be as absurd to suppose the Bible issuing instructions to slaveholders for the treatment of slaves, as if they could righteously hold slaves, as it would to suppose similar instructions given to horse-thieves for the treatment of their stolen property, or to fornicators for the treatment of their mistresses, as if fornication and horse-stealing were no crimes.

That may be said in regard to the word δουλος, and kindred terms in the New Testament, which has been beautifully and truly remarked by Professor Tholuck concerning some other phrases in Greek, used for religious ideas, that " in connection with the Christian dispensation they are all surrounded with new light, and advanced to a higher sense. The lexicographer of the New Testament has, therefore, first of all, to make the Old Testament idea the object of his research, and to express it exactly; then, by a careful comparison of the parallel passages, and from the consciousness of Christian feeling, to obtain a clear view of the Christian signification; and finally to point out what is the point of connection between the idea of the New Testament and that of the Old."*

* Tholuck on the Lexicography of the New Testament. The article translated from the Latin by Dr. Robinson, is to be found in the first volume of the Biblical Repository, pp. 552–568.—Also Dr. Robinson, Philology of the N. T. Bib. Rep., vol. 4.

EVIDENCE FROM THE GOSPEL OF MATTHEW.

The first occurrence of the subject of *service*, in any form, is in Matthew viii. 5–13, the application of the centurion to Jesus for the healing of his *servant*. The word here used three times for the servant in question, is παῖς, answering to the Hebrew נַעַר, *naar*, *boy*, or *youth*. Bloomfield remarks on the passage, that παῖς is often used, both in the classical and

The reader may consult, also, on this subject, in the same volume, J. A. H. Tittman's admirable article on the grammatical accuracy of the writers of the New Testament. He here remarks on the importance of Ernesti's direction "to inquire respecting words and phrases expressing things about which the Greeks were accustomed to speak; and first, whether such single words are spoken in the same sense in which the Greeks used them." This article was published in the first volume of the Biblical Repository, in 1831. See also in the same volume the article of Hahn on Interpretation.

Likewise, Prof. Turner's Lectures on the Claims of the Hebrew Language and Literature. He remarks that "the Greek of the New Testament is Hebraistic." "If words occur in the New Testament, the meaning of which is modified by that of analogous words in Hebrew, it becomes necessary for every one who would thoroughly comprehend his Greek Testament to study his Hebrew Bible."

See also Hug on the Prevalence of the Greek Language in Palestine in the age of Christ and the Apostles Hug's Introduction to the New Testament. "In the holy city itself whole congregations of Jews who spoke Greek were established." Bib. Rep., vol. i, p. 530–552.

Also J. A. H. Tittman. Causes of Forced Interpretations of the New Testament. See particularly the remarks on the word δικαιος and its cognates. "The Alexandrine dialect was the language employed by the Greek interpreters of the Old Testament." "The style of the New Testament is mixed and made up of words and idioms borrowed from several languages, and particularly from the Hebrew." The importance of the true historical as well as the grammatical interpretation is noted. Bib. Rep., vol. i., pp. 470–487.

Pfanukuche. Aramean language in Palestine in the age of Christ and the Apostles. The writer notes "the unexampled firmness with which the Palestine Jews, after their return from the Babylonish exile, remained faithful to their ancient manners and customs." Also, under the dominion of the Romans in Palestine, "the entire internal administration of the government, the courts of justice, etc., remained without any important change; the nation were permitted to retain their code of laws, so inseparable from their religions." Bib. Rep., vol. i., p. 33.

Consult also Prof. Tholuck on the Method of Theological Study and Interpretation. Bibliotheca Sacra, vol. i., pp. 200, 340.

Also Prof. Stuart on the meaning of Κυριος. Bib. Rep., vol. i., p. 736.

Hellenistic Greek, for δοῦλος, servant, like *puer* in Latin. It is manifest that there is no indication of slavery here.

In Matt. ix. 38, " The *laborers* are few ; pray that he would send forth laborers ;" the word used by our Lord is εργάται, answering to the Hebrew עֹבֵד, *ovedh*, a working man ; the Greek word here certainly meaning servants, hired laborers, but not slaves.

Matt. x., 23, " The *servant* is not above his lord ; enough for the servant that he be as his lord ;" δουλος is used in both cases ; no meaning of slavery attached to it, but signifying a free, voluntary service, the service of Christ.

Matt. xii., 18, " Behold my *servant*, whom I have chosen, my beloved," etc., ο παις μου ; in the Hebrew, עַבְדִּי, my *servant*.

Matt. xiii., 27, 28 ; the parable of the householder sowing good seed. "The *servants* said unto him," δοῦλοί, with no indication of any but free service.

Matt. xviii., 23–35 ; the parable of the king and the wicked servant, who owed ten thousand talents. Here the words used are δοῦλος and σύνδουλός, employed nine times, but with no signification of slave or slavery, since it is the king who takes accounts of servants entrusted with the disbursement of vast sums of money, and who have fellow-servants owing them in like manner, in accounts of business. It is not a process of servitude, but of official business, or mercantile transactions, here brought to view, and of debts among freemen under responsibilities to the law. Bloomfield remarks on the word δούλων, here used, that it does not mean *slaves*, but officers in the receipt or disbursement of money, of what sort it is not certain.

Matt. xx., 1–16.—Here we have an important passage, the parable of the *householder* hiring his *laborers* for his vineyard. It is in the market place that he hires them, going forth, morning, noon and afternoon, for that purpose ; and the representation intimates that there were many standing idle, waiting to be hired, offering their services.   There is no hint, no intimation of there being any such thing as *slavery* known, any such servants as slaves to be bought and worked as property, without wages.   There is no slave-market, and the servants are hired from themselves, and neither bought nor hired from any third persons.   There is no such possibility or custom conceived of.   These servants were freemen, who hired themselves out, and this, manifestly, was the prevailing, customary style of service, just as in England at this day, or in free New England, where no such thing as slavery is known.

And the master of the vineyard agrees with the servants for so much by the day, and in the case of the latest hired, he promises to give to them whatever is *just* as their *wages*. He does not intimate that he will give them a peck of meal a week, and a fustian jacket and trowsers, and that the provision of such food and clothing as he chooses for them will be wages sufficient for their work. Whatsoever is *just*, I will give you.   Upon this very principle, and with a view to this very passage, the injunction was issued by the apostle, " Masters, give unto your servants that which is just and equal ;" such wages as their labor demands, such as will be a just equivalent for their work.

The word used in this parable is εργάται, *workmen*, laborers, as in Matt. ix., 38.

Matt. xx., 26 ; "Whosoever will be great among you, let him be your minister," διάκονος, *servant*, "and he that will be first among you, let him be your *servant*," δουλος, *servant of all work ;* not necessarily slave ; and the exigency of the case forbids that our blessed Lord could have commanded any of his disciples to be as *slaves* one to another, as *chattels*, as each other's property.   Call no man master in such a sense.   It was not that kind of miserable, utter degradation, at the will of another, that was here enjoined, but humility, and the service of love, as in Galatians, Ye are called unto liberty by love, to serve one another, not to be one another's slaves.   A free service is here enjoined, the service of freemen and not of slaves, the service of voluntary love, in lowliness of mind, each esteeming others better than themselves.

Matt. xxi., 33–42; the parable of the householder planting a vineyard, and building a tower, and letting it out to husbandmen, and then sending his *servants* to collect his rents; τους δουλους, the *servants*, used three times, verses 34, 35, 36. It certainly does not mean *slaves*, for the scene of the parable is in Judea, the vineyard is a Jewish vineyard, the servants are supposed to be Jews, and not enslaved heathens; and the whole parable is as truly a representation of social life, in the relation between masters, or employers, and those employed by them, as the preceding parable of the householder going forth to hire workmen for his vineyard. There was not an individual who heard this discourse of Christ who could have understood him to mean any other than hired servants, servants on wages, but not slaves. The householder sent these servants to the husbandmen, to receive of the fruit of the vineyard. They were entrusted with the collection of the rents in the productions of the land leased, or rented.

The householder being a Jew, the demonstration is perfect, his servants being Jews, that they could not be slaves, and, therefore, the word δουλους is demonstrated as possible to be applied, as beyond all question it was applied, to such servants as were free servants, and not slaves. The Jewish law forbade any Hebrew from being held as a slave, over and above the principles and statutes, that, likewise, strictly applied, would forbid holding any human being as a slave.

Matt. xxii., 2–14. Here the parable is of the king who made a marriage supper for his son, and sent forth his *servants* to summon the invited guests to the wedding. The phrase used for servants is τους δουλους, and it is employed five times, in verses 3, 4, 6, 8, and 10. There is no reason to suppose that it means *slaves*; and in the 13th verse the word employed is διακονοις, attendants or servants, just as διακονος and δουλος are interchanged in the preceding case, Matt. xx., 26, "Then said the king to his *servants*, Bind them hand and foot," etc. These last would be more likely to be slaves than the first ; yet the word in the last case is διάκονος, and in the other δοῦλος. There is no proof whatever that slaves are here indicated; but if they were, it is not a scene in Judea, but abroad, in the dominions of some oriental potentate.

Matt. xxiii., 12. "But he that is greatest among you shall be your *servant*," διάκονος ; a repetition of the injunction of humility in Matt. 20 : 26, and the word employed signifying a free, voluntary laborer or attendant.

Matt. xxiv., 45–51. "Who then is a faithful and wise *servant*, whom his lord hath made ruler over his household," etc. Here the words employed are δοῦλος and συνδούλους, and the word δοῦλος is employed four times, in verses 45, 46, 48 and 50. There is no meaning of slave in it, for, again, it is supposed to be a scene of household life among the Jews, who kept no slaves, and at whose feasts and scenes of recreation and enjoyment the very relatives and members of the household thought it no degradation to serve with the servants, if there were need of such service, as in the case recorded in John xii., 2, where "they made him a supper, and Martha served." The servants in this case are faithful and wise, types of the willing and faithful disciples and servants of the Lord, voluntary servants and not slaves. The good and the bad are contrasted, and their responsibility to their Lord is solemnly set forth.

So in Luke xvii., 7, where our Lord was speaking to the Jews, to his apostles, and generally to the disciples (it was in the neighborhood of Jerusalem), "Which of you having a servant ploughing, or feeding cattle," etc., δοῦλον and δοῦλοι ; and the service is signified by the word διακόνει, not δουλεύει. The agricultural life and service of Judea, as in the days of Boaz, with the picture of his servants at their work, was a life of free service ; there were no slaves. There is no evidence of any change for the worse, in this respect, from the time of Boaz to the days of our Lord Jesus.

Matt. xxv., 14–30. This is the parable of the man traveling into a far country, and calling his servants, and delivering to them his goods, his money, to trade with for him in his absence. The words here used are δουλος and δουλους, employed six times, in verses 14, 19, 21, 23, 26 and 30. It was not the employment of *slaves* to invest capital, and make money thereon, or to act as brokers, or exchangers, or commission merchants. There is no proof here that slaves were meant, or were in the minds either of the speaker or the hearers. On the contrary, as our blessed Lord was discoursing of things familiar to his hearers, and which were well understood as illustrated by things familiar to their own observation, the presumption is that neither he nor they referred to, nor would think of, any other kind of factors or servants in such commission business than voluntary, free servants, employed for wages, on a compact of their own.

Matt. xxvi., 51; "Struck a *servant* of the High Priest." Here the word used for servant is δουλον, certainly not a slave, for the Jewish priests kept no slaves; the law did not permit it. This man was a Jew, and could not possibly have been a slave. No Hebrew could be, or could be held, as a slave, and this man was certainly a free servant, follower, retainer, perhaps one of the υπηρεται, or officers of Judas' band. Yet he is called a δουλος, and the case is proof absolute that the use of that word does not of itself prove the existence of slavery.

Matt. xxvi., 58. Peter, in the high priest's palace, went in and sat with the *servants*, to see the end. Here the word used for servants is υπηρετων, used of the same class and condition as the word δουλος, in verse 51. It is said to mean here the ministers, attendants, or beadles of the Sanhedrim. But the Sanhedrim had no slaves. The servant of the high priest, whose ear Peter cut off, may have been one of these very officers, one of the ὑπηρεται. There is no evidence to the contrary.

The δουλοι were a more generic class, the ὑπηρεται specific; and in John xvii., 18, we have the two together. " And the *servants* and *officers* stood there, who had made a fire of coals; for it was cold; and they warmed themselves; and Peter stood with them, and warmed himself." But again, in verse 26, the kinsman of Malchus, the servant of the high priest, whose ear Peter cut off, is called one of the *servants* of the high priest, εἰς τῶν δούλων. And in the third verse Judas is said to have received a band and officers from the chief priests and Pharisees, comprising the whole rabble that rushed upon Jesus in the garden, and whom Peter encountered with his sword. The δοῦλος, whose ear he cut off, would appear to have been one of the ὑπηρετὰι, but neither of these were slaves.

Generally the attendants upon any work, the working agents, were called ὑπηρέται. John xviii., 36, our Lord says, "If my kingdom were of this world, then would my *servants* fight"—ὑτηρέται. But our Lord's disciples and servants are called δίακονοι, δοῦλοι, or ὑπηρέται, the words being interchangeable, as for example, John xii., 26, my servant, δίακονος; John xiii., 16; Luke xvii., 10; John xiii., 16, and xv., 15; the *servant* not greater than his lord—not *servants* but friends —we are unprofitable servants, δουλοι—and so in other places. Luke i., 2, ministers of the word, ὑπηρέται. In Liddell and Scott, ὑπηρέτης is set down as a laborer, helper, assistant, servant, underling, inferior officer. "In Xenophon, ὑπηρέται were a number of men in immediate attendance on the general, as aides-de-camp or adjutants. Cyr. 2, 4, 4; 6, 2, 14, etc., etc." Compare Matt. xx. 26, page 360.

Matt. xxvi., 69. Peter sitting in the palace, a *damsel*, παιδισκη, comes to him. She is called, in Mark xiv., 66, one of the *maids* of the high priest, μία τῶν παιδισκῶν, and in Luke xxii., 56, a certain *maid*, παιδίσκη, and in John xviii.,

16, 17, her that kept the door, the *damsel*, παιδίσκη ή θυρωρος. " The word properly signifies *a girl ;* but, as in our own language, it is often, in later Greek, used to denote a *maid servant.* The office of porter, though among the Greeks and Romans it was confined to *men*, was among the Jews generally exercised by women."—BLOOMFIELD in loc.

See also Acts xii., 13, 14. There the doorkeeper, or the servant whose business it was to attend upon the door, was a Jewish damsel, παιδίσκη, named Rhoda, herself one of the disciples, and on such terms of intimacy with the circle of brethren and sisters praying in the house, that she ran back instantly among them, and told them that Peter had come, and was at the gate, knocking ; so intimately acquainted with Peter that she knew him by his voice, as he stood outside the gate and demanded admittance, and so full of joy at his arrival that, actually forgetting to open the gate, she ran into the midst of the prayer-meeting with the news. Now these maids, or damsels, whether of the high priests, or of the disciples, in their families, were not slaves, but answered to the condition of the free maid servants under the Mosaic laws in the Old Testament.

USAGE IN THE GOSPEL OF MARK.

Mark, i., 20. They left their father Zebedee in the ship with the *hired servants*, μισθωτων. No slaves here ; yet servile work to be done by *servants* for wages. The difference between μισθωτος and δοῦλος may have been the same as between the Hebrew שָׂכִיר, *hired servant*, and the עֶבֶד, *servant*, neither being slaves, but free.

Mark ix., 35. If any one will be first among you, he shall be last of all, and *servant* of all, διάκονος ; in other places, as Matt. xx., 26, δοῦλος.

Mark x., 43. Whosoever will be great among you, shall be your minister, διάκονος ; and whosoever will be the chiefest among you, let him be the servant of all, δοῦλος.

Mark xii., 2, 4 ; the parable of the husbandman letting out the vineyard, and sending his *servants* to receive the fruits, as in Matt. xxi., 34. The word for servant is δοῦλον, certainly not a *slave*, the same being of a Jewish husbandman.

Mark xiii., 34. The Son of man on a far journey, giving authority to his *servants*, and to every man his work ; δουλοις, not *slaves* in a Jewish household.

Mark xiv., 54, 65. Peter sitting with the *servants*, and the *servants* smiting Jesus, ὑπηρέται.

We may note in this gospel, as in Matthew's, concerning the application of δοῦλος to denote the affectionate, voluntary servant in the household of faith, in the family of Jesus, that our blessed Lord never would have employed a word so base as that of *slave* to signify a relation so free, honorable, voluntary and glorious as that of the Christian brother, the loving servant for Christ's sake, in Christ's love, the child of God, the happy, willing, loving servant of the Saviour. God is not a slaveholder, but a Father. Satan is the great SLAVEHOLDER, but God rejects the service of a slave, and will have only the voluntary, loving service of a freeman. The Greek word δοῦλος, employed by the divine Spirit in the New Testament to signify a servant of God, and applied even to the divine Redeemer in his work of matchless, voluntary love, received its elevated meaning from the Hebrew עֶבֶד, and is no more to be debased with the idea of slavery than the Hebrew law and language itself. The word δοῦλος is a Hebrew proselyte, and has been baptized, and thus only is admitted into the Christian family, its Pagan wickedness being washed away.

CHAPTER XXXII.

Evidence from Luke.—Pictures of Free Jewish Households.—Parable of the Prodigal Son.—Nothing of Slavery to be Met with.—Only Free, Voluntary Service, as Under the Old Testament Laws.

In the first chapter of Luke we find δούλη used for *maiden* and *handmaiden of the Lord,* certainly not *slave.* (i. 38, 48.) And παιδὸς, *child* (54), for his *servant* Israel, and the same (69) for his *servant* David. Ch. ii., 29. "Lord, now lettest thou thy *servant* depart," etc., δοῦλον σου, not thy *slave.* Luke vii. 2, 3, 7, 10, the centurion's *servant* who was sick. Here the word used in verses 2, 3, 8 and 10, is δοῦλος. But in verse 7, the centurion himself speaks, and calls his *servant* παῖς μοῦ. It has been contended that being a centurion he must have had slaves ; but even if he had, there is no proof of it, and no proof that this παῖς was a slave, or that there was a single slave in his household. The word παῖς is proof absolute that the word δοῦλος does not necessarily indicate a slave. We find παῖς and δοῦλος often used indifferently. In Matthew, viii., 5–13, in the same case, the centurion uses the word παῖς in verses 6, 9, and his servant is not called δοῦλος at all ; and the sacred historian uses the word παῖς, not δοῦλος, in verse 13, his *servant* (παῖς) was healed the same hour.

Now the argument here is triumphant, so far as the proof that δοῦλος may be used as signifying the same with παῖς, that is, may be used of a free servant, and does not necessarily imply a slave. There is no proof whatever that the *servant* of this centurion was a *slave,* but every indication to the contrary. Supposing this man a proselyte, then his household must have been ordered according to the Jewish law, according to God's covenant with Abraham. But his servant may have been a freeman, and freemen were still termed δουλος, so that this Greek word may mean a free person.*

Luke x., 2, 7, *laborers* for the harvest; and, "The *laborer* is worthy of his hire," ἐργατάι, ἐργάτης. The occurrence of this proverb intimates a state of society in which the working class are all hired laborers, workers for wages, *servants*, not *slaves*. It is a proverb that grows out of the custom of free and not slave labor; but it comes directly from the word of God, and in connection with the Old Testament laws on this subject, it here proves that involuntary servitude, unpaid labor, the labor of slaves without hire, is wrong. It is a sin against God, the denunciation of which covers every case. "Wo to him that useth his neighbor's service without wages, and giveth him not for his work." If it was not permitted to take a man's *service* without wages, much more not to take *himself* as a *chattel*, a *slave*. If it was forbidden, in every case, so to oppress a man as to compel him to labor without hire, much more was it forbidden, much more was it criminal in the sight of God, and a much greater cruelty against man, to degrade the man himself to the condition of a horse, or an ox, compelling him to labor perpetually without wages, as a *slave*.

In other words, if to steal the man's wages was forbidden, how much more to steal the man himself. And especially when, as in the case of American slavery, the stealing of the man is followed by the stealing of his children, and his children's children, to all generations, as a legal consequence and necessity, the children of the stolen parents being affirmed to have been born in slavery, and therefore having no right to any other *status*, that *status* itself being affirmed, even by divines, to be the holy providence of God, irreversible and righteous! What exasperation and complication of iniquity!

* ESCHENBERG. Grecian Antiquities, § 99. EDWARDS. Slavery in Ancient Greece. Bib. Rep., vol. 5.

Luke xii. 37–47, the parable of the *servants* waiting for the Lord's return from the wedding. Blessed are those servants, or δοῦλοι; and the word *servants* is used six times in that form, δοῦλος. That it does not mean *slaves* is very clear from the 37th verse, where it is said that their Lord would gird himself, and make them to sit down to meat, and come forth and serve them. The οἰχονόμος in this parable, the faithful and wise steward, verse 42, is called, 43, 45, 46, δοῦλος, and his fellow servants are called, verse 45, παῖδας καὶ παιδίσκας, and the household described being a Jewish family and household, the words used mean just what the same words would mean in the Old Testament, a household of free servants, with the head servant, or steward, over the whole. Such an office, as far back as the days of Abraham, was that of the eldest servant of his house, Eliezer of Damascus, Gen. xv. 2 and xxiv. 2. Always, in all Hebrew families, it was a free and honorable office and service, and the stewardship was over free servants, according to the strictness of the Jewish law, and not slaves.

Our Lord depicted, in this parable, a family under that law, and not a Greek or Roman family or household, not the domestic institutions of any heathen nation, but of the Jews; and of the Jews as subject to the Mosaic laws, and maintaining them. The responsibility of the servants, and of the steward as a faithful and wise servant over the rest, was what Peter and the other disciples, who asked if the parable applied particularly to them, could well understand, in the system of free, voluntary Hebrew service, but nowhere else; and nowhere else could any original be found of the grateful, affectionate communion and relation of mutual confidence, labor and reward, between the master of the household and his servants. If the household service of the Hebrews had not been a free service, if their servants had not been voluntary servants for wages, those customs would have been totally unfit for an illustration of the service of the Saviour and of the household of faith. The service and responsibility of freemen, working for reward, and not of degraded chattels without wages, were as necessary for the ground-work of these beautiful parables as the system of Jewish sacrifices was essential for a prophetic illustration of the atonement by the Messiah.

The same is true of the domestic pictures contained in the fourteenth chapter, which are all Jewish, founded on the very scenes beheld by the Saviour in the house of one of the chief Pharisees, with whom he was a visitor. The whole parable, verses 16–24, is of Jewish life. It is a Jew, like the Pharisee that had invited our Lord, who is supposed to have made a great supper, and bidden many; and the servants whom he sends are Jewish servants, who could not possibly be slaves; there could be no such thing as slavery in existence in a Jewish household, under the law of God.

It is not a luxurious, proud Roman noble's household of chattel slavery and pomp that our blessed Lord is here describing, but a household of which the very family in whose presence he was teaching, at whose board he was sitting, of whose hospitality he was partaking, formed the counterpart; and he was appealing to their own well-known and familiar habits and usages. In this parable, as in the preceding, the word δοῦλος is the word employed for *servant*, as it is the Greek word commonly used in the Septuagint translation of the Old Testament, where the servants of the Hebrews are mentioned; and it means the same kind of servant here that it does there, the free Hebrew servant, but not the slave. The word δοῦλος no more means *slave* in New Testament Greek than it meant slave in the Greek of the Septuagint, where it was employed to denote the voluntary, free, hired and paid servants in the families of the Hebrews.

Luke xii. 36–47. " Blessed are those *servants*, δοῦλοι, whom the Lord, when he cometh, shall find watching." The description is of free servants, not slaves, these latter not being the subjects of reward for good behavior. It is a pic-

from the corresponding noun, to prove that the service indicated is that of slavery. It may be that of persons perfectly free. The SEPTUAGINT uses the word δουλευσει in Ex. xxi., 6, and elsewhere of the service of a Hebrew, voluntary and free.

Fourth, to these considerations it may be added that when the prodigal son was reduced to misery in his wanderings into a far country, he went and joined himself (ἐκολλήθη), engaged himself, bound or apprenticed himself, to a citizen of that country, who sent him into his fields to *feed swine*. This was analogous to the case supposed in Lev. xxv., 47, of a Hebrew falling poor, and selling himself to a heathen. If the transaction had been described in the customary language of the country of old, it would have been that his employer bought him, and that he sold himself. If that citizen had described the transaction, he would have said, " I have purchased me a new swine-herd to-day; I met a wandering Jew, and bought him for so much money, and sent him at once to feed swine." Yet the purchase was a voluntary contract, as voluntary on the part of the prodigal selling himself as on the part of the farmer *hiring*, or as the Hebrew phrase was, *buying* him. The whole parable is a most striking picture of a state of society where freedom and not slavery prevailed. The μισθιοι, the hired servants, did not have to pay their own board out of their wages, nor was it considered that they had just and equal wages, because they had an allowance for their food, and sufficient sackcloth for their garments. They had food enough and to spare, besides their just and equal wages.

The poor miserable prodigal, even after his engagement as a swine-herd, was still a free servant, on a voluntary engagement, although perhaps his master would have described him as being *his money*, and as having been *bought* by him. Yet he was at perfect liberty to leave his service, and return to his home if he chose, as the result proves. His master had no power or claim over him as *property*, and no hint is given of any imagination or purpose of sending a marshal or a bloodhound after him as a fugitive slave. He takes his line of march direct for his father's house without so much as consulting with his master.

Luke xvi., 1–13, the parable of the rich man who had a steward, the unjust steward. Compare the οἰκονόμος in this parable with that in chapter xii., 42, and it is found that the office is the same, and the servant holding it is beyond question a freeman, as among the Jews he never could be otherwise, for they received their customs neither from Greeks nor Romans, nor any other Pagans, but from Moses and from God.

That the steward here was a perfectly free servant, is plain from his very trial and dismissal by his master, his employer, and his own complaint, that having had the stewardship taken away from him, he was no longer in his master's employment, no longer had any claim of salary for service, no longer, therefore, any means of subsistence; for he was not accustomed to labor, he was too proud to beg, and, being turned out of his stewardship for malversation of office, no other man would hire him. Now there is nothing described of this steward peculiar; such as he was, except, it is to be hoped, his rascality, such were all stewards, such they always had been, from the time of Abraham's Eliezer, who was no more a slave than this man in our Lord's parable was a slave. The office and the service were always those of freemen. Yet the service is referred to under the word δουλεύειν, proving that that word in the New Testament means a free service, and not the service of a slave.

This is strikingly confirmed by our Lord's own argument in verse 13, "No servant can serve two masters; for either he will hate the one and love the other, or else he will hold to the one and despise the other. Ye can not serve God and Mammon." Ye can not δουλεύειν God and Mammon.

Here (verse 13) the word for *servant* is οἰκέτης, and its application is generic, all sorts of servants; yet in all cases it is sup-

posed to be a free service, a service of voluntary choice and
contract, for upon that point the pith and gist of the argument
depend. The service supposed is *not* a compulsory one, about
which the servant can have no will nor choice, nor about his
master, or the choice of a master ; as it is well known no slave
is ever consulted as to whether he will choose to serve his own
master or prefers to run away, or enter into the employment
of another. This attribute of choosing one's employer is the
attribute of a *freeman*, not of a *slave*. And while the word
used is οἰκέτης, which here certainly means a free servant, and
is taken generically for all servants, the word descriptive of
the service is δουλευειν, which, therefore, can not possibly here
mean slave-service, or to serve as a slave.

It is, therefore, proved that a man might be held δουλευειν,
to perform the office of a δουλος, and yet be a free servant,
free to choose his service and his employer, free to continue
in his employer's service, or to quit it, and bind himself to
another, or, in the language of the parable, hold to another,
just as he pleased. Nothing can be more satisfactory than
this demonstration ; the more so because it is generic, intended
purposely to cover all cases, and the same word, used to signify the service of man, is also used to signify the free voluntary service of God, and that word is δουλευειν. If the argument had been concerning *slavery* or *slaves*, it would certainly
have run in this style, namely, that no man can serve two masters, for he is the property of one only, and has no will or
choice of his own.

The possibility of a question between the service of two
masters, the possibility of hesitating or doubting, is founded
on the fact of being able to choose, the fact of the service being voluntary, and not compulsory, a compact with one of the
two, which can not be made with both. Being made, the
whole service of the man choosing that master belongs to him,
and on the part of a faithful servant will be given to him, for
it can not be given to two, and especially if the two are op-

posed, the servant must inevitably be loyal to the one and opposed to the other.

Luke xvii. 5–10. The apostles, in answer to their prayer, "Lord, increase our faith," are addressed by our Lord with the apothegm, or illustration of the way in which their faith is to be increased by working. "Which of you, having a *servant* plowing or feeding cattle, will say unto him, when he has come from the field, go and sit down to meat?" etc., etc. Here the word for *servant* is δοῦλος, and it is employed three times, in verses 7, 9, 10, and the word for *service* is not δουλευειν, but διακόνει, verse 8. Several things of importance in the argument are gathered here.

1. These δουλοι were of the same class with the οἰκέται mentioned in the preceding chapter as free servants. They were οἰκέται, *servants* belonging to the house, and employed to wait upon table. But they were also δουλοι, employed as plowmen and herdsmen, laboring in the field and in the care of the flocks. They were μισθιοι, hired servants, although at the same time δουλοι, as in the parable of the prodigal son; and they were οἰκέται, house servants, at the same time, their service in the house being a διακονιαν, or ministry personal at the table of the master.

2. These are supposed to be *servants of the apostles; that* is the very case put by our blessed Lord; and, therefore, from the necessity of the case they could not be *slaves*, for no Hebrew could either be a slave himself, or hold others as slaves, as property. This was forbidden in their law, and our Lord would no more have supposed the possibility of one of the apostles holding slaves than of his having a dozen wives.

3. The apostles are called δουλοι, and are put upon the same level, as to our Lord, with the servants of their own households, that is, persons engaged to a voluntary service, which they rightfully owe, not as being property or chattels, but as having chosen their own lord and master, on being chosen by

him. The whole argument from this case is of extraordinary power.

Luke xviii. 22–29, and xix. 8, are passages presenting some interesting considerations bearing on our investigation. " Sell all that thou hast, and distribute unto the poor," was our blessed Lord's command to the rich ruler. It is manifest that human beings could not have been included by our Lord in this man's property, by the sale of whom, and distribution of the profits, he was to have treasure in heaven. And so, when he said, " There is no man that hath left house, or parents, or brethren, or wife, or children for the kingdom of God's sake," there is no enumeration of slaves as any part of the man's possessions to be relinquished, as there must have been if they were the most valuable of his properties. And just so in the case of Zaccheus, " Behold, Lord, the half of my goods I give to the poor; and if I have taken away any thing from any man by false accusation, I restore him fourfold," it is not to be supposed here that this converted man gives the half of his slaves, or the profits of their sale, to the poor, or that he has any slaves among his property. The incidental argument against the possibility of slavery is worth noting in these graphic pictures of society.*

Luke xix. 13–22. In this passage we have the parable of a nobleman going into a far country, to receive a kingdom, and to return. And he calls his *servants*, δουλους, or ten of his servants, and commands them to take charge of his business (occupy) till he returns. " The word (Πραγματευσασθε) signifies literally and in the classical writers, to be engaged in business; but here it is used as a deponent in the sense to do business with by investment in trade." The noun is used both in the classical writers and the Septuagint to denote a

---

* The case may remind us of the anecdote concerning a slave owned by two men, one of whom, being professedly a devout Christian slave-holder, was accustomed to pray, " Lord, bless our slave Tom, especially my half of him!"

merchant. But the term in Matthew is εργαξεσθαι.—BLOOM-
FIELD, *in loc.*

When he returns, he reckons with his *servants*, these merchants in charge of his property, δούλους, verse 15. Well
done, good *servant*, δοῦλε, verse 17; and he gives him authority of over ten cities, and the next over five. Then in
verse 22, Thou wicked *servant*, δοῦλε.

It is to be remarked here, 1. It is a clear case of the word
δοῦλος not meaning a *slave*. It is not to be pretended that
these servants, δοῦλοι, were *slaves*. The business committed
to them, the occupations in which they were engaged, and the
governments with which they were intrusted, forbid any such
supposition.

2. The answer of the servant with the one talent would
have been impossible to put into the mouth of a slave to his
master. It is the answer of a man who conceives himself at
liberty to refuse the service, if he pleases, and to give what
reason he pleases. And accordingly the punishment here is
merely the taking away of the commission and the property
from him, and bestowing it upon another, while the unwilling
servant is dismissed. He is not treated as a slave.

Luke xx., 9–12. A certain man planted a vineyard, etc., the
parable of the wicked husbandman. At the season he sent a
servant, verse 10, δοῦλον, and verse 11, another servant,
δοῦλον. Here the husbandman is a Hebrew, the scene being
of Jewish life and occupation, and the servants such as the
Jews were accustomed to employ, such, for example, as we
find in the beautiful descriptions of rural life in the book of
Ruth. There is no possibility of construing δοῦλον in this
place as meaning *slave*. It has the same sense, borne by the
same word, in the multitude of cases in the Septuagint, as in
the New Testament, signifying a *servant*, but not a *slave*.

Luke xxii., 26, 27. "He that is chief as he that doth serve.
For whether is greater, he that sitteth at meat, or he that
serveth? But I am among you as he that serveth," διακονῶν.

Compare John xiii., 16. The *servant* is not above his master, δοῦλος being used the same as διακονος, and in this case the signification of slave in either passage impossible. Compare, also, Phil. ii., 7. "Took upon him the form of a *servant*," certainly not of a slave, but a servant, who voluntarily endures "for the joy set before him."

Luke xxii., 50. A servant of the high priest, δοῦλον. Compare Matt. xxvi., 51, and John xviii., 10. The servant in this case being a Jew, Malchus by name, we have another demonstration of the employment of the Greek word δοῦλος to signify not a slave, but a free servant. For such Malchus certainly was.*

Luke xxii., 56, 57. "But a certain *maid* beheld him," (παιδισκη). The word here employed is the same used in Luke xii., 45, the men servants and *maidens*, in John xviii., 17, in Acts xii., 13, in Matt. xxvi., 69, in Mark xiv., 66, 69. That it here means a free servant, certainly not a slave, is rendered probable by the style of Peter's address : "Woman (γυναι), I know him not." This was the manner in which our Lord addressed his own mother at the marriage† (John ii., 4), and on the cross (John xix., 26). It is not the mode of addressing slaves, not the word that Peter would have used, had it been a slave he was answering.‡ Compare the cases of its use in Matt. 15., 28, Luke xiii., 12, John iv., 21 ; xix., 26 ; xx., 13, and 1 Cor. vii., 16. The manner of address is that of courtesy, kindness, respect.§

Παιδισκη is used so often, in the Septuagint, of free maidens (as in Ruth iv., 12, of the wife of Boaz), that its use in the New Testament (especially Gal. iv., 22–31) must be judged accordingly. Only in Acts xvi., 16, is there any application of it to a slave, the slave only of a heathen.

---

* See LIGHTFOOT on the passage, works, vol. xii. p. 397.

† BLOOMFIELD, on John, N. T. "A form of address used even to the most dignified persons."

‡ See γυναι, as used by HERODOTUS, Thalia. 134.

§ ALFORD, N. T. Note on John i., 4. Also ROBINSON, Lex., *in verb.*, γυνη.

CHAPTER XXXIII.

JOHN ii., 5, 9. The marriage at Cana, and the servants. His mother saith unto the *servants,* διακόνοις, verse 5. But the *servants* knew, διάκονοι, verse 9. Here, also, it is a Jewish household. There are no *slaves* in the family, but the usual retinue of *servants* on a bridal occasion. Had the word δοῦλοι been used, the meaning would have been the same, not *slaves,* but the *servants,* hired as free servants, according to the Jewish law.

John iv., 36. " And he that reapeth receiveth wages." The reapers were not a peculiarly privileged class of laborers or servants, but were on the same level with all other workmen. The receiving wages is named as a matter of course. The possibility is never even intimated of men being compelled to work without wages, and wages are the certain mark of freedom and free labor.

John iv., 46–51. The nobleman at Cana, whose son was sick at Capernaum. The term for nobleman is Βασιλικὸς, *courtier, nobleman,* according to Robinson and others, " but whether holding any office or not," says Bloomfield, " or whether a Jew or a foreigner, is uncertain." "The man seems to have been a Jew."—ALFORD, *in loc.* Capernaum was some twenty-five miles from Cana, and while he was returning home, the servants of his family met him, δοῦλοι. In Cana the servants are called διάκονοι, in Capernaum, δοῦλοι. Being both Jewish families, the servants were doubtless free in the one case as in the other. There was a synagogue at Capernaum where our Lord publicly taught, and where this whole believing family may have heard him.

John viii., 34, 35, 36. The *servant* of sin, δοῦλος. We were never in bondage to any one, said the Jews, but are the children of Abraham. How then sayest thou, Ye shall be made' free ? So far as the state of *slavery* is here brought into view, it is with reprobation and horror of it, as a state to which no man could be justly assigned but for crime. Our Lord's argument is, that freedom from earthly bondage is indeed a blessing, but that a man might be what is called a free man, and free born, as they claimed to be from Abraham, and yet the slave of sin and Satan. But there was another and a higher freedom, the spiritual, by the truth and the love of it, and obedience to righteousness; and if the Son made them free, then they would be free indeed.

John x., 12, 13. "The hireling fleeth because he is a hireling," μισθωτὸς, a hired servant. Compare Luke x., 7, "the laborer is worthy of his hire." It is clear that those employed in the class of employments here designated were not *slaves*, but free hired servants. Compare Luke xvii., 7, "which of you, having a *servant*, δοῦλον, feeding cattle," etc., ποιμαινοντα, *feeding sheep*, from which it appears that the house servants and the field servants were of the same grade, and were hired servants, and not slaves. The argument is very forcible.

John xii., 2. At Bethany, where they made for our Lord a feast, and Martha *served*, διηκόνει, did the work of an attendant, a *servant*.

John xii., 26. "Where I am, there shall my *servant* be," διακονος. The word is used to signify a free service, and not the service of a slave. But the word δοῦλος being employed in the same connection, for the same service, also means a free servant.

John xiii., 16. The *servant* is not greater than his Lord. Here the word used is δοῦλος, and the service is the διακονιαν, or ministry, the doer of which is called, in verse 26 of chapter xii., διακονος, not a slave, but a free servant. Our blessed

Lord himself performed the work of a servant in washing his disciples' feet. And on that occasion he said, I am among you as one that serveth, διακονῶν. Luke xxii., 27. "And if I, your Lord and Master, have washed your feet, ye also ought to wash one another's feet. For the *servant*, δοῦλος, is not greater than his master." Nothing can be clearer than that the word here does not mean a slave, but a free, voluntary servant.

John xv., 15, 20. "I call you no more *servants*, δοῦλους, but friends. The servant, δοῦλος, is not greater than his Lord." Compare John xii., 26, and Matthew x., 25. The comparison of passages proves incontrovertibly that it is a free, voluntary service, and that the word δοῦλος is used concerning such a *servant*, and not to signify a slave.

John xviii., 10, 18, 26, 36. Peter struck a *servant*, δοῦλος, of the high priest. The servant's name was Malchus. In verse 26 one of the *servants*, δοῦλον, the kinsman of Malchus. In verse 18, the *servants*, δοῦλοι, and the *officers*, ὑπηρέται. In verse 3, a band and officers of the priests and Pharisees. Malchus was one of these, and is called δοῦλος. He could not have been a *slave*, and so here is another incontrovertible instance in which the word δοῦλος is applied to a person beyond controversy a free man. The name of the servant of the high priest is Jewish, as noted by Lightfoot, "Malchus, a name very much in use among the Jews, Neh. x., 4, 27."* Malchus and his kinsman being Jews, could not possibly have been *slaves*, but, though called δοῦλοι, were free men in the condition of *servants*.†

---

* LIGHTFOOT, Hebrew and Talmudical exercitations on John. Works, v., 12.

† In confirmation of this and the preceding testimony as to usage, we have the knowledge that freedmen themselves, among the Greeks, were still termed δοῦλοι, and seldom, if ever, obtained the rights of citizens. The word, therefore, could not mean *slaves*, exclusively. ESCHENBERG, Gr. Antiq., 99.

"Slaves," says Archb. POTTER, "as long as they were under the government of a master, were called οἰκέται, but after their freedom was granted

EVIDENCE FROM THE ACTS OF THE APOSTLES.

Acts ii., 44, 45. "They had all things common.—And they sold their possessions and goods, and parted them to all men, as every man had need." There were thousands in this community, and they were speedily increased by thousands more. If slavery had been an institution of God, slaves would inevitably have been among the most valuable of the possessions of these men. Did they sell their slaves, and put the money into their Christian treasury? Did Barnabas do this? It is well known that the early Christians applied their offerings sometimes to the purchase of their brethren out of heathen slavery. Did they regard them in the church as goods and chattels?* The absurdity of the supposition is palpable.

Acts ii., 18. And upon my *servants* and handmaidens will I pour out my Spirit, δούλους and δούλας, certainly not *slaves-*

Acts iv., 25, thy *servant* David, παιδός.

Acts iv., 29. Grant unto thy *servants*, δούλοις, not *slaves*, for they are the servants of the Most High.

Acts x., 7. The case of Cornelius, the centurion in Cesarea: "Two of his household *servants*," οἰκετων, by no means necessarily *slaves;* and as to "*those who waited on him*," it is noted by Bloomfield that centurions were allowed to use some of their *soldiers* in the capacity of *domestics.*—BLOOMFIELD, *in loc.* If this man were a Jewish proselyte his household were under the law of the Jewish Scriptures. Compare Luke xvi., 13. This word οικετης is employed in the Septuagint where *slave* could not be meant. Robinson gives as its just meaning

them, they were δοῦλοι, not being, like the former, a part of the master's estate, but only obliged to some small services. POTTER, Antiq. of Greece, vol. ii., page 78.

NEANDER, Church Hist. Works of Christian Piety, vol. iii., 356.

* CHRYSOSTOM, cited in Neander, affirms that there was no such thing among the Christians as the sale of a slave, but that the masters set them free. He enjoins the purchase and completion of their freedom, and giving them trades, that they might support themselves. Slavery, he says, would cease if there were a true Christian feeling. NEANDER. Life of CHRYSOSTOM, 414.

a house companion. Liddell and Scott, *an inmate of one's house*, with instances of its being used for the free women and children, and *opposed* to δοῦλος.

Acts xii., 13, 14. "And as Peter knocked at the door of the gate, a damsel came to hearken, named Rhoda. And when she knew Peter's voice, she opened not the gate for gladness, but ran in and told how Peter stood before the gate." (See on Matt. xxvi., 69, page 364.) This damsel, παιδίσκη, was a servant in a Jewish family, but not a slave. She was a Christian servant, and the familiarity and affectionate intimacy and equality of her intercourse in the household, with her joyful recognition of Peter by his voice, and her subsequent conduct, are characteristic of freedom, not slavery.

Acts xvi., 16, 17. The damsel, παιδίσκη, possessed with the spirit of divination, following Paul and Silas, and crying, These are the *servants* of the Most High God, δοῦλοι. It was a pagan, heathen city, where this transaction took place; and this damsel is said to have brought much gain to her masters, who were ignorant idolaters, practicing both slavery and divination, as well as idolatry, for gain. She was doubtless a miserable slave, held in common by them, and exhibited for the gain of such a diabolical development. In exorcising her of the demoniac possession, Paul reduced her price, so that, comparatively, she was worth nothing to her masters, who drew Paul and Silas unto the market place, with the accusation of being troublers of the city. As in the uproar against Paul at Ephesus, the *trade* was troubled, and no crime could be greater than a reduction in the price of this stock, or the shaking of its permanence and security in the service of Satan. JOHN BROWN entering into the city could not have produced greater terror and wrath than Paul and Silas, delivering this poor slave from the thraldom of Satan, and restoring her to her senses.

CHAPTER XXXIV.

EVIDENCE FROM THE EPISTLES TO THE ROMANS AND CORINTHIANS—USAGE OF WORDS IN THESE EPISTLES—MORAL ARGUMENT FROM BOTH.

ROMANS i., 1. Paul, a *servant* of Christ, δοῦλος. Compare 2 Cor. iv., 5 ; 1 Cor. vii., 22 ; Gal. i., 10 ; Phil. i., 1 ; Col. i., 7 ; iv., 7 ; 1 Thess. iii., 2 ; 1 Tit. i., 1 ; Phil. i. ; James i., 1 ; 2 Peter i., 1 ; Jude i. ; Rev. i., 1. The Lord Jesus not being a slaveholder, and having declared the sense in which his apostles, ministers and disciples are his servants, that is, his freemen, serving him from the heart, choosing him, and cleaving to him, by divine grace, willingly, as their Lord and Master, the word δοῦλοι applied to them, or δοῦλος to any one of them, can not prove that they were *slaves*, but proves only that this word was incontrovertibly in use to designate free persons, as, indeed, the instances of its usage abundantly demonstrate. God would never have chosen, to signify the exalted, holy, voluntary, loving service and adoration of a free heart toward the Saviour, a word that meant the chattelism of beasts, the compulsory service of a slave.

Rom. vi., 16–22. "To whom ye yield yourselves servants to obey, (δούλους and δοῦλοί εἰς ὑπακοὴν,) his servants ye are, to whom ye obey, δοῦλοι, whether of sin unto death, or of obedience unto righteousness." This is an exceedingly important passage, even to the end. Several things are to be considered : 1. The service to which this word δοῦλος and the word ὑπακοὴν are applied, is voluntary, of free choice, whether the service is that of Satan or of God. *Ye yield yourselves servants.*

2. There is the privilege with the ability of changing both the service and the master at pleasure, and entering into a new engagement, freely, voluntarily.

3. When this change is made, it is called becoming the servants of righteousness, or, as in verse 19, yielding your members as servants to righteousness, a voluntary act.

4. The servants of sin are called free from righteousness, and the servants of God are called free from sin, showing the service, either side, a voluntary service.

5. The word for obedience and service thus rendered is in verses 16 and 17 υπακουω, and in verses 18 and 22 δουλευω. Here, then, is another case of the verb δουλευω being applied to the service of a freeman, as well as the noun δοῦλος to the quality and state of a freeman. Compare Luke xv., 29, where the son says to his father, These many years do I serve thee, δουλεύω, the service of a freeman; and Luke xvi., 13; No *servant* can serve, δουλευειν, two masters; ye can not serve, δουλευειν, God and Mammon. Also note in this connection the fact of δοῦλοι and μισθιοι being applied to the servants of the same household, as equivalent terms. The proofs of this usage, as taken from the Septuagint, and intimating the same views in regard to slavery in the New Testament as in the Old, are multiplied.

6. The *wages*, finally, are mentioned. The service is a service on wages, which is the service of a free, hired servant, and not a slave. The wages of sin is death; the service voluntary; the wages earned and paid. Δοῦλος, δουλευω, and ὀψωνια (wages) are here applied to one and the same system of voluntary, paid labor. Compare 1 Cor. xix., 19, For though I be free from all men, yet have I made myself servant unto all that I might gain the more; εδουλωσα, *made myself a servant*, yet, at the same time, ἐλεύθερος, *a free man.* Compare also Rom. vii., 6, *we are set free from the law, that we should serve,* (δουλευειν,) *in newness of spirit.* There can be no question, therefore, that the words δουλος

and δουλευειν are both used of a free service, the voluntary service of a freeman.

Rom. xiv., 14. Who art thou, that judgest another man's servant? οἰκέτην. To his own master he standeth or falleth. It is the servant of God that is here spoken of, and the service a free service.

Rom. xvi., 1. Phebe, a *servant* of the church, διάκονον.*

EVIDENCE FROM FIRST CORINTHIANS.

1 Cor. iv., 1, 2; ministers of Christ and stewards, ὑπηρέτας and οἰκονόμους. It is required in stewards that a man be found faithful, οἰκονόμοι. Compare Luke xii., 42, 43, that faithful and wise *steward*, οἰκονόμος. Blessed is that servant, δοῦλος. The argument here, from the use of the words, is plain and powerful. The steward was a freeman, not a slave (compare Luke xvi., 1), and the word δοῦλος is used as synonymous with οἰκονόμος, of the same meaning, applied to the

* Stuart on Rom. xii., 7, and xvi., 1. On the general Greek usage in Romans and the whole N. T. see THOLUCK on this epistle, ch. i. vs. 1, 17; ch. ii. v. 13; iii. vs. 4, 19; vi. vs. 16–19. "The pious Jews loved to use Bible phrases in speaking of the things of common life." "The Jews in general, and Paul among the rest, were fond of speaking in the language of the Old Testament." Ch. ix. vs. 3, 24, etc; ch. xi. 12; ch. xii. 7.

See also HUG's Introd. to the New Testament, pp. 13, 15, 26, 339, 361, 541, etc., and Stuart's Notes, 675.

Also DR. ROBINSON's admirable article on the Philology and Lexicography of the New Testament, Bib. Rep., vol. iv., pp. 154–182.

Also, on διακονος, see LARDNER, v. 7, p. 45. Lardner quotes the testimony of Pliny, and remarks, concerning his torture of the two *maid ser-* vants (*duabus ancillis, quæ ministræ dicebantur*, the two *maid servants*, who were called *deaconesses*), "I can not easily believe that deaconesses in Christian churches were slaves. Nor do I think it very likely that they should be domestic or hired servants. We now all know what is meant by a deaconess, in Christian writings. But I suspect that Pliny was misled by the ambiguity of the Greek word διακονος, which is sometimes used for slaves, or such as performed the lowest services usually appropriated to slaves. I say I am apt to think that Pliny was not sufficiently aware of the different meanings of the word διακονος, *deacon*, in common use, and in the ecclesiastical sense. Phebe, our sister, a servant of the church. It does not follow that she was either a slave or a hired servant to any one member of it." V. vii., pp. 45, 22.

same free person. Ὑπηρέται, οἰκονόμοι and δοῦλοι are applied indiscriminately to signify the servants of Christ, and διακονος often in the same way. (See Robinson on the words.)

Here it is proper to note the forced interpretation of *bondsmen* applied by some, as for example, *Conybeare and Howson*, as the designation in English of the service, office and employment of the apostles and preachers of the gospel. They have taken the bad and lowest signification of the terms, from Pagan usage, in regard to *slaves*, and applied *that slavish signification*, to the highest, freest, most honorable and voluntary commission and work of Christ's servants among mortals.! They have gone so far as to render 1 Cor. vii., 23, " Christ's *slave*, for he has paid a price for you all."* And they have translated Paul's injunction to use freedom, thus: " Nay, though thou have power to gain thy freedom, seek rather to remain content;" at the same time acknowledging that " the Greek might be so rendered as to give directly opposite precepts." Whence then this preference for slavery, and this dreadful attempt to foist it in, and fasten it upon, the blessed words and doctrine of divine inspiration?

1 Cor. vii., 21–23. " Art thou called being a servant? δοῦλος. Care not for it; but if thou mayest be made free, use it rather. For he that is called in the Lord being a servant, δοῦλος, is the Lord's freeman ; likewise also, he that is called, being free, is Christ's *servant*, δοῦλος. Ye are bought (redeemed, ἠγοράσθητε,) with a price; be not ye the servants, δοῦλοι, of men ?" The argument here is the same as that in regard to a wife who is called, but is the wife of an unbelieving husband. If he be pleased to dwell with her, let her not leave him, for she may be the means of saving him. But if he depart, she is not under bondage, she is free from him, and from all obligation to him. So if a servant is called, being a servant, he is not to be troubled by that condition of

---

* CONYBEARE and HOWSON, Life and Epistles of Paul, vol. i., pp. 39, 159, 436, etc.

bondage, as if it were obligatory upon him, for if he may be made free, if he *can* be made free, or become free (εἰ καὶ δύνασαι ἐλευθερος γενεσθαι), he is at liberty to avail himself of that, he is commanded to become free, rather than remain a slave. Several things are to be considered.

1. It is not merely a permission, but a command, *Use it rather*.

2. The reason, the ground, of this command is, that the slave, when converted, is the Lord's freeman ; but if he uses the privilege of his freedom from men, he is still Christ's servant.

3. He is redeemed by Christ, and must not be the slave of men.

4. If the state of freedom is his privilege and duty, then, on the other hand, it follows incontrovertibly that it is the duty of every master to yield to him that privilege, to let him go free. If, as a Christian, he is free, and is commanded to use his freedom rather than remain in bondage, then much more it is the duty of his master, as a Christian, not to restrain him of that freedom, not to prevent him from that duty, not to deny him that privilege. If the state of freedom is so much better for the servant, or slave, that he is bound to use it, if he can become free, then by the same obligation his master is bound to give it to him, as justice and equality, as his due, bound to do to him as he would have him do to himself. This acknowledgement, or gift of freedom, is the first thing considered in the obligation of masters giving to their servants that which is just and equal. The first thing, and without which nothing can be just and equal, is to treat them as free, to yield to them their freedom, and to deal with them as free.

5. It is to be marked that while a general command is issued to converted persons to remain in the same calling in which they were found when called to the knowledge of Christ, one exception is made, and only one is mentioned,

that of slavery.   Out of that calling a man is to hasten as
soon as possible, and as being the Lord's freeman; and for
plain reasons, not only of natural and Christian right, but
because the state of slavery is so infinitely disastrous and
degrading to the moral being, so unfavorable to piety, so inevitably interfering with a man's duty to God.   That a man
may hope to keep his Saviour's commandments, and grow in
grace, he must, as quick as possible, get out of the state of
slavery.   If thou *canst* be made free, use it rather.   Deliver
me from the oppression of man; so will I keep thy precepts.
Deliver me, that I may keep them.*

1 Cor. xii., 13.   For by one Spirit are we all baptized into
one body, whether Jews or Gentiles, *whether bond or free,*
εἴτε δοῦλοι εἴτε ἐλεύθεροι.   And whether one member suffer,
all the members suffer with it, verse 26.   On this ground particularly the injunction to remember them that are in bonds
as bound with them, has its special sacredness of obligation, as
a duty devolving on all Christians, and which, if it were to
the letter fulfilled, would, without any other instrumentality,
in the growth of the Christian church, do away with slavery
from the whole world.   But, alas! this power is destroyed
by so large a portion of the so called Christian church taking
the side of the oppressor, and instead of remembering them
that are in bonds as bound with them, remembering them

* See OLSHAUSEN, Comm. on 1 Cor., ch. vii., vs. 20–24.   Also DODDRIDGE, Exp. on verse 23.   Doddridge expounds the verse, " *Do not become the slaves of men, since so many evils and dangers and snares are inseparable from such a situation.*"   POOLE, Annot. gives the same interpretation. " *Make use of thy liberty rather.*"   See also LIGHTFOOT on verse 23.   Hebrew and Talmudical Exercitations on Corinthians.   Works, vol. xii. p. 498.   See also PATRICK, LOWTH and WHITBY, *in loc.* "That the charity of Christians was employed to buy their brethren out of slavery we learn from the apologies of Justin Martyr and Tertullian, who tell us that the offerings at the sacrament were, amongst others, employed for that use."   See also NEANDER on the Church in Corinth.   History of the Planting of Christianity, 263, Bohn's ed.   Also NEANDER on Slavery.   Church Hist. vol. i., p. 372.   GROTIUS, Annot. on 1 Cor.

CHAPTER XXXV.

Gal. iii., 28. There is neither bond nor free; all one in Christ Jesus; δοῦλος, ἐλεύθερος, not meaning, necessarily, *slave* nor free, but if so, then an argument against slavery. These distinctions were to be done away in the church. Once obliterated and abolished there, their abolition would speedily follow in the world, and slavery would cease everywhere, would no longer be possible any where.

Gal. iv., 7. Thou art no more a servant, δοῦλος, but a son. In connection with this, take the first verse of the same chapter, " The heir, as long as he is a child, differeth nothing from a servant, δοῦλος, though he be lord of all." It is evident that the apostle does not mean by δοῦλος a slave. He would not say that the heir differs nothing from a slave; he would not say of Christ, the Lord of all, that he differs nothing from a slave. The meaning of δοῦλος here is of subjection to law, and to tutors and governors, till the time of assuming the heirship; even as a Hebrew servant, or δοῦλος, by the law, though not a slave, was under subjection to his master, till the appointed period of such service and subjection was fulfilled. Just so the Son of God was made under the law, to redeem them that were under the law, not under slavery, that we might receive the adoption of sons.

The condition of slavery is not here referred to, neither in the whole argument that follows, but simply of bondage to the observances of the ceremonial law, and to the law as a condition of life contrary to the law of faith. "Tell me," says the apostle, "ye that desire to be under the law" (it was a voluntary thing), "do ye not hear the law?" He then illustrates the allegory of Abraham's two sons, the one by a *maid servant*, παιδισκη, improperly rendered *bond-woman*, since that is not the meaning of the Hebrew term, which is translated by the Septuagint, παιδισκη, and by the English translators, in the first instance, simply *maid* (Hagar, Sarah's *maid*), though afterwards they translated the very same word *bond-woman*, but without any ground in the original for such change. The *mistress* would be called ελευθερα, a free woman, in distinction from the *maid servant*, not because the maid servant was a *slave*, but, by the terms of Hebrew domestic service, was under subjection to her mistress during the time of her contracted service. The mistress of a Hebrew household would be called ελενθερα in distinction from all her Hebrew servants, who would each be called παιδισκη, but not slave; and they also would be each ελενθερα, a free woman, according to the law, when the legal term of service had expired. Not one thing more than this distinction is here brought into view, as is manifest from the opening of the chapter, where the son and heir is represented under the appointed condition of a *servant*, until the fullness of time for release from it.

This is further illustrated and proved by the contrast, *under the flesh*, and *under the promise*. It will not be contended that Ishmael was a slave; yet, if it is slavery and slave law that is here in view, he certainly was, if Hagar was a slave. But Hagar was simply a maid-servant, and Ishmael, being her son, was not entitled to the promise, which belonged to Abraham's seed by Sarah, his wife. Paul compares the condition of Hagar and her seed with that of the children of the flesh, who are not the children of God, unless they become such by faith in the Lord Jesus, but are under subjection to the law, not as slaves, but by a just and righteous subjection. Mount Sinai, as a personification of the law, " gendereth to bondage," and Hagar answers to Jerusalem and the Jews, who are all in this bondage under the law, until by faith in Jesus they are redeemed from under the law, and receive the adoption of sons. " For it is written that Abraham had two sons, the one by a maid-servant, the other by a free woman. But he who was of the maid-servant was born after the flesh; but he of the free woman was by promise. Which things are an allegory.—What saith the Scripture? Cast out the maid-servant and her son; for the son of the maid-servant shall not be heir with the son of the free woman. So then, brethren, we are not children of the maid-servant, but of the free. Stand fast, therefore, in the liberty wherewith Chrst hath made us free, and be not entangled again with the yoke of bondage. Ye have been called into liberty; only use not liberty for an occasion to the flesh, but by love serve one another, δουλευετε. If ye be led by the Spirit, ye are not under the law." Note here the word δουλευετε employed to signify the free voluntary service of love, a service of freedom, not the service of slavery.

Now the arbitrary manner in which the translators of the Old Testament have put a difference between Hagar in the 16th and Hagar in the 21st chapters of Genesis, may be seen at a glance. No reason can be given for translating the Hebrew words שִׁפְחָה or אָמָה by the English word *maid* in one chapter and *bond-woman* in another, especially considering that the Septuagint translation παιδισκη is the same in both cases, and the Hebrew words are synonymous. (See 1 Sam. xxv., 41.) In the 16th chapter (1–3) we read as follows: Sarai had an *handmaid.* Go into my *maid* (Sept. παιδισκη); and Sarai took Hagar, her *maid,* and gave her to her husband Abraham to be his wife. Verse 5, I have given my *maid;* verse 6, Behold thy *maid;* verse 8, the angel says, Hagar, Sarai's *maid.*

In the 21st chapter the word אָמָה, maid, is rendered *bond-woman* (Sept. παιδισκη) several times. No reason can be given for such a rendering in English. There is no justification for

it, either in the Old or New Testament. "So, then, brethren," concludes the apostle, we are not children of the bond-
woman (παιδισκη) but of the free, ελευθερα." The contrast is
not between slavery (which is the unrighteous bondage of
chattelism) and freedom, but between the righteous obligations of the law, impossible to be met by nature, and the freedom of the gospel, the liberty in Christ by divine grace.
Stand fast, therefore, in the liberty wherewith Christ hath
made us free, and be not entangled again with the yoke of
bondage. Ye have been called unto liberty, the liberty of
love.

Now the whole moral argument here is overwhelming
against slavery. "Christianity," remarks Neander,* " ef
fected a change in the conditions of men, from which a dissolution of this whole relation was sure eventually to take place.
This effect Christianity produced, first of all by the facts to
which it was a witness, and next by the ideas which by means
of these facts it set in circulation. The original unity of the
human race was restored in Christ. Servants and masters, if
they had become believers, were brought together under the
same bond of a heavenly union, destined for immortality. They
became brethren in Christ, in whom there is neither bond nor
free, members of one body, baptized into one Spirit, heirs of
the same heavenly inheritance. Masters saw in their servants
no longer their slaves, but their beloved brethren. Christianity could not fail to give birth to the wish that every man
might be placed in such a situation as would least hinder the
free and independent use of his intellect and moral powers,
according to the will of God. Accordingly the apostle St.
Paul, speaking to the servant, says (1 Cor. vii., 21), "If thou
mayst be made free, use it rather."

In the persecution under Diocletian, it appears that in some
instances free-born Christians were made slaves, and put to
the lowest and most degrading of servile employments. A

---

* NEANDER'S Church History, vol. i., p. 372, Bohn's Ed.

part of the persecuting edict ran thus: "In judicial proceedings the torture may be used against Christians, whatsoever their rank may be; those of the lower rank to be divested of their rights as citizens and freemen; and slaves, so long as they shall remain Christians, are to be incapable of receiving their freedom."* This last item would intimate that Christians had been accustomed to give freedom to the enslaved. We here see a Pagan emperor divesting men of their rights as citizens and freemen because of their religion. In our own Christian country we see the government and the Chief Justice of our national tribunal administering the same kind of treatment to Christian men because of their *color*. Under Diocletian the rescript of justice ran thus: Christians have no rights that the Romans are bound to respect. Under the government of the United States it runs thus: Black men have no rights that white men are bound to respect. Which is most infamous and wicked, the ignorant intolerance of the old Pagans or the enlightened inhumanity and barbarism of the modern Christians?

Some of the commentators seem so enamored of the language of slavery that they degrade the illustrations of the apostles by it. Conybeare and Howson translate παιδαγωγος, in Gal. iii., 24, as *the slave who leads the child to the house of the schoolmaster*, and they suppose Paul to have been under such a slave.

"His education was conducted at home rather than at school; for, though Tarsus was celebrated for its learning, the Hebrew boy would not lightly be exposed to the influence of Gentile teaching, or, if he went to a school, it was not a Greek school, but rather to some room connected with the synagogue, where a noisy class of Jewish children received the rudiments of instruction, seated on the ground with their teacher, after the manner of Mohammedan children in the east, who may be seen or heard at their lessons near the

* NEANDER, Church History, vol. i., p. 205.

mosque. At such a school, *it may be*, he learned to read and to write, going and returning under the care of some attendant, according to that custom, which he afterward used as an illustration in the Epistle to the Galatians (and perhaps he remembered his own early days when he wrote the passage) when he spoke of the law as the slave who conducts us to the school of Christ."*

There is no ground for such a translation. On the contrary, it violates both what we know of Hebrew domestic manners, there being no such thing in any Jewish family as such a slave, and is contrary to the laws of interpretation in regard to tropical language, such as confessedly that of the apostle here is. The *pedagogue* in this passage, and 1 Cor. iv., 15, is certainly (see Robinson and Bloomfield on the word) a tutor, or teacher, and tropically the law is so called. To translate the word as *slave*, and suppose that Paul's childhood was passed under the care of such a slave, to and fro from the synagogue, would be something like supposing from the mention of the lion of the tribe of Judah, that the families of that tribe kept such a lion, and were accustomed to regard it with particular veneration, and thence applied the title to their expected Messiah.

Speaking of the relation of Christianty to government, Neander remarks that " Christianity (in the time of Paul) taught men to render an obedience that had its root in the love of God, and pointed ultimately to HIM ; therefore a free obedience, as far removed from a slavish fear of man on one hand, as from a lawless self-will on the other. The same spirit of Christianity which taught men to obey for God's sake, taught also that God should be obeyed rather than man, and that every consideration, even of property and life itself, should be disregarded in all cases where human power demanded an obedience contrary to the laws and ordinances of God. In such cases the Christians displayed that true spirit of freedom against which despotic power could avail nothing."†

* CONYBEARE, Life and Epistles of Paul, vol. i., 54.

† NEANDER, General Hist. of the Christian Religion and Church, vol., i. p. 359.

Conybeare and Howson have also rendered Gal. vi., 17, " I bear in my body the scars which mark my *bondage* to the Lord Jesus." And they attempt to justify this translation by saying that στιγματα signifies literally the scars of the wounds made upon the body of a *slave* by the branding-iron, by which he was marked as belonging to his master.* They think the scars of the wounds suffered for Christ's sake are to be rendered as such branding-marks of slavery. How strange that so forced and degrading an illustration should be chosen when another, so much more natural, and at the same time honorable, was near at hand. We are informed in Lucian† that the Thracians and others counted these στιγματα as the badges of honor among freemen. Archbishop POTTER quotes Theodoret as of opinion that the Jews forbade the branding of themselves with *stigmata,* because the idolaters by that certification used to consecrate themselves to their false deities.‡ The στιγματα, referred to by the apostle, can not, therefore, be regarded as a proof of slavery, or its imitation, but of a voluntary and honorable religious consecration. Such marks Paul bore about with him, the marks of his consecration to the service of his Saviour, but not the marks of his having been branded as Christ's bond-slave. It is also important to be noted that the στιγματα were branded not upon slaves, as slaves, but as marks of punishment and disgrace upon thieves and *fugitives.*§ But Paul was never a fugitive from Christ's service.

* Life and Epistles of Paul, vol. ii., p. 152.

† LUCIAN, Syrian Goddess, Works, vol. iv.

‡ POTTER, Grecian Antiquities, vol. ii., 75, 76.

§ See BLAIR's Inquiry, 48, 110 ; also BECKER, Gallus, 231, Slave Family.

CHAPTER XXXVI.

EVIDENCE FROM THE EPISTLE TO THE EPHESIANS.—INSTRUCTIONS TO HUSBANDS AND WIVES, PARENTS AND CHILDREN.—ROMAN LAWS IN REGARD TO THESE RELATIONS.

EPHESIANS iv., 28. "Let him that stole, steal no more; but rather let him labor, working with his hands the thing that is good, that he may have to give to him that needeth." It would be singular, if while such an injunction as this were supposed to apply to such a thing as a man's purse or pocket handkerchief, it should have no authority or obligation in regard to himself, or his own person; that is, if for a man to take another's purse should be considered thieving, while to take the man himself and *sell him*, should be an honest transaction, nay, a fulfillment of the law of charity! When the apostle says, "Let him that stole steal no more," menstealers as well as money-stealers would be included. And let men labor themselves rather than steal the labor of others.

Ephesians v., 22. "Wives, submit yourselves unto your own husbands, as unto the Lord," etc. This passage, as applied to human society, makes slavery and Christianity incompatible. The sacrament of marriage does not belong to slaves; if servants can be slaves, they must cease to be husbands and wives; they can possess none of the privileges, enjoy none of the blessedness, experience nothing of the inviolable love and sacredness of this celestial union, nor can they assume or be bound by its obligations. Human law for them abrogates or nullifies the divine law, and puts them out of its authority and protection. It is the judgment of slave law "*that slaves have no marital rights*," can not contract marriage, can not, therefore, be guilty of any violation of that ordinance by any promiscuousness of concubinage. The diabolical destruction of the institution of marriage by American slavery, the defiance and violation of God's law, the teaching and enforcement of concubinage, fornication, adultery, licentiousness, if there were not a single other feature to condemn it before God and man, would be enough, of itself, to brand it as sin, and only sin, continually; demonstrating the system as nothing but a machinery for the permanent violation of the seventh commandment, as well as the eighth, and through them of every commandment of the decalogue.

If the instructions of husbands and wives belong to servants, then servants must be free, and slavery is condemned by the Word of God, as not an ordinary crime, but a vast fountain of wickedness. If they do not so belong, then the obligations and privileges of the decalogue are not universal, and Christianity is demonstrated not to be from God, but to be a system of gross and shameful respect to persons, making that to be sin in one class which is righteousness in another, and taking away the dearest rights of one class to make them the property of another. A monopoly of the most sacred affections, sentiments, and passions of life, taken away from the social existence of four millions, rendering them, by such fraud, inevitably vicious and miserable, making the state of social purity and happiness for them impossible, and that monopoly given to three hundred thousand owners for their profit, would, of itself alone, if such an infinite monstrosity were attempted to be palmed off as a divine revelation, prove the volume containing it to be the product of sin, the work of the father of lies and murderer from the beginning. To think of that sacrament of wedded love, which the Lord Jesus has so infinitely exalted and magnified by comparing it with his own love for the church, being degraded into a stock-power, at the command of three hundred thousand merchants in human flesh, for the breeding of slaves as property!

Let the closing verse of this sacred passage be read and

applied to such a system! "Nevertheless, let *every one of you in particular* so love his wife even as himself; and the wife see that she reverence her husband." The impossibility of such an obligation and such a blessedness for creatures in the condition of American slaves, under bondage to owners as their property for their sole benefit, is but one among the terrible consequences of the crime of slaveholding, but one instance or example of the havoc it makes with the holy precepts of the Word of God. Yet theologians at the North split hairs upon it on the question whether it be sinful in itself, *malum in se*, while theologians at the South accept and maintain it as the righteousness of God, and the most perfect state of human society, with the maxim *partus sequitur ventrem* as the Urim and Thummin of the system on the bosom of its ministering priests.

Ephesians vi., 1–4. "Children, obey your parents in the Lord, for this is right. Honor thy father and mother. And ye fathers, provoke not your children to wrath, but bring them up in the nurture and admonition of the Lord." These sacred injunctions no more belong to slaves, as property, and are no more possible to be fulfilled by them than the former. In slavery children can owe no obedience to their parents, can not tell, indeed, in many cases, who their parents are, neither can parents possess any authority, or right of affection, or of service, or of instruction, over their children, they being merely and solely the property of their owners, as mere merchandise, for their sole benefit and pleasure. The effect of this, in the destruction even of the parental instinct, is impressively demonstrated by Rev. Dr. Adams in his work on the South Side of Slavery; as also to such an extreme in the destruction of the filial sentiment from the child to the father, making it absolutely unintelligible, demonstrating the impossibility even of the *relation* of *father* being understood by slave-children, that he could not undertake to speak to a class of such children in reference to the words, OUR FATHER *who art in heaven*, with any hope of making them comprehend the the blessed meaning of those words! It would scarcely be possible to conceive a more overwhelming demonstration of the dreadful nature of slavery in itself, but especially as wrought, concentrated, and established in a system by law and religion in our own country, vaunted as the most perfect form of Christian socialism, and the most effective missionary institute of heaven!

It is not possible that Christianity could ever tolerate such a system. If we admitted that Christianity tolerated slavery in order to subvert it, as some have argued, then on the same grounds we must admit that Christianity tolerated conjugal slavery, and filial slavery, as well as servile slavery, for under the Roman law, which prevailed in those lands wherein Christianity was first taught to the Gentiles, slavery inhered in the relations of wife and son, as well as in that of servant. But if the precepts of Christ could not .be interpreted into consistency with a Christian's treating his wife as a slave, or treating his son as a slave, neither can they be interpreted into consistency with a man's treating his Christian brother as a slave.*

Under the Roman laws, " in his father's house the son was a mere thing, confounded by the laws with the moveables, the cattle, and the slaves, whom the capricious master might alienate or destroy, without being responsible to any earthly tribunal. At the call of indigence or avarice, the master of a family could dispose of his children or his slaves." But the condition of the slave was far more advantageous in this respect, Gibbon adds, because the slave was free on being the first time manumitted ; but the son might be sold by his father a second and a third time into slavery. He had the power of life and death over him ; " examples of such bloody executions were sometimes praised, and never punished."†

* Dr. Hague, Christianity and Statesmanship.
† Gibbon, Decline and Fall, chap. xliv.

Under the same laws the wife was equally the slave of the husband, " who was invested with the plenitude of paternal power, so that by his judgment or caprice her behavior was approved, or censured, or chastised; he exercised the jurisdiction of life and death; and it was allowed that in cases of adultery or drunkenness the sentence might be properly inflicted." " So clearly was woman defined not as a *person*, but as a *thing*, that if the original title was deficient she might be claimed, like other moveables, by the use and possession of an entire year."*

Now if the relation of slavery is sanctioned, as some have argued, by the instructions in the gospel to masters and servants, under the Roman law, so is the power and right of the father and the husband over the life and liberty of the son and the wife, as part and parcel of the filial and marital relation, sanctioned by the instruction to fathers and husbands. There is no condemnation of the Roman law in either case; no injunction forbidding husbands to kill or sell their wives or their children. Does the fact of the relation of father and son, husband and wife, being recognized in the New Testament sanction or sanctify those enormities, or make the son and the wife slaves? No more does the relation of master and servant being recognized in the New Testament make the servant a slave, or sanction or permit the claim of the master over him as a chattel, as his property. The same argument of human law that makes the servant a slave makes the son and the wife a slave.

" Be ye not the servants of men," says the apostle Paul. " It is far from his intention," says Lightfoot on the passage, " to take away the relation that is between masters and servants."† But the injunctions upon masters do absolutely abolish the relation that is between masters and *slaves*,

---

* GIBBON, ch. 44. BLAIR, Inquiry into the State of Slavery among the Ro-   mans. FUSS, Rom. Ant., §§ 83, 84, 86.
   † LIGHTFOOT, vol. xii., p. 498.

making it impossible for a Christian to hold a slave, or to treat a human being as property. The true primitive Christians, acting upon Christ's precepts, must have carried them into a complete abolition of slavery in their households, and this example at length produced its effect among all the races under the Roman empire. Paul's Epistle to Philemon, as we shall see, was just a development and application of these principles.

In later times we have some striking testimonies of the same principles. Neander quotes the Abbot Isidore of Pelusium writing in behalf of a fugitive, and addressing the master thus : " I did not suppose that a man who loves Christ, who knows the grace which has made all men free, COULD STILL HOLD A SLAVE !" He quotes also from " the venerable Monk Nilus," citing the example of Job's benevolent and righteous conduct to his servants, and demanding compassion for the race of slaves, " whom the mastership of violence, destroying the fellowship of nature, had converted into tools." The essence of slavery is here brought to view, the conversion of an immortal being into a chattel; *a mastership of violence*, inconsistent with the professions of Christianity.*

Augustine also protested against treating slaves as things. " The Christian," said he, " *dare not regard a slave as his property*, like a horse, or silver, although it may happen that a horse fetches a higher price than a slave, and still more an article of furniture made out of gold or silver." It is related of Eligius, Bishop of Noyon, that " when he heard that vessels were arrived full of slaves for sale, captives of Roman, Gallic, British, and Moorish descent, but particularly Saxons, who were driven like so many cattle, he hastened to the spot, and sometimes ransomed a hundred."†

At the same time it is scarcely to be doubted that such in-

---

* NEANDER, General History of the Church, vol. iii., p. 356.   † NEANDER's Memorials of Christian Life, pp. 306, 377.

stances were rare, and indicate the highest Christian consciousness above the corruption of the age. They are as light-houses upon rocks amidst the sea, and they shine amidst many abominations. It could not be expected that, while the corruptions of Christianity were deepening, this great virtue of the rebuke, resistance and excommunication of slavery would be maintained, according to the spirit of the gospel. There came to be, in various parts of the Roman empire and among its fragments, a race of serfs, *adscripti glebæ*, in France, England and other nations, treated in almost every respect like the slaves of ancient Rome. The records of successive councils of the Christian church, as traced by Guizot (especially in French history) and by others, show the long continuance of this iniquity in a most oppressive form.* Of the Roman emperors, Hadrian and Antoninus Pius were the first who endeavored to abolish the power of life and death held by masters over their slaves.† This power, even with the father over his children, was held until the time of Constantine; and even this emperor allowed parents who were very poor to sell their infants instantly on their birth.‡ Meantime human beings were constantly reduced to slavery by wars, and the cases of their redemption or deliverance, through the interference of the church, stand recorded as remarkable examples. The monastic institutions and spirit were opposed to slavery, even while in the church it was tolerated. The ordinance of Louis le Hutin, in France (anno 1315), for the enfranchisement of the serfs, cited by Michelet and Guizot,§ while

---

* GUIZOT, History of Civilization, vol. 2.—Compare MURATORI, cited in BLAIR, 238.

† FUSS, Ant. Rom., ch. 1, § 54.—BLAIR, Inquiry, 85.

‡ FUSS, ch. i., § 86.

§ MICHELET, History of France, vol. i. The ordinance of Phillipe le Bel, in 1311, is still more remarkable. "Seeing that every human creature who is made in the image of our Lord ought to be free by natural right, and that in no country this natural liberty or freedom should be so effaced or obscured by the hateful yoke of servitude," etc. (Vol. i., page 398.) "A grand spectacle," exclaims the historian, "to see proclamations made from the throne itself of the imprescriptible right of every man to lib-it followed the spirit of Christianity, ran before the practice of Christians. This ordinance begins like our Declaration of Independence. "Since, according to the right of nature, every one should be born free, and that by certain usages and customs, which have been introduced and kept from great antiquity in our kingdom, and by adventure, many of our common people are fallen into conditions of servitude which greatly displeases us; we, considering that our kingdom is called the kingdom of the FRANCS, and wishing that the thing in truth should agree with the name, by deliberation of our great council have ordained, and do ordain, that generally throughout our kingdom, as far as in us lies, and in our successors, such servitudes should be abolished, and that freedom should be given to all those who are fallen into servitude, either by origin, or by marriage, or by residence." Centuries before this, Hilary of Poictiers had said to the emperor, in an epistle, "The whole labor of your sovereignty should have for its object to secure for all over whom it extends the sweetest of all treasures, liberty. There is no mode of appeasing troubles until every one be emancipated from all the fetters of servitude."*

Michelet refers to the passage of slavery (the canker and destruction of the Roman empire) into serfdom, or the growth of serfdom out of slavery, rooting the laborer to the soil. He cites the Justinian code. "The tenant follows the law of his

erty." The asylum of the churches, and the freedom bestowed by them, were respected long before. Nevertheless, it is proved that serfs were held as ecclesiastical property, and Christians, who would not suffer Jews to hold slaves, held them themselves. Yet in a council at Lyons, in the year 567, it is decreed that those who neglect to restore to liberty those that have been made captives by violence and treason shall be excommunicated.

In 550, "As we have discovered that several people reduce again to servitude those who, according to the custom of the country have been set at liberty in the churches, we order that every one shall keep possession of the liberty he has received, and if this liberty is attacked, justice must be defended by the church." GUIZOT, Civiliz., vol. ii.

* AGES OF FAITH, vol. i., 232. GIBBON, ch. 36.

birth; although in point of condition apparently free-born, he is the slave of the soil on which he is born." "A tenant secreting himself, or seeking to desert from his patron's estate, is to be held in the light of a fugitive slave."* Such is the serfdom, or slavery, traced by Guizot in the councils of the church in France through nearly six centuries, from the fourth to the tenth.† At the same time the example of personal industry by the monks commences an innovation of free and voluntary labor, which is to be the basis of a free modern existence. "The rule of St. Benedict sets the first example to the ancient world, of labor by the hands of freemen."‡

Ephesians vi., 5–9. "Servants (δοῦλοι) be obedient to them that are your masters (κυριοις)§ according to the flesh, with fear and trembling, in singleness of your heart, as unto Christ; not with eye-service, as men-pleasers, but as the servants (δοῦλοι) of Christ, doing the will of God from the heart, with good will doing service (δουλεύοντες) to the Lord, and

---

* MICHELET, History of France, vol. i., 56.

† GUIZOT, Modern Civilization, vol. ii., 458–511.

‡ MICHELET, i., 62. "Charlemagne gratifies his teacher, Alcuin, with a farm of twenty thousand slaves." The Crusades began a revolution of liberty in central France. "The serfs had their own page of history."

§ CONYBEARE and HOWSON (Life and Epistles of Paul, vol. ii., p. 422) assert that "the word κυριος, Lord, always implies the idea of servants." A strange assertion, as see, ROBINSON, Lex. on the word, No. 3. See also, in this connection, PROF.' STUART on the meaning of κυριος, Bib. Rep., vol. i., pp. 733–776. Comparison of κυριος and δεσποτης, p. 736.

Conybeare and Howson also translate the word δοῦλοι, here and in 1 Tim. vi., 1, also Colossians and elsewhere, as bondsmen, and they have put in the margin, "duties to slaves." Thus, in fact, they would take from the Scriptures what was meant to be the guidance of God for servants in all ages and places, to all time, and restrict these precious passages to persons under a temporary and wicked bondage, forbidden in the word of God, and destined to be utterly abolished! If these passages apply to slaves, to those who are the property of their owners, then they have no application whatever to servants in England, in Switzerland, in Germany in Italy, in France, in Sweden, in free New England; any where and everywhere in the world, where there are no slaves, there these instructive precepts are in effect blotted from the Bible as superfluous, or indicating only a wickedness that has passed away.

not to men, knowing that whatsoever good thing any man doeth the same shall he receive from the Lord, whether bond or free (εἴτε δοῦλος εἴτε ἐλεύθερος). And ye masters, do the same things unto them, forbearing threatening, knowing that your master also is in heaven; neither is there respect of persons with him." Compare Col iv., 1, "Masters give unto your servants (δούλοις) that which is just and equal, knowing that ye also have a master in heaven."

There is no intimation of slavery here, but on the contrary, the rule laid upon masters forbids the supposition of slavery, making it impossible to consider servants as slaves, or to treat them as such, as property; the masters being commanded to regard and treat their servants just as the servants are commanded to regard and treat their masters, according to the will of Christ, with a single and supreme regard to his pleasure. They could neither be claimed nor treated as property without the most direct violation of the law of God, and disregard of the will of Christ. They could not be claimed as property without assuming a mastership and command over them which Christ alone possessed. The word δοῦλος contrasted with ἐλεύθερος by no means proves the significance of *slave*, since that was the very mode of comparison and contrast become the ordinary Jewish servant, who could not possibly be a slave, and the freeman. The servant hired for six years would be called δοῦλος, in contrast with his master as ἐλεύθερος, or with any person not in domestic or household service. The contrast, *bond* and *free*, was a customary contrast between simple service and the state of freedom from such service, and inasmuch as the word here translated *bond* is δοῦλος, in every other instance in the passage translated *servant*, there is no reason for changing this translation. If it read in English, "*whether servant or free*," the whole sense of the passage would be perfectly conveyed. There is no intimation or proof whatever of slavery *in the language*, while, on the other hand, there is an absolute interdiction of slavery *by the precept*, by the whole tenor and meaning.

ADAM CLARKE'S energetic testimony against slavery, under this passage, is here to be noted. "Though δοῦλος frequently signifies a slave or bondman, yet it often implies a servant in general, or any one bound to another, either for a limited time or for life.* In heathen countries slavery was in some sort excusable; amongst Christians it is an enormity and a crime, for which perdition has scarcely an adequate state of punishment."—Comm. on Eph. vi., 5.

---

* THIRLWALL (History of Greece) affirms that Aristotle sometimes employed the word δοῦλοι to signify the whole mass of the people who were not citizens.

The late DR. THOMSON, of Edinburgh, maintained, with great power of eloquence, the righteous love of liberty inspired by the gospel, and the inherent iniquity of the relations of slavery. "I appeal," said he, "to the inherent and efficacious power of Christianity, as determining all in whom it really dwells to aspire after liberty as the object of their keen ambition, to cleave to it as the object of their fond and decided attachment. If you introduce the principles and sentiments of Christianity into the heart of any individual, you introduce into his heart the very elements of freedom; you infuse that which he feels to be at eternal variance with every species of bondage; you prepare him for throwing off the yoke, with an energy which may be calm and secret, but which is also potent and irresistible in its operations. Let his faith be strong in the truths of revelation, and let him experience their practical influence, and the consequence is, that without waiting to compare what he is with what he ought to be, or calculating on the advantages of exchanging the one situation for the other, he is constrained, as it were, by instinct to aim at the transition, and to seek for disenthralment from the tyranny that presses him to the earth. There is something within him which is abhorrent of whatsoever goes to constitute him a slave. His soul has acquired an elasticity that bids him rise with the silent and resistless force of nature to that place in the creation of God in which alone, as his congenial clime, he can breathe, live, and be happy."

CHAPTER XXXVII.

Epistles to the Philippians and Colossians.—That which is Just and Equal.—
Nature of the Rule, and its Conclusions,—It Abolishes Slavery.—Epistle to
the Thessalonians.

Philippians i., 1. "Paul and Timotheus, the servants (δοῦλοι) of Jesus Christ." (See on Rom., p. 383, and 1 Cor., p. 386).

Phil. ii., 7, spoken of Christ, who "took upon him the form of a *servant* (δοῦλον)." Here is an incontrovertible instance in which δοῦλος can neither mean *slave*, nor be translated by the word *slave*. It would be false to the reality, and a violence against the meaning of the passage, to say that our blessed Lord took upon him the form of a *slave*. He is said to have been formed in fashion as A MAN, not as a *slave*, and to have humbled himself as A MAN, not as a *slave*. He could not be said, in any sense, to have taken upon him the form of a slave, unless he had been born a slave, of a slave mother, according to the infamous slave law, "*partus sequitur ventrem ;*" unless he had been born the *property* of a slave-owner, the chattel of a master, who would have the right by law to have sold him and his mother together, or him as a child, without respect to his mother. This, therefore, is a case in which δοῦλος does certainly mean merely and only a person in the condition of a servant, not a slave. In taking the form of a man, he took the form of a servant of God, a servant under subjection to the law of God, but not the form of a chattel of man, a slave owned as property by his master. Such a sense of the word is to be rejected with abhorrence.*

EVIDENCE FROM THE EPISTLES TO THE COLOSSIANS AND THESSALONIANS.

Colossians i., 7. "Epaphras, our dear *fellow-servant* (συν-δόυλου)." Compare iv., 12. "Epaphras, a *servant* (δοῦλος), of Christ," and iv., 7, "Tychicus, a faithful minister and fellow-*servant* in the Lord, διάκονος και σύνδουλος."

Col. iii., 11. "Neither Barbarian nor Scythian, bond nor free," δοῦλος, ἐλεύθερος. The same remarks apply here as on Eph. vi., 8. There is no intimation of slavery or its sanction in the Church, but an exclusion and condemnation of it.†

Col. iii., 18–24. The same body of instructions as in Eph. v., to husbands, wives, parents, children, and servants. "Wives, submit yourselves unto your own husbands, as it is fit in the Lord." Impossible in the state of slavery. "Children, obey your parents in all things, for this is well pleasing unto the Lord." Impossible in the state of slavery. "Servants (δοῦ-λοι), obey in all things your masters, according to the flesh; not with eye-service, as men-pleasers, but in singleness of heart, fearing God." "For ye serve the Lord Christ (δου-λεύετε)." This does not mean *ye are enslaved* to the Lord Christ, but ye *serve* him, as his freemen, from the heart. Com-

---

* CAMPBELL on the Gospels, Preliminary Discourses. Dis. iv., vol. i. Also vol. ii., ch. xx. "It is solely from the scope and connections that we must judge when it should be rendered in the one way, and when in the other." See also POOLE, Annot. on Phil. Compare HOWE on the Faithful Servant, works, 965.

† See CHRYSOSTOM's Homilies, cited by NEANDER, in his Life of Chrysostom, pp. 413–416. "There was no slave in the old times; for God, when he formed man, made him not bond, but free. Behold, slavery came of sin. Slavery is the punishment of sin, and arose from disobedience. But when Christ appeared, he removed this cause, for in Christ Jesus there is neither bond nor free." Chrysostom elsewhere intimates that if a pure Christian feeling were prevalent, slavery would cease. Compare NEANDER's Church History, vol. iii., p. 356. Also MEMORIALS of Christian Life, page 196.

pare the whole with Eph. vi. 5–9, and the remarks on the meaning of the word δοῦλος in the same connection there.

Col. iv., 1. "Masters, give unto your *servants* (δοῦλοις) that which is just and equal; knowing that ye also have a Master in heaven." This commandment would abolish slavery throughout the world. It is impossible to give to a servant that which is just and equal, and yet treat him as a slave. In making him a slave, all justice and equality is denied him. In claiming him as a slave, and treating him as property, which is the essence of slavery, nothing is given him but cruelty; every right of a human being is withheld frcm him; nothing but injustice and inequality are forced upon him.

There is no law of justice or equality in behalf of the slave; no obligation on the part of his owner toward him is ever pretended, but for his (the owner's) sole benefit. It is even declared that slaves have no marital rights, much less any right to wages, or any of the privileges or natural possessions of a freeman. The slave has no right even to his peck of meal a week, if his owner chooses to withhold it. The plea of justice and equality toward American slaves is just merely the fanaticism of Abolitionism. True; and this is the fanaticism of the New Testament; and this one injunction of Paul to masters, as to the treatment of servants, would break up and abolish the system of American slavery forever, and prevent the possibility of the crime of slaveholding wherever the law of God is regarded and obeyed.

For, 1. The very first article of justice and equality toward a servant requires that he be treated as a human being, and not as a brute, or chattel, but as a human being having a right inalienable to life, liberty, and the pursuit of happiness; a right to dispose of his own services, and a right to a just recompense therefor.

2. The rule of justice and equality in regard to servants, as to all classes of men, was to be found in the Word of God, and not in men's own perverted ideas of self-interest, or the right

of conquest or of power; not in any Roman, Greek, or Pagan code of laws, but in the Divine law. This, and this alone, was the acknowledged guide of the conscience of the Christian. To this, therefore, he must refer to learn what, in God's sight, was the treatment of servants pronounced just and equal, and required of all.

3. The treatment of men as merchandise was forbidden in that law. To make any man a slave, or to hold him as such, or to sell him, was forbidden on pain of death. Therefore to treat a servant as a slave was to be guilty of a crime against him punishable with death. That which is just and equal could not be given to him in any way while he was treated as a slave; for his very manhood and all its rights were taken from him.

4. The law of God required that, without respect to persons, "Thou shalt love thy neighbor as thyself; and whatsoever ye would that men should do to you, do ye even so to them." If men would not themselves be made slaves, or suffer their own children to be made slaves, then they ought not to make slaves of others.

The consequence is plain, that both by natural right and by the law of God, to which the apostle always refers as the acknowledged supreme rule of duty, this precept must have rendered slavery impossible. Had there been not another word in the New Testament on the subject of slavery, this one precept would abolish it, would brand it as a crime, would forbid it as a cruelty and injustice incompatible with Christianity, and which, if any professed Christian were guilty of it, must exclude him from the Christian church as an extortioner and a man-stealer.*

* Compare, on page 350, the notice of Isidore and Augustine's abhorrence of slavery, and declarations of its incompatibility with Christianity. Among the works of Christian piety, Isidore names the redeeming of slaves from bondage, "The noble disposition (a man of noble disposition) frees those whom violence has made slaves." NEANDER, Church History, vol. iii. CHRYSOSTOM, rebuking the rich and the nobles, who pretended

GIVE UNTO YOUR SERVANTS THAT WHICH IS JUST AND EQUAL, was a fit inscription over the gate of the New Testament in this branch of morals and of domestic economy ; as over the gate of the Old Testament, the inscription, HE THAT STEAL-ETH A MAN, AND SELLETH HIM, OR IF HE BE FOUND IN HIS HANDS, SHALL SURELY BE PUT TO DEATH. Between these two slavery is abolished for ever.

2 Thes. iii., 10–12. " For even when we were with you, this we commanded you, that if any would not work, neither should he eat. For we hear that there are some which walk among you disorderly, working not at all, but are busy bodies. Now them that are such we command and exhort by our Lord Jesus Christ, that with quietness they work, and eat their own bread." These precepts show that a state of society was founded and formed by the gospel, in which manual labor for the earning of one's bread was so far from being inconsistent with the dignity and freedom of manhood, that if any one refused it, and would live without labor, the law of Christianity itself would leave him to starve in his chosen gentility and indolence. The publication of this rule may have been found especially necessary to correct the supposition, that because masters were forbidden from making slaves of their

to permit a crowd of slaves to follow them, out of philanthropy, said, " If ye cared for these men ye would buy them, let them learn trades, that they might support themselves, and then give them freedom." The Christian spirit of Chrysostom revolted against the traffic in human flesh, as well as against slavery. Referring to the communion of possessions at Jerusalem, the Christians selling their goods, and supposing the possibility of their example being followed, he cautions the people against imagining any "sale of slaves, *for that did not exist in those times,* but equitably they were permitted to be free." — CHRYSOSTOM,

Hom. in Acts Apost., xi., cited by NEANDER in Life of Chrysostom.

" If any one ask," said Chrysostom, " whence came slavery into the world (for I have known many who desired to learn this), I will tell him. Insatiable avarice and envy are the parents of slavery ; for Noah, Abel, Seth, and their descendants, had not slaves. Sin hath begotten slavery ; then, wars and battles, in which men were made captives." There were those in Chrysostom's time, as in ours, who appealed to father Abraham. " But ye say that Abram had slaves. Aye, *but he treated them not as such.*"

servants, therefore the servants were released from the necessity of working, or the duty of obeying their lawful masters. The privileges of the gospel freedom were guarded on all sides from licentiousness. It was as much the duty of the servant to work, and to do his work faithfully, as it was of the master to pay his wages, giving to his servants that which is just and equal.

The law of love was to bind each class to the other, in mutual dependence and obligation, and all together to Christ. The socialism of the gospel expels slavery on the one side and pride on the other; servility on the one side and arrogance on the other; and the true freedom of the gospel transfigures society with the happiness and content of heaven. With what heaven-instructed impartiality does the apostle apply the principles of justice and of love at one and the same time to the highest and the lowest. After enjoining a behavior from servants towards their masters inspired with good will, and fraught with deferential observance of duty in singleness of heart as unto Christ, doing service as to the Lord and not to men, he adds, *And ye masters do the same things unto them.* Where on earth was the character of the servant and the quality of service ever so exalted, so combined and dignified, with the highest independence? It is a picture of social equality, with the preservation of just distinctions, in harmony and love, to which there has never been an approach outside of divine revelation. And, indeed, the wondrous treatment of the subject, at the same time that slavery is branded as a crime worthy of death, is in itself a proof of divine inspiration.

CHAPTER XXXVIII.

1 TIMOTHY i., 9, 10, 11. "Knowing this, that the law is not made for a righteous man, but for the lawless and disobedient, for the ungodly and profane, for the murderers of fathers and murderers of mothers, for man-slayers, for whoremongers, for them that defile themselves with mankind, for MEN-STEALERS, for liars, for perjured persons, and if there be any other thing that is contrary to sound doctrine, according to the glorious gospel of the blessed God, which was committed to my trust."

Paul is here instructing Timothy how to preach the gospel, and he informs him that he must do it by the faithful application of the law to all the sins forbidden by the law, some of the worst of which sins he enumerates, and among them the sin of MAN-STEALING, referring unquestionably to Ex. xxi. 16, "He that stealeth a man, and selleth him, or if he be found in his hand, he shall surely be put to death." That the reference is explicitly to this law there can be no manner of doubt, since the context of crimes, murderers of fathers, murderers of mothers, man-slayers, etc., is the very catalogue in the chapter of the law in Exodus, in which the crime of man-stealing is defined and forbidden.

The apostle declares that it is as much the duty of the preacher of the gospel to preach against that crime, with and under the gospel, as it is to preach against murder, adultery, lying, profaneness, and all other sins. It is the legitimate office of the gospel to proclaim the law against man-stealing, and certainly to apply it in all its meaning, against every form of the crime, against holding a man as a slave, and against making merchandise of him, as well as against the original stealing of him.   The forcible continuance of a man in the condition of a slave, a stolen man, would be just a repetition and continuance of the original man-stealing, and, therefore, the application of this law, under and by the authority of the gospel, and for the purpose of the gospel, to bring men away from such sins, and to save them in Christ, must be made to the slaveholder; and it would inevitably forbid, break up, and destroy the crime of slaveholding, as a crime inconsistent with Christianity, forbidden of God, and set down by him in the same catalogue with that of the murder of fathers and mothers.

In this view, a more tremendous passage against slavery does not exist than this.   It binds the preachers of Christ and him crucified to make the application of the law of God against this crime a part of their gospel preaching.   They can not be faithful preachers of the gospel without preaching, in the name and by the authority of Christ and his cross, against this sin of making merchandise of men, of holding or selling human beings as property, as slaves.   Let the gospel be preached according to Paul's instructions, and let the churches apply the discipline of Christ accordingly to the sinners under this category, and slavery would be abolished from our land.

The Greek word for men-stealers is ἀνδραποδισταῖς.   Liddell and Scott define the word thus: a slave-dealer; also one who kidnaps freemen or slaves, to sell them again.   The Greek verb, ἀνδραποδίζω, signifies to reduce to slavery, to enslave; in the passive, to be sold into slavery. Dr. Robinson defines the word as follows: a slave-dealer, man-stealer, 1 Tim. i., 10; compare Ex. xxi., 16; Deut. xxiv., 7.—Pol. 12, 9. 2; Xen. Mem. 1, 2, 6.

The authorities show that the word means a slave-dealer,

and also a man-stealer ; and the apostle, by using this word as a synonyme of that crime which in Ex. xxi., 16 is forbidden on pain of death, shows that any man making merchandise of men is guilty of that crime ; the slave-dealer, the slave-trader, the slave-buyer, the slave-seller is the man-stealer.

The man who sanctions and employs the slave-dealer, receiving from him a man as merchandise, or putting into his hands a man to be sold as merchandise, is himself the guilty party, the man-stealer. Any man who has any thing to do with the crime, either as go-between, or buyer, or seller of a man, or holding him as property, is implicated in the guilt of man-stealing. They who pass laws sanctifying this iniquity only increase the guilt ; they who practice it under the laws that sustain it can not extricate themselves in that way from the crime, but are guilty of it before God. The nation that defends and practices it by law is a nation of MEN-STEALERS.

The attempt to evade the terrible power of this passage, by directing it against *slave-stealers*, as if the stealing of a slave was what God has forbidden, while the stealing of a man is not forbidden at all, is futile, because the reference of the apostle is to the Hebrew law against man-stealing,[*] and not to any law against *slave* stealing, there being no such law. It was enough to forbid the stealing of a man ; for that prevented the possibility of there being such a thing as a slave to steal. If there had been such a thing, then the stealing of a slave would have been a crime simply because it was the stealing of a man, and not because it was the stealing of a slave ; the stealing of a man from himself, and not the stealing of a slave from his master. There is no law in the Old Testament or the New against *slave* stealing ; there is against man-stealers. There are no such criminals recognized as

---

[*] GROTIUS, Opera, Comm., *in loc.* Grotius refers to both forms of the law in Ex. xxi., 16, and Deut. xxiv., 7. He adds that the stealing of a freeman is the highest kind of theft. *Maxi-* *mum est furti genus hominem liberum furari.* The imagination of *slave* stealing being here referred to did not enter into his mind.

slave-stealers ; but there are as men-stealers, and it is men-stealers, and men-merchants, men buyers and sellers that are condemned to death. And Paul commands that the law of God and the gospel of Christ be preached against this crime. It is an argument of wonderful power against slavery.

ADAM CLARKE'S note on this passage is comprehensive. " Ανδραποδισταις, *slave-dealers ;* whether those who carry on the traffic in human flesh and blood ; or those who steal a person in order to sell him into bondage ; or those who *buy* such stolen men and women, no matter of what color or what country ; or those who sow dissensions among barbarous tribes, in order that they who are taken in war may be sold into slavery ; or the nations who legalize or connive at such traffic— all these are MAN-STEALERS, and God classes them with the most flagitious of mortals."*

CONYBEARE and HOWSON (vol. 2, p. 464) translate the word as Clarke does, *slave-dealers.* They add, *this is the literal translation of the word.* If, then, the gospel of God is to be preached against *slave-dealers,* it is because the traffic in human beings, as property, is condemned of God in his law as a crime. Any man is a *slave-dealer* who buys or sells, or buys

---

* See also LUCIAN'S DIALOGUES. The Sale of Philosophers. Jasper Mayne's translation, 1638. Oxford, fol., p. 382. "MERCURY. You, fellow, with the scrip over your shoulder, stand forth, and walk round the assembly. O yes ! I sell a stout, virtuous, well-bred, free mortal ! Who buys him ?

"MERCHANT. Do you sell a freeman, Crier ?

"MERCURY. Yes !

"MERCHANT. Are you not afraid he should accuse you of MAN-STEALTH, and summon you before the Areopagus ?

"MERCURY. He cares not for being

sold, but thinks himself nevertheless free."

See also FUSS, Roman Antiquities, ch. i., 53. Also BLAIR'S Inquiry on the State of Slavery, pp. 32, 52, 45. The traffic in slaves was carried to a greater height in Rome during its days of prosperity and luxury than any where else ; the market being furnished from all parts of the world, but chiefly from Greece and Asia, and men free by birth being kidnapped everywhere to supply it.—POTTER, Antiq. Greece, vol. ii., 81, by whom Aristophanes is cited, using the word ανδραποδιστων for the traffic.

and holds a man as a slave ; so that inevitably the slaveholder comes under this condemnation. And this is GROTIUS' interpretation of the law.

It would be impossible to set the gospel against slave-dealers if it were not contrary to the gospel to hold men as slaves, to make merchandise of men. The only reason for the infamy attaching to the profession and character of a slave-dealer, is because slavery itself is criminal and infamous, just as a pimp is an infamous character, because adultery is infamous. If the holding of slaves were righteous, the dealing in them would be righteous also ; if the slaveholder can be received into good society, the slave-dealer is equally worthy of it ; if the slaveholder can be admitted into the Christian church, the slave-dealer can also. On the other hand, if slave-dealing is criminal, it is because slaveholding is a crime, and if the slave-dealer is infamous, the slaveholder is likewise. The apostle, therefore, in setting up the slave-dealer as a personification of crime and infamy, along with the murderer, for the condemnation of the law and the gospel, and thus excluding him from the Christian church, does the same with the slaveholder, for what belongs to the one belongs of necessity to the other. If the church excludes the one, it must the other.

The practice by nations of a crime denounced by the Lord God as worthy of death in individuals, the sanctioning and pursuing by law of what God has forbidden under any and all circumstances, has never on earth been so terribly illustrated as in the nineteenth century of the Christian era, in the United States of America. At this day the crime of kidnapping, the crime of stealing men and converting them into property for gain, is being committed openly by professedly Christian States, without scruple, without compunction, without shame, in unparalleled defiance both of God and man. Christian States are by law doing precisely what the United States laws denounce and punish as piracy ; seizing free citizens, and selling them as slaves.

The example of a pagan nation before the coming of Christ

is here followed under the light of Christianity. In pagan
Greece Pericles is said to have proposed a law that only those
who were born of parents that were Athenians on both sides
should be reputed free citizens of Athens. Having prevailed
upon the people *to give their consent*, little less than five thousand free citizens were at-once deprived of their freedom and
sold as slaves.* Our State piety has improved on the obedience of paganism, and our rulers, under the teachings of the
gospel according to slavery, *do not have to ask the people* for
leave to sacrifice their liberties, but first pass the law, and then
compel the people to obey it.

1 Tim. vi., 2. "Let as many *servants* (δοῦλοι) as are under
the yoke (ὑπὸ ζυγὸν) count their own masters (δεσπότας) worthy of all honor, that the name of God and his doctrine be not
blasphemed. And they that have believing masters, let them
not despise them, because they are brethren, but rather do
them service, because they are faithful and beloved, partakers
of the benefit. These things teach and exhort." This passage
is a proof of the completeness of divine inspiration in guarding
against the abuse of doctrines that might have been perverted
to evil, though perfect in good. After the injunctions against
slavery, the reference to the Hebrew law branding it as a
crime worthy of death, and the precept, "If thou mayst be
made free, use it rather," a *stampede* of slaves from their
heathen masters might have been apprehended, which could
have been attended (before the diffusion and knowledge of
the truth and will of God in Christ concerning it) with nothing
but disaster. The Word of God faithfully proclaimed against
this as other sins, was to put an end to slavery; and when
heathen masters became Christian, and were acquainted with
the laws of God in the Scriptures, then they would see and
acknowledge the wickedness of this crime.

But until then the converted slaves were enjoined to obey

---

* Archb. Potter, Grecian Antiquities, vol. ii., p. 55. Blair's Inquiry.

their ignorant heathen masters, so far as they could do it consistently with the law of God and their supreme allegiance to their Saviour, and as far as possible to honor them, that they might not suppose that the Christian doctrine was a doctrine teaching disobedience, idleness, insolence, or pride and insubordination from servants to superiors. To avoid any danger of such perversion, any occasion of thus blaspheming God and Christianity, the converted slaves were enjoined even to be doubly careful and diligent to please their masters, for just the same reason that a wife was enjoined to use the same carefulness toward an unbelieving or heathenish husband, in order that if possible the unbelieving husband, ignorant of the Word, might be won to Christ by the sweet behavior of the wife. Just so with the converted slave, and his yet unenlightened, unconverted master. As long as he staid with him, he must endeavor doubly to honor and to please him, in order to win him, if possible, to an examination of the religious teaching and spirit which could produce such lovely fruits of patient obedience and faithfulness.

But it was only in regard to unbelieving heathen masters that this was spoken. It is such only who are supposed to continue to hold slaves. For the moment a man came to the knowledge of the truth as it is in Jesus, his eyes were opened by the word of God to see that the holding of men as property, the making merchandise of men, was a crime placed of God along with that of murder. The moment a man was converted, the gospel command came also upon him to give unto his servants that which was just and equal, and he learned that they were no longer slaves, but brethren beloved, and entitled to the rights of freemen under God's law. That which was just and equal involved, first of all, an entire relinquishment of all claim of property in them and over them. A servant under such a master was no longer *under the yoke*, but freed from it by having a *believing* master.

And now, in regard to this class of servants, who knew their freedom by the divine law, and knew that their masters also knew it, and were forbidden of God to treat them as slaves, but required to treat them as brethren; remembering that the same Lord was their Lord and Master, and no respecter of persons; in regard to this class, admitted so suddenly into such an unaccustomed liberty, elevated to such an equality with their masters in Christ, the danger was of being puffed up with pride, and despising their masters, instead of rendering them due honor and obedience. They were, therefore, cautioned against despising their masters, because they were brethren, and being such were deprived by the law of God of all unrighteous despotic authority over them; and they were warned to render that obedience now out of love, which before, beneath the yoke of slavery, they had been compelled to render out of fear and by compulsion. They must now be faithful to their masters as to Christ, and out of love to Christ, rendering them service because they also were believers in Jesus, Christian brethren, partakers of his love.

The servants *under the yoke* could not break the yoke, but must bear it patiently. But when the law of God came to the conscience of the master, and when he was converted, then came the conviction of the criminality of slavery, and the command *to break every yoke*, and to give liberty, every man to his neighbor, and every man to his brother. None but heathen masters maintained that yoke.*   Christian masters

---

* Compare the Epistle to Philemon for the practical proof of emancipation. Also the testimonies previously adduced. ADAM CLARKE (Comm. on 1 Tim. vi., 1) remarks that " the word δουλοι here means slaves converted to the Christian faith; and the ζυγον, or yoke, is the state of slavery; and by δεσποται, masters or despots, we are to understand the *heathen* masters of those Christianized slaves."

The having a heathen master is presented by the apostle as synonymous with being under the yoke; the having a Christian master is synonymous with being freed from the yoke.

"We find that even among the slaves there were Christian converts, to whom, though he recommends submission and contentment, yet he intimates that if they could get their freedom, they should prefer it; and he strongly charges those that were free not to become again the slaves

were required to break it, and it would seem from this very text that they did break it; for this is the very point of contrast between believing and unbelieving masters, that while the latter maintained that yoke of slavery, by the former it was broken.

The servants of Christian masters were no longer slaves, but free servants, brethren beloved; and Christian masters were no longer slaveholders, but forbidden to be such, and required, as in the case of Philemon, to regard and treat their servants no longer as slaves, but above that condition, as brethren in Christ, and not slaves at all, not permitted to be treated as such in any way. The law of God forbids it, and how much more the gospel of Christ, the love of Christ, in addition to that law, and in fulfillment of it.

BLOOMFIELD remarks on 1 Tim. vi., 1, that "it was obvious that the *spirit* of the gospel is adverse to slavery. Indeed, in proportion as its injunctions are obeyed, it tends to *root out a practice in which folly and injustice are alike conspicuous.*" This admission is enough. There can not, by any possibility, be any precept in the gospel of God sanctioning or commanding a practice which the spirit of the gospel condemns, a practice conspicuous for folly and injustice, and known, by the testimony of the gospel, to be a crime.

Bloomfield adds that "it was natural for persons so ignorant as slaves to regard the gospel as freeing men from all obligations intrinsically and fundamentally inconsistent with justice and equity." And who is there, with a right knowledge of the law of God, that can regard the gospel in any other way? No enlightened Christian man can regard as obligatory by

of men, which, in a Christian, would be a disgrace to his redemption by Christ."

"The Christian religion does not abolish our *civil* connections; but slavery, and all buying and selling of the bodies and souls of men, no matter of what color or complexion, is a high offense against the holy and just God, and a gross and unprincipled attack on the liberty and rights of our fellow-creatures.—CLARKE on 1 Cor. vii., 23.

the gospel what is intrinsically and fundamentally unjust. It needed not the ignorance of a slave to regard the gospel as freeing men from such obligations, for it was the enlightenment of every Christian to know that what is in itself intrinsically and fundamentally unjust is forbidden by the gospel. If slavery is "intrinsically and fundamentally inconsistent with justice and equity," then it is inherently sinful, *sin per se*, and only for the sake of honoring Christ, by obedience to heathen masters, was the relation itself to be endured by the subject of it, and then only in such things as were not unrighteous before God.*

Bloomfield says, on Eph. vi., 5, "The apostle does not interfere with any established relations, however morally and politically wrong, as in the case of slaves." It is a good admission, that slavery is a relation morally and politically wrong. But that admission is fatal to the idea that the apostle does not interfere. The gospel is in every part an interference with whatever is morally wrong, and forbids it. If there be *any thing* contrary to sound doctrine, according to the gospel, against that, says the apostle, our preaching is to be directed. It being admitted that the relation of slavery is morally wrong, it is morally impossible that Christians should be permitted to sustain that relation. It is morally certain that the gospel forbids it, and that, under the gospel,

---

* See also CALVIN, comm. on Titus ii., 9. He restricts the duty of obedience to those things that are right (*quæ recta sunt*), and excepts every thing that is not according to the will of God (*ne quid nisi secundum Deum*).

Also CALVIN on Ex. ii., 14. "It is the common duty of all believers when the innocent are harshly treated to take their part, and as far as possible to interpose, lest the stronger should prevail. It can scarcely be done without exasperating those who are disposed to evil; but *nothing* ought to allow us to be silent, while justice is violated by their frowardness. For in this case silence is a kind of consent."

See also NEANDER, Church Hist. Relation of Christianity to Government. "God should be obeyed rather than man, and every consideration, even of property and life itself, should be disregarded, in all cases where human power demanded an obedience contrary to the laws and ordinances of God," vol. i., p. 359.

no person can rightfully be a slaveholder. The relation being admitted to be morally wrong, it is morally certain that the early churches could not have permitted slaveholding in their communion. Hence the power of such a spontaneous testimony as that of Augustine, against treating servants as things, as property; and that of Isidore, that he did not suppose that any Christian could keep a slave.

Neander remarks of the relation of slavery, that "a relation must necessarily fall of itself which is opposed to the Christian universal philanthropy, and to the ideas spread by Christianity respecting the equal destiny and dignity of all men, as created in the image of God, and called to rule over nature."*

The spirit of Christianity never could abolish that which the law of Christianity established as just and right. The argument is absurd, which at one and the same time pretends a sanction of slavery in the Word of God, and then claims that if it be let alone, if there be no agitation or disturbance, the spirit of the gospel will in due time destroy it. If it be sanctioned in the Word of God, then the spirit of the gospel can not be against it. But both law and spirit condemn and forbid it.†

The laws which the great Deliverer and Redeemer of mankind gave for the government of his kingdom were those of universal justice and benevolence, and as such were subversive of every system of tyranny and oppression.‡ "To suppose, therefore, as has been rashly asserted, that Jesus or his apostles gave their sanction to the existing systems of slavery among the Greeks and Romans, is to dishonor them. That the reciprocal duties of masters and servants (δοῦλοι) were in-

---

* NEANDER'S Memorials of Christian Life, p. 62.

† SAALSCHUTZ, *Das Mosaische Rechte,* vol. ii. This German writer on the Mosaic legislation corrects some fundamental errors, and shows the false-ness of the impression that slavery finds a place in God's Word.

‡ See the admirable views of the Christian argument in DR. ANDREW THOMSON'S Sermon and Speeches, page 7.

culcated, admits, indeed, of no doubt. But the performance of these duties on the part of the masters, supposing them to have been slave masters, would have been tantamount to the utter subversion of the relation. The character of the existing slavery was utterly inconsistent with the entire tenor of the moral and humane principles of the precepts of Jesus."*

But no matter if the character and quality of that slavery had been less severe ; the relation itself is always inconsistent with Christianity. Hence the righteous testimony of one of the very few ecclesiastical bodies that have at any time spoken authoritatively and plainly against this sin, " the United Presbyterian Church of North America," against the sin of slaveholding, as " a disqualification for membership in the church of Christ." " It is the relation itself, which we have examined in the light of Scripture, and which we have found to be so inconsistent with it, and not the many cruel laws which blacken the statute-books of the slaveholding States, and the many gross and fearful evils that result from this relation."†

" I flatter myself," said the eloquent Dr. Andrew Thomson of Edinburgh, " that I have said enough to show that those who take shelter under Christianity, as if that afforded any countenance to the slave system, are either ignorant or regardless of that revelation of Divine mercy ; that when they appeal to the Scriptures as sanctioning what they are so unwilling to renounce, they do nothing less than put a blasphemous commentary on the contents of that sacred volume."‡

Titus ii., 9, 10. " Exhort servants (δούλους) to be obedient unto their own masters, and to please them well in all things, not answering again, not purloining, but showing all good fidelity, that they may adorn the doctrine of God our Saviour in all things." The same remarks are to be made on this

---

* WRIGHT, Kitto's Cyclop. Art. *Slave.*
† TESTIMONY of the United Presb. Ch. of N. Am., 1858, p. 31.
‡ ANDREW THOMSON, Slavery condemned by Christianity, page 91.

passage as on the passages in Ephesians and Timothy, containing the same instructions. They are suitable for all time, for all generations, for all possible conditions of society, to the end of the world; for there is no intimation, or indication, or sanction of slavery in them; the relation of masters and servants being intended of God to belong to free Christian society, as long as the world stands, but of masters and *slaves*, never; this relation being forbidden, not only in the original law condemning to death the man who holds his fellow-man as property, but also in the command to masters to give unto their servants that which is just and equal.

The exhortations to servants to obey their masters no more intimate that it was right for those masters to hold them as *slaves*, than the command to love your enemy intimates that it is right for any one to be your enemy, or than the command to bless them that curse you, and do good to those that persecute you, intimates that it is right for men to curse you and to persecute you. It might as soundly and properly be argued that malignant enemies and persecutors of Christians may themselves be good Christians, and that the relation of a cruel enemy and persecutor to the victim of such cruelty was a Christian relation, as that the holders of Christians as property may be good Christians, or the relation of a slaveholder to the slave a Christian relation.

The old Hebrew law, and not the Roman law, or the Grecian law and custom in Crete or Athens,* is the glass through which this relation must be viewed. Viewed thus, it is instantly seen to be criminal before God; it is seen as condemned in his Word, and there is no possibility of any thing forbidden in the moral law of God in the Old Testament being sanctioned by the gospel in the New. God's Word, and not the custom or law of society, is the tribunal at which every custom and law among men must be tried. He who

---

* THIRLWALL, History of Greece, Slavery in Crete, ch. 7, 121, and in Athens, 187. GROTE, Hist. Greece, vol. iii., ch. xi.

appealed for the guide and sanction of his own life to the Old Testament, and referred to that supreme rule in the words, IT IS WRITTEN, never could have sanctioned in custom that which God, in writing, had forbidden ; and that God had forbidden the claim of property in man is indisputable.* It is that claim, and the application of it, in law and in practice, that constitutes the essence of slavery, and without which slavery could not exist.†

* BLACKSTONE, Commentaries, vol. i., B. i., ch. xiv. Repugnancy of slavery to reason and the principles of natural law. That such a state should subsist anywhere, he says, is thus repugnant. And all the three origins of the pretended right of slavery, assigned by Justinian, he shows to be false and iniquitous, contrary to the law of nature and of reason. "Upon these principles the law of England abhors, and will not endure the existence of slavery within the nation." It is not to be endured that a slaveholding Christianity should set revealed religion against the natural conscience of mankind, or by a false interpretation of the gospel set that against the law, or by perversion of both, make each appear contrary both to God and nature.

† DR. ANDREW THOMSON, Sermon and Speeches. "Shame on those who have so far taxed their ingenuity, and so far consulted their selfishness, and so far forgotten their Christian name, as to apologize for the existence of slavery by extolling the incomparable superiority of spiritual freedom, and dragging in the aid and countenance of Scripture, misstated or misunderstood. Slavery! the tempter, and the murderer, and the tomb of virtue! It must be put an end to, and without delay, for every day's procrastination only adds to the guilt of those who indulge in it, and sets at defiance the very first principles and maxims on which a true Christian feels himself constrained to act." (Pages 28 and 40.)

CHAPTER XXXIX.

"PAUL, a prisoner of Jesus Christ, unto Philemon, our fellow laborer, and to the church in thy house." The epistle was written during Paul's first imprisonment at Rome, and was sent, together with the epistles to the Ephesians and Colossians,* by Tychicus and Onesimus, about the ninth year of the Emperor Nero, or 63 of our Lord.† Philemon's residence was in Colosse, as appears from Col. iv., 9, where Onesimus, the servant of Philemon, is said to be one of the Colossians. Theodoret says that Philemon's house was still standing in Colosse in his time, that is, in the commencement of the fifth century.‡ Grotius supposed that Philemon was an elder in the church at Ephesus. Michaelis regarded him as a deacon. Doddridge supposes him to have been one of the pastors of the church at Colosse, colleague with Archippus.§ Lardner thinks it not certain whether he were an elder or a private Christian. If he had been an elder, Lardner thinks he must have known his duty better than to have needed so pressing an exhortation to receive a Christian brother.‖ Paley and

* PALEY, Hor. Paul., ch. vi. See also KITTO, Cycl., Art. ONESIMUS.

† But LIGHTFOOT supposes the year 60. Works, vol. iii., 301.

‡ LARDNER, Works, vol. vi., 77.

§ DODDRIDGE, Preface to Phil. and Notes. Fam. Exp., 948.

‖ LARDNER, vol. vi., 78, 131.

Lardner suppose that Paul had before known both Philemon and Onesimus.* And Beausobre and Lardner supposed that Onesimus' knowledge of Paul, as the friend of Philemon, induced him to visit Paul at Rome.

Paley says that Onesimus was the servant or slave of Philemon. But Paley's acute observations in the comparison of the epistles to the Ephesians, Colossians, and to Philemon, make it plain that the two latter, and, perhaps, all three epistles, may have been intrusted to Tychicus and Onesimus in one and the same commission; a thing not very likely if Onesimus was coming back as a slave to Philemon, to be his property for ever.† The supposition has been almost universal that Onesimus was set free by Philemon; but, in fact, Paul's own epistle is a rescript for the freedom of Onesimus, if he had ever been a slave; and the very commission with which he was immediately entrusted shows that he was considered as free by Paul and Tychicus and the Colossians. When Ignatius wrote his epistle to the Ephesians, about the year 107, their bishop's name was Onesimus; and Grotius concludes him to be the same Onesimus who was converted and sent back by Paul. Lardner thought that some persons might be unwilling to admit that Philemon himself could have been a bishop or elder of the church, "because he was a man of substance, who had one slave at least, or more."‡

---

* PALEY. HORÆ PAULINÆ, 229.

† POLI, Synopsis, vol. v., 1108. "Returned as one free; not as was customary with fugitives, to send them back bound, or under a keeper." Again, "Non ut retractum, ex fuga, aut remissum, sed aut sponte reversum," of his own accord returning, and not as one apprehended in flight. Yet one of the suppositions made by this commentator concerning Onesimus is that "he may have been a natural brother of Philemon, begotten by his father of a slave girl, for such offspring were slaves, following the condition of the mother."

‡ LARDNER, vol. vi., 78. It was a just and natural conclusion, a Christian conclusion. But the argument is equally forcible against his being a member of the church, and still maintaining the claim of property in man. The laws of Christianity forbade that claim; and if those laws were made known by the apostles, they must have been respected, at least until the corruptions of Christianity carried away its integrity and purity as with a flood.

But Macknight supposes that Philemon, on the contrary, had a number of slaves, on whom, if he pardoned Onesimus too easily, the escape from punishment for running away would have had a bad effect. And the methods of punishment were notoriously dreadful. But Macknight conceives that Paul presented to Philemon "the obligation he lay under to him, for having made his unprofitable slave a faithful and affectionate servant to him for life. By telling Philemon that he would now have Onesimus for ever, the apostle intimated to him his firm persuasion that Onesimus would never any more run away from him."* And even Doddridge says, "that he might not only be dear and useful to thee during all the remainder of his life as a servant, whose ear, as it were, is bored to the door of thine house (to allude to the Hebrew custom, Ex. xxi., 6), but a source of eternal delight," etc. And Hug says, "that Paul was restoring property which was then of considerable value, and was, moreover, returning it to its owner in an improved condition."† And Poole, in answer to the question, Why did not Paul in plain terms ask Philemon to emancipate his slave? says, "Perhaps it would have been too costly a demand. For slaves were very useful to their masters, and made a good part of their possessions."‡

Such are some of the preliminary suppositions and prejudices with which men have set Paul the apostle to the business of writing a pro-slavery document to comfort a rich Christian slaveholder with the assurance that his property in human flesh was more secure than ever. Had this Epistle been rendered through the eye of the Old Testament, under the guidance of which it was written, very different conclusions would have been drawn from it. Let us examine the proof.

Verses 8–21. "Wherefore, though I might be much bold in Christ to enjoin thee that which is convenient, (9.) yet for

* MACKNIGHT, Apostolical Epistles, 498.
† HUG's Introd. to the N. T.; Ep. to Phil., 555.
‡ POLI, Synop., vol. v.

love's sake I rather beseech thee, being such an one as Paul the aged, and now also a prisoner of Jesus Christ. (10.) I beseech thee, for my son Onesimus, whom I have begotten in my bonds; (11.) which in time past was to thee unprofitable, but now profitable to thee and to me; (12.) whom I have sent again; thou, therefore, receive him; that is, mine own bowels. (13.) Whom I would have retained with me, that in thy stead he might have ministered unto me in the bonds of the gospel; (14.) but without thy mind would I do nothing, that thy benefit should not be as it were of necessity, but willingly. (15.) For perhaps he therefore departed for a season, that thou shouldst receive him forever. (16.) NOT NOW AS A SERVANT, but above a servant, a brother beloved, especially to 'me, but how much more unto thee, BOTH IN THE FLESH AND IN THE LORD. (17.) If thou count me, therefore, a partner, receive him as myself. (18.) If he hath wronged thee, or oweth thee aught, put that on mine account. (19.) I, Paul, have written it with mine own hand, I will repay it; albeit I do not say to thee how thou owest unto me even thine own self besides. (20.) Yea, brother, let me have joy of thee in the Lord; refresh my bowels in the Lord. (21.) Having confidence in thy obedience, I wrote unto thee, knowing that thou wilt also do more than I say."

Of this it is to be noted that it is the conclusion and climax of all Paul's instructions on the subject of slavery. It might have been asked by the disciples, to whom any of his Epistles had come, referring to the treatment of servants, " But what are we to do, under the Roman empire, with the laws of God in regard to fugitives?* We are told that if the slave may

---

* JOSEPHUS, Book 6, chap. vi., Jud. Bell.—Laws of the Jews. That these laws were still of force, Paul himself teaches in 1 Tim. i, 9, by his reference to the whole body of moral precepts and forbiddings, and his instructions to have them enjoined in the preaching of the gospel. If the laws of God against MEN-STEALERS, murderers, and defilers of themselves with mankind were not abrogated, neither were those against the betrayers of fugitives; if the ανδραποδισται were objects of the divine reprobation, so were the *fugitivarii*, the *man-hunters*, the ανδρακυνναγοι. JOSEPHUS,

be made free, he is to use it rather, and that we must not be the slaves of men. But now suppose he runs away, what are we Christians to do with him?

The answer of Paul says, practically, in this Epistle,

1. You are to shelter him, and not to oppress him.

2. On no account give any notice of him, nor betray the wanderer, but he shall abide with thee, in one of thy gates, in that place where it liketh him best.*

3. Instruct him in the gospel, and by the grace of God convert him to Christ.

4. If he had had a Christian master, and you are confident in that master's piety and benevolence, then you may give notice to such a master (and send your letter or message by the fugitive himself) that you have sent him back to be emanci-

---

referring to the fact of the Jewish laws being acknowledged, records a speech of Titus to the Jews, noting the liberality of the Romans in this respect. "We have preserved to you the laws of your forefathers, and permitted you to live as it should please you, by yourselves or with others, permitted you also to collect your sacred tribute."

Now it is not to be supposed that the laws contained in the books of Exodus or Deuteronomy, or in the twenty-first and twenty-third chapters of those books, were considered as abrogated, while those of Leviticus were enforced; or that, while the laws against perjurers were binding, those against delivering up the fugitive, those protecting the fugitive from oppression and securing his freedom, were of none effect. The laws of Rome can not be proved to have been considered by Paul and his fellow Christians as more binding than the laws of God.

* JOSEPHUS, Antiq., B. xv., ch. 9. Josephus remarks concerning Herod, that "the liberality and submissive behavior which he exercised toward Cæsar and the most powerful men of Rome, *obliged him to transgress the customs of his nation,* and to *set aside many of their laws.*"

Suppose such a testimony as this to have been given respecting Paul, that judging himself brought under Roman law, and obliged to cultivate the favor of the court, and to avoid giving offense, he had been compelled in some things to set aside and transgress the law of God, though he had commanded Timothy to preach it! The supposition is shameful. Yet such, in fact, is the course of conduct attributed to him, in supposing that out of regard to the Roman law he would set at nought the Divine law, and at the command of Cæsar return into slavery a fugitive whom God had commanded him to protect.

pated; that by the law of God his master is bound to receive him, and treat him as a brother, but no longer as a slave; that in every respect, just as Paul would have a right to be treated as a freeman, just so has he. You are to commit the fugitive to his own care, and not to denounce him to the authorities, nor commit him to the keeping of any marshal. He is not to be rendered up as if he were a prisoner, or had committed an offense, but is to be intrusted, as a Christian brother, and a freeman, with the letter missive, demanding his free papers.

These things are clear from the analysis of this Epistle. Some other things are equally clear.

1. From verses 8–10, the assertion is clear that Paul could of right, in Christ's name, enjoin upon Philemon by commandment the freedom and brotherly kindness which, for love's sake, he asks for Onesimus.

2. From verse 11 the conclusion is clear that slavery is unprofitable, while freedom and piety are profitable.

3. From verses 11, 15, 16, the conclusion is manifest that freedom, and not slavery, is the cause of piety; that not slavery, but the escape from it, and the hearing of the gospel in freedom, is the true missionary institute, attended with converting grace. If Onesimus had remained with Philemon, and been treated as a slave, there is no proof that he would ever have been converted. He is said to have "departed" from Philemon, and getting to Rome he met with Paul, and being affectionately received and protected by him, he opened his heart to him, and was converted.

4. From verse 13 it is evident that Paul held that he had a right to have retained Onesimus, if Onesimus chose to be in his service, and that he was not bound by any pretended right of Philemon in him as property, or in his services, against his own will. "Whom I would have retained with me, that in thy stead he might have ministered unto me in the bonds of the gospel." If Onesimus had been considered as Philemon's property, then the very design of retaining him, without buying

parture the same language (εχωρισθη) as is used in Acts i., iv., and xviii., 12, of the departure of the disciples and of Paul from Jerusalem and Athens, and Romans viii., 35, Who shall *separate* us from the love of Christ? It is inconceivable, if Onesimus was the property of Philemon (and if so, then the most sacred of all property), and had stolen himself out of Philemon's power, committing thus the crime of man-stealing, that Paul should not so much as hint at any thing criminal or wrong in this action, but should leave it to be considered an innocent departure. The commentators call it a *euphemism ;* but Paul was not wont thus to conceal a great crime under soft and flattering language. Had it been a crime in Onesimus to depart from Philemon, Paul would have stated it.

7. Some other things he does distinctly state, namely, that Onesimus is to be received back, *not now as a servant*, οὐκέτι ὡς δοῦλον, *no more* as a servant, or slave (see ROBINSON, Lex., ουκετι, *no more, no further, no longer*), distinctly, *not again as a slave*, no more a slave, but above a slave, a brother beloved. If Paul sought to express as clearly as possible the fact that Philemon was to be free, was no more to be a slave, could no longer be held as such (even if he had been before), he could not have used more pointed language. The thing is as positive as words can make it, *no longer as a slave*. It is an example of the impossibility of a Christian being a slaveholder, and of the manner in which fugitives from slavery were always to be treated by Christians, as brethren, and not as slaves.

8. To prevent all possibility of doubt, to cut off all opportunity of evasion by resorting to the pretense that this freedom was merely Christian freedom in the Lord, or the privilege of being beloved as a brother in Christ, notwithstanding the continuance of slavery, it is distinctly added and declared that Onesimus is to be received by Philemon not merely as by Paul, in the character of a brother beloved in Christ, but as a brother also in the flesh; not as a servant, but above a servant, a brother beloved, BOTH IN THE FLESH *and in the Lord.*

This can have no other meaning than that Onesimus could no longer sustain the relation of a slave to Philemon in the flesh any more than in the Lord, but was a brother in both senses, so that he could not be a slave, nor could Philemon as a Christian hold him as such any more than he could have been supposed to hold his own brother as property, or use him as merchandise.

9. To all this is added another requisition and characteristic of perfect equality and freedom, "If thou count me a *partner* (κοινωνον) receive him as myself." For the meaning of this, compare 2 Cor. viii., 23. "Whether any do inquire of Titus, he is my *partner* and fellow-helper." Also Luke v., 10. "The sons of Zebedee, *partners* with Simon." Make a common friend and partner of both of us, him as myself. (See Robinson on the word and its cognates, in Lex. of N. T.)

10. "If he hath wronged thee, or oweth thee aught, put that on mine account." It is not here asserted that Onesimus *had* wronged Philemon. On the contrary, it is very clearly intimated (as well as in verse 15) that his *departure* was *not* a wrong; had *that* been a wrong, it would have been (if Onesimus were of right a slave) the highest kind of robbery, and Paul could not have questioned it. What an insult it would have been to send back Onesimus as a criminal, guilty of such robbery, and at the same time coolly to write concerning him to his owner, If he hath wronged thee, charge it to me! If, according to the interpolations of some paraphrasts, Onesimus had been the property of Philemon, and the value of that property had been greatly increased by his conversion (the presence of the Holy Spirit in him constituting him a much more precious piece of property than he was before, which is the hideous sense that some commentators put upon the 11th verse), then the proposition of Paul to set Onesimus free would have been just a demand upon Philemon for the sacrifice of a considerable sum of money; and on the same principles of generosity and justice on which Paul offers to pay any

thing that Onesimus might be owing to Philemon, Paul **must** also have offered to purchase *Onesimus*, and pay for *him*. To demand that Philemon should give him to Paul, and then for Paul to offer to pay a few pitiful debts that Onesimus was owing to Philemon, would be somewhat like asking a man to give you five hundred dollars, and then offering to settle for him a neglected bill of his last year's water-tax.

11. There is no intimation of Onesimus having robbed Philemon, and fled from him as a thief. Such suppositions and assertions are gratuitous and unfounded, as Bloomfield, Macknight and others have noted. There is not the slightest intimation in the epistle to the Colossians, where Onesimus is mentioned, of any allegation against him, nor of his being a slave, any more than Tychicus ; but he is mentioned as a faithful and beloved brother, along with Aristarchus, Marcus, Justus, Epaphras, " who is one of you" (the very same words used in regard to Onesimus), in the same epistle in which it is declared that in the church there is neither distinction of Greek nor Jew, bond nor free, and in which masters are commanded to give unto their servants that which is just and equal. Onesimus is no more considered a slave than Epaphras.

12. Paul's confidence in Philemon's *obedience* is to be noted. The command was, as well as request, to receive Onesimus, not as a servant, but as a brother. Paul had no right to command Philemon to do any thing but what the law of God and the gospel of Christ enjoined upon him. But in this he makes no question of his obedience. The dignity of his authority in Christ is thus united with the persuasive tenderness and courtesy of Christian love.* That Onesimus was considered by Paul as free is plain from his being intrusted, along with Tychicus (both mentioned by name in Col. iv., 7, 9), with the apostle's letter and messages to the saints and faithful brethren in Colosse. No difference whatever is put by Paul between Onesimus and Tychicus. They are both called faithful and

---

* This point is noted by PALEY, in Horæ Paulinæ, with emphasis.

beloved brethren, and it is added, "They shall make known unto you all things which are done here."

At the same time Onesimus was intrusted with the epistle to Philemon, and he must have known its contents, and the conditions on which, with his own consent, Paul was sending him on this mission. He was free; nor could Philemon have retained him as a servant, except with his own and Paul's con sent; as a *slave* he could not have received him at all, but was forbidden from maintaining any such claim or relation, not only by the present epistle, but by the principle laid down in that to the Colossians, iv., 1, Masters, give unto your servants that which is just and equal. If, as a slave, Paul was sending back Onesimus, and if, as a slave, Philemon was to receive him, greatly increased in value, and bound to him for ever as his property, then the idea of Paul writing a letter to Philemon, humbly and affectionately beseeching him to do this for Christ's sake and for love's sake, is one of the greatest absurdities that could be imagined.

For, consider the case of a slave worth a thousand or fifteen hundred dollars having escaped from a plantation at the South, and becoming a Christian at the North, his value being thus increased, say five hundred dollars, would any pious slave-catcher think it necessary, would the minister of religion, under whose instructions the slave was converted, think it necessary to write a humble, beseeching letter, entreating him, for Christ's sake, to receive back the fugitive as part of his plantation stock, and permit him to work for him without wages as his property? Meantime the master has offered publicly a hundred dollars reward or more to any who would aid him in recovering his valuable property. How does the system work where we see it in practice? Do slave-catchers have to entreat the masters for the sake of Christ to condescend to receive back their valuable chattels? It is ordinarily the case that they are glad enough to get them, though at the cost of great toil, expense and agitation.

It is not to be endured that such absurdities should be

fastened upon an inspired epistle, or that conduct, sentiments and arguments should be imputed to Paul, such as would disgrace an intelligent heathen.   Yet, so ingrained has the common mind been with the supposition of the rightfulness of slavery, the moral sense so poisoned, so drugged with the idea of slavery being a system sanctioned of God, and through this incarnation of iniquity in the conscience so deadened to the shame of such sentiments imputed to the inspired writers, that even Conybeare and Howson have translated Paul's words (rendered in our translation, *that thou shouldst receive him for ever*) by the phrase, " that thou mightest POSSESS him for ever," and in the phrase following, they have interpolated the words " *being thine*" (not in the original), and instead of our common translation, which is " a brother beloved, especially to me, but how much more unto thee, both in the flesh and in the Lord," they have added in the translation " *being thine*, both in the flesh and in the Lord."

But these writers have also translated Paul, in 1 Cor. vii., 21, as enjoining Christians to prefer slavery to freedom, even if they could have their choice !   Not a few of the commentators have, in respect to this subject, taken their stand point in the lowest level of Paganism, and have attempted to draw Christianity down upon that platform.   Instead of consulting the Old Testament Scriptures, and interpreting the New accordingly, disclosing the elevation of Judean and Christian society, produced by the Scriptures, and the divine spirit in them, above that of the whole world besides, they have adopted one of the worst vices of Pagan civilization as sanctioned of God, and then have put the interpretation of the gospels and epistles to the torture, in order to accommodate the Christian Scriptures to that sanction.   We might have said the worst vices of a Pagan *barbarism ;* for what can be worse, what more diabolical on earth, than the system of slavery known to have come to its perfection in Greece and Rome, to which these interpreters would affix the seal and

authority of divine inspiration ?   They have carried the very
words of the Holy Spirit to be stamped by the depravities of
the Pagan world, and then circulated them, under such an
image and superscription, as the exponents of Christianity.

A consultation of some who have written on this epistle
will give a vivid idea of the deadening and debasing power
of slavery over the conscience and mind, wherever this wickedness is defended or excused as right, and maintained as
consistent with the gospel.   The distortion and degradation
of the moral sense are incredible.   But nothing in this line
could surprise us from writers who could paraphrase the fifth
verse of the sixth chapter of Ephesians thus : " As the gospel
does not cancel the civil rights of mankind, I say to *bond-
servants*, obey your masters, WHO HAVE THE PROPERTY OF
YOUR BODY, with fear and trembling, as liable to be punished
by them for disobedience."* And yet, the very same commentator adds a note on the word *man-stealers* thus : " They
who make war for the inhuman purpose of selling the vanquished as slaves, as is the practice of the African princes, are
really *man-stealers*.   And they who, like the African traders,
encourage that unchristian traffic, by purchasing the slaves
whom they know to be thus unjustly acquired, are partakers
in their crime."†   But how can slaves be ever acquired in any
other way than unjustly ?   The purchase of slaves acquired
in war is perhaps the least iniquitous *mode* of man-stealing ;
but if the traffic be unchristian, it can be so only on the
ground of the fact both of natural justice and divine revela-

* MACKNIGHT, Apostolical Epistles,
Eph., ch. vi.

† MACKNIGHT on 1 Timothy i., 10.
And yet, on chapter vi, Macknight
reasons as if slaveholding was a right,
to which masters are entitled by the
law of nature, or the law of the country, which the Christian religion of
course confirms!   And a part of his
paraphrase of the third verse is, that

" if any one teach that under the gospel slaves ought to be made free, he
is puffed up with pride, knowing nothing."   He renders verse 6, " But god-
liness with a competency is great
gain ;" and according to the scope of
this reasoning, the paraphrase would
rightly add that a certain number of
slaves is the divine idea of a Christian
competency.

tion, that human beings can not be property, and that the treatment of them as such is a crime in God's sight, and by God's law worthy of death.*

The KEY TO THIS EPISTLE is in the grand OLD HEBREW FUGITIVE LAW in Deut. xxiii., 15, 16. "THOU SHALT NOT DELIVER UNTO HIS MASTER THE SERVANT WHICH IS ESCAPED FROM HIS MASTER UNTO THEE." Nearly all the commentators have neglected this law, have refrained from referring to it, and have sought to break open the epistle without using the key, or with false keys modeled by the slave power, so that they could rifle its contents by their own private interpretation for the sanction of slavery. Some have done this ignorantly, in unbelief; others are still doing it, in the bold avowal of the opinion that slavery is an institution of God, and that any shelter given to a fugitive slave is a violation of that religion and law which says, "Betray not the fugitive; take away from the midst of thee the yoke; give liberty every man to his brother and every one to his neighbor." Not in the law only, but in the prophets; not in Deuteronomy only, but in Isaiah and Jeremiah and the Psalms, Paul's favorite books of consultation and of study, he would find such passages as the following, in connection with the statutes against holding and treating human beings as merchandise, and against oppressing and defrauding them: "Take counsel; execute judgment; make thy shadow as the night in the midst of the noonday; hide the outcasts; betray not him that wandereth. Let mine outcasts dwell with thee; be thou a covert to them from the

---

* BLACKSTONE on the Rights of Persons, B. i., ch. xiv. Also, Introduction, Law of Nature and of Revelation, sec. 2. See also TUCKER'S Light of Nature, and COLERIDGE on Self-Evident Truths, and the necessity of their repromulgation. THE FRIEND, Essay 8. Also, HUMBOLDT, Cosmos, vol. ii., 567, 568, and vol. i., 368. Also, Speeches of FOX and WILBERFORCE.

"Political freedom was a great blessing; but compared with personal, it sunk to nothing. Personal freedom was the first right of every human being. It was a right of which he who deprived his fellow creature was absolutely criminal in so depriving him, and *which he who withheld was no less criminal in withholding.*"

face of the spoiler; for the extortioner is at an end, the spoiler ceaseth, the oppressors are consumed out of the land, and in mercy shall the throne be established."*

Paul could not pass by such passages, nor ignore, nor misinterpret God's laws against every form of man-stealing, though some of his interpreters can. It is a singular example of blindness and perversion, when the light of the Old Testament is carefully excluded from an epistle in the New. In every other case of examination of the meaning of the New Testament, wherever there is any reference in the subject or the language to any Old Testament passage, the commentators have, of course, referred back to it. But in this very plain case of the epistle to Philemon as connected with the law in Deuteronomy, and the precepts in Isaiah and other books, the commentators have turned away from that light, and kept it from the subject, avoiding, with singular pertinacity, all allusion to the appointed mode of treating fugitives in the Old Testament, while maintaining that they must be punished as runaway slaves in the New, and that the utmost that the religion of the gospel could do for them, toward shielding them from such cruelty, was humbly to beg their masters to refrain from such punishment! While the piety of the Old Testament is thus presented as noble, elevated and humane, that of the New is caricatured, in contrast, as mean, servile and oppressive. It is an insufferable slander of dishonesty and craftiness, a handling of the word of God deceitfully, a debasement of the most precious coin of divine inspiration, for avaricious and inhuman purposes.

Now it would be almost as gross a piece of ignorance or obstinacy, and of superficial investigation, under the power of prejudice, for a man to undertake an exposition of the epistle to the Hebrews, and of the nature of Christ's priesthood, without referring to the Levitical priesthood and the laws concerning that, as for a man to expound the epistle to Phile-

---

* Is. xvi, 3, 4, 5.

mon without referring to the Mosaic laws in regard to the
treatment of servants and fugitives. It can not be ignorance ;
for some of these very writers, as we have seen, quote, as illustrative of Onesimus being received by Philemon forever, (as
they affirm in their slave sense,) the custom of boring the ear
of a Hebrew servant, when he entered into a new contract to
serve his master till the jubilee ; and they intimate that Onesimus was sent back by Paul to have his ears bored and nailed
to Philemon's service as his property for life ! To such an incredible length has the prejudice in behalf of slavery gone,
while the provisions in behalf of justice and mercy are concealed or forgotten ! And so the word of God is ingeniously
(and sometimes unconsciously) tortured, to compel some appearance of the sanction of the greatest iniquity of modern
times !

Paul must have had God's law in respect to the treatment
of fugitives directly before him in the case of Onesimus, and
he could not have avoided consulting it for light. It was a
guide to him in this particular instance ; and his epistle to
Philemon proves him to have acted according to it, under the
confidence of Philemon's own Christian character, committing
to him the performance of the appointed duty of benevolence
to Onesimus as a Christian brother and freeman, permitted to
dwell where it might like him best, in that place where he
should choose, and not oppressing him. Paul himself, in the
first place, gives him shelter in his own hired house. He
does not betray him. He does not deliver him up into the
power of his master as a fugitive. He does not send word to
him to come up to Rome, prove property in his slave, pay
charges, and take him away. He kindly protects and in-
structs him. He then at length sends him back, with his own
consent, as a trusted and honored messenger and brother, as
free as Tychicus (Col. iv., 7, 9), with a message for the brethren at Colosse, and a command to Philemon from divine inspiration, as well as the affectionate entreaty of Paul's love

concerning his freedom. He does not accuse Onesimus of running away wrongfully, does not intimate that he committed any wrong in escaping. He states, on the contrary, that perhaps it was by the merciful providence of God that he departed from him for a season that he might be received back, no more as a servant, but above a servant, a brother beloved.* He commands Philemon to receive him as he would Paul himself, as a partner. Whatever wrong Onesimus may have done to Philemon, whatever he may have been owing to him, Paul does not intimate that it was in running away from him, but during his unprofitable state of bondage to him, which state now ceases ; and in order that there might be no shadow of claim remaining from Philemon against Onesimus whereby he might have said, I will keep you still in bondage till you work out your debt, Paul takes all Onesimus' debts upon himself, whatever they might be, and becomes security for him.† The result is, ONESIMUS A FREEMAN.‡

* SAALSCHUTZ, *Mos. Recht.* Laws of Moses, p. 715. Saalschutz remarks upon the singular felicity of the laws by which, if a heathen slave happened to have been sold in Judea, he could escape from his master, and the whole Hebrew world were forbidden to do any thing toward bringing him back, but were bound of God to shelter the fugitive. It was impossible that Paul could have despised that law.

† POLI, Synopsis, vol. v., in Epist. ad Phil. Poole does not once refer to the law of God forbidding the delivering up of fugitives, but he does refer to the Roman law requiring it, and remarks "that the reason why Paul was not willing to keep Onesimus was because of the very heavy penalties of the Roman laws against receiving or retaining fugitive slaves." Men would seem to imagine that Paul was more afraid of breaking the law of Rome than of God.

‡ WALLON, Histoire d'Esclavage dans l'Antiquité, vol. iii., ch. 1. This writer declares that in the example of Paul and the precepts of the New Testament, Christianity had already accomplished the emancipation of the slave. "Paul received the fugitive, taught him, and sent him to his master, NO MORE A SLAVE, but a brother, equal, *both before the world and before God.*" The duty and the work of emancipation are here complete and perfect.

JOSIAH CONDER, in his work on the Literary History of the New Testament, p. 440, also affirms that " in the epistle to Philemon, who has been, *by an absurd abuse of terms, styled a slaveholder*, St. Paul has pronounced a more emphatic condemnation of slaveholding by Christians than could have been conveyed by more direct prohibitions."

CHAPTER XL.

HEBREWS xiii., 3. "Remember them that are in bonds, as bound with them." Doubtless, from the phraseology employed in this passage, and in others where the same words occur, the primary application of it is to those in imprisonment for Christ, or *bound with this chain*, (Acts xxviii., 20,) as was Paul at Rome, or those condemned by their persecutors to labor in the mines, or under chains; but in general it comprehends those under the galling yoke of slavery, those whose heathen masters knew no rule of conduct toward their slaves but that of the supreme ownership and inexorable severities of the Roman law, by which they were treated not as persons but as things, as slaves are in America.* These were to be remembered in prayer, and in every way of possible compassion, just as the Christians themselves, to whom Paul was writing, would desire to be remembered, if they were in this deplorable condition, by those who enjoyed the blessedness of freedom. The words employed are δεσμίων and συνδεδεμένοι; but every slave is in a bondage incomparably worse than was that of Paul, the prisoner of Jesus, and under chains of ownership as a thing, a chattel, more galling, more dread-

---

* Compare STROUD, Slave Laws, Condition of the Slave in Civil Society, ch. iii., with FUSS, Rom. Antiq., sec. 54, 55, 56, and GROTE, History of Greece, vol. iii., pp. 94, 95. Also BLAIR'S Inquiry of Slavery among the Romans, 32, 45. Also GIBBON, Hist., chapters ii., xvi., xxxvi. Christians not put to death were treated with imprisonment, exile, or slavery in the mines. The mines of Numidia contained nine bishops in slavery, with many others.—CYPRIAN, cited in GIBBON. Also WALLON, Hist. d'Esclavage.

ful, more iniquitous, than was that chain which fastened Paul's wrist, even in his own hired house, to the arm of his Roman keeper.

James ii., 1. "Have not the faith of our Lord Jesus Christ, the Lord of glory, with respect of persons." The worst kind and degree of such respect is that against color, reducing the colored race to a despised, oppressed, enslaved class, and carried to such an extreme that the dreadful assertion is not only tolerated but defended, that black men have no rights that white men are bound to respect.* A Christianity that can accept or endure this as justice will admit and defend any iniquity, any cruelty against the race so set apart for scorn and oppression, so condemned to a living death by a public moral assassination.† It will force upon them a social system that crushes them into the condition of chattels, in the torture of life-long labor without wages, under a contempt not felt toward *things*, and that animals can not be made to feel. It will force upon them a church and a religion that by law keeps them in ignorance, forbids their being taught to read, excludes them from the sacrament of marriage, makes the Sabbath a mockery, or a mere block and pulley for hauling taut and securing the fastenings of the system.‡ This is that respect of persons, forbidden of God, but carried in slavery to the extreme of turning

---

* SIR JAMES STEPHENS, Slavery in the West Indies, vol. i., p. 364. Under the section of Maxims of Colonial Slave Law, the author presents some terrible proofs of the power and propagation of such caste and prejudice. He cites as the law of usage "that no white person can by any means whatever be reduced to slavery; but that every man, woman and child, whose skin is black, or whose mother, grandmother, or great-grandmother was of that complexion, shall be presumed to be a slave, unless the contrary is proved."

† Contrast this old West India legislation, and similar law and usage in America, with the law and custom under Louis XI. of France. (See SMYTH'S Lectures on Mod. Hist.,vol. i., p. 110.) "An age of superstition and violence." "In all cases where the proofs for and against the serfage are equal, let the decision be in favor of liberty."

‡ HUMBOLDT, Kingdom of New Spain, vol. i., p. 174, etc., presents illustrations of the power and misery of slave-caste perpetuated, but he says that in Mexico the laws are always

persons into things. In the church, by command of Christ, there was to be neither Barbarian, Scythian, bond nor free; but all one in him. But slavery denies or destroys even the fundamental law that God has made of one blood all nations and races, and substitutes in its stead a discord of partial cruelty worse than any depraved Manichean imagination ever attributed to the all-wise Creator and Governor.*

James v., 4. "The hire of the laborers kept back by fraud." The whole of this passage is terrible. The fraud of taking men and using them as slaves, not only keeping back their wages, but giving them nothing, and making it a point of law that nothing is due to them, buying and selling, not only their labor, but themselves, their bodies and souls, as merchandise, is the highest possible example of this wickedness. In addition to all other cruelties, the wages of which they have been defrauded, but which the eye of Supreme Justice has marked

---

interpreted in favor of liberty, and the government favored the increase of freemen. This was written in 1809. HUMBOLDT gives a description of what he witnessed of the disregard of color and of caste in the Academy of Fine Arts in Mexico, where rank, color and race were compounded, the Indian, the Mestizo, and the Whites, the sons of the lowliest artisans and of the highest lords were seated together. (Vol. i., p. 241.)

* SMYTH, Lectures on Mod. Hist., vol. i., 170, refers to "the effect of *habit* in banishing all the natural feelings of mercy, justice, benevolence, as in the instances of slave-dealers, etc., as perfectly frightful." Compare WRIGHT, Slavery at the Cape of Good Hope, p. 15, the effect of law and usage sanctioning concubinage and adultery. STEPHENS, Slavery in W. I., under the head of *Unjust and Merciless Laws*, vol. i., sec. 6, p. 208, dis-

closes the inalienable and incurable cruelty and selfishness of the system. "The first founders of slavery in the English as well as Dutch colonies held it to be incompatible with the condition of a Christian man, and such as pagans and infidels could alone be lawfully subjected to." While this prejudice existed, a man by becoming a Christian might possibly escape from the condition of a slave. They therefore, in Jamaica, as early as 1696, passed a law to prevent such a result. "Be it enacted that no slave shall be free by becoming a Christian." In America there is an improvement on this. Be it enacted that slavery is the highest style of Christianity, "undoubtedly good, and only good; the only good in the whole affair of negro existence in America."—Southern Presb. Review May, 1857.

as owing to them by the law, Give unto your servants that which is just and equal, make up an account against their oppressors for which God alone can bring them to a settlement. Let any man once compute, if possible, the amount of the wages of the four millions of slaves in this country, accumulating for so many years, and kept back by fraud; the amount due by the law of justice and equality, according to which God commands that all servants should be treated. It would amount, at the lowest rate, to more than the value of all the real estate of their masters at this hour.

And yet, if they had been treated justly, if their wages had been paid them, as free laborers from the outset, the wealth of their masters, the value of the lands, the quantity and worth of their products, would have been incalculably accumulated. The North and the South would have been richer by thousands of millions; for the payment of just wages, and the treatment of the laborer according to God's laws of freedom and benevolence, are the only conditions on which the earth will yield her increase with the security of the divine blessing. Without these conditions the curse of the Lord, as in this epistle, is on the field and the wealth of the wicked, and an eating rust as of fire is in the prosperity and at the vitals of the nation, whose laws and subjects make merchandise of men.

1 Peter ii., 16. "As free, and not using your liberty for a cloak of maliciousness, but as the servants of God." Compare 2 Peter ii., 19, "While they promise them liberty, they themselves are the servants of corruption; for of whom a man is overcome, of the same is he brought in bondage."

When the apostle says *as free*, he speaks in opposition to slavery, and in perfect correspondence with Paul, in 1 Cor. vii., 22, 23 (be ye not the servants of men), and Gal. v., 1, 13, "Ye have been called unto liberty." But it is absurd for any man who is a slave to sin, to sensual desire, and to angry passion, to talk about liberty, for he knows nothing of it, and being conquered by his own corruptions, is by them sold as a

slave to Satan, just as men taken captive in war were by the
Pagan nations tasked and sold as slaves.   But the servants
of God are redeemed from all slavery, and are bound to hate
every form of it.

1 Peter ii., 18.   "Servants (οἰκέται) be subject to your
masters with all fear ; not only to the good and gentle, but
also to the froward."   There is here a similar distinction as
in 1 Tim. vi., 1, 2, between servants under the yoke, and those
that have believing masters.   And much the same reason is
given for such subjection as is presented in the first verse of
the next chapter for the subjection of wives to their own
husbands, although such husbands might be unbelieving ; the
reason, namely, of the power of a sweet and loving obedience,
to the honor of God and the gospel, attracting men to him
and to it, winning them by such meek, submissive, holy conversation, and bringing them to Christ by the power of such
practical piety, when otherwise they might have continued
ignorant of the word.

Calvin thinks that by the use of the word οἰκέται instead
of δοῦλοι, in this passage, it is probable that free domestics
are to be understood as well as slaves.*   But if slaves at all,
then would not the particular proper word have been used in
place of the more general ?†   Eusebius, Beza, Cave and others
have supposed that Peter wrote his epistles to Jews ;‡ if so,
there is good reason why he should not have written to slaves,
since they had none.   But Lardner and others believe him to
have written " to all Christians in general ; Jews and Gentiles
living in Pontus, Galatia, Cappadocia, Asia and Bithynia, the

---

* CALVIN, Comm. in Ep., 1 Pet., ch.
ii.   " Quoniam non hic habetur δοῦλοι,
sed οἰκέται, possumus intelligere li-
bertos una cum servis."

† JOSEPHUS, Contra Apion, B. 2,
sec. 19, uses for the Jewish servants
the word οἰκετων.   But in sec. 30, of

the same book, he uses δοῦλοις in
speaking of the punishment of crime.

‡ CAVE, Lives of the Apostles, 211.
" He wrote to the Jewish converts,
to direct them in the relations both
of the civil and the Christian life."

greatest part of whom must have been converted by Paul."[*]
Bishop Sanderson argues that Peter was addressing the Jews,[†]
and showing them "that being indeed set at liberty by Christ,
they are not therefore any more to enthral themselves to any
living soul or other creature; not to submit to any ordinance
of man as slaves, that is, as if the ordinance itself did, by any
proper, direct and immediate virtue, bind the conscience.[‡]
But yet, notwithstanding, they might and ought to submit
thereunto, as the Lord's freemen, and in a free manner."

Their native, inexpugnable hatred of slavery, the Jews had
received from the Old Testament, as well as from the law
written on the heart.[§] But the gospel taught Christian servants, even when treated as slaves, to be submissive and
gentle, even to the froward, and when under the yoke, for
the sake of the Lord Jesus, and for the honor of his cause.
Love to Christ could unite such submission (in all things in
which it was not contrary to his will) with the most perfect
spirit of true independence, and the most undiminished abhorrence of oppression.

[*] LARDNER, vol. vi., p. 260.

[†] See also BLOOMFIELD, N. T.
"Chiefly Jews, but partly Gentiles."

[‡] See CALVIN on Exodus i., 17.
"Sustained and supported by the
reverential fear of God, they boldly
despised the commands and threatening of Pharaoh." Calvin remarks
on the wickedness of those, "whom
the fear of men instead of God gov-
erns, and who, under pretext of due
submission, obey the wicked will of
governors in opposition to justice and
right, being in some cases the ministers of avarice and rapacity, in others
of cruelty; pleading the frivolous excuse that they obey their princes according to the word of God; as if
every earthly power which exalts itself against heaven ought not rather more justly be made to give
way."

[§] JOSEPHUS, Wars of the Jews, B.
7, ch. viii. "We have preferred
death before slavery," δουλειας. "We
are bound to die," Eleazer argued;
"but not to be slaves; death is necessary, but slavery unnatural and un-
necessary." He was advising, in the
defense of the fortress of Masada,
that they should rather die than yield
to the Romans, by whom they would
inevitably either be put to death or
sold as slaves. His speech is a faithful demonstration of the love of liberty instilled into the heart by the
"lively oracles," and which in the
Christian would be combined with
supreme submission to the will of
God.

CHAPTER XLI.

REVELATIONS xiii., 10. "He that leadeth into captivity shall go into captivity." There is a striking reference in this to Is. xxxiii., 1 : "Wo to thee that spoilest, and thou wast not spoiled, and dealest treacherously, and they dealt not treacherously with thee! When thou shalt cease to spoil, thou shalt be spoiled ; and when thou shalt make an end to deal treacherously, they shall deal treacherously with thee." The carrying of men into captivity, the forcing of them into bondage, the making slaves of them, and compelling them to serve as slaves, as was done generally with captives in war,* is one of the gigantic forms of oppression and cruelty on earth most plainly condemned of God. The horrors and woes consequent upon it have been interminable.† But if the making of slaves

---

* JOSEPHUS, Bell. Jud., B. vi., ch. 8. He speaks of the multitude of captives being so vast that the price for them was very low, while the purchasers were few. A very literal fulfillment of the prediction in Deut. xxviii., 68 : "Ye shall be sold unto your enemies for bondmen and bondwomen, and no man shall buy you." Josephus calculates the number carried away captive on the taking of Jerusalem at 97,000, (ch. ix., sec. 3,) and this, it has been supposed, is a moderate computation.

† See WALLON, BLAIR, STEPHENS, BROUGHAM, GIBBON, GROTE, NIEBUHR, FUSS, POTTER, BURIGNY, BECKER, and others. The almost inconceivable miseries and crimes resulting from the recognition of slavery as a legitimate status in Greece and Rome, and from the sale and distribution of captives in innumerable wars, and from the conversion of freemen into serfs and chattels, and of free parents into the fountain heads of perpetual streams of slavery, are but partially disclosed by GROTE. (Hist. Greece, vol. iii., ch. ii.) WALLON, (Histoire d'Esclavage, vol. ii., the chapters on Sources of Slavery, and State of the Slave under Law,) STEPHENS, (Penal Slavery and Max-

under pretence of conquest over enemies is sinful in God's sight, how much more the taking and holding of slaves by individuals for gain, under pretence of having purchased them with money! The making merchandise of men was a crime in God's sight worthy of death; and no man can be a slave-holder without being guilty of this crime. The slaveholder kidnaps and carries away captive a human being every day and hour in which he holds a human being against his own will as a slave, as property. The Greek word in 1 Tim. i., 10, translated MEN-STEALERS, is rendered in GROTIUS and others by the Latin word *plagiariis*. And the Latin word *plagiarius* is rendered by FACCIOLATUS as one who not only steals, but retains a freeman in slavery, against his consent, *invitum in servitute retinet*. Any man who claims another man as his property is therefore such a *man-stealer*, ανδραποδιστής. He falsely assumes to be the owner of the personality of which the man himself, under God, is the sole owner. Hence the word *plagiarist* in our language, one who falsely proclaims himself the author of another man's books. Slaveholding is the *plagiarism* of immortal beings from God; and the stealing of the children from their parents, and making merchandise of *them*, is at once the meanest, most cruel, and yet the most unnoticed, unrebuked form of this inquity.* The opprobrium connected with the word *man-stealer* ought to rest also

ims of Colonial Slave Law), and other writers. Incidentally, sometimes, a terrible revelation is made. Every extreme of severity made possible by slave law finds its realization in fact, and makes a fixture of existence in character. *Quot servi tot hostes* was a proverb, or *quot hostes tot servi, as many enemies, so many slaves,* capable of another and terrible meaning, afterward realized. But this was the war maxim. Slave merchants followed the great armies like vultures. After a battle and victory the general would appoint a day for the public sale of the captives; then came the strife for the best and cheapest bargains in wholesale purchases, and then the slaves were herded in gangs to their various destinations, or city slave-markets.

* COLUMELLA proposed rewards, bounties, for the breeding of slaves; and the number of *vernæ, home-born,* was sometimes almost incredible. See BLAIR'S Inquiry, and WALLON, Histoire, vol. ii., ch. ii. Also BECKER'S Gallus, 213.

on the word slaveholder. A man-stealer is any one who makes merchandise of human beings. A slaveholder is such a merchant, such a slave-trader. He bought his human beings as chattels; he will sell them as chattels But worse yet, a slaveholder is one who propagates and perpetuates the crime, and whereas perhaps he bought the parents, whereas he went through the formula of *purchasing* them, and *therefore* holds them as property; he scouts even this formula in regard to their posterity, but seizes, claims, and holds the babes, new-born, the children, and makes merchandise of them, without even the pretence of paying a farthing for them.*

Rev. xviii., 13. This was one of the great crimes found in great Babylon, when the time of her destruction and punishment was come. "The merchandise of slaves and souls of men," σωμάτων και ψυχὰς ἀνθρώπων. "The merchants of these things, which were made rich by her, shall stand afar off, for the fear of her torment, weeping and wailing." The reference here is to Ezekiel xxvii., 13, the merchandise of Tyre, and the merchants of Javan,† Tubal and Meschec, who traded the persons of men (souls of men) and vessels of brass in the market. In this slave trade‡ souls are tossed about as

---

* PLUTARCH, Life of Cato, relates that he was in the business of buying up slaves on speculation, especially youths, from the slave merchants who bought them at the army auctions; he did this in order to increase their value by training them, and then to sell them at an advanced rate. Our slave-breeding States improve on all these methods, and concentrate them into a home manufacture.

† WALLON, Histoire d'Esclavage dans l'Antiquité, vol. ii., part ii., Sources of Slavery. Ionia is referred to in the text, and the slaves brought thence were highly valued for their beauty. But Delos became one of the greatest slave marts of antiquity.

‡ STEPHANUS, Thesaurus. Ανδρα-ποδιστης is rendered by Stephanus by the Latin *mancipator*, whoever reduces any man to slavery. He adds illustrations of its significance as *those who supply slaves to the merchants*, that is, literally, *slave-dealers*. Thessaly, he states, was full of such men in that business.

BRETSCHNEIDER, on the origin cf the word ανδραποδιστω, with its derivation, interprets it thus: *hominem capio, et servum vendo*, literally, *I take a man and sell a slave*, and he refers directly to Ex. xxi., 16, and Deut. xxiv., 7. He that stealeth, holdeth, or maketh merchandise of a man, shall be put to death. SCHLEUSNER also

things, and the merchandise of slaves is the merchandise of souls, נֶפֶשׁ אָדָם, souls of men.

There is no distinction as to guilt, drawn in the Scriptures, between a foreign and domestic slave-trade. On some accounts the guilt of the foreign seems the blackest, and our laws have condemned it as piracy. Our laws at one and the same time brand the bringing of men *into* slavery as piracy, and the *rescuing* of them *from* slavery at home as piracy and treason. John Brown, as captain of a slaver, bringing a cargo of slaves to Cuba or Louisiana, would have received a reward. John Brown attempting to deliver a dozen slaves from slavery, is hanged.* Abroad the slave-trade is denounced as a traffic of demons; at home it is extolled as a business that becometh saints. Abroad it is the instigation of the devil; at home it is the climax of social civilization and Christianity, and the missionary providence of God.

But it is must be admitted that if either form of this great wickedness is crime, the domestic is the worst, because, 1. It is a breeding, propagating form, with frighful rapidity in the increase. 2. It is committed and continued under the light of the gospel, and with pretence of a sanction therein. 3. It is established by law, which is always an immeasurable exaspera-

refers the word, for illustration, to those very passages in the Old Testament in the laws of Moses, where God sentenced the man-stealer, and the man who made merchandise of man, to death.

* There is no instance of any punishment ever being inflicted on any man for making slaves, or bringing them from Africa to this country. Near the time when John Brown was hanged in Virginia for attempting to rescue slaves from slavery, a man named BROWN was being tried, *on a second indictment*, in Savannah, for the crime of bringing Africans into the United States and holding them as slaves.

The jury stood eight for acquittal and four for conviction, and doubtless the man-stealer goes scot free. But in proximity with this comes the following record of the penalty of death against a poor unfortunate creature, not for any crime before God or man, but simply for aiding a human being to escape from bondage: "Charleston, South Carolina, January 29. Francis Mitchell, porter of the steamship Marion, was yesterday sentenced to be hung on the 2d March for *assisting a slave in his attempt to leave the State!*" No language can describe the wickedness and injustice of such elective and oppressive cruelty.

tion of any sin. 4. Being so sanctioned, and transmitted legally to posterity, each successive generation of slave traders, as the masters and owners of property belonging to them by inheritance, claim an increasing right in such property, and have less and less conscience of the sin, and lay their grasp with less and less compunction upon the next crop or generation of human beings as their possession, and as having been justly foreordained by them for bondage, and under a benevolent providence, born to be the victims of the system of slavery and of the domestic slave-traffic.

This, with its connections, is the vastest form of merchandise and mercantile speculation, except perhaps the traffic in hay and cattle, carried on in the United States. All parts of the nation, north and south, east and west, are fearfully involved in it.* The merchants stand afar off in fear and torment, in terror of the breaking up of this great Babylon. It is contended by a vast party that the union of the States depends upon the integrity and unassailable security of this traffic. The complicity in it is as a vein of gangrene running from head to foot in the body, which can be traced by the inflammation and discoloration, and is frightfully diffusive and malignant.

The palsying and perverting power of this sin upon the conscience is appalling. Holding the truth in unrighteousness, it becomes a lie, and men who thus hold it are given over to strong delusion to believe a lie. We have read of a stream

---

* Extensive mortgages are held on slave property, perhaps at the extreme north. Hence a part of our sensitiveness. A slave master and planter in Louisiana, the ostensible owner of a large number of slaves, declared to a mercantile friend his convictions of the wickedness, wretchedness, and ruin of the system of slavery, and avowed that if he could do it, he would set free every slave in the United States, whatever might be the consequences. "Why do you not emancipate your own?" was the very natural question of his friend. "If such are your convictions, why not begin at home?" "Why sir," was the answer, "they are every one of them *mortgaged to merchants in New York*, and if I should set them free, they would foreclose, and grasp them instantly, and they would all be sold under the hammer!"

that encrusts every thing that falls in it, or grows by it, with flint, and just so the instincts of humanity itself, as well as the precepts of religion, are turned into stone by the flowing of this infernal fountain over them. The Christian conscience, steeped in the habits and sophistries of slave-life, comes out a fossil, on which the slaveholder grinds his sharpest arguments. The sanctioning and shielding of such abominations can not possibly be less offensive to God than the suffering that woman Jezebel to teach in the early churches, and to throw the seduction of her sophistry over the immoralities of paganism. The ministers of the gospel who listen to these doctrines, and consent to silence the gospel in regard to them, are infected by them. The very essence of morality is changed, and the mind and conscience are defiled. A man lays himself down to bathe in this stream, and his moral sense turns into *adipocire.* The finger of slavery presses upon his intelligence and emotion, and there is no rebound; the mark stays, as upon an image of hog's lard; there is a deep indentation. The man of *adipocire* goes into the pulpit; his very sermons are a dead tissue; his conscience, his sentiments, are as lifeless as pale wax, as smooth, as cold, as susceptible of being moulded to order for the forms of political expediency.

Rev. xix., 18. Describing the supper of the great God, the fowls are summoned to eat the flesh of all " free and bond, small and great." Compare chapter vi., 15, " every bondman and every freeman." A southern writer, the author of what is called a Scriptural view of the moral relations of African slavery, adduces these passages in proof " that there will be bondmen on the earth when the last trumpet sounds. This fact being admitted, the writer says that " the hope of liberating all the slaves upon the whole earth must be visionary indeed." The conclusion is this, that African slavery is a divine institution, and that any scheme of abolition is a wild, fanatical interference with that which is destined of God to stand still till the last day.

By this kind of argument the mention of murderers in Rev. xxi., 8, and whoremongers and idolaters, and liars, proves that there will be murderers and liars at the end of the world, and therefore murdering and lying are divine institutions, and any interference with them in the hope of delivering the earth from such wickedness is visionary and foolish. A perfect delirium seems to have seized upon the understandings of those who have consecrated themselves to the defense of this gigantic cruelty and sin; but it is a DELIRIUM TREMENS. Perhaps they are in the position of those described by Paul in his second epistle to the Thessalonians, as wrought upon of Satan with all deceivableness and unrighteousness, because they received not the love of the truth that they might be saved; and for the same cause given over of God to strong delusion to believe a lie, because they believed not the truth, but had pleasure in unrighteousness. They are an example, such as we could hardly have deemed possible under the light of the gospel, of men so lost to all sense of guilt and shame in the practice and defense of the greatest of national and individual cruelties, that like the old Jews at the climax of their debasement and crisis of their overthrow, under God's retributive judgments in the age of Jeremiah, they can deliberately and defiantly plead that "they are delivered to do all these abominations.*

* WHEWELL on the Elements of Morality, sec. 108, 109, 522, 524. "Slavery is contrary to the fundamental principles of morality." Again, "Slavery is utterly abhorrent to the essence of morality, and can not be looked upon as a tolerable condition of society, nor acquiesced in as what may allowably be. Wherever slavery exists its abolition must be one of the greatest objects of every good man, 522, 529. Compare HUME, Populousness of Ancient Nations. It is interesting to note the infidel philosopher and the Christian moralist viewing this gigantic iniquity from a point outside its personal sweep, uniting in its abhorrence and condemnation. "A chained slave for a porter," says Hume, "was usual at Rome. Had not these people shaken off all sense of compassion towards that unhappy part of their species, would they have presented their friends, at their first entrance, with such an image of severity of the masters and misery of the slaves?" But this searedness and stupidity of the moral

Burke somewhere speaks with contempt of the " exploded fanatics of slavery," who believed in its indefeasible right. The career of slavery in this country, and the insolent shame-lessness with which its doctrines of devils are intruded on mankind, to the corruption of all religion and confusion of all morals, would have been a fit subject for Burke's powerful denunciations. There would be no danger of exaggeration in the description of this system, and of its effect upon so-ciety, and of the reign of terror under which it must inevita-bly bring the whole community, for the support of those in power, who are the personal managers and leaders of so inso-lent and savage a despotism, the known policy of which is " to destroy the tribunal of conscience, and bring to their *lanterne* every citizen whom they suspect to be discontented by their tyranny."*

When the possession of power obtained by such means, and resting on such personal robbery and destruction of hu-man rights, is made the interest of a great party, and the ex-pediency and even sanctity of the system of cruelty and wrong are maintained for the sake of political supremacy, for the sake of wielding the patronage and dividing the emolu-ments of the government of a great nation, the corruption of such a party must be deep, rapid and frightful, to a degree never yet demonstrated in history. The depravity of men, the violence of their passions, and the moral atrocity of their principles, will be developed, along with the haughtiness and holiness of their professions, as in a hot-house; for religion itself, in the most insolent hypocrisy, goes side by side with this system of the moral assassination of millions, and is even its pretended foundation to the glory of God. The party so supported must, in the very nature of things, and by a moral

---

sense were pardonable in comparison with the defiance of God and of com-mon humanity, involved in the attempted justification and sanction of this system by the Christian relig-ion.

* BURKE's works, vol. 3. Letter to a Member of the National Assembly.

necessity arising out of its position, and its means of permanence in power, be a party radically regardless of justice, and
ready, in any emergency, to set precedents of cruelty and
oppression in the place of law, and to contrive a machinery
of government, with inquisitorial committees of Congress,
armed with powers, and clamps of federal legislation, breaking
down, one after another, every State right, every personal
protection, all remnant of State sovereignty, by the sheer despotism of party organization ; each individual being animated
with the spirit of a slaveholder towards all who oppose the
sin which is the life and soul of such a usurpation. Let this
insolent domination be extended to the pulpit and the freedom of the word of God, and all that has ever been recorded
of Star Chamber tyranny in Great Britain would be trifling
in comparison with the consequences of the erection of that
lynch law, that now triumphs in the slave States, into a systematic politico-ecclesiastical tribunal at the North, under the
plea of peace, piety, and the salvation of the Union. To this
extreme things are rapidly tending, and men, whose daily
boast is of liberty, are forging their own fetters, and burning
incense to this Moloch. They know not what they are preparing for themselves and for their children.*

"The Romans," said Fisher Ames, on a memorable occasion, endeavoring to warn his countrymen, "were not only
amused, but really made vain, by the boast of their liberty,
while they sweated and trembled under the despotism of emperors, the most odious monsters that ever infested the earth.
It is remarkable that Cicero, with all his dignity and good
sense, found it a popular seasoning of his harangue, six years

---

* BURKE on the Democratic Tyranny. Works, vol. iii., p. 146. "In
a democracy the majority of the citizens is capable of exercising the
most cruel oppressions upon the minority, whenever strong divisions prevail in that kind of policy, as they
often must; and that oppression of
the minority will extend to far greater
numbers, and will be carried on with
much greater fury, than can almost
ever be apprehended from the dominion of a single scepter."

after Julius Cæsar had established the monarchy, and only six months *before* Octavius totally subverted the commonwealth, to say that it was not possible for the people of Rome to be slaves, whom the gods had destined to the command of all nations. Other nations may endure slavery, but the proper end and business of the Roman people is liberty."* Such is the rhetoric, such the music and the melody, such the flattery and fawning, with which to-day the people of the United States are offering their wrists for manacles to the despotism of a more odious and dreadful oligarchy than ever ruled in Greece or Rome; the despotism of three hundred thousand slaveholders, who hold twenty million whites in bondage, through the enslavement of four million blacks.

* AMES' Works, Dangers of American Liberty.

CHAPTER XLII.

APPEAL OF THE MORAL ARGUMENT.—BEGUN IN THE OLD TESTAMENT.—COMPLETED IN THE NEW.—DREADFUL CONSEQUENCES OF ITS DENIAL.—ATROCITIES OF SLAVERY AND SLAVE LAW UNDER THE LIGHT OF THE GOSPEL.

THE moral argument from Scripture on this subject appeals to the common conscience of all mankind, and at every step enlists the common sense of humanity in its behalf. The defense of slavery has to be undertaken and pursued against conscience, against benevolence, against law, natural and divine, against history, against both the letter and spirit of the Scriptures, against the Old and New Testament theology, against the gospel, against God. The consentaneousness of both parts of divine revelation on this subject, in condemnation of this crime, is perfect; and it is an incidental proof of divine revelation, when an article of morality, conveyed at first through the medium of the social life of a particular nation, divinely arranged for that purpose, passes, on the dropping away of the letter of that law, into a higher universal life and energy for all mankind, for all nations, as the ripe fruit hangs upon the tree after the blossoms have vanished, after the leaves have disappeared, What the law severely and inexorably forbade in the Old Testament, the Christian life of the New renders impossible to a pure Christianity and to all good men. What the law enjoined of love to the stranger, the gospel takes up as belonging, in Christ, from each to all, from all to one another, as one family in him; and the law of the spirit of life in Christ Jesus accomplishes, by spontaneous

Christian love, what the letter of the antique law could only indicate and command.*

If on this point the morality of the New Testament were inferior to that of the Old, while on every other point it is superior ; if on this point the divine standard were changed ; if there could be such mutability in the elements of justice and the requisitions of benevolence; if, when the preparatory dispensation, the husk, was taken away, instead of disclosing a fruit, it revealed a poison, or a dry innutritious cob, of less worth than the husk itself; this would have been an inconsistency fatal to the claims of a divine revelation. The argument of Paul, in the second epistle to the Corinthians, stakes the claims of the *ministry* of the New Testament on the superiority of the *gospel* of the New Testament, as a gospel of the Spirit, everywhere and in every particular carrying the letter into life. The old glory of the letter was to be done away, because the new ministration of the Spirit, promised by it, growing out of it, and perfecting it, far exceeded it in glory, as a ministration of righteousness, and not of law merely, but of the fulfillment of the law, by the glorious energy of the spiritual life.

If now the life, instead of transfiguring the letter, instead of throwing back a divine radiance of love upon it, in which its intended and prophetic glory might be visible, had fallen below it, had come short of it, this would have been a fatal failure and contradiction ; much more, if in any important particular the divine announcement of the letter had been falsified, abrogated or repealed in the life ; much more, if the life had taken up into itself, as part and parcel of its own piety, a practice which the letter had distinctly, and for all mankind,

---

* GRANVILLE SHARPE. Law of Retribution against Tyrants, Slaveholders and Oppressors, pp. 6, 319. In this admirable volume the benevolent author presses the Old Testament historical and legal Scripture argument with great accuracy of learning and acuteness and power of reasoning. At the same time an application, irresistible for its pungency and faithfulness, is made to the conscience.

condemned, as involving a guilt, and constituting a crime, equal to that of murder.

It is not possible, therefore, adequately to describe the mischief and misery inflicted on Christianity by the assertion that the gospel sanctions slavery. It is inevitably a destruction of the evidence of divine revelation. This horrible corruption of Christianity in modern times concentrates the abominations of all earlier corruptions. Prideaux says, "It may almost raise a doubt whether the benefit which the world receives from government be sufficient to make amends for the calamities which it suffers from the follies and maladministrations of those that manage it." The same may be said of the iniquity and madness of those who are undertaking to manage the Christianity of the gospel as a slaveholding Christianity. It is a virulent practical infidelity, sustained by crime. They who support such a Christianity are the infidels; and they who deny it are the believers, they who deny and reject with scorn and hatred such a libel against God, such a monstrous perversion of His Word, and cleave to the letter and spirit of the law and gospel.*

* DYMOND, Essays on Morality, ch. xviii. "Whether it is consistent with the Christian law for one man to keep another in bondage without his consent, and to compel him to labor for that other's advantage, admits of no more doubt than whether two and two make four. It were humiliating, then, to set about the proof that the slave system is incompatible with Christianity, because no man questions its incompatibility, who knows what Christianity is, and what it requires."—387. Compare WHEWELL, on the immorality of slavery, (Elements, Vol. 1,) and MACKINTOSH on the natural right of freedom, Works, Vol. 3, 138. "It is not because we have been free, but because we have a right to be free, that we ought to demand freedom. JUSTICE AND LIBERTY HAVE NEITHER BIRTH NOR RACE, YOUTH NOR AGE."

Compare GISBORNE, on the natural right to freedom, as constituted of God. A striking passage from Gisborne is quoted in DEWAR's Moral Philosophy. Sir James Mackintosh, defending the Missionary Smith, so persecuted for his opinions against slavery in the West Indies, referred to Dr. Johnson. "Mr. Smith has expressed the opinion that slavery never could be mitigated, but must die a violent death. These opinions the honorable gentleman calls fanatical. Does he think Dr. Johnson a fanatic, a sectary, or Methodist, or an enemy to established authority?

Now to suppose that while the letter of the Old Testament was against the relation of slavery or slaveholding, and required its abolition, the spirit of the New sanctioned the continuance of the relation, and only forbade its abuse, would be to degrade the moral standard of the New below that of the Old. It is impossible to deny that by the very letter of the law, "He that stealeth a man and selleth him, or if he be found in his hands, he shall surely be put to death," the relation of slaveholding, as a relation in and by which a human being is claimed as property and treated as merchandise, is sinful in itself; whether designated as a civil or a moral relation, it is immoral and unjust, and contrary to God's law, in and by itself. And this letter of the law is defined, represented, illustrated and applied, by the prophets, by the moral teachings of the Old Testament in various forms, and the spirit in the New Testament is demonstrated as conformable to the letter in the Old, sustaining it in every part, and carrying into practice its extreme meaning as its right meaning.

What then shall be said of the modern defenders of slavery, who set the New Testament *against* the Old, and hesitate not to declare that Christ and the apostles would not abolish slavery because it was a civil established relation, not to be interfered with by the gospel, but just and right! And whereas Christ declared that he came not to impugn or destroy the law, but to fulfill, they do, in this important respect, in an article of common morality, appeal to Christ's authority *against* the law, maintaining that to be just and righteous, under the gospel, which by and under the law was the extremest injustice and wrong.

But after having thus maintained that the relation of slave-

But he must know, from the most amusing of books, that Johnson proposed as a toast at Oxford, Success to the first revolt of negroes in the West Indies. He neither meant to make a jest of such matters, nor to express a deliberate wish for an event so full of horror, but merely to express in the strongest manner his honest hatred of slavery."—MACKINTOSH'S Works, 3, 405.

holding is in itself right, they also argue, with singular inconsistency, that Christ and the apostles left it *to be done away
by the spirit of the gospel,* by the spirit of Christianity in its
onward march and development. But how can the spirit of
Christianity be against a relation and a practice which in itself is not wrong, and if not wrong, then certainly just and
right ?   If the letter of Christianity is not against slavery,
then its spirit is not. If the spirit of Christianity is bound
to abolish slavery, it is because the law of Christianity rep-
robates and forbids it. And if the spirit of Christianity *can*
abolish slavery, it can only be by going in God's name and
authority against it, by employing God's word against it.
The Bible, from Genesis to Revelation, is a continuous line
of living fire against this iniquity.   The denunciations of it
are the more terrible and sweeping, because not only the original edict described the crime as parallel with murder, but all
its elements in turn, and the crimes resulting from it, are denounced in the same dreadful manner ; so that, in the wholesale, and in particular, the application is indisputable, and the
power indefeasible and immeasurable. It only needs that the
church and ministry should make use of this power, and
slavery would speedily be swept from existence.

But in our insane defence of slavery we render it necessary
either to pervert and corrupt both the law and the gospel, or
to forbid their utterance, to silence the church and the ministry on this subject, to muzzle the pulpit, and spike the word
of God.   What one of the purest and most eloquent of our
country's early patriots predicted on another occasion,* by
this madness " we make what is called law an assassin, we cut
asunder what law ought to protect, and teach the people to
scoff at their morals, and to unlearn their education to virtue."
The debasement of character becomes universal when men
are compelled to cut and square the very teachings of God to
meet the imperious demands of a detestable institution, which

* FISHER AMES. Works. Dangers of American Liberty.

being in itself sin and inhumanity, requires the disavowal of all that is holy and human in its supporters, and for their safety renders essential the abridgement of the freedom of speech both in the pulpit and in social life. Men submissive to these vices teach their consciences the art of defending them.

The celebrated Humboldt, in the course of his investigations in the regions of the Spanish wars and conquests in America, discovered a document in the will of the great Cortez, which, he says, is worthy of preservation and promulgation to mankind.* Speaking of his slaves, in the thirty-ninth and forty-first articles of his testament, Cortez adds the following memorable words: "As it is doubtful if a Christian can conscientiously employ as slaves Indians who have been made prisoners of war, and as this point has never been rightly cleared up till this day, I order my son, Don Martin, and those of his descendants who shall possess my property after me, to take every possible information as to the rights which may be legally exercised towards prisoners. The natives who have been forced to yield personal service ought to be indemnified, if it shall be decided that those personal services ought not to have been demanded." Humboldt adds to this testimony the following sarcastic words: "We must own that three centuries later, notwithstanding the civilization of a more enlightened age, the rich proprietors in America have less timorous consciences even on a death bed. In our days it is not the devotees but the philosophers who call in question the justice of slavery."†

But the law of nature and of nations denounces it, as well as the Word of God, affirming that slavery stands wholly and

* HUMBOLDT, Kingdom of New Spain, Vol. I., B. 2., ch. vii.

† THIERRY, History of the Norman Conquest, sec. 5, 293, refers to similar testimonies. On the approach of death those that held serfs in slavery repented of it as a thing displeasing to God. Deeds of emancipation were drawn up with the following preamble: "Seeing that in the beginning God made all men by nature free, but afterwards the law of nations brought some of them under the yoke of slavery, we believe it would be pious and meritorious in the sight of God to liberate such persons to us subjected. Know, therefore, that we have freed and liberated from

solely upon force against right, and being contrary to nature,
it follows that every moment that it is maintained, the relation
so continued is an ever new and active violation of the law of
nature. It is on this ground mainly that the principle is so
strongly stated in Coke upon the laws of England,* that a
man is to be regarded as impious and cruel who is not in favor
of liberty as against slavery, and that the common law in all
cases gives the right to liberty. When we think of a practice
thus denounced by the law of nature and of nations as a cruel
and impious violation of nature, passing into a habit of life,
and being claimed as a right of property and possession by
Christians, by those who, in addition to the law of nature and
of nations, have the law of God for their guide, we may cease
to wonder at the debasing and terrible effect of such cruelty
and injustice on the character of those who persist in it as
sanctioned by the gospel. The testimony of Hume is striking.
"The little humanity commonly observed in persons accustomed from their infancy to exercise so great authority over
their fellow-men, and to trample upon human nature, were
sufficient alone to disgust us with such unbounded dominion.
Nor can a more probable reason be assigned for the severe, I
might say barbarous, manners of ancient times, than the practice of domestic slavery, by which every man of rank was
rendered a petty tyrant, and educated amidst the flattery,
submission and low debasement of his slaves."† In such a
case, the higher they rose, the lower he descended; the more
intelligent and valuable they were, and the greater the crowd
of them, the worse the character of the master, who, as their
owner, had illimitable power over them, to use them at his

---

all yoke of servitude these our knaves,
them and all their children, born or
to be born."

   * Coke upon Lyttleton. Common
Law is Common Right. Impius et
crudelis judicandus est, qui libertati
non favet. Nostra jura in omni casu,
libertati dant favorem. See also

Smyth, Lect. Mod. Hist. Laws of
Louis IX., Vol. I., 110.

   † Hume's Essays. Populousness of
Ancient Nations. Compare Jefferson
on Virginia, and Becker, Charicles,
Exc. Slaves; and Gallus, The Slave
Family. Also, Blair's Inquiry, 148.

will, for his gain or pleasure. The French historian of slavery has described in an impressive passage the corruption of morals in the free classes of society in Greece and Rome in consequence of the habits of slavery, and the excitement and accumulation of human depravity under such opportunities of unrestrained indulgence of the passions.* "To carry this depravity to the highest pitch, there was only needed in the bosom of society a creature like a man, but divested by opinion of all moral obligations proclaimed by the human conscience or predicated upon it. A being whom they could turn to vice as to virtue without outraging his nature, in whom all excesses were lawful the moment they were commanded by his owner. Such a being was a slave, and such depravity did not hesitate to use him for its purposes." For the details of the demonstration of such depravity, the very museums of antiquity, as well as the Roman satirists, are open to us.†

When to all this there is added the frightful consideration that slavery propagates a posterity in its own likeness, that it secures a system and a supply increasing and perpetual of such depravities and subjects of depravity, we understand the grounds of the Divine wrath against it. We can understand also how a writer like Mr. Coleridge, a consummate master of language and logic, the logic of living principles, and accustomed to philosophical precision as well as power of imagination in the dress of thought, should have set down slavery as of blacker guilt than either rapine or murder.‡ Blacker guilt, because a fountain guilt ; because it is " the raising up of the foundations of many generations" in cruelty, in adultery, in robbery and moral assassination. Blacker guilt, because neither fraud nor murder, when committed on the first victim, are consolidated into a system and ratified and protected by law, and made just and holy for the second generation of

* WALLON. Histoire d'Esclavage, Vol. II. Compare STROUD, Slave Laws.
† BECKER. Charicles and Gallus, the Slave, and the Slave Family. Compare HUME, Populousness of Ancient Nations, Works, Vol. III, and THOLUCK, Moral Influence of Heathenism.
‡ See THE FRIEND, Essay 8, or COLERIDGE'S Works, Vol. III.

murderers upon the second generation of their victims.*
Blacker guilt, because neither fraud nor murder are perpetuated by propagation, with the law that the children of the
robbed and murdered follow the condition of their robbed
and murdered parents, and are to be themselves legitimately
robbed and murdered by right of descent, by necessity of the
law of slave generation, *partus sequitur ventrem.* Blacker guilt
than either murder or rapine, because while rapine and murder
finish their work with their present victims, slavery retains those
victims for the breeding of the crime, and by means of the stealing of babes passes the crime to a new generation under the
form and assumption of virtue, social habit, piety and law !

And therefore has Coleridge declared that the agitating
truths with which Thomas Clarkson, and his excellent confederates, the Quakers, fought and conquered the LEGALIZED
BANDITTI OF MEN-STEALERS, the numerous and powerful perpetrators and advocates of slavery, are to be at all hazards re-
published with a voice of alarm and impassioned warning.
"Truths of this kind being indispensable to man, considered
as a moral being, are above all expedience, all accidental consequences ; for as sure as God is holy, and man immortal, there
can be no evil so great as the ignorance or disregard of them."

CONCLUSION.

The necessity for the repromulgation of these truths, and
of the battle with them against slavery by the Word of God,
is increasing every day and hour in the United States, as a
necessity of our own life and freedom. We are under the

---

* DYMOND. Essays on Morality,
ch. xviii., 388. "The sufferer has
just as valid a claim to liberty at my
hands as at the hands of the ruffian
who first dragged him from his home.
Every hour of every day the present
possessor is guilty of injustice. Nor
is the case altered with respect to
those born on a man's estate. Nay,

even if the parents had been rightfully
slaves, it would not justify me in
making slaves of their children."

Compare WHEWELL, Elements of
Morality. " In the eye of morality
all men are brothers, and the crime
of maintaining slavery is the crime of
making or keeping a brother a slave."
Whewell presents in a most impres-

pressure of the rapidly advancing judgment of God, in that question, "If ye have not been faithful in that which is another man's, who shall give you that which is your own?" The crime and guilt of slavery are becoming frightfully exasperated in atrocity, and complicated, by the laws of the free States against the negro race, and by the new statutes of slave States, ordering the sale of free negroes as slaves, on penalty of quitting the State by such a time specified.

The horrible inhumanity and iniquity created and enforced by the slave laws of this country, and burned into the colored race, generation after generation, by decisions entitled justice, are never more painfully apparent than when brought in contrast with the maxims of English and Common Law in regard to liberty. By law, in South Carolina, it is always presumed that every negro and mulatto is a slave, unless the contrary be made to appear, and the burden of proof is on the poor creature claimed as a slave. "The wretch who, by art or force, is enabled to claim him as a slave, is exempted from the necessity of making any proof how he obtained him, the unhappy person said to be a slave being presumed to be so by the law of the land!" Chief Justice Taylor, of North Carolina, charged, in the case Gobu *vs.* Gobu, as correct, "the presumption of every black person being a slave." "It is so," said he, "because the negroes originally brought into this country were slaves, and their descendants must continue slaves." In 1740, it was enacted in South Carolina, "That all negroes and mulattoes, who now are, or shall hereafter be in this province, and all their issue and offspring, born or to be born, shall be, and they are hereby declared to be, and remain for ever hereafter, absolute slaves, and shall follow the condition of the mother."*

sive light the monstrosity, and awful moral consequences, of maintaining slavery, on the pretence that the negro is not of the human family. "Even his crimes are not acknowledged as wrongs, lest it should be supposed that as he may do a wrong, he may suffer one." Ch. xxiv., v. 1.

* STROUD's Slave Laws, ch. iii., 122–130. Compare WAILON, Hist.

With this atrocious doctrine of presumption against liberty there is held forth a perpetual bounty on the crime of man-stealing, and between law and custom there arises a complication of wickedness, as the habit of society in a slave State, which is frightful to consider, and for the description or sentence of which no language of reprobation can be too strong.

And here are Christian States, so called, deliberately enacting the very crime of kidnapping, which the government of our country has branded as piracy, and has forbidden in Africa, or on the high seas, on pain of death. Though the criminals are never punished, yet the law stands. And now that very crime of man-stealing, which the government denounces as piracy, and which God has condemned in the individual as equivalent with murder, is adopted by the State, and commanded and committed by law, as an article of State policy! Such is the latest form and exasperation of this sweeping and remorseless iniquity.

This State and corporate crime drives many poor creatures into the shame and misery of selling themselves into slavery, or permitting themselves to be made slaves, though sensible that in so doing they give themselves up to the will and machinery of the system and its managers, to make slaves not only of them but of their posterity. The crime and its dreadful consequences are increased immeasurably by the fatal brand imprinted on the children. The Christian State compels the man to constitute himself the head of a system of adultery and cruelty extending to his children and his children's children. The seller of himself as a slave inflicts the same oppression and misery on those who come after him. But those who compel him into this horrible choice, and those who defend the infinitely dreadful system, will bear their judgment in the other world.

State of the Slave under Law, and STEPHENS, of the Slave under Colonial Law. The atrocities of Grecian and Roman Slavery as drawn out in Blair, Becker, Hume and others, are almost innocent in comparison with the same every day being practised in Christian America.